First World War

and Army of Occupation

War Diary

France, Belgium and Germany

24 DIVISION
Divisional Troops
Royal Army Medical Corps
72 Field Ambulance
1 September 1915 - 30 April 1919

WO95/2202/1

The Naval & Military Press Ltd
www.nmarchive.com
Published in association with The National Archives

Published by

The Naval & Military Press Ltd

Unit 10 Ridgewood Industrial Park,

Uckfield, East Sussex,

TN22 5QE England

Tel: +44 (0) 1825 749494

www.naval-military-press.com

www.nmarchive.com

This diary has been reprinted in facsimile from the original. Any imperfections are inevitably reproduced and the quality may fall short of modern type and cartographic standards.

Contents

Document type	Place/Title	Date From	Date To
Heading	WO95/2202/1 72 Field Ambulance		
Heading	72nd Field Ambulance Sep 1915-1919 Apl		
Heading	24th Division 72nd Field Ambulance Vol I		
Heading	War Diary Of Officer Commanding 72nd Field Ambulance From September 1st 1915 To September 30th 1915 Volume 1		
War Diary	Brookwood	01/09/1915	01/09/1915
War Diary	Southampton	01/09/1915	01/09/1915
War Diary	S S South	01/09/1915	01/09/1915
War Diary	Western Miller	01/09/1915	01/09/1915
War Diary	Havre	02/09/1915	02/09/1915
War Diary	Monterolier Bucay	03/09/1915	03/09/1915
War Diary	Abbeville	03/09/1915	03/09/1915
War Diary	Maresqel	03/09/1915	03/09/1915
War Diary	Neuville	03/09/1915	14/09/1915
War Diary	Sempy	14/09/1915	14/09/1915
War Diary	Neuville	14/09/1915	19/09/1915
War Diary	Preures	20/09/1915	22/09/1915
War Diary	Reclinghem	22/09/1915	22/09/1915
War Diary	Berquette	23/09/1915	24/09/1915
War Diary	Bethune	25/09/1915	28/09/1915
War Diary	Oblinghem	29/09/1915	29/09/1915
War Diary	Berguette	30/09/1915	30/09/1915
Heading	24th Division 72nd Field Ambulance Vol 2 Oct 15		
Heading	War Diary Of Officer Commanding 72nd Field Ambulance From October 1st To October 31st 1915		
War Diary	Berguette	01/10/1915	02/10/1915
War Diary	Godewaersvelde	02/10/1915	02/10/1915
War Diary	Houtkerque	02/10/1915	06/10/1915
War Diary	Reninghelst	06/10/1915	31/10/1915
Heading	24th Division Nov 15		
Heading	Diary Of Officer Commanding 72nd Field Ambulance For Month Of November 1915		
War Diary	Reninghelst	01/11/1915	23/11/1915
War Diary	Steenvoorde	23/11/1915	25/11/1915
War Diary	Noord Pene	25/11/1915	26/11/1915
War Diary	Houlle	26/11/1915	27/11/1915
War Diary	Nordausques	27/11/1915	30/11/1915
Heading	24th Div 72 F. A. Dec 15		
Heading	War Diary Officer Commanding 72nd Field Ambulance From 1-12-15 To 31-12-15		
War Diary	Nordausques	01/12/1915	31/12/1915
Heading	24th Div 72nd Field Amb Vol 5		
Heading	War Diary Of (Capt. G.B. Edwards) Officer Commanding 72nd Field Ambulance From 1st January 1916 To 31st January 1916		
War Diary	Nordausques	01/01/1916	06/01/1916
War Diary	Poperinghe	06/01/1916	31/01/1916
Miscellaneous	72nd Field Ambulance		

Heading	War Diary Of Officer Commanding 72nd Field Ambulance From 1st February 1916 To 29th February 1916		
War Diary	Poperinghe	01/02/1916	29/02/1916
Heading	War Diary Of Commanding 72nd Field Ambulance From 1-3-16 To 31-3-16 Volume 7		
War Diary	Poperinghe	01/03/1916	18/03/1916
War Diary	Meteren	18/03/1916	29/03/1916
War Diary	Bailleul	30/03/1916	31/03/1916
Heading	War Diary Of Officer Commanding 72nd Field Ambulance From 1st April 1916 To 30th April 1916		
War Diary	Bailleul	01/04/1916	20/04/1916
War Diary	St. Jans Cappel	21/04/1916	30/04/1916
Heading	War Diary Of Major G.B. Edwards O.C. 72nd Field Ambulance From 1.5.16 To 31.5.16		
War Diary	St. Jans Cappel	01/05/1916	31/05/1916
Heading	War Diary Of (Major G.B. Edwards) Officer Commanding 72nd Field Ambulance		
War Diary	St Jans Cappel	01/06/1916	07/06/1916
War Diary	Bailleul	08/06/1916	17/06/1916
War Diary	24 D R S S. 16c. 24 (28)	17/06/1916	28/06/1916
Diagram etc	Plan of Camp		
Diagram etc			
Heading	War Diary Of (Major G.B. Edwards) Officer Commanding 72 Field Ambulance		
War Diary	Bailleul S 16c 2.4 (28) 24 D.R.S	01/07/1916	06/07/1916
War Diary	M 23 d 29 Sheet 28 1/20,000	06/07/1916	09/07/1916
War Diary	Bailleul S 16. C 2.4 (Sheet 28 1/20,000)	09/07/1916	31/07/1916
Heading	War Diary Of Major G.B. Edwards Officer Commanding 72nd Field Ambulance		
War Diary	Dive Copse (62 D) J 24 b 8.6	01/08/1916	10/08/1916
War Diary	Sappers Corner L 9d 80 62d	11/08/1916	14/08/1916
War Diary	L 9d 8.0 62 D	15/08/1916	18/08/1916
War Diary	Bronfay S 22d 9.0 57 C	21/08/1916	22/08/1916
War Diary	Bronfay Farm S 22d 9.0 57 C		
War Diary	Carnoy A 13d 5.9 62 C	19/08/1916	20/08/1916
War Diary	Sappers Corner	23/08/1916	23/08/1916
War Diary	Dive Copse	23/08/1916	26/08/1916
War Diary	D 30b 3.7 62 D	27/08/1916	30/08/1916
War Diary	F 6a 1.0 62 D Mametz	31/08/1916	31/08/1916
Heading	War Diary Of Major G.B. Edwards Officer Commanding 72 Field Ambulance		
War Diary	Mametz F 6a 22 Sheet 62 D	01/09/1916	06/09/1916
War Diary	Buire D 30b 2.8 (62 D) on March	06/09/1916	08/09/1916
War Diary	Eaucourt	09/09/1916	19/09/1916
War Diary	Valhuon N 8 Sheet 36 B 1/40000	20/09/1916	23/09/1916
War Diary	Houdain	24/09/1916	25/09/1916
War Diary	Les 4 Vents W 9	25/09/1916	30/09/1916
Heading	War Diary Of Lieut Col. G.B. Edwards Commanding 72nd Field Ambulance		
War Diary	Les 4 Vents W. 9 (36 B)	01/10/1916	27/10/1916
War Diary	Braquemont L 25b 34 (36 B)	28/10/1916	30/10/1916
Diagram etc			
Heading	War Diary Of (Lieut Col G.B. Edwards) Officer Commanding 72nd Field Ambulance		
War Diary	Braquemont L 25b. 44 (36 B)	01/11/1916	09/11/1916

War Diary	L 25b 44 (36 B)	10/11/1916	30/11/1916
Heading	War Diary Of (Lieut Col G.B. Edwards) Officer Commanding 72nd Field Ambulance		
War Diary	Bracquemont L 25 B (36B)	01/12/1916	31/12/1916
Heading	War Diary Of Lieut Col G.B. Edwards Officer Comdg 72nd Field Ambulance		
War Diary	Bracquemont L 25 b (36B)	01/01/1917	13/01/1917
War Diary	L 25 b (36 B)	14/01/1917	31/01/1917
Diagram etc			
Heading	War Diary Of Lieut Col. G.B. Edwards Officer Comdg. 72nd Field Ambulance		
War Diary	L 25b (36 B)	01/02/1917	12/02/1917
War Diary	Allouagne D 7a 25 (36 B)	13/02/1917	14/02/1917
War Diary	D7.a 2.5 (36 B)	15/02/1917	28/02/1917
Heading	War Diary Of Lieut Colonel G.B. Edwards D.S.O. Officer Commanding 72nd Field Ambulance		
War Diary	Allouagne D7a 3.7 36 D	01/03/1917	04/03/1917
War Diary	Labeuvriere D17a 4.4 36 B	04/03/1917	31/03/1917
Heading	War Diary Of Lieut Colonel G.B. Edwards Officer Commanding 72nd Field Ambulance		
War Diary	Labeuvriere D17a 4.6 36 B	01/04/1917	06/04/1917
War Diary	D17a 4.4 36 B	07/04/1917	21/04/1917
War Diary	La Couture	22/04/1917	24/04/1917
War Diary	Delette	23/04/1917	30/04/1917
Heading	No 72 F A May 1917		
Heading	War Diary Of (Lieut Col. G.B. Edwards D.S.O.) Officer Commanding 72nd Field Ambulance		
Miscellaneous	B.E.F. Summary Of Medical War Diaries Of 72nd Field Ambulance		
Miscellaneous	72nd F.A. 24th Division B.E.F.		
War Diary	Delette Sheet 5A	01/05/1917	09/05/1917
War Diary	Boeseghem	10/05/1917	10/05/1917
War Diary	Boeseghem 5A	11/05/1917	12/05/1917
War Diary	Godewaersvelde Sheet 27 Q 12b 1.4	13/05/1917	13/05/1917
War Diary	Brandhoek G 12b 5.9 Sheet 28	13/05/1917	23/05/1917
War Diary	G 12b 5.9 Sheet 28	24/05/1917	31/05/1917
Miscellaneous	B.E.F. Summary Of Medical War Diaries Of 72nd Field Ambulance		
Miscellaneous	72nd F.A., 24th Division B.E.F.	01/05/1917	01/05/1917
Heading	Cover for Documents. Nature of Enclosures. Surgery 20 Eyes		
Heading	War Diary Of Lieut-Col. G.B. Edwards D.S.O. 72nd Field Ambulance		
War Diary	R 5a 5.0 Sheet 27	01/06/1917	04/06/1917
War Diary	M.3a.5.2 Sheet 28	05/06/1917	15/06/1917
War Diary	H 24a 50.9 Sheet	16/06/1917	30/07/1917
Heading	War Diary Of (Lt Col. G.B. Edwards D.S.O.) Officer Commanding 72nd Field Ambulance		
War Diary	Lumbres Sheet A5. B4.4	01/07/1916	17/07/1916
War Diary	Renescure	18/07/1916	18/07/1916
War Diary	V 11 C. 3.6 Sheet 28	19/07/1916	19/07/1916
War Diary	Q 19. C. 36 Sheet 27	20/07/1916	23/07/1916
War Diary	Dickebusch H 34a 6.9 Sheet 28	24/07/1916	31/07/1916
Heading	War Diary Of Lieut Colonel G.B. Edwards D.S.O. Officer Commanding 72nd Field Ambulance		
War Diary	Dickebusch H 34a 6.9 Sheet 28	01/08/1917	03/08/1917

War Diary	H 34a 6.9 Sheet 28	03/08/1917	31/08/1917
Heading	War Diary Of Lieut Colonel G.B. Edwards D.S.O. Officer Commanding 72nd Field Ambulance		
War Diary	Dickebusch H 34a 6.9 Sheet 28	01/09/1917	06/09/1917
War Diary	H 34a 6.9 Sheet 28	06/09/1917	13/09/1917
War Diary	Fletre W 17d 39 Sheet 27	14/09/1917	21/09/1917
War Diary	Beaulencourt N 11c 7.3 Sheet 57c	21/09/1917	24/09/1917
War Diary	Doingt I 36a 2.0 Sheet 62c	25/09/1917	28/09/1917
Heading	War Diary Of Lieut Colonel G.B. Edwards D.S.O. Officer Commanding 72nd Field Ambulance		
War Diary	Doingt I 36a 2.0 62c	01/11/1917	30/11/1917
Heading	War Diary Of Lieut Colonel G.B. Edwards Officer Commanding 72nd Field Ambulance		
War Diary	Doingt I 36a 20 Sheet 62c	01/11/1917	30/11/1917
Heading	War Diary Of Lieut Colonel G.B. Edwards D.S.O. Officer Commanding 72nd Field Ambulance		
War Diary	Doingt I 36a. 2.0 Sheet 62c	01/12/1917	31/12/1917
Heading	War Diary Of Lieut Colonel G.B. Edwards D.S.O. Officer Commanding 72nd Field Ambulance		
War Diary	Doingt I 36a 2.0 Sheet 32c	01/01/1918	31/01/1918
Heading	War Diary Of Lieut Colonel G.B. Edwards D.S.O. Officer Commanding 72nd Field Ambulance		
War Diary	Doingt I 36a Sheet 32c	01/02/1918	28/02/1918
Heading	War Diary Of Lieut Colonel G.B. Edwards D.S.O. Officer Commanding 72nd Field Ambulance		
War Diary	Aubigny Map 62c O 2d. 6.0	01/03/1918	01/03/1918
War Diary	Devise V 3a 63 62c	02/03/1918	11/03/1918
War Diary	Devise	12/03/1918	12/03/1918
War Diary	Poeuilly Q 28b. 90 Map 62c	13/03/1918	18/03/1918
War Diary	Poeuilly Map 62c	19/03/1918	21/03/1918
War Diary	Poeuilly	21/03/1918	21/03/1918
War Diary	St Cren	22/03/1918	22/03/1918
War Diary	Marchelepot	23/03/1918	23/03/1918
War Diary	Chaulnes	24/03/1918	24/03/1918
War Diary	Rosieres I3 Amiens 17	25/03/1918	25/03/1918
War Diary	Cayeux H3 Amiens 17	26/03/1918	26/03/1918
War Diary	Cayeux	27/03/1918	27/03/1918
War Diary	Cayeux Loumuin	28/03/1918	28/03/1918
War Diary	Rouvrel St. Sauflieu	29/03/1918	29/03/1918
War Diary	St. Sauflieu	30/03/1918	31/03/1918
Heading	War Diary Of Lieut Colonel C.H. Denyer M.C. Lieut Colonel		
War Diary	St. Sauflieu D3 Amiens 1-100,000	01/04/1918	03/04/1918
War Diary	St. Sauflieu Amiens Ecole de Tevne Filles Rue Porte de Paris	04/04/1918	04/04/1918
War Diary	St Sauflieu to Amiens	04/04/1918	04/04/1918
War Diary	Amiens	05/04/1918	06/04/1918
War Diary	St Valery Sur Somme	07/04/1918	11/04/1918
War Diary	St Valery Sur Somme	12/04/1918	15/04/1918
War Diary	Pinchvalise	16/04/1918	17/04/1918
War Diary	Valhuon Lens E1	18/04/1918	19/04/1918
War Diary	Valhuon Divion	20/04/1918	20/04/1918
War Diary	Divion	21/04/1918	30/04/1918
Heading	War Diary Of Lieut Colonel C.H. Denyer Officer Commanding 72nd Field Ambulance from May 1st 1918 to May 31st 1918		

War Diary	Aix Noulette R 22a. 2b Sh 36 B	01/05/1918	09/05/1918
War Diary	Aix Noulette	09/05/1918	31/05/1918
Heading	War Diary Of Lieut Colonel C.H. Denyer M.C. Officer Commanding 72nd Field Ambulance		
War Diary	Aix Noulette	01/06/1918	30/06/1918
Heading	War Diary of Lieut Colonel C.H. Denyer M.C. Officer Commanding 72nd Field Ambulance		
War Diary	Aix Noulette R. 22a. 2.6 Sheet 44 B	01/07/1918	06/07/1918
War Diary	Aix Noulette	07/07/1918	31/07/1918
Heading	War Diary Of Lieut Colonel C.H. Denyer M.C. Officer Commanding 72nd Field Ambulance		
War Diary	Aix Noulette R22.a. 2.6 Sh 44 B	01/08/1918	08/08/1918
War Diary	Aix Noulette	20/08/1918	31/08/1918
Heading	War Diary Of Lieut Colonel C.H. Denyer M.C. Officer Commanding 72nd Field Ambulance		
War Diary	Aix Noulette Map. Ref. R22a. 2.6	01/09/1918	04/09/1918
War Diary	Aix Noulette	04/09/1918	29/09/1918
War Diary	Hersin	30/09/1918	30/09/1918
Heading	War Diary Of Lieut Colonel C.H. Denyer M.C. Officer Commanding 72nd Field Ambulance		
War Diary	Warluzel	01/10/1918	05/10/1918
War Diary	Louveral	06/10/1918	06/10/1918
War Diary	Boulon Wood	07/10/1918	19/10/1918
War Diary	Avesnes Les Albert 6 U 28.a.0.8 Sh	20/10/1918	22/10/1918
War Diary	Avesnes Les Aubert	26/10/1918	31/10/1918
Heading	War Diary Of Lieut Colonel C.H. Denyer M.C. Officer Commanding 72nd Field Ambulance		
War Diary	Avesnes Les Aubert	01/11/1918	03/11/1918
War Diary	Ferme Avesnes	04/11/1918	05/11/1918
War Diary	Wargnies Les Petit The Chateau	06/11/1918	16/11/1918
War Diary	Wargnies to Maresches	17/11/1918	17/11/1918
War Diary	Maresches to Roeulx	18/11/1918	18/11/1918
War Diary	Roulx to Bruille	19/11/1918	19/11/1918
War Diary	Bruille to Magny	21/11/1918	21/11/1918
War Diary	Masny	23/11/1918	24/11/1918
War Diary	Masny to Landas	25/11/1918	25/11/1918
War Diary	Landas to Ouvignies	26/11/1918	26/11/1918
War Diary	Ouvignies	26/11/1918	30/11/1918
Heading	War Diary of Lieut Colonel C.H. Denyer M.C. Officer Commanding 72nd Field Ambulance		
War Diary	Ouvignies	01/12/1918	01/12/1918
War Diary	G 4a 2.8 Sh 44	02/12/1918	02/12/1918
War Diary	Belgium Port of Sheet 1,40,0000	03/12/1918	09/12/1918
War Diary	Ouvignies	12/12/1918	12/12/1918
War Diary	Tournai	14/12/1918	31/12/1918
Heading	War Diary Of Lieut Colonel C.H. Denyer M.C. Officer Commanding 72nd Field Ambulance		
War Diary	Tournai	01/01/1919	31/01/1919
Heading	To 72 Field Ambulance		
War Diary	Tournai Belgium	02/02/1919	28/02/1919
Heading	72nd F.A. Mar 1919		
Heading	War Diary Of Lieut Colonel C.H. Denyer M C Officer Commdg 72nd Field Ambulance		
War Diary	Tournai Belgium O 27.a.9.8 Sheet 37	01/03/1919	05/03/1919
War Diary	Tournai Belgium	07/03/1919	25/03/1919

War Diary	Tournai to Gruson France M 33a Sh 37 1.40,000 Belgium Pt of France	26/03/1919	31/03/1919
Heading	War Diary Of Lieut Colonel C.H. Denyer M.C. Officer Commanding 72nd Field Ambulance		
War Diary	Gruson M 33a 3b 37 Belgium PT France	01/04/1919	30/04/1919

WO/95/2202/1

72 Field Ambulance

24TH DIVISION
MEDICAL

72ND FIELD AMBULANCE

SEP 1915 - ~~DEC 1918~~
1919 APRL

24th Division

Summarised

121
7121

Sept '15.
S

72nd Field Ambulance
Vol I

Sept 15.
Dec '18

CONFIDENTIAL

WAR. DIARY.

OF.

OFFICER. COMMANDING 72nd FIELD. AMBULANCE.

FROM SEPTEMBER 1st 1915 TO SEPTEMBER 30th 1915.

VOLUME. I

W.C. [illegible]
Capt R.A.M.C.
O.C. 72nd Field Ambulance

Army Form C. 2118.

WAR DIARY
or
~~INTELLIGENCE~~ ~~SUMMARY.~~
(Erase heading not required.)

(1)

Instructions regarding War Diaries and Intelligence Summaries are contained in F. S. Regs., Part II. and the Staff Manual respectively. Title pages will be prepared in manuscript.

Place	Date September 1915	Hour	Summary of Events and Information	Remarks and references to Appendices
BROOKWOOD	1/9/15	3-5AM	First train load of 92nd Field Ambulance (5 officers, 1 W.O. 104 NCO's & men, 28 horses, 7 four-wheeled and 2 two-wheeled wagons) left BROOKWOOD STATION	
— " —	"	5-5AM	Second train load (5 officers, 1 W.O. 105 N.C.O's & men, and same amount of horses and wagons) left same station	
SOUTHAMPTON	"	5-5AM	First train arrived	
"	"	6-55AM	Second train arrived	Day Cloudy & overcast, Some rain at intervals
"	"	9-30AM	Whole of horses and wagons of Ambulance embarked	
SS "SOUTH-WESTERN MILLER"	"	3-30PM	Whole of personnel Embarked, Complete less 4 officers & 45 men who Embarked on S.S. "Empress Queen"	
"	"	4-30PM	Ship left dock. [illegible]	W.C. [illegible] Capt RAMC
HAVRE	2/9/15	12-30AM	Ship arrived off HAVRE	
"	"	7-0AM	Disembarkation commenced. The Field Ambulance remained in the Shed on the Wharf for the rest of the day	
"	"	5-30PM	Field Ambulance marched to the GARE DE MARCHANDAISE arriving at 6-5 P.M.	
"	"	10-19PM	Train left Station. Day cloudy, rain at times	W.C.N.

2353 Wt. W2544/1454 700,000 5/15 D. D. & L. A.D.S.S./Forms/C. 2118.

(2)

Army Form C. 2118.

Instructions regarding War Diaries and Intelligence Summaries are contained in F. S. Regs., Part II. and the Staff Manual respectively. Title pages will be prepared in manuscript.

WAR DIARY
or
~~INTELLIGENCE SUMMARY~~.
(Erase heading not required.)

Place	Date	Hour	Summary of Events and Information	Remarks and references to Appendices
MONTEROLIER BUCHY	3/9/15	3-30 AM	Train arrived here – stop of 30 minutes. Men were not given tea owing to lateness of hour	
ABBEVILLE	"	8.50 AM	Train arrived here 10 minutes late. Men were given tea, & biscuits issued out. Stop of full 45 minutes given by R.T.O.	
MARESQUEL	"	12-10 PM	Train arrived here, detraining started at once. Completed by 1-15 P.M. in pouring rain, Men given tea, this took considerable time owing to miserable weather.	
	"	2-50 PM	Field Ambulance marched off in pouring rain through BEAURAINVILLE, LESPINOY-SUR-CANCHE, BRIMEUX, BEAUMERIE to NEUVILLE which was reached at 5-50 P.M.	Reference Ordnance & Survey Maps ARRAS & MONTREUIL 1911
NEUVILLE	"	5-50 PM	Field Ambulance went in to billets at once. Men wet through & no facilities for giving them any hot food.	WCA
"	4/9/15		Redistribution of billets. 135 NCOs & men in lofts of a house in main street, 45 others in a barn further up street. Headquarters in Mairie. Weather dull, & overcast.	WCA
"	5/9/15		Divine Service in the Morning – the rest of the day resting. Completion of drying men's clothes. Weather much finer.	WCA

2353 Wt. W2544/1454 700,000 5/15 D. D. & L. A.D.S.S./Forms/C. 2118.

Instructions regarding War Diaries and Intelligence Summaries are contained in F. S. Regs., Part II. and the Staff Manual respectively. Title pages will be prepared in manuscript.

WAR DIARY

or

~~INTELLIGENCE SUMMARY.~~

(*Erase heading not required.*)

(3)

Army Form C. 2118.

Place	Date	Hour	Summary of Events and Information	Remarks and references to Appendices
NEUVILLE	6/9/15	9.0 AM	The "Alarm" was given and it took the Ambulance 48 minutes to get completely ready, everything packed up to march off. They did a Route March of 8 miles, no one falling out.	W.C.H.
"	7/9/15		The morning was spent in checking the Equipment of the different Sections, a few minor deficiencies which were not drawn on mobilisation have been indented for	
"	~~7/9/15~~ "	2.0 to 4.0 PM	The N.C.O.s & men bathed in the River CANCHE. Weather brilliantly fine. Concert for men in School.	W.C.H.
"	8			
"	8/9/15	9-10 AM	Ambulance trained in Wagon Drill.	
	"	10.12 AM	Lecture on "Contents of Panniers" to all N.C.O.s & men.	
	"	2.0 PM	The "Alarm" was called & the whole Unit turned out ready to march off, this took 35 minutes, and at 2-35 PM the Ambulance started off on a 6 mile Route March. Another glorious day.	W.C.H.
"	9/9/15	6-7 AM	The whole Unit given Physical Drill - this takes place each day at this hour.	
"	"	AM 9 - 12 PM	Whole Ambulance practiced in loading, & unloading of the wagons, so that each man knows exactly where each article is packed.	

1577 Wt. W10791/1773 500,000 1/15 D. D. & L. A.D.S.S./Forms/C. 2118.

Army Form C. 2118.

(4)

Instructions regarding War Diaries and Intelligence Summaries are contained in F. S. Regs., Part II. and the Staff Manual respectively. Title pages will be prepared in manuscript.

WAR DIARY
or
~~INTELLIGENCE~~ SUMMARY.

(Erase heading not required.)

Place	Date	Hour	Summary of Events and Information	Remarks and references to Appendices
NEUVILLE	9/9/15	2-4 PM	Pitching & striking Operating Tents, practised by Sections.	
"	"	3 PM	Cases for Hospital from Concentration areas sent by Motor Ambulance Wagons to NORTH General Hospital ETAPLES.	
"	"	6-8 PM	A Cinematograph apparatus kindly lent by the YMCA in MONTREUIL was put up in the Schools and a show given to the men with songs in between each film.	Weather continues perfect, cloudless sky, heat not too great. WCN
NEUVILLE	10/9/15	6-7 AM	Physical Drill	
"	"	9 AM-1 PM	Route March of 12 miles. The men instead of having their great coats in a roll around their necks, carried them as a pack on the back, they stood the march well only one falling out although the heat was considerable.	
"	"	2-4.30 PM	A & B Sections had a hot bath in a sail bath formed out of a wagon cover rigged up in a secluded spot. The water was heated up in a copper in a house close by, and in degchies on an open fire. The men had a good wash & it was much appreciated by them. 'C' Section were lectured to on the contents of Panniers.	
	"	6-8 PM	A concert was given by the men, with the assistance of some officers in the Schoolroom	Another glorious day, absolutely cloudless sky & cool wind. WCN

1577 Wt. W10791/1773 500,000 1/15 D. D. & L. A.D.S.S./Forms/C. 2118.

Army Form C. 2118

(5)

WAR DIARY
or
~~INTELLIGENCE~~ SUMMARY.
(Erase heading not required.)

Instructions regarding War Diaries and Intelligence Summaries are contained in F. S. Regs., Part II. and the Staff Manual respectively. Title pages will be prepared in manuscript.

Place	Date	Hour	Summary of Events and Information	Remarks and references to Appendices
NEUVILLE	11/9/15	6-7AM	Physical Drill	
		9AM to 12-NOON	Medical Inspection;- inspection of kits, first field dressing, Brassards etc,	Another magnificent day with sufficient wind to keep the temperature moderate
	"		Lieut HS Groves lectured to each Section on "Protection against Gas". This officer had attended a lecture by Lieut. Col. Watson RAMC on this subject, the day before at Brigade Headquarters, at the same time he & 6 men were put in a trench full of Chlorine; they were wearing gas helmets & their efficacy as a protection was amply proved.	
	"	2-4 PM	The men bathed in the River CANCHE	WCA
NEUVILLE	12/9/15	9-0AM	Sunday; a day of Rest. Divine Service for C of E & Nonconformists. Patch Pockets for GasHelmets issued out to men to be sewn in their own tunics.	Glorious weather continues. WCA
	13/9/15	6-7AM	Physical Drill	
			Acting on instructions from ADMS 24th Division, "B" Tent Sub Division was opened as a Reception Hospital in the Schools for cases of sick needing hospital treatment, but who were unlikely to need treatment for more than 3 days	

1577 Wt. W10791/1773 500,000 1/15 D. D. & L. A.D.S.S./Forms/C. 2118.

Instructions regarding War Diaries and Intelligence Summaries are contained in F. S. Regs., Part II. and the Staff Manual respectively. Title pages will be prepared in manuscript.

WAR DIARY
or
INTELLIGENCE SUMMARY.
(*Erase heading not required.*)

(6)

Army Form C. 2118.

Place	Date	Hour	Summary of Events and Information	Remarks and references to Appendices
NEUVILLE	13/9/15	AM 9-12 15 PM	A & C. Tent Sub Division practised preparing Dressing Stations in barns, & receiving wounded – Bearers Stretcher Drill.	Weather very fine in early part of day, clouded over later, with a little rain
"	"	2-4.30 PM	Route March	
"	"	3-0 PM	6 cases sent to No 24 General Hospital ETAPLES. (2. 13th Middlesex, 2-8th Queens & 2. 11th Essex.	WCR
NEUVILLE	14/9/15		Orders from ADMS Division received previous day that there was to be a Divisional Field Day today, & 72nd FIELD AMBULANCE was to march to SEMPY, and be there in reserve, forming a Dressing Station there, & sending out bearers to get touch with firing line when it came up in level with SEMPY.	
"	"	7-30 AM	72nd FIELD AMBULANCE (less Lieut. W. J. WEBSTER, 2 Sergeants & 1 man of "B" Tent Sub Division, personnel of Reception Hospital) marched out from NEUVILLE, through MARLES-SUR-CANCHE, MARANT, AIX-EN-ISSART to SEMPY, the outskirts of which was reached at 9.45 AM, the unit being due in SEMPY by order at 10.0 AM. The CO whilst searching round for a suitable building to open a Dressing Station ~~they~~ received orders that the Field Day was off, & to march back to billets!	Reference Ordnance Survey Maps ARRAS & MONTREUIL 1911
SEMPY	"	10.30 AM	Field Ambulance marched off, reaching NEUVILLE at 12.30 PM.	
NEUVILLE	"	2-4.30 PM	First Aid & improvised splints practised. 'C' Section – lot back	A dull & overcast day fine drizzle during early part of morning
"	"	3-0 PM	8 cases sent to Hospital at ~~Etaples~~ ETAPLES – 2. 24 Divl Ammunition Column. 4. 12th ROYAL FUSILIERS. 2. 24th SIGNAL CORPS)	
			WCR	

1577 Wt. W10791/1773 500,000 1/15 D. D. & L. A.D.S.S./Forms/C. 2118.

Instructions regarding War Diaries and Intelligence Summaries are contained in F. S. Regs., Part II. and the Staff Manual respectively. Title pages will be prepared in manuscript.

WAR DIARY
or
~~INTELLIGENCE~~ SUMMARY.

(*Erase heading not required.*)

(7)

Army Form C. 2118.

Place	Date	Hour	Summary of Events and Information	Remarks and references to Appendices
NEUVILLE	15/9/15	6-7 AM	Physical Drill - men provided with coffee & ½ biscuit before going on Parade	A fine day dull & cloudy later
"	"	AM 9-12-15 PM	Tent Sections (less "B") practised opening Dressing Stations in barns, & reception and treatment of wounded.	
"	"	2-4-15 PM	Lecture on Contents of Panniers.	
		3.0 PM	6 cases transferred to 24th General Hospital ETAPLES	WCA
NEUVILLE	16.9.15	6-7 AM	Physical Drill.	
	"	AM 9-12.30 PM	The Ambulance did a Route March for about 5 miles down the ETAPLES road & back.	
		2.0 to 4.15 PM	The unloading & loading practised by Sections, all the transport wagons thoroughly cleaned up.	A dull day to start with, with fine rain, cleared up later
		3.0 PM	3 cases sent to 24th General Hospital ETAPLES.	WCA
"	17/9/15	6-7 AM	Physical Drill	
	"	AM 9-10.12.30 PM	A & B Tent Sub Division with all three Bearer Sub. Divisions marched out a distance of 3 kilometers along the ST. OMER road, the TENT Sub-Division pitched Dressing Stations on some sloping ground about 400 yards S. of the road. Some bearers were put out as patients on the surrounding countryside & brought in by the rest of the bearers to the Dressing Station. The work on the whole was very well done, but time was too short for the work to be completely done	Reference Map as above (MONTREUIL) MAP WCA

1577 Wt. W10791/1773 500,000 1/15 D. D. & L. A.D.S.S./Forms/C. 2118.

Instructions regarding War Diaries and Intelligence Summaries are contained in F. S. Regs., Part II. and the Staff Manual respectively. Title pages will be prepared in manuscript.

WAR DIARY
or
~~INTELLIGENCE SUMMARY.~~
(*Erase heading not required.*)

(8)

Army Form C. 2118.

Place	Date	Hour	Summary of Events and Information	Remarks and references to Appendices
NEUVILLE	17/9/15	2-4-15 PM	"A" & "B" Sections had a hot bath, "C" Section having a lecture on "Contents of Panniers".	
"	"	3-0PM	Sick cases sent Hospital at ETAPLES.	
"	"	9-50PM	Orders received from 71st Brigade, that ~~Brigade would~~ concentrate at the MONTECHOR cross roads at 12-0 (midnight) 17th - 18th inst & move by route AIX-EN-ISSART - ST DENOUX - X of ST DENOUX to a covered position E of track running N & S through Second S of BOUBERS-LES-HESMOND troops being ready to leave rendezvous at 4-45 AM on the 18th inst.	71st Brigade Operation Order No 1
			The packing up of the Ambulance took some considerable time as it was anticipated that in all probability a move would be ordered to our new billeting area at PREURES after operations were over. This necessitated issuing out iron rations & gas helmets to all as they could not be carried on the wagons. They had ~~not~~ been issued previously as it had been considered more desirable to keep them ~~intact~~ in store.	Fine hot sunny day
"	"	11-40PM	Field Ambulance marched off along ST OMER road & caught up rear of transport of 9th BEDFORDS at the MONTECHOR cross roads at 12-15 AM.	A thick misty night & progression on Road very slow WCN
"	18/9/15		The night was very misty, it was difficult keeping contact with unit in front. The march with constant checks, was made through AIX-EN-ISSART (reached at 1-40 AM), ST DENOUX (reached at 2-45 AM. At 3 30 AM a halt was made on a rough track running due E from ST DENOUX about 1½ miles from that place.	

Instructions regarding War Diaries and Intelligence Summaries are contained in F. S. Regs., Part II. and the Staff Manual respectively. Title pages will be prepared in manuscript.

WAR DIARY

or

~~INTELLIGENCE~~ SUMMARY.

(*Erase heading not required.*)

(9)

Army Form C. 2118.

Place	Date	Hour	Summary of Events and Information	Remarks and references to Appendices
NEUVILLE	16/9/15		This track was so rough & the ground covered on the March considerable, as a result the transport animals were "done up", & a message sent to the Brigade who had moved to a field about 1 mile further down the track, to that effect and asking for orders. The order came to march to SEMPY & wait for the Brigade there.	ARRAS MAP
	"	7.0AM	Just as Unit was marching off the ADMS Division came along & ordered the unit to proceed about 1 mile along the road running NE from ST. DENOEUX, wait for casualties, & at 9-0AM march back to billets in NEUVILLE. This was done & the Field Ambulance arrived back NEUVILLE at 12-30 PM. The rest of the day spent in resting. Later on in evening orders received from ADMS for 2 Sections & Headquarters to move the next day to PREURES, the 3rd Section to remain behind, hand over billets & patients to join main unit next day.	A fine hot day WCH
NEUVILLE	17/9/16	1.30PM	Field Ambulance – less LIEUT. W. J. WEBSTER & "B" Tent subdivision – marched off from NEUVILLE through ESTREE – MONTCAVREL – to PREURES which was reached at 4.50 P.M. The officers were billeted in the school, the men in another school-room & barns, all being very clean & comfortable.	A magnificent day, a delightful cool breeze which made marching a pleasure MONTREUIL Map WCH

1577 Wt. W10791/1773 500,000 1/15 D. D. & L. A.D.S.S./Forms/C. 2118.

Army Form C. 2118.

WAR DIARY
or
~~INTELLIGENCE~~ SUMMARY.
(*Erase heading not required.*)

(10)

Instructions regarding War Diaries and Intelligence Summaries are contained in F. S. Regs., Part II. and the Staff Manual respectively. Title pages will be prepared in manuscript.

Place	Date	Hour	Summary of Events and Information	Remarks and references to Appendices
PREURES	20/9/15		The morning was spent in settling into billets & re-allotting some of the areas slightly. Orders had been received the night before, that the Field Ambulance would practice the collection of wounded this afternoon in conjunction with RMOs of the Brigade.	
"	"	12-30 PM	LIEUT. W J WEBSTER & 'B' Tent Sub-Division arrived from NEUVILLE.	
		1-30 PM	Field Ambulance (less 'A' & 'B' Tent Sub-divisions) marched out of billets through HUCQULIERS - to MANINGHEN cross roads which was reached at 2-55 P.M. A rendezvous there being ordered for 3.0 P.M. An hour was spent here waiting for orders when a Major in the 9th WEST KENTS came up & said that 40 men had been put at his disposal as casualties & that we had better get to work. He & I put out the casualties over a perimeter of about 1½ miles, the Regimental M.O's & stretcher bearers followed & formed Aid posts from which the bearers of all 3 bearer Sub-divisions collected the wounded & took them to a Dressing Station opened up by 'C' Tent Sub-Division of the Ambulance about 1½ miles back from the front line. A valuable 1½ hours had been wasted waiting for orders, so the whole thing had to be done in a rush, but the work was well done on the whole.	A fine day much colder
"	"	8.20 PM	Field Ambulance arrived back in billets	
"	"	9-30 PM	Confidential Communication from 24th Division arrived - that Division was moving off on the march the next day.	WCA

1577 Wt. W10791/1773 500,000 1/15 D. D. & L. A.D.S.S./Forms/C. 2118.

Instructions regarding War Diaries and Intelligence Summaries are contained in F. S. Regs., Part II. and the Staff Manual respectively. Title pages will be prepared in manuscript.

WAR DIARY
or
~~INTELLIGENCE~~ SUMMARY.
(*Erase heading not required.*)

Army Form C. 2118.

(11)

Place	Date	Hour	Summary of Events and Information	Remarks and references to Appendices
PREURES	21/9/15	10.0AM	Field Ambulances paraded for instructional purposes, R.M.O.s of the Brigade were instructed by me in the Duties of a R.M.O. in action. 40 men of the 8th QUEEN'S regiment were sent out as patients, collected by the Bearers of the Field Ambulance, acting as regimental stretcher bearers. Cases brought down to Regimental Aid Post & then to an imaginary Dressing Station of a Field Ambulance.	
"	"	11.45AM	Proceeded to Headquarters 24th Division at ROYON for instructions from ADMS as to disposal of sick on the march.	
"		6.5PM	72nd Field Ambulance marched out of billets through HUCQUELIERS—MANINGHEM PETIT ST MICHEL to cross roads at ST PHILBERT—the starting point of the Brigade; this was reached at 8-45PM, 5 minutes after appointed time, the 104th Co. R.E. whom we were to follow having already moved off. We came up to them 2 miles farther on. The march was continued through RIMEUX to DENNEBROEUCQ	ARRAS Map A fine day
	22/9/15		which was reached at 12.30 AM. Here LIEUT. DE BEAUPRÉ our billeting officer met us & conducted us to billets in RECLINGHEM, 1½ miles to the EAST.	WCN
RECLINGHEM	"		The morning was spent cleaning up, & resting. 9 cases from the 8th WEST KENTS & 8th QUEENS sent to 24th GENERAL HOSPITAL ETAPLES.	
		6.5PM	Field Ambulance marched out of billets due NORTH to cross roads at PONCHE, then due E up a very stiff hill, which the transport had great difficulty in negotiating, to cross roads SE Point 140 which was passed at the appointed time 8.20PM.	

1577 Wt. W10791/1773 500,000 1/15 D. D. & L. A.D.S.S./Forms/C. 2118.

Instructions regarding War Diaries and Intelligence Summaries are contained in F. S. Regs., Part II. and the Staff Manual respectively. Title pages will be prepared in manuscript.

WAR DIARY
or
INTELLIGENCE SUMMARY.
(Erase heading not required.)

(12)

Army Form C. 2118.

Place	Date	Hour	Summary of Events and Information	Remarks and references to Appendices
RECLINGHEM	22/9/15		The march - a very long & dreary one - was continued through the night through ENGUINEGATTE - BASSE BOULOGNE - WITTERNESSE - LE HAMEL ISBERGUES to BERGUETTE which was reached at 1-30 A.M. Many men in the Brigade fell out on the march, the men of the Ambulance were very weary, but none fell out.	HAZEBROUCK Map. A glorious day, but night much warmer. WCA
BERGUETTE	23/9/15		The day was spent resting, the men being very tired. 8 cases from regiments in the Brigade sent to No. 22 Casualty Clearing Station AIRE.	A dull & cloudy day with rain at intervals
"	24/9/15		The day spent in refitting and checking iron rations, gas helmets etc.	
"	"	6-15PM	Field Ambulance marched out of Billets through GUARBECQUE across the railway to starting point at cross roads at last E in LE MIQUELLERIE which was reached at 8.15PM ½ hour before time. The 71st BRIGADE passed by first, then 74th FIELD AMBULANCE then 73rd FIELD AMBULANCE, the 72nd moving off behind them at 9.30 P.M. Another long & dreary march through BUSNES GONNEHEM, CHOCQUES to BETHUNE which was reached at about 1.0 AM, the Ambulance being billeted in stables on the CHAMP-DE-MARS.	HAZEBROUCK Map WCA. Another dull & cloudy day with rain at intervals. WCA
BETHUNE	25/9/15	9.0AM	A conference called by the ADMS. 24th Division (LIEUT-COL. S.W. BLISS RAMC) with the OCs of the 3 Field Ambulances of the Division. It was explained that the Division was expected to go into action that day in extension of an attack which had	

1577 Wt. W10791/1773 500,000 1/15 D. D. & L. A.D.S.S./Forms/C. 2118.

Instructions regarding War Diaries and Intelligence Summaries are contained in F. S. Regs., Part II. and the Staff Manual respectively. Title pages will be prepared in manuscript.

WAR DIARY
or
~~INTELLIGENCE SUMMARY.~~
(Erase heading not required.)

(13)

Army Form C. 2118.

Place	Date	Hour	Summary of Events and Information	Remarks and references to Appendices
BETHUNE	25/9/15		been started that morning E of VERMELLES, the proposed disposition of the Field Ambulances was explained & directions given for Evacuating Casualties.	
	"	10.30 AM	I proceeded to Headquarters 72nd Brigade to ascertain movements & found that the BRIGADE was shortly moving off to VERMELLES. I returned at once to the Field Ambulance & ordered the whole of the Bearer Division with LIEUTS GROVES & DE BEAUPRE under LIEUT EBERTS to march off at once behind the BRIGADE & keep touch with it, at the same time I ordered LIEUT HOGG with "A" Tent Sub Division to march off 2 hours later, proceed to SAILLY-LE-BOURSE, & then move on himself & keep touch with the Bearers – this order was cancelled shortly after as the ADMS ordered off 73rd Field Ambulance to follow 73rd BRIGADE (which was to be detached from 24th DIVISION & attached to the 9th DIVISION) & the rest of the 72nd Field Ambulance & Tent Divisions of 74th Field Ambulance to march off to Point F 20d 2.3 on Map 36B, to park in a field at that spot & await further orders.	FRANCE 'B' Series Map 36 C Maps FRANCE 'B' Series 36 B & 36. C.
	"	2.30 PM	72nd & 74th Field Ambulance marched off & arrived at appointed spot at 3.30 PM. I at once went on ahead to VERMELLES to get touch with my Bearers. I found Headquarters of 24th Division & 72nd Brigade in VERMELLES the regiments of the Brigade, the Bearers of 74th Field Ambulance, & the whole of the 73rd Field Ambulance. Apparently ~~[illegible]~~ the 72nd Field Ambulance Bearers had marched round another route in to VERMELLES as I was leaving it, as a consequence I was unable to find them.	

1577 Wt. W10791/1773 500,000 1/15 D. D. & L. A.D.S.S./Forms/C. 2118.

Instructions regarding War Diaries and Intelligence Summaries are contained in F. S. Regs., Part II. and the Staff Manual respectively. Title pages will be prepared in manuscript.

WAR DIARY
or
~~INTELLIGENCE~~ SUMMARY.

(*Erase heading not required.*)

Army Form C. 2118.

(14)

Place	Date	Hour	Summary of Events and Information	Remarks and references to Appendices
BETHUNE	25/9/15		I returned to Headquarters of the Ambulance shortly afterwards & a little later went to Divisional Headquarters in BETHUNE to report to the ADMS. who informed me that 72nd BRIGADE had pushed on to VENDIN-LE-VIEIL, and that I was to get my bearers in touch with the Brigade. On return to headquarters of the Ambulance there was still no news of the Bearers – I heard next day that LT EBERTS had sent off a note to me at 5.30 P.M. on the evening of the 25th; but the orderly was unable to find headquarters & did not deliver the note till 8.0 AM on the 26th –	
	"	8.30 PM	I went on again to VERMELLES to Report Centre of the Division, taking with me LIEUT HOGG. Here we learnt that the 72nd Brigade had marched out from VERMELLES at 8.0 P.M. (VENDIN-LE-VIEIL was merely it's objective) to LE ROUTOIRE farm. LIEUT HOGG & I went on there, meeting on the way the transport of 71st & 72nd Brigades. We found at LE ROUTOIRE farm an advanced Dressing Station of the Field Ambulances of the 1st DIVISION. It was a ruined farm with very limited & bad accommodation, & it was obvious that it was no good one trying to open a Dressing Station there. We returned to Headquarters of the Ambulance expecting that the next day the 1st Division would be relieved by the 24th & that 72nd FA would take over the Dressing Station at LE ROUTOIRE farm.	A dull & cheerless day with much rain – roads very bad. WCH

2353 Wt. W2544/1454 700,000 5/15 D. D. & L. A.D.S.S./Forms/C. 2118.

Instructions regarding War Diaries and Intelligence Summaries are contained in F. S. Regs., Part II. and the Staff Manual respectively. Title pages will be prepared in manuscript.

WAR DIARY
or
INTELLIGENCE SUMMARY.

(Erase heading not required.)

Army Form C. 2118.

(15)

Place	Date	Hour	Summary of Events and Information	Remarks and references to Appendices
	26/9/15	9.0AM	Received message from Lt EBERTS that he & the Bearers were in VERMELLES. I proceeded with the orderly who had brought the ~~message~~ note to VERMELLES & found the 2 bearer sub-divisions with 3 Ambulance wagons, the 3 Officers with the other bearer Sub-division had gone out towards the trenches. They returned about 10 minutes after I got there, apparently they had proceeded a short way along the HULLUCH road, which was under heavy shrapnel fire, losing STAFF SERGT. DUNN and 7 men wounded one (PTE. LEEK) severe (through the abdomen) They had been taken to the 27th Field Ambulance Dressing Station in the Brewery. I went to see them there before they were sent down. I then went to see the ADMS. for further orders - he was in SAILLY-LE-BOURSE. I found CAPT. Rose O/C 74th Field Ambulance there. The ADMS directed that CAPT. ROSE should open a Dressing Station at LE ROUTOIRE farm & that I should send my Bearers out at once if possible, if not after night fall. The DADMS, (MAJOR WESTON), CAPT. ROSE and I went off to go to LE ROUTOIRE farm to reconnoitre it, but found that the whole area was under heavy shell-fire & we couldn't get there. We returned & the ADMS. directed that CAPT. ROSE should find a suitable house in VERMELLES for a dressing station, and that I should give him one officer to help him, Sending out my Bearers at first opportunity.	
	"	4-0PM	Capt. ROSE opened Dressing Station in house opposite Brewery, with one Tent Sub-division & LIEUT. HOGG from 72nd F.A.	

2353 Wt. W2544/1454 700,000 5/15 D. D. & L. A.D.S.S./Forms/C. 2118.

Instructions regarding War Diaries and Intelligence Summaries are contained in F. S. Regs., Part II. and the Staff Manual respectively. Title pages will be prepared in manuscript.

WAR DIARY

or

~~INTELLIGENCE SUMMARY.~~

(Erase heading not required.)

Army Form C. 2118.

16

Place	Date	Hour	Summary of Events and Information	Remarks and references to Appendices
	26/9/15	6-30PM	All the Bearers from 72nd & 74th F.A.s under Lts EBERTS & DUNCAN with 6 Horse ambulance wagons went to LE ROUTOIRE farm & from there operated behind their respective Brigades.	
	"	8-30PM	All the Motor Ambulances Wagons of the two Ambulances, which I had previously sent for, came up & Evacuation of cases from Dressing Station to No1. CASUALTY CLEARING STATION at CHOCQUES started.	
		9-15PM	I returned to Headquarters of the F.A. & found that the ADMS. had given orders for a Reception ~~Hospital~~ Station to be opened by a Tent Sub Division for cases that had been told to walk down to the Casualty Clearing Station, so that they could have some rest & nourishment before going down further. Two bell tents were put up for a start, & 7 cases had been admitted. On the way down I had called in at SAILLY-LE-BOURSE to report to the ADMS. what had been done, but found he had moved.	
	"	10-15PM	I proceeded to VERMELLES again to try & find the ADMS but found that communications had broken down, & on returning 3 hours later to F.A. Headquarters met the whole Field Ambulance coming up the road, orders having come from ADMS to go to LONE TREE. This I could not find on the map so stopped the Ambulance at PHILOSPHE on the outskirts of VERMELLES, and later, finding the ADMS, received orders from him to send the personnel & equipment of one Tent Sub Division with 3 officers to open a Dressing Station at LE ROUTOIRE,	

2353 Wt. W2544/1454 700,000 5/15 D. D. & L. A.D.S.S./Forms/C. 2118.

Instructions regarding War Diaries and Intelligence Summaries are contained in F. S. Regs., Part II. and the Staff Manual respectively. Title pages will be prepared in manuscript.

WAR DIARY
or
~~INTELLIGENCE~~ SUMMARY.
(*Erase heading not required.*)

Army Form C. 2118.

(17)

Place	Date	Hour	Summary of Events and Information	Remarks and references to Appendices
BETHUNE	26/9/15	10-15 PM Cont	the rest of the Ambulance to return & park in a field to be chosen by me close to SAILLY-LE-BOURSE & on the N side of the road SAILLY-LE-BOURSE – NOYELLES-LES-VERMELLES. This I did choosing a field at Point L36 q.6.8 reporting same to ADMS. I then returned to VERMELLES & despatched "A" Tent sub division with sufficient equipment & rations, under LIEUT. HOGG with LIEUTS. CATHCART & LAING to help him to LE. ROUTOIRE farm to open a Dressing Station; then returned with the remainder of the FA to the spot chosen.	FRANCE B Series Map 36 B
	27/9/15	12.30 AM	I proceeded to LE ROUTOIRE farm to see the Dressing Station & found things going well under very adverse conditions, the clerking being especially difficult.	Another cheerless day, but not much rain W.C.A.
		6-15 PM	The ADMS came to Headquarters of the Field Ambulance & directed that I should confer with CAPT. ROSE O/C 74th Fld. Amb. with a view to sending out all the bearers of both Ambulances to search the ground N & S of the HULLUCH Road behind the area operated over by the Brigade (which would be relieved in the morning) to make sure that there were no casualties left. I went up to VERMELLES to see CAPT. ROSE & arranged with him that his Bearers under LT. DUNCAN should search the area	

Instructions regarding War Diaries and Intelligence Summaries are contained in F. S. Regs., Part II. and the Staff Manual respectively. Title pages will be prepared in manuscript.

WAR DIARY
or
INTELLIGENCE SUMMARY.
(*Erase heading not required.*)

Army Form C. 2118.

(18)

Place	Date	Hour	Summary of Events and Information	Remarks and references to Appendices
	27/9/15	6-15PM	N of the HULLUCH Road & the 72nd F.A. Bearers under LT. EBERTS should search the area S of the HULLUCH Road. I wrote out orders to this effect, & directed LT EBERTS to send a combined report to me, by 530 AM in the morning, that both areas were clear.	A miserably dull & rainy day WCM
	28/9/15	7-0AM	LT EBERTS report received & forwarded to A.D.M.S.	
		10 AM	Orders received from ADMS for "A" Tent sub Division to withdraw from LE ROUTOIRE farm together with the whole Bearer sub-division & return to Headquarters of Fld Amb. During the time the dressing station was opened at LE ROUTOIRE farm 166 cases passed through of whom 3 (No 2448 C/Sgt ROBSON, 3rd COLDSTREAM GUARDS – No 1200 Pte STEWART 4/CAMERON HIGHLANDERS – No 10837 Pte OLIVER SOUTH WALES BORDERERS) died in the dressing station, they were buried by the official burial party who took their identity discs, & the pay-books were retained by the clerk in the Dressing Station – These pay-books have been forwarded. 7 cases were admitted to the small Reception Hospital opened near BEUVRY for temporary treatment of cases walking down to the CASUALTY CLEARING STATION. The rest of the morning was spent in resting, the officers & men of 'A' Tent sub-Division,	

2353 Wt. W2544/1454 700,000 5/15 D. D. & L. A.D.S.S./Forms/C. 2118.

Instructions regarding War Diaries and Intelligence Summaries are contained in F. S. Regs., Part II. and the Staff Manual respectively. Title pages will be prepared in manuscript.

WAR DIARY
or
INTELLIGENCE SUMMARY.

(*Erase heading not required.*)

Army Form C. 2118.

(19)

Place	Date	Hour Cont	Summary of Events and Information	Remarks and references to Appendices
"	28/9/15	10 AM	and the Bearer Division were very weary after many hours constant work, & very little sleep. The work of all the Officers & men especially the Bearers was splendid, & they worked hard with an enthusiasm & whole hearted purpose that was very gratifying to see in a new Unit in their first experience actually in the zone of operations.	A dull & overcast day with almost constant drizzle. The roads in a bad condition
		3.0 PM	All Officers called to a conference at ADMS's Office on the work done during the last few days, this conference had to be stopped as, at the commencement, orders came in to the Division to move at shortest notice.	
		8.40 PM	Field Ambulance marched out from billets to starting point of transport of Brigade, behind whom they were to march, to cross roads at Point L2d6.5., the march was continued through VERQUIGNEUL - VERQUIN to ANNEZIN where orders where found for F.A to proceed to OBLINGHEM & to billet there	FRANCE B Series Map 36 B. HAZEBROUCK Map WCN
OBLINGHEM	29.9.15	1.30 AM	This place reached, and after a long search for billets the men were accomodated in a huge barn in a big farm, the Officers all sleeping on the floor of the sitting room in the farm-house.	
"		1.30 PM	The Fld. Amb. marched out from billets to the starting point cross roads 600 YARDS S.E. of S CHOCHQUES.	HAZEBROUCK Map

2353 Wt. W2544/1454 700,000 5/15 D. D. & L. A.D.S.S./Forms/C. 2118.

Instructions regarding War Diaries and Intelligence Summaries are contained in F. S. Regs., Part II. and the Staff Manual respectively. Title pages will be prepared in manuscript.

WAR DIARY
or
INTELLIGENCE SUMMARY.
(Erase heading not required.)

(20)

Army Form C. 2118.

Place	Date	Hour	Summary of Events and Information	Remarks and references to Appendices
OBLINGHEM	29/9/15	1.30 PM	This was reached shortly before the appointed time (2.15 pm) when it was found that the 104th Co. RE who were to march in front of us had gone on ahead and the first LINE TRANSPORT of 72nd BRIGADE was behind us, we joined in behind them & continued the march through CHOCQUES, HILLIERS, HAM-EN-ARTOIS to BERGUETTE, which was reached at 7.30 PM, A very dreary cheerless march	Another miserable day, raining most of the time W.C.A.
BERGUETTE	30/9/15		Day spent in resting & refitting. The men were very tired & weary after that hard work of the previous days, with two rather long marches on top of it.	A much finer day. Considerable drop in the temperature W.C.A.

2353 Wt. W2544/1454 700,000 5/15 D. D. & L. A.D.S.S./Forms/C. 2118.

Oct. 1915

24th Division

72nd Field Ambulance
Vol 2

Oct 15

CONFIDENTIAL

WAR. DIARY.

OF.

OFFICER. COMMANDING.
72ND FIELD AMBULANCE.

FROM, OCTOBER 1ST TO. OCTOBER 31ST 1915

72ND FIELD AMBULANCE

Army Form C. 2118.

WAR DIARY
or
~~INTELLIGENCE~~ SUMMARY.
(*Erase heading not required.*)

(1)

Instructions regarding War Diaries and Intelligence Summaries are contained in F. S. Regs., Part II. and the Staff Manual respectively. Title pages will be prepared in manuscript.

Place	Date	Hour	Summary of Events and Information	Remarks and references to Appendices
BERGUETTE	1/10/15	10 AM	Orders came in from 72nd Brigade for the Ambulance to march off behind the 1st Line Transport 72nd Brigade & 104th 60. R.E. to pass starting point at Cross roads 400 YARDS N of U in LA ROUPE by 12-45 P.M.	HAZEBROUCK Map
	"	10-30 AM	The DADMS 24th Division came to F.A. Headquarters with the information - that only the Horse Transport of the Ambulance would march, the personnel of the Ambulance with Cook's Wagon would entrain with the rest of the Personnel of the Brigade on the next day - the 2nd inst.	
	"	11-20 AM	Transport under LIEUTS. CATHCART and HOGG marched out of billets. The rest of the day spent by the men resting & cleaning up and by the office in completing returns of recent casualties.	a dull cloudy day much colder rain at intervals WCA
BERGUETTE	2/10/15	4-30 AM	Reveille	
	"	5-15 AM	Breakfast.	
	"	6-25 AM	Cooks cart packed up & started off to BERGUETTE STATION for entrainment at 7-0 AM	
	"	7-5 AM	The Field Ambulance marched off out of billets being due at the station at 7-25 AM and entrainment at 7-40 A.M. The station was reached a few minutes before time & it was found that the train before had not left.	
"	"	8.10 AM	Train left.	

2353 Wt. W2544/1454 700,000 5/15 D. D. & L. A.D.S.S./Forms/C. 2118.

Army Form C. 2118.

Instructions regarding War Diaries and Intelligence Summaries are contained in F. S. Regs., Part II. and the Staff Manual respectively. Title pages will be prepared in manuscript.

WAR DIARY
or
~~INTELLIGENCE~~ ~~SUMMARY.~~

(*Erase heading not required.*)

(2)

Place	Date	Hour	Summary of Events and Information	Remarks and references to Appendices
GODEWAERS-WELDE	2/10/15	9-15AM	Train arrived at this station & troops detrained (8th E. SURREY's also being in train) The march was started at once through WATOU TO HOUTKERQUE.	HAZEBROUCK Map
HOUTKERQUE "		1-0PM	This place reached. No billets could be obtained for the men, so 20 Tents were obtained from Brigade Headquarters, & one operating tent pitched for the Sergeants. Officers billeted in the town.	A finer day, but still colder, sharp frost at night. WCA
HOUTKERQUE	3/10/15		A rest & a general clean up, the wagons – horsed & motors – were thoroughly cleaned which they needed badly.	A fine day, a little rain later.
"		7-0PM	Orders came from Brigade that G.O.C. 24th Division would inspect the troops & transport the next day the 4th inst. at 12-0 (noon). Orders were therefore issued accordingly for the parade of 72nd Field Ambulance.	WCA
	4/10/15	1-10PM	MAJOR-GENERAL J.E. CAPPER, G.O.C. 24th DIVISION – who had taken over command that day of the Division from MAJOR-GEN. SIR. J.G. RAMSAY K.C.B. – inspected the 72nd Field Ambulance after having previously inspected the troops of the Brigade and the 104th Co RE. The General seemed pleased with everything but the condition of the horses, but it was explained to him that they had had a lot of hard work the last 10 days with most irregular feeding.	
"		6-45PM	Orders came in from Brigade for the move next day – the 5th to POPERINGHE, orders issued accordingly	A showery day, finer later on, colder. WCA

2353 Wt. W2544/1454 700,000 5/15 D. D. & L. A.D.S.S./Forms/C. 2118.

Instructions regarding War Diaries and Intelligence Summaries are contained in F. S. Regs., Part II. and the Staff Manual respectively. Title pages will be prepared in manuscript.

WAR DIARY
or
~~INTELLIGENCE~~ SUMMARY.

(*Erase heading not required.*)

Army Form C. 2118.

3

Place	Date	Hour	Summary of Events and Information	Remarks and references to Appendices
HOUTKERQUE	4/10/15		The Brigade-Major 72nd Infantry Brigade requested an investigation & report on the water-supply of the area occupied by the Brigade at HOUTKERQUE owing to reports having been received that there was Enteric fever in the District. I went in to the question with the Mayor and found that these reports were not justified, there was no history of any prevailing fever, but the question of water supply was one rather of quantity than quality. The supply was entirely from shallow wells which with the sudden strain thrown upon them by the influx of a considerable number of British troops were liable to give out. I therefore recommended that the water carts of all Units of the Brigade should proceed every evening between 4-0 & 6-0 o'clock to WATOU to fill the carts at a public pump there. This was never carried out as the Brigade moved out of the area shortly after.	WCN
"	5/10/15	10-30 AM	Orders came in from 72nd Brigade cancelling previous order of night before for the Brigade to move to POPERINGHE. The Field Ambulance was packed up ready to move, everything was then unpacked again. The rest of the day spent in a thorough overhauling of the clothing & equipment of the men, & a list made of deficiencies for replacement.	France B series Sheet 27.
"		9.0 PM	Orders received from 72nd Brigade that Brigade would march to new area next day 6th inst. 72nd Field Ambulance to be clear of Starting point (E 21 a 9.8) by 11.30 AM marching after 104th Coy R.E.	A better day, rather dull & cloudy. No rain. WCN

3353 Wt. W2544/1454 700,000 5/15 D. D. & L. A.D.S.S./Forms/C. 2118.

Instructions regarding War Diaries and Intelligence Summaries are contained in F. S. Regs., Part II. and the Staff Manual respectively. Title pages will be prepared in manuscript.

WAR DIARY
or
~~INTELLIGENCE SUMMARY.~~
(Erase heading not required.)

4

Army Form C. 2118.

Place	Date	Hour	Summary of Events and Information	Remarks and references to Appendices
HOUTKERQUE	6/10/15	11-15 PM	72nd Field Ambulance marched out of billets & passed starting point at appointed time, March continued through WATOU (passed at 12-15 PM) POPERINGHE passed at 1-30 PM. to RENINGHELST which was reached at 3-10 PM	BELGIUM & FRANCE B. Series Maps Sheets 27 & 28
RENINGHELST			72nd Field Ambulance took the School previously occupied by the 52nd Field Ambulance as a Dressing Station, also some barns behind as billets for the men. LIEUT. R.W. HOGG with LIEUT. H.S. GROVES 1 N.C.O. & 30 men took over the Divisional Baths & Equipment thereof in the Brewery.	A fine day WCA
"	7/10/15		The morning was spent in cleaning up the schools, & the Brewery & the surroundings, and patients were taken in later on in the morning 2 Officers & 3 men whom we had brought with us the night before were evacuated by No 5 M.A.C. to No 10 Casualty Clearing Station at POPERINGHE. LIEUT. HOGG & I proceeded to GODEWAERSWELDE to see O/C. 52nd Field Ambulance & the officer who had previously been in charge of baths. On our return we found that LIEUT. GROVES had started bathing men on request of G.O.C. 24th Division – 200 were bathed altogether & given clean clothing.	

2353 Wt. W2544/1454 700,000 5/15 D. D. & L. A.D.S.S./Forms/C. 2118.

Instructions regarding War Diaries and Intelligence Summaries are contained in F. S. Regs., Part II. and the Staff Manual respectively. Title pages will be prepared in manuscript.

WAR DIARY
or
~~INTELLIGENCE SUMMARY.~~
(Erase heading not required.)

5

Army Form C. 2118.

Place	Date	Hour	Summary of Events and Information	Remarks and references to Appendices
RENINGHELST	7/10/15	6-30PM	Orders came in through ADMS. 24th Division from ADMS 9th Division (the Brigade being attached to the 9th Division temporarily) for (i) 2 Officers & "A" 1. Tent Sub Division to proceed early next morning to BOESCHEPE to take over Rest Station & baths from 29th Field Ambulance. (ii) 1 Officer & 20 other ranks to proceed to LA CLYTTE with two Motor Ambulances wagons to be attached to 29th Field Ambulance for instruction purposes	A dull cloudy day but no rain WCH
"	8/10/15	7-30AM	LIEUT. W. B. CATHCART with 1 W.O. 2 NCO's & 17 other ranks marched off with 2 Motor Ambulance Wagons to LA CLYTTE. LIEUT. W. J. WEBSTER and LIEUT. H. F. H. EBERTS with B. "Tent Sub. Division 2 G.S. Wagons, 1 limbered cart, and 1 Water cart marched off to BOESCHEPE.	
"		11-30AM	I proceeded to BOESCHEPE & found that 'B' Tent Sub. Division had taken over the Cinema House & schools, also the Baths in the Brewery, with billets for the men in a Chateau. The keys of the Baths together with an inventory of equipment were left behind by 53rd Field Ambulance, but no cart for carting the water from a pond to the well in the Brewery so the Baths could not be opened.	

2353 Wt. W2544/1454 700,000 5/15 D. D. & L. A.D.S.S./Forms/C. 2118.

Instructions regarding War Diaries and Intelligence Summaries are contained in F. S. Regs., Part II. and the Staff Manual respectively. Title pages will be prepared in manuscript.

WAR DIARY
or
~~INTELLIGENCE SUMMARY.~~
(*Erase heading not required.*)

Army Form C. 2118.

6

Place	Date	Hour	Summary of Events and Information	Remarks and references to Appendices
RENINGHELST	8/10/15		6 cases evacuated by No. 5 M.A.C. – 14 cases remaining in hospital. 27 Officers & 483 men of the Division were given baths to-day, water was cresoled, but no soap allowed owing to fouling of stream down below where horses water	Another dull, depressing day but no rain WCA
"	9/10/15	8-0 AM	LIEUT. W.B. CATHCART and party of 20 other ranks moved with Tent sub-Division of 29th Field Ambulance from LA CLYTTE to OUDERDOM, establishing a dressing station there. 4 cases evacuated from this hospital by No 5 M.A.C., 17 cases remaining in hospital in the evening. The Personnel of the 24th Divisional Train were given baths at Baths taken over by "B" Tent Sub: Division at BOESCHEPE – 74 in number. 17 Officers & 815 men bathed at Baths here.	A finer day, colder. WCA
"	10/10/15		Orders from ADMS. to replace Tent Sub-Division personnel at OUDERDOM by Bearer personnel. LIEUT. H.S. GROVES, 1 Sergeant & 11 men sent up to replace LIEUT. W.B. CATHCART, SGT. MAJOR COGGINS and 11 other ranks. LIEUT. CATHCART was up in the Railway Dug-out (Advanced Dressing Station) and could not be relieved by LIEUT. GROVES from OUDERDOM till next night. Admitted to Hospital 10, To Duty – 3, Evacuated to C.C.S. – 2. Remaining – 22. Baths working very well, 29 Officers & 636 men bathed to-day.	Weather getting finer each day, Warmer. WCA

Instructions regarding War Diaries and Intelligence Summaries are contained in F. S. Regs., Part II. and the Staff Manual respectively. Title pages will be prepared in manuscript.

WAR DIARY
or
~~INTELLIGENCE~~ SUMMARY.

(*Erase heading not required.*)

7

Army Form C. 2118.

Place	Date	Hour	Summary of Events and Information	Remarks and references to Appendices
RENINGHELST	11/10/15		Admitted to Hospital - 6, Evacuated - 2. To Duty - 3. Remaining - 23.	Finer, & warmer.
"	"	3-30PM	LIEUT. E.J. DEBEAUPRE proceeded to take temporary medical charge of 8th Buffs	
"	"	10-0PM	LIEUT W.B. CATHCART returned from OUDERDOM. 17 Officers & 383 men were bathed.	WCA
"	12/10/15		Admitted to Hospital - 22, Evacuated - 1. To Divisional Rest Station - 12. Duty - 1. Remaining - 31.	A fine day Cloudy, with slight rain towards evening.
		1-0PM	LIEUT. A.W. BRETHERTON. and Fle Ash returned from temporary Duty with NO I Casualty Clearing Station at CHOCQUES.	
			32 Officers & 716 men bathed to-day.	WCA
"	13/10/15		Men of the Ambulance otherwise unemployed have been put on to carrying on the erection of thatched hutments for winter Quarters.	Very fine day, much warmer
			No. of cases admitted - 21, and 2 officers, Evacuated - 1 Officer & 2 men. To Duty - 7. Remaining - 1 Officer & 43 men.	
			LIEUT. E.J. DEBEAUPRE rejoined this unit from temporary duty with 8th BUFFS.	
			Number bathed to-day - 25 Officers & 971 men.	WCA

2353 Wt. W2544/1454 700,000 5/15 D. D. & L. A.D.S.S./Forms/C. 2118.

Instructions regarding War Diaries and Intelligence Summaries are contained in F. S. Regs., Part II. and the Staff Manual respectively. Title pages will be prepared in manuscript.

WAR DIARY
or
~~INTELLIGENCE SUMMARY.~~
(Erase heading not required.)

8

Army Form C. 2118.

Place	Date	Hour	Summary of Events and Information	Remarks and references to Appendices
RENINGHELST	14/10/15		Work continued satisfactorily as before. A start has been made with gathering brick-rubble and old timber to put up a permanent standing for the horses of the Unit. Hospital – Cases admitted = 18 men + 2 Officers. To Divisional Rest-Station = 26. Evacuated = 3 Officers and 4 men. To Duty = 2 men. Remaining = 25. Number bathed to-day = 24 Officers and 615 men.	Fine weather continues WCA
"	15/10/15		More brick-rubble collected from DICKEBUSCH & "Shale" from POPERINGHE.	
	"	10.0AM	G.O.C. 24th DIVISION inspected the Hospital & Sanitary arrangements Hospital – Cases admitted = 3 Officers + 41 men. To Divisional Rest-Station = 21 men. Evacuated = 3 Officers + 15 men. To Duty = 1 man. Remaining = 30 (+1 man brought in dead). Number bathed to-day = 28 Officers, and 1181 men.	Weather still very fine WCA
"	16/10/15		Horse standing started with, foundation of "Shale, and above it, a thick layer of old brick & cement. – Size 50 yards by 8 yards. It will be roofed in with a thatched roof, and eventually entirely closed in as the weather gets colder. Hospital – Cases admitted: 3 Officers + 13 other ranks, Evacuated = 2 Officers + 4 Other Ranks To Duty = 2 Other Ranks. Remaining = 1 Officer = 30 Other ranks. To Divisional Rest Station = 34 O.R.. Number bathed today = 32 Officers + 769 Other ranks,	Weather still gloriously fine, no rain for a long time WCA

2353 Wt. W2544/1454 700,000 5/15 D. D. & L. A.D.S.S./Forms/C. 2118.

Instructions regarding War Diaries and Intelligence Summaries are contained in F. S. Regs., Part II. and the Staff Manual respectively. Title pages will be prepared in manuscript.

Army Form C. 2118.

WAR DIARY
or
INTELLIGENCE SUMMARY.
(*Erase heading not required.*)

(9)

Place	Date	Hour	Summary of Events and Information	Remarks and references to Appendices
RENINGHELST	17/10/15		Work on construction of horse-standing, hutments, etc continues rather slowly owing to lack of material. Hospital - Cases admitted = 27 OR, Evacuated = 9 other ranks, To Divisional Rest Station = 17 OR, To Duty 5 OR. Remaining = 1 Officer 14 OR. Number bathed today: 31 Officers & 663 men.	Glorious weather continues WCN
"	18/10/15		Work continues. Paths are being remade. A commencement made today with incineration of faeces, this works well, but there is some difficulty of disposing of the urine, as the soil is not absorbent, & the subsoil water at a high level. - Hospital - Cases admitted = 3 Officers & 26 OR Evacuated = 3 Officers & 14 OR. To DRS = 11 OR. To Duty 1 OR. Remaining = 1 Officer & 14 OR. Numbers bathed today = 28 Officers & 877 men.	Another fine day WCN
"	19/10/15		Cementing of flooring of horse's standing commenced today, about 4 yards being done. 3 Huts now completed. - Hospital - Cases admitted = 38 OR Evacuated = 1 Officer & 11 OR. To DRS = 20 OR. To Duty 4 OR. Remaining 17 OR Numbers bathed to-day = 4 Officers & 363 men.	Fine day
"		1-0 PM	LIEUT. H. MAJOR 4th MIDDLESEX admitted dead to this hospital. A hand grenade exploded accidentally, when practising, inflicting very grave wounds from which this Officer died shortly after.	WCN

2353 Wt. W2544/1454 700,000 5/15 D. D. & L. A.D.S.S./Forms/C. 2118.

Army Form C. 2118.

Instructions regarding War Diaries and Intelligence Summaries are contained in F. S. Regs., Part II. and the Staff Manual respectively. Title pages will be prepared in manuscript.

WAR DIARY
or
~~INTELLIGENCE SUMMARY.~~
(Erase heading not required.)

(10)

Place	Date	Hour	Summary of Events and Information	Remarks and references to Appendices
RENINGHELST	20/10/15		Work continues on the same lines	
"	"	12-30PM	LIEUT. MAJOR was buried by his regiment in a part of the civil Cemetery set aside for British troops. Hospital - Cases admitted = 38 OR. Evacuated = 11 OR. To Divisional Rest Station = 28 OR. Remaining = 16 OR. Number bathed to-day - 48 Officers & 716 men.	Cloudy later in the day Much warmer WCA
"	21/10/15		6. G.S. Wagons & 3 Limbered Carts went in to YPRES to-day & collected a lot of brick rubble & timber for the Horse-standing & hutments. Five stoves obtained from C.R.E. for the hospital wards, and 2 fireplaces re-constructed, the Hospital is efficiently heated for the present weather. - Hospital - Cases admitted = 1 Officer & 47 O.R. Evacuated = 1 Officer. To D.R.S. = 17 O.R. To Duty = 1 O.R. Remaining = 45 O.R. Number bathed to-day: 37 Officers & 908 Men.	Glorious Weather WCA
	22/10/15	11-0AM	A Medical Board was held at the Hospital on 2nd/Lieut. J.L. WARD, 12th SHERWOOD FORESTERS according to instructions received from A.D.M.S. 24th Division, to report on the physical fitness of that officer for a commission in the Regular Forces. The Board passed him as fit.	

2353 Wt. W2544/1454 700,000 5/15 D. D. & L. A.D.S.S./Forms/C. 2118.

Army Form C. 2118.

Instructions regarding War Diaries and Intelligence Summaries are contained in F. S. Regs., Part II. and the Staff Manual respectively. Title pages will be prepared in manuscript.

WAR DIARY
or
INTELLIGENCE SUMMARY.

(Erase heading not required.)

(11)

Place	Date	Hour	Summary of Events and Information	Remarks and references to Appendices
RENINGHELST	22/10/15	11-0AM	The composition of the Board was as follows:- Major W.G. Nimmo - President; Lieut W.B. Cathcart, " A.W. Bretherton - Members. Hospital - Cases admitted = 1 Officer & 49 OR. Evacuated 49 OR. To DRS = 18 OR. To Duty 1 OR. Remaining 1 Officer & 26 OR. Number of cases bathed = 40 Officers & 827 other Ranks.	Fine weather W.G.N.
"	23/10/15		Work on horse standing & other improvements continues. A great problem in the winter is going to be - the disposal of urine. A urine pit (covered in) constructed by the 5th Fld Amb was opened up to-day & it was found that it was not absorbing, the two feet of earth above the pit being saturated with urine. It is proposed to seperate the urine from faeces in latrines by construction of a trough behind a pole just in front of the latrine buckets, the urine draining off into buckets containing saw-dust, which is eventualy burnt on the incinerator, also the faeces which are now burnt very effectualy after the liquid contents of the pans have been strained off in to a Soakage pit - this latter is not satisfactory. Hospital - Cases admitted = 31 OR. Evacuated = 8 OR. To DRS = 8 OR. To Duty = 5 OR. Cases Remaining = 1 Officer & 8 OR. Numbers bathed to-day = 53 Officers & 990 OR.	Fine weather W.G.N.

2353 Wt. W2544/1454 700,000 5/15 D. D. & L. A.D.S.S./Forms/C. 2118.

Army Form C. 2118.

Instructions regarding War Diaries and Intelligence Summaries are contained in F. S. Regs., Part II. and the Staff Manual respectively. Title pages will be prepared in manuscript.

WAR DIARY
or
~~INTELLIGENCE SUMMARY.~~ (12)

(Erase heading not required.)

Place	Date	Hour	Summary of Events and Information	Remarks and references to Appendices
RENINGHELST	24/10/15		Divine Service	
		9.30 AM	Parade C of E. in Y.M.C.A. TENT	
		10-15 AM	" Nonconformist " "	
"		9-30 AM	" R. C. in Local Church.	
			Hospital - Cases admitted = 37 O.R. Evacuated = 9 O.R. To D.R.S. = 17 O.R. To Duty = 1 Officer + 1 O.R. Remaining = 46 O.R. Number bathed = 46 Officers + 719 O.R.	Fine Weather WCA
"	25/10/15		Work practically stopped to-day owing to the weather, the cement not setting. Some fine red sand & gravel drawn from a quarry between BOESCHEPE & GODEWAERSVELDE, this will greatly help the cement-work. Hospital - Cases admitted = 32 O.R. Evacuated = 9 O.R. To D.R.S. = 30 O.R. To Duty = 2 O.R. Remaining = 36 O.R. Number bathed to-day = 40 Officers & 782 O.R.	Weather broke during night; constant downpour of rain for 18 hours WCA
"	26/10/15		Slight improvement in the weather consequently more work has been done, the horse-standing is steadily progressing. A lot of work will have to be done on the paths & roads to make them possible during the winter. The Skeleton frame-work of one wooden hut drawn to-day for accomodation of personnel of the Unit. The straw thatched huts are not satisfactory, they have been imperfectly thatched and as a consequence the roofs are not water tight - this will be eventually overcome by lining the inside with tin obtained from old	

2353 Wt. W2544/1454 700,000 5/15 D. D. & L. A.D.S.S./Forms/C. 2118.

Instructions regarding War Diaries and Intelligence Summaries are contained in F. S. Regs., Part II. and the Staff Manual respectively. Title pages will be prepared in manuscript.

WAR DIARY
or
~~INTELLIGENCE~~ SUMMARY.

(*Erase heading not required.*)

(13)

Army Form C. 2118

Place	Date	Hour	Summary of Events and Information	Remarks and references to Appendices
RENINGHELST	26/10/15		biscuit tins. The floor, however, is very damp, and can never be otherwise with the men tramping in and out with damp boots. Hospital – Cases admitted = 1 Officer and 22 O.R. Evacuated = 1 Officer & 2 O.R. To D.R.S = 18 O.R. To Duty = 4 O.R. Remaining = 34 O.R. Number bathed today = 40 Officers and 782 O.R.	A better day, some rain at intervals. WCA
"	27/10/15	12-0 NOON	KING GEORGE V visited the area of the 24th Division and inspected a composite Battalion of troops in the Division under the Command of the G.O.C. of the Division. Hospital – Cases admitted = 44 O.R. Evacuated = 10 O.R. To D.R.S. = 15 O.R. To Duty = 1 O.R. Remaining = 52 O.R. Number bathed to-day 32 Officers & 705 O.R.	Slight improvement in weather but a good lot of rain at intervals. WCA
	28/10/15		6 G.S. Wagons & 3 limbered wagons sent in to YPRES under LIEUT. W.B. CATHCART, sufficient brick rubble obtained to carry on work for a week. Work was much interfered with by the poisonous weather. Hospital – Cases Admitted = 3 Officers & 37 O.R. Evacuated = 3 Officers & 17 O.R. To D.R.S. = 41 O.R. To Duty = 3 O.R. Numbers bathed today = 52 Officers & 842 O.R.	Perfectly dreadful weather, constant rain, ground a Quagmire. WCA

Instructions regarding War Diaries and Intelligence Summaries are contained in F. S. Regs., Part II. and the Staff Manual respectively. Title pages will be prepared in manuscript.

Army Form C. 2118.

WAR DIARY

or

~~INTELLIGENCE SUMMARY.~~

(Erase heading not required.)

14

Place	Date	Hour	Summary of Events and Information	Remarks and references to Appendices
RENINGHELST	29/10/15		A much better day, work proceeded with, the standing for horses nearing completion. The framework of one wooden hut put up. Satchels for smoke helmets issued to all ranks & orders issued that the "tube pattern" always to be carried in the satchel on the man. Hospital - Cases admitted = 1 Officer & 38 OR. Evacuated = 1 Officer To D.R.S. = 20 OR. To Duty = 1 OR. Remaining = 45 OR. Number bathed today = 74 Officers & 1114 OR.	A better day, but some rain at intervals
"	30/10/15		There is some difficulty in obtaining sand-stone owing to the fact that the approach to the pit from which it is gathered is in a very bad condition owing to the recent rain. No more supply of coal "Shale" from POPERINGHE is available, so the construction of paths & roads is being hung up. Hospital - Cases admitted = 2 Officers & 40 OR. Evacuated = 22 OR. To D.R.S = 9 OR. To Duty = 5 OR. Remaining = 2 Officers & 49 OR Number bathed today = 67 Officers & 784 OR.	Rain to start with, quite fine later

Army Form C. 2118.

Instructions regarding War Diaries and Intelligence Summaries are contained in F. S. Regs., Part II. and the Staff Manual respectively. Title pages will be prepared in manuscript.

WAR DIARY
or
~~INTELLIGENCE SUMMARY.~~

(*Erase heading not required.*)

.15

Place	Date	Hour	Summary of Events and Information	Remarks and references to Appendices
RENINGHELST	31/10/15	9.0AM	Divine Service Roman Catholics in RENINGHELST CHURCH	
	"	10-15AM	" " " Nonconformists & Presbyterians in Y.M.C.A TENT	
	"	6.0PM	" " Church of England - Evensong in Y.M.C.A. TENT (Voluntary)	
			Hospital - Cases admitted = 60 OR. Evacuated = 2 Officers & 37. OR	Weather worse again, more rain & mud
	"		To D.R.S. = 6 OR. To Duty = 4 OR. Remaining = 62. O.R.	
			Number bathed to-day = 36 Officers & 323 OR.	WCA

1577 Wt. W10791/1773 500,000 1/15 D. D. & L. A.D.S.S./Forms/C. 2118.

24th Division

72nd F.A.
Vol: 3

121
7656

Nov 1915

Nov. 15.

CONFIDENTIAL DIARY

OF OFFICER COMMANDING

72ND FIELD AMBULANCE

FOR MONTH OF NOVEMBER 1915.

72nd FIELD AMBULANCE

Army Form C. 2118.

Instructions regarding War Diaries and Intelligence Summaries are contained in F. S. Regs., Part II. and the Staff Manual respectively. Title pages will be prepared in manuscript.

WAR DIARY
or
~~INTELLIGENCE SUMMARY.~~
(Erase heading not required.)

(1)

Place	Date	Hour	Summary of Events and Information	Remarks and references to Appendices
RENINGHELST	1/11/15		Completion of new wooden-hut delayed owing to the shortage of wood & the horse-standing has gone very slowly the last few days owing to the inclement weather. The separation of urine & faeces in the latrines is working very well, but the disposal of urine is a great problem, an attempt has been made to place saw-dust in urine tubs & burn it on the incinerator but this takes a considerable quantity of sawdust & the supply is limited. The urine is now being poured into a huge closed pit close to the hospital which seems to be absorbing satisfactorily. Hospital - Cases admitted = 5 Officers & 28 O.R. Evacuated - 5 Officers & 21 O.R. To D.R.S = 14 O.R. Remaining = 45 O.R., Numbers bathed today = 42 Officers & 584 O.R.	A perfectly awful day, constant rain, ground like a quagmire. WCN
"	2/11/15		Another miserable day which interfered very much with work, the cement is not setting properly owing to the constant rain.	
		12.30PM	No 7940 L/Cpl TILL W. 1st NORTH STAFFORDS, suffering from shrapnel wound of right chest (penetrating) & face, admitted to hospital his condition was practically hopeless - he died at 4 o'clock. Hospital - Cases admitted = 44 O.R. Evacuated = 14 O.R. To D.R.S. = 9 O.R. To Duty = Nil. Remaining = 66 O.R. Number bathed to-day = 42 Officers & 682 O.R.	Another bad day, almost continuous rain. WCN

2353 Wt. W2544/1454 700,000 5/15 D. D. & L. A.D.S.S./Forms/C. 2118.

Instructions regarding War Diaries and Intelligence Summaries are contained in F. S. Regs., Part II. and the Staff Manual respectively. Title pages will be prepared in manuscript.

Army Form C. 2118.

WAR DIARY
or
INTELLIGENCE SUMMARY.
(*Erase heading not required.*)

(2)

Place	Date	Hour	Summary of Events and Information	Remarks and references to Appendices
RENINGHELST	3/11/15		A better day, work made good progress, the half of horse-standing nearing completion, the other half ought to be finished in two days time 3 thatched + one wooden hut completed, 1 thatched hut in process of construction & 1 wooden hut to be commenced to-morrow.	
		11.30 AM	No 7940 L/Cpl. TILL was buried by Rev. E. L. FROSSARD in part of RENINGHELST Cemetery set aside for British troops - this is the last grave available. Hospital - Cases admitted = 3 Officers & 35 O.R. Evacuated = 3 Officers + 22 O.R. To D.R.S = 12 O.R. To Duty = 1 O.R. Remaining = 65 O.R. 1 Case Died. Number bathed to-day = 49 Officers + 706 O.R.	A better day, rain at frequent intervals. W.C.A.
	4/11/15		Work has been interfered with by the weather, the cement work in the horse-standing has not set owing to the perpetual rain. Hospital - Cases admitted - 3 Officers + 44 O.R., Evacuated = 1 Officer + 28 O.R. To D.R.S = 15 O.R. To Duty = 6 O.R. Remaining = 2 Officers + 60 O.R. Number bathed to-day = 8 Officers + 35 O.R. The reason why such a small number were bathed, was that the dam in the stream was carried away in the early morning by the volume of water coming down, and had to be built up again before water could be pumped up into the boilers.	Another bad day, a good deal of rain. W.C.A.

Army Form C. 2118.

Instructions regarding War Diaries and Intelligence Summaries are contained in F. S. Regs., Part II. and the Staff Manual respectively. Title pages will be prepared in manuscript.

WAR DIARY
or
INTELLIGENCE SUMMARY.
(Erase heading not required.)

(3)

Place	Date	Hour	Summary of Events and Information	Remarks and references to Appendices
REMINGHELST	5/11/15		The first wooden hut was completed today, and the 4th thatched hut nearing completion. The framework of a second wooden hut obtained to-day when this is finished all the personnel of the Unit will be accomodated in huts, this will set free one section at present billeted in an attic above the hospital, this attic will then be used as an extra ward. Hospital – cases admitted = 2 Officers + 46 O.R. Evacuated = 4 Officers 26 O.R. To D.R.S = 4 O.R. To Duty = 14 O.R. Remaining = 62 O.R. Numbers bathed to-day = 68 Officers & 792 O.R	A better day, much finer & Colder WCH
"	6/11/15		Work continued. Two of the thatched huts now completely "tinned" inside with old oil tins. Hospital – cases admitted = 40 O.R (including 5 cases of Trench foot) cases Evacuated = 30 O.R. To D.R.S. = 2 O.R. To Duty = 6 O.R. Remaining = 1 Officer & 51 O.R. Number bathed to-day = 66 Officers & 901. O.R.	A much finer day, Colder. Frost in the early morning WCH

2353 Wt. W2544/1454 700,000 5/15 D. D. & L. A.D.S.S./Forms/C. 2118.

4

WAR DIARY
or
~~INTELLIGENCE SUMMARY~~.
(Erase heading not required.)

4

Army Form C. 2118.

Instructions regarding War Diaries and Intelligence Summaries are contained in F. S. Regs., Part II. and the Staff Manual respectively. Title pages will be prepared in manuscript.

Place	Date	Hour	Summary of Events and Information	Remarks and references to Appendices
RENINGHELST	7.11.15	2-30PM	Divine Service Church of England in 72nd Infantry Brigade Recreation Room	
	"	10-15AM	Nonconformist & Presbyterian in Y.M.C.A. Tent	
	"	9-0AM	Roman Catholics in RENINGHELST Church	
			Hospital Cases admitted = 1 Officer & 26 OR. Evacuated = 28 OR. To D.R.S = 1 OR To Duty = 10 OR. Remaining = 1 Officer & 51 OR. Number bathed to-day = 60 Officers & 552 OR.	a very fine day, no rain, frost at night WCN
"	8.11.15		The weather is beginning to effect the men in the trenches, cases of "Trench Foot" started to come in towards the end of last week, to-day 11 cases have been admitted. The hospital has been very full for the last 10 days, 4 wards are now open, and soon as billets can be obtained for 1 section, another attic will be opend up as a ward. Hospital Cases admitted = 1 Officer & 31 OR Evacuated = 2 Officers & 29 OR To Duty = 8 OR Remaining = 45 OR. Number bathed to-day = 38 Officers & 867 OR.	Fine weather the ground is drying up rapidly WCN

2353 Wt. W2544/1454. 700,000 5/15 D. D. & L. A.D.S.S./Forms/C. 2118.

Army Form C. 2118.

5

Instructions regarding War Diaries and Intelligence Summaries are contained in F. S. Regs., Part II. and the Staff Manual respectively. Title pages will be prepared in manuscript.

WAR DIARY
or
~~INTELLIGENCE SUMMARY.~~

(Erase heading not required.)

Place	Date	Hour	Summary of Events and Information	Remarks and references to Appendices
RENINGHELST	9.11.15		39 cases of Trench Foot admitted to this Ambulance to-day, most of these being from the 9th Division - the great majority in one Battalion 11th HIGHLAND LIGHT INFANTRY. It has been a very busy day in hospital 101 cases having been admitted, & at dinner-time there were 130 patients in to feed whereas only 74 rations had been drawn, the resources of the Ambulance being taxed to the utmost. The four wards were fully occupied & there was a constant stream of cases coming in & being evacuated. Hospital cases admitted = 2 Officers & 61 OR. Evacuated = 1 Officer & 15 OR. To DRS = 7 OR. To Duty = 1 Officer & 10 OR. Number bathed = 56 Officers & 740 OR.	A windy day with considerable rain at intervals NCN
	10.11.15		Patients still come in in considerable numbers, the congestion in hospital becoming worse owing to the fact that the Divisional Rest Station at BOESCHEPE has been full for some days, only a few cases of scabies being taken in. - Hospital - cases admitted = 1 Officer & 101 OR. Cases evacuated = 31 OR. To DRS = 61 OR (there were twenty sent 9th DRS being cases from 9th Division) To Duty - 10 OR. Remaining = 1 Officer & 72 OR.	
		7-30AM	One man - No 2680 Pte MORGAN E. 9/E. SURREY REGIMENT. - died in Hospital, a result of Rifle wound of head, having been admitted about an hour beforehand. Number bathed to-day = 46 Officers & 739 OR.	Another bad day, almost continuous rain NCN

2353 Wt. W2544/1454 700,000 5/15 D. D. & L. A.D.S.S./Forms/C. 2118.

Army Form C. 2118.

Instructions regarding War Diaries and Intelligence Summaries are contained in F. S. Regs., Part II. and the Staff Manual respectively. Title pages will be prepared in manuscript.

WAR DIARY 6

or

INTELLIGENCE SUMMARY.

(Erase heading not required.)

Place	Date	Hour	Summary of Events and Information	Remarks and references to Appendices
RENINGHELST	11/11/15		Cases still coming in in considerable numbers, the Divisional Rest Station is beginning to open again – 10 ordinary cases being sent to-day. Hospital Cases admitted = 61 OR Evacuated = 44 OR. To DRS 100R To Duty = 2 OR Remaining = 1 Officer & 77 OR. Number bathed today = 59 Officers & 638 O.R.	Almost constant rain ground a quagmire WCN
"	12/11/15		Number of cases admitted keeping up to that of last few days & evacuation has been brisk. A small extension has been made of the shed outside used as a dining hall for the patients but is quite inadequate in size, most of the patients having to have their meals in the wards. The horse-standing is now complete but cannot be covered until all the hutments for men are completed. There is one thatched hut hung up for want of straw, and the framework of a wooden hut which cannot be completed owing to the lack of timber. Good progress has been made with the roads & paths during the last few days, but the ground is in an appalling condition, inches deep in mud, we are very well off in this respect compared with other camps, however, most of them being a sea of mud & water, Some of the men still under canvas. The disposal of urine is becoming an urgent matter, the big covered in pit constructed by the 52nd Fld. Amb. is rapidly filling up and it is impossible to get enough sawdust to put in the urine pans	

2353 Wt. W2544/1454 700,000 5/15 D. D. & L. A.D.S.S./Forms/C. 2118.

Instructions regarding War Diaries and Intelligence Summaries are contained in F. S. Regs., Part II. and the Staff Manual respectively. Title pages will be prepared in manuscript.

WAR DIARY
or
INTELLIGENCE SUMMARY.
(*Erase heading not required.*)

7

Army Form C. 2118.

Place	Date	Hour	Summary of Events and Information	Remarks and references to Appendices
RENINGHELST	12.11.15		to incinerate afterwards - unless there is a plentiful supply of sawdust the incinerator cannot deal with it. Hospital - cases admitted = 2 Officers & 65 OR Evacuated = 2 Officers 34 OR To DRS = 13 OR. To Duty = 6 OR. Remaining = 88 OR. No 3757 L/Cpl Burns R 8th BLACK WATCH died at 1-0 PM yesterday having been brought in at 8-30 A.M suffering from Grenade wound of Head - compound fracture with hernia cerebri. He was buried at 4.0 PM. Number bathed to-day = 42 Officers + 648 OR.	almost continuous rain, much warmer. WCN
"	13.11.15		Hospital - Cases admitted = 2 Officers + 58 OR Evacuated = 50 OR To DRS = 12 OR To Duty = 13. OR Remaining = 2 Officers + 71 OR. Number bathed to-day = 54 Officers + 626 O.R.	A better day, fine, rain at intervals WCN
"	14.11.15		Cases increasing in number almost constant stream of traffic in & out, 12 cases to-night had to be placed in an attic above the Hospital occupied by 6 Section Personell.	
		3.0 PM	A.D.M.S. 24th Division sent for me & informed me that there was to be a big artillery demonstration by the Artillery of 5th Corps at 5.0 PM tomorrow onwards, & instructed me to get the Hospital as empty as possible so as to be ready if the enemy retaliated and there were numerous casualties at the same time to have all my bearers ready move off at ~~the~~ short notice should they be needed to re-inforce the 73rd Fld Amb. Arrangements were made by me accordingly.	

2353 Wt. W2544/1454 700,000 5/15 D. D. & L. A.D.S.S./Forms/C. 2118.

Instructions regarding War Diaries and Intelligence Summaries are contained in F. S. Regs., Part II. and the Staff Manual respectively. Title pages will be prepared in manuscript.

WAR DIARY
or
~~INTELLIGENCE SUMMARY.~~
(Erase heading not required.)

8

Army Form C. 2118.

Place	Date	Hour	Summary of Events and Information	Remarks and references to Appendices
RENINGHELST	14.11.15		Hospital – cases admitted = 1 Officer & 80 OR Evacuated = 3 Officers & 35 OR To DRS = 16 OR. To Duty = 7 OR Remaining = 93 OR. Number bathed to-day = 54 Officers & 785 OR.	A very fine day, clear almost cloudless sky. No rain much colder. W.C.A.
"	15.11.15		The Hospital was evacuated this morning, according to orders, with the exception of 6 patients to be discharged to Duty tomorrow. All arrangements have been made to send up bearers if necessary, iron rations & gas helmets thoroughly gone in to & every man's water bottle full.	
"		11.0AM	No 3882 SAPPER E.G. PITT 104th Co. R.E. who was brought in dead to this Ambulance yesterday morning was buried by the REV. W. DICK in the BRITISH Cemetery in RENINGHELST.	
"		12.30PM	The body of CAPT. H.M.C. STAPYLTON O/C "C" Battery 107th BRIGADE R.F.A. was brought to this Ambulance – he had died of wounds (shell wounds Right Thigh) the afternoon before shortly after being hit. He was buried by the REV. W. DICK in the British Cemetery in RENINGHELST at 3-0 P.M. Everything was very quiet on the front last night so evidently the bombardment did not come off Hospital – Cases admitted = 2 Officers & 88 OR. Evacuated = 113 OR. To DRS = 24 OR. To Duty = 16 OR Remaining = 2 Officers & 29 OR. Numbers bathed to-day = 51 Officers & 915 OR.	A fine day much colder. W.C.A.

1577 Wt. W10791/1773 500,000 1/15 D. D. & L. A.D.S.S./Forms/C. 2118.

Instructions regarding War Diaries and Intelligence Summaries are contained in F. S. Regs., Part II. and the Staff Manual respectively. Title pages will be prepared in manuscript.

WAR DIARY
or
~~INTELLIGENCE SUMMARY.~~

9

(*Erase heading not required.*)

Army Form C. 2118.

Place	Date	Hour	Summary of Events and Information	Remarks and references to Appendices
RENINGHELST	16/11/15		Hospital almost empty at the start but cases were being admitted regularly throughout the day.	
		9.0 AM	No 6743 PTE. HUCKS C. 8th ROYAL WEST KENT REGIMENT admitted in a practically moribund condition, with a big hole in the skull and hernia cerebri the result of an explosive rifle wound. He did not die till the early hours of the morning. I proceeded to ST. OMER this afternoon to attempt to get some comforts for the patients in Hospital from the BRITISH RED CROSS SOCIETY, but it took such a long time getting there that there was not enough time left to get anything – it would have been a long job.	
			Hospital – Cases admitted = 2 Officers & 56 OR Evacuated = 2 Officers + 43 OR TO D.R.S = 10 OR To Duty 10 OR Remaining = 2 Officers & 22 OR. ~~Remaining~~ Numbers bathed to-day = 38 Officers + 777 OR.	A fine day generally; but some rain in the afternoon WCA
"	17/11/15	11.15 AM	PTE. HUCKS was buried in the British Cemetery in RENINGHELST by the Rev. D. G. B. POOLE.	
"		7.15 PM	No 16040 PTE SYMONDS. S. 7th NORTHANTS REGIMENT admitted with shrapnel wound of abdomen – he died a few minutes after admission	
			Hospital – Cases admitted = 2 Officers & 77 OR. Evacuated = 2 Officers & 46 OR. TO D.R.S – 10 OR. To Duty = 5. OR. Remaining = 2 Officers & 37 OR. 1 Man died Numbers bathed to-day = 30 Officers & 673 OR.	A fine day on the whole; heavy hail storm with stones as big as marbles about mid-day WCA

2353 Wt. W2544/1454 700,000 5/15 D. D. & L. A.D.S.S. Forms/C. 2118.

Instructions regarding War Diaries and Intelligence Summaries are contained in F. S. Regs., Part II. and the Staff Manual respectively. Title pages will be prepared in manuscript.

WAR DIARY
or
~~INTELLIGENCE SUMMARY.~~
(Erase heading not required.)

10

Army Form C. 2118.

Place	Date	Hour	Summary of Events and Information	Remarks and references to Appendices
RENINGHELST	18/11/15	NOON 12-0PM	No 16040 PTE SYMONDS was buried by the Rev EW SCOTT in the British Cemetery at RENINGHELST.	
	"	5-50AM	No 11034 PTE BUSH HF 1st ROYAL FUSILIERS was admitted with a rifle wound of the head he died at 8-55AM & was buried at 4-0PM by the Rev. B.H.H BROWN in the British Cemetery.	
			No 9775 SGT W. TRUEMAN 1st NORTH STAFFORDS was admitted in a moribund condition suffering from a rifle wound of the head.	Fine day much colder frost at night
			Hospital – Cases admitted = 2 Officers & 75 OR Evacuated = 2 Officers & 49 OR TO DRS – 16 OR. Remaining = 2 Officers & 45 OR Died=1	
			Number bathed today = 51 Officers & 503 OR.	WCA
"	19.11.15	2-30AM	Sgt TRUEMAN died and was buried at 2-0PM by the REV. W. DICK in the British Cemetery.	
	"	12-30PM	The ADMS. 24th Division informed me that the 72nd Field Ambulance would move on the night of 23rd – 24th to be clear RENINGHELST on the POPERINGHE road by 3-45 PM marching at the rear of a composite 72nd BRIGADE. Instructions were given me for preparations to be made for the move.	Still very cold, but some rain at times
			Hospital – Cases admitted = 2 Officers & 42 OR TO DRS = 11 OR To Duty – 7 OR. Remaining = 85 OR.	
			Number bathed to-day = 48 Officers & 976 OR.	WCA

2353 Wt. W2544/1454 700,000 5/15 D. D. & L. A.D.S.S./Forms/C. 2118.

Instructions regarding War Diaries and Intelligence Summaries are contained in F. S. Regs., Part II. and the Staff Manual respectively. Title pages will be prepared in manuscript.

WAR DIARY
or
~~INTELLIGENCE~~ SUMMARY.
(Erase heading not required.)

12

Army Form C. 2118.

Place	Date	Hour	Summary of Events and Information	Remarks and references to Appendices
RENINGHELST	22/11/15	12-30PM	Taking LIEUT A.W. BRETHERTON with me I fetched LIEUT HOGG from the AQMG's office & took him to his own own room placing him in open arrest. Hospital – Cases admitted = 1 Officer & 48 OR. Evacuated = 1 Officer & 49 OR. To D.R.S. = 3 OR. To Duty = 13 OR. Remaining = 56 OR. Number bathed to-day = 31 Officers & 226 OR.	very cold & a hard frost most of the day with a thick fog. WGR
	23/11/15		Many cases admitted during the night. 26 cases of the 3rd Division handed over to No 7 Fld. Amb.	
		11.0AM	Advance Party of No 7. Fld. Amb. arrived & took over the hospital from this Unit.	
	"	9.0AM	The Baths were handed over by LIEUT. R.W. HOGG to LIEUT. J.R. MWSSON MO i/c 3rd Division Sanitary Section. Hospital – Cases admitted = 3 Officers & 64 OR. Evacuated = 3 Officers & 85 OR. To D.R.S = 3 OR. Handed over to No 7. Fld. Amb = 26 OR. Remaining = 6 OR.	
	"	4.30PM	The 72nd Fld. Amb. paraded in the main street of RENINGHELST in front of the Officers Mess, the transport being on the HEKSKEN – RENINGHELST road with the head at the junction of that road with the main street of RENINGHELST. Orders had been received the night before to march at the rear of the 72nd Brigade just after the 7th NORTHAMPTONS, the head of the Brigade to reach Point G 34 a 22 at 4-45 P.M.	Belgium & France Maps "B" Series Sheet 28

2353 Wt. W2544/1454 700,000 5/15 D. D. & L. A.D.S.S./Forms/C. 2118.

Army Form C. 2118.

Instructions regarding War Diaries and Intelligence Summaries are contained in F. S. Regs., Part II. and the Staff Manual respectively. Title pages will be prepared in manuscript.

WAR DIARY
or
~~INTELLIGENCE SUMMARY.~~

(*Erase heading not required.*)

13

Place	Date	Hour	Summary of Events and Information	Remarks and references to Appendices
RENINGHELST	23/11/15		The Head of the Brigade passed by this Unit at 4-55 P.M., but it was not until nearly 6-0 P.M. that this unit march off. The march was made through POPERINGHE (reached at 7.15 PM). ABEELE (reached at 8.45 PM) here there was a 20 minute halt. STEENVOORDE was reached at 10-45 P.M. The Field Ambulance going into Billets at 28a RUE DE CARNOT. The whole Ambulance was in billets and the men being provided with hot soup by 11-45 P.M.	HAZEBROUCK MAP
STEEN-VOORDE	"		4 Horse Ambulance Wagons were lent by the 3rd Division Fld Amb to pick up men suffering from the effects of life in the trenches, who fell out on the march, the Motor Ambulance wagons of this unit following up behind to pick up those missed by the Horse Ambulance. In this way about 80 men were picked up, conveyed to STEENVOORDE where they were sent off to join their units.	The weather during last night became much warmer the fog disappearing. The roads were in a very muddy condition, a slight drizzle of rain at intervals. WCh
	24/11/15	10-0AM	No 30536 CORPL MONRO was brought up on a charge of "Whilst on active Service neglect of Duty – failing to prepare breakfast by the appointed time" – Punishment awarded – "To revert to the ranks"	
	"	10-5AM	No 52011 PTE PAGE was brought up on a charge of "When on active service being drunk" Punishment awarded – "21 days Field Punishment No 1 and 21 days forfeiture of Pay" – The day was spent in resting & cleaning up. 31 cases of sick were collected from different units in the Brigade, & evacuated to No 15 Casualty Clearing Station HAZEBROUCK.	

2353 Wt. W2544/1454 700,000 5/15 D. D. & L. A.D.S.S./Forms/C. 2118.

Army Form C. 2118.

Instructions regarding War Diaries and Intelligence Summaries are contained in F. S. Regs., Part II. and the Staff Manual respectively. Title pages will be prepared in manuscript.

WAR DIARY
or
INTELLIGENCE SUMMARY.
(*Erase heading not required.*)

14

Place	Date	Hour	Summary of Events and Information	Remarks and references to Appendices
STEENVOORDE	24/11/15	8-0PM	Orders received from Brigade as follows:- (1) D group will march to it's new area as follows on November 25th 1915 - 2. 72ND Field Ambulance - march off 10-30AM Route STEENVOORDE - forked road ¼ mile NE of L in CASSEL - OXELEARE - BAVINCHOVE to NOORDPEENE (3) One Ambulance will march in rear of 12 SHERWOOD FORESTERS. Two Ambulances will march in rear of 9th ROYAL SUSSEX. Field Ambulance orders were issued accordingly	72nd Infantry Brigade order No 7. A bleak & blustering day, very cold, much rain at intervals. WCA
"	25.11.15	7-0AM	Reveille	
		8-0AM	Breakfast	
		10-0AM	Horse transport hooked in.	
		10-15AM	Field Ambulance paraded	
		10-45AM	Field Ambulance marched off - the late start being due to other units starting late and congestion of traffic at entrance to Square of STEENVOORDE.	HAZEBROUCK Map 1/100,000
			The march was a slow & tedious one, owing to constant stoppage in front. OXELEARE was not reached till nearly 1 o'clock. CASSEL STATION (BAVINCHOVE) at 1-30 PM. here a delay of 1/4 hour occurred owing to shunting of a goods train. From that point the road was clear & more rapid progress was made & NOORDPEENE was reached at 2-40PM, where the Field Ambulance went in to excellent billets, the men being in five barns & a dry empty house	
NOORDPEENE		9-0PM	Orders received from 72nd Infantry Brigade as follows:- The 72nd Fld. Amb. will move off from NOORDPEENE at 11-30. A.M Route - WATTEN - BLEUE MAISON - GANSPETE to EPERLECQUES. 31 cases of sick in the Brigade evacuated to No 15 C.C.S. HAZEBROUCK	72nd Inf Bgde Order No 8. A cold & windy day with much rain at intervals. WCA

2353 Wt. W2544/1454 700,000 5/15 D. D. & L. A.D.S.S./Forms/C. 2118.

Instructions regarding War Diaries and Intelligence Summaries are contained in F. S. Regs., Part II. and the Staff Manual respectively. Title pages will be prepared in manuscript.

WAR DIARY
or
~~INTELLIGENCE SUMMARY.~~
(Erase heading not required.)

15

Army Form C. 2118.

Place	Date	Hour	Summary of Events and Information	Remarks and references to Appendices
NOORDPENE	26/11/15	6-15AM	Following message received from 72nd Brigade "according to orders just received from 24th Division the destination of this unit will be HOULLE AAA Starting Point & times remain as already detailed"	
		9-30AM	12 sick from the Brigade (1 lying & 11 sitting cases) transferred by Motor Ambulance Wagons to No 20 Casualty Clearing Station ST OMER	
		11.0AM	Horse transport hooked in.	
		11.15AM	72nd Field Ambulance paraded	
		11-30AM	72nd Field Ambulance moved off, passing cross-roads ½ mile S of last E in LEDERZEELE (the Brigade starting point) at 12-50 P.M.	
		1-40PM	½ hours halt for food of men & horses was made about 1 mile W of the above named cross roads WATTEN was passed through at 3-45 PM, BLEUE MAISON at 3-45 PM, GANSPETTE a few minutes later and HOULLE was reached at 4-30PM.	
HOULLE			All the available room for billets for men in HOULLE was taken up by the 9/ROYAL SUSSEX so the men of this unit had to be billeted in an old mill in HOULLE - a very dark & dingy billet, but with the aid of a considerable amount of straw they were made fairly warm & comfortable.	
			The men did not get their dinners until after 6-0 P.M. over 1½ hours after getting into billets - this shows the absolute necessity for the provision of a Field Cooker for a Unit like a Field Ambulance. I sent in an application for one over two months ago but no notice appears to have been taken of my application	WCN

2353 Wt. W2544/1454 700,000 5/15 D. D. & L. A.D.S.S./Forms/C. 2118.

Army Form C. 2118.

WAR DIARY
or
~~INTELLIGENCE SUMMARY~~.
(Erase heading not required.)

16

Instructions regarding War Diaries and Intelligence Summaries are contained in F. S. Regs., Part II. and the Staff Manual respectively. Title pages will be prepared in manuscript.

Place	Date	Hour	Summary of Events and Information	Remarks and references to Appendices
HOULLE	27/11/15	12-30AM	72nd Infantry Brigade, orders just received (4) The remaining units of the 72nd ~~Inf~~ Brig. will march in one column as under:- 1st Line Transport will follow in rear of their Units - Starting Point Cross roads ¼ mile EAST of M in NORTLENLINGHEM The head of each unit will pass the starting point as under:- 72nd Field Ambulance 11-0 AM	72nd Infantry Brigade No 9
		9-0AM	4 Sick of 8/Queens evacuated to NO20 Casualty Clearing Station ST OMER.	
		9-30AM	Horse transport hooked in	
		9-45AM	72nd Field Ambulance paraded	
		9-55AM	" " " Marched off	
		10-10AM	A halt was made for 25 minutes, as the unit was too early, at junction of roads about ¼ mile N of Point 40 on the map	A very cold bright day no rain
		11-0AM	Starting Point passed.	
NORDAUSQUES		12-30PM	72nd Field Ambulance arrived in billets in this place. The area is somewhat congested as in the same village are billeted the Headquarters 72nd Infantry Brigade & the 8TH Queens regiment. Two sections billeted in a large new building (an Engineers Work-shop) and the others in a barn above empty houses just opposite	
"		6-0 to 7-0PM	Capt. G.B.EDWARDS RAMC took a Summary of evidence on the case of LIEUT. R.W. HOGG - Names of witnesses:- 1. CAPT. W.B. CATHCART - 72nd Field Ambulance 2. LIEUT. R. SMITH - 8th QUEENS 3. LIEUT. A.W. BRETHERTON 72nd Field Ambulance	A fine cold day

2353 Wt. W2544/1454 700,000 5/15 D. D. & L. A.D.S.S./Forms/C. 2118.

Instructions regarding War Diaries and Intelligence Summaries are contained in F. S. Regs., Part II. and the Staff Manual respectively. Title pages will be prepared in manuscript.

WAR DIARY
or
~~INTELLIGENCE SUMMARY~~. 17

(Erase heading not required.)

Army Form C. 2118.

Place	Date	Hour	Summary of Events and Information	Remarks and references to Appendices
NORDAUSQUES	28/11/15		Rearrangments of men in billets & inspection of General Sanitation. Commenced handing over charge of the Ambulance to CAPT. G. B EDWARDS. RAMC according to instructions received from DMS 2nd ARMY through ADMS 24th Division	A very fine & cold day, sharp frost. WCN
"	29/11/15		Process of handing over command to Capt G.B. Edwards RAMC continued.	A wretched day almost continuous rain WCN
"	30/11/15		Handed over command of 72nd Field Ambulance to Capt G.B Edwards RAMC and reported departure for ETAPLES to ADMS 24th Division according to instructions received from DMS 2nd Army.	W C Nimmo Major RAMC

2353 Wt. W2544/1454 700,000 5/15 D. D. & L. A.D.S.S./Forms/C. 2118.

24th Bn

Dec/15

72nd F.A.
Vol: 4

72 F.A

121/7824

CONFIDENTIAL

WAR DIARY OF CAPTAIN. G.B. EDWARDS

OFFICER COMMANDING

1/2ND FIELD AMBULANCE

FROM. 1-12-15 TO 31-12-15

72 FIELD AMBULANCE

Instructions regarding War Diaries and Intelligence Summaries are contained in F. S. Regs., Part II. and the Staff Manual respectively. Title pages will be prepared in manuscript.

WAR DIARY
or
~~INTELLIGENCE SUMMARY.~~

(Erase heading not required.)

Army Form C. 2118.

(1)

Place	Date	Hour	Summary of Events and Information	Remarks and references to Appendices
NORDAUSQUES	1.12.15		Took over command of 72nd FIELD AMBULANCE from Maj. W C NIMMO on afternoon of 30.11.15. I was struck with the fact that in selecting billets for the personnel of the Ambulance on 27.11.15 on arrival at NORDAUSQUES no arrangements had been made to treat any possible sick from the Brigade billeted in the area & not place selected by the billeting party. Obtained a small private schoolroom & converted it into a temporary hospital for 20 slight cases. O.C. B section detailed to take charge of the Brigade sick.	
			Published Orders for the Orderly Officer, Orderly Sgt & instructions for men in billets. Detailed fire picquet. Kit & clothing inspection A & B sections.	
"	2.12.15	3.30 PM	Lecture in Boys school on Poisonous gases employed by the Enemy.	
		4 PM	Kit inspection C Section & ASC. All deficiencies checked & indents made out to complete	[signature]
"	3.12.15.		Visited all billets, stables & buildings occupied by the Ambulance. Made plans & chose sites for permanent latrines (pail system) Ablution benches, incinerators etc. All horses in stables, harness room provided.	
		4 PM	Received list of deficiencies in Medical & Surgical equipment of sections & deficiencies & repairs for transport both horse & mechanical	
			Detailed LIET. H F. H. EBERTS as officer in charge of Motor Ambulances in addition to his other duties	[initials]
"	4.12.15.	11. AM.	B & C sections moved into new billets from their original one which has been taken over by the Brigade & is being converted into a recreation room. B Section billeted in barn near river & opposite Hospital. C Section in a cottage 200 yds behind A Section.	
			All sections are employed in collecting material for construction of permanent sanitary arrangements.	
			Made plan of village showing position & numbers occupying various billets, stables, etc, & detailed plan of billets.	
			Lieut. A.W. BRETHERTON & L.Cpl No. M/2101[illegible] BALL. Motor Transport on 8 days leave to ENGLAND	[initials]

2353 Wt. W2544/1454 700,000 5/15 D. D. & L. A.D.S.S./Forms/C. 2118.

72 FIELD AMBULANCE

Instructions regarding War Diaries and Intelligence Summaries are contained in F. S. Regs., Part II. and the Staff Manual respectively. Title pages will be prepared in manuscript.

WAR DIARY
or
~~INTELLIGENCE SUMMARY.~~
(Erase heading not required.)

Army Form C. 2118.

(2)

Place	Date	Hour	Summary of Events and Information	Remarks and references to Appendices
NORDAUSQUES	5.12.15		Drew 1800 bricks from HELLEBROUCQ for constructional purposes.	JMcL Captain
	6.12		Work on incinerators, latrines etc well underway. Cement indented for & obtained. Sand collected from pits at C of LA RECOUSSE LIEUT. R.W.E. HOGG temporary duty with 1 NORTH STAFFORDS.	JMc
	7.12		Two small boilers fitted in room being converted into Bath house.	JMc
	8.12.	11. AM	Two FODEN THRESH disinfectors arrived to disinfect clothing, blankets etc of 72 I. Brigade. Man in charge stated that he had to return to ST OMER leaving here at 3 P.M. He could disinfect 160 blankets in 40 minutes as there were over 4,000 blankets besides hundreds of kits & underclothing requiring to be disinfected. I sent a message to ADMS asking for the disinfectors to remain here & complete the work pointing out the want of time & inconvenience caused by not being able to continue the work. Received reply that it was not possible to arrange at present 72 Inf Brigade ask for report on billets with map to be rendered by 6 P.M. 10.12.15.	72 I Bde 2784 8/12 JMc
	9.12		Flooring for latrines, ablution places, ablution bench, & gravel approaches to these places completed. The undermentioned details arrived from ROUEN No 37814 Sgt. AKERMAN. H.D. N 43322 PTE. BATE. R No 44910 Pte DURHAM C No 57242 Pte DUFFELL. H.W. No 50032 Pte GILSON. A.	JMc
	10.12		Last night very heavy rain. B section flooded out of billets. New billet found about 300 yards to the right of NORDAUSQUES – ST OMER road. B section moved into new billet. Maps of billets & report asked for by the Brigade forwarded to 72 I Brigade. Felt for covering in latrines etc indented for & obtained Incinerator for destruction of excreta & refuse completed.	JMc

2353 Wt. W2544/1454 700,000 5/15 D. D. & L. A.D.S.S./Forms/C. 2118.

72 FIELD AMBULANCE

Instructions regarding War Diaries and Intelligence Summaries are contained in F. S. Regs., Part II. and the Staff Manual respectively. Title pages will be prepared in manuscript.

WAR DIARY
or
~~INTELLIGENCE SUMMARY.~~
(Erase heading not required.)

(3)

Army Form C. 2118.

Place	Date	Hour	Summary of Events and Information	Remarks and references to Appendices
NORDAUSQUES	11/12/15.		LIEUT de BEAUPRE. E.T. & Rev. MINNEAR. G.E. on 8 days leave to ENGLAND 1. Officers rider arrived to complete establishment	JMh
"	12.12.15		LIEUT A.W. BRETHERTON returned from leave	JMh
"	13.12.15		LIEUT H.S. GROVES returned from temporary duty with the 9th EAST. SURREY REGT. CAPT. W.B. CATHCART detailed to drive to 49 DIVISION & enquire into the Field Ambulance arrangements in view of our taking over from them later on. Sent to O/c Records name 3rd Section recommendation for promotion to Sgts. & Staff Sgts	JMh
	14.12.15		Selected 8 mules to be taken to ST MARTIN AUX LAERTES & exchanged for 8 L.D. Horses. when the transport Sgt Major arrived at the appointed place he found that the horses were heavy draught & that there were not enough to be exchanged so he brought the mules back	
		9 am	Sent Captain CATHCART to report at ADMS office to go with the DADMS to visit the 49 Div & obtain particulars as to their methods of collecting casualties & any other useful information. Captain CATHCART returned about 8 P.M. & rendered his report to me	JMh
	15.12.15		Bath house completed & is very satisfactory the men having made a very good job of it B & C Section are using the bathhouse to day & A Section & HQs tomorrow. Received memo from DAQ asking for return of 240 leather jerkins issued to this unit & which are surplus to scale (none being allowed).	JMh

2353 Wt. W2544/1454 700,000 5/15 D. D. & L. A.D.S.S./Forms/C. 2118.

72 FIELD AMBULANCE

Instructions regarding War Diaries and Intelligence Summaries are contained in F. S. Regs., Part II. and the Staff Manual respectively. Title pages will be prepared in manuscript.

WAR DIARY
or
~~INTELLIGENCE SUMMARY.~~
(Erase heading not required.)

Army Form C. 2118.

(4)

Place	Date	Hour	Summary of Events and Information	Remarks and references to Appendices
NORDAUSQUES	16.12.15	9 AM.	LIEUT. R.W. HOGG ~~[illegible]~~ rejoined this unit from temporary duty with 1st North STAFFORDS.	
"	16.12.15		LIEUT. H.F.H. EBERTS temporary duty with 8 Bn The Queens Memo from ADMS 24 Division stating that one FODEN LORRY would be at my disposal tomorrow 17th & following day make arrangements to get full use. Forwarded memo to OC 8th Queens & arranged for disinfector to work at that regiment	GMh
		9.35 PM.	LIEUT R.W. HOGG reported to me that he had found No 8132 Pte HUMPHREYS. A 1st NORTH STAFFORDS drunk in the road & that he had placed him in arrest in the Guard room.	GMh
	17.12.15	11. AM	Forwarded charge sheet & evidence (documentary) charging No 8132 Pte HUMPHREYS. A 1st North STAFFORDS "whilst on Active Service Drunkenness." to OC. 1st N STAFFORDS & asking for an escort.	
		10 AM.	FODEN LORRY. arrived man stated he had only a little coal & not enough to work all day. This morning my QrMr reported to me that there was no coal to be had today or I have sent him round to the disinfector to find out how much is required & to see if it can be obtained, Arranged that the QrMr 8th Queen's will supply the coal.	GMh
	18.12.15		Nothing to report	

2353 Wt. W2544/1454 700,000 5/15 D. D. & L. A.D.S.S./Forms/C. 2118.

Instructions regarding War Diaries and Intelligence Summaries are contained in F. S. Regs., Part II. and the Staff Manual respectively. Title pages will be prepared in manuscript.

72 Field Ambulance

WAR DIARY
or
~~INTELLIGENCE SUMMARY.~~
(*Erase heading not required.*)

(5)

Army Form C. 2118.

Place	Date	Hour	Summary of Events and Information	Remarks and references to Appendices
NORDAUSQUES	19/12/15		A.D.M.S. visited the billets & commented favourably on the arrangements which had been made.	
			Lieut. E.J. de BEAUPRE returned from leave. Also Rev. G.E. MENNIER.	SM
	20/12/15		One Sunbeam car on returning from ST OMER. broke down. report forwarded to O.C. 7 A.M.W.	SM
	21/12/15		PTE. No 3801 W. DYKES on leave to England until 28/12/15	
			Report received from ½ ASC Sect AG Base re L/Cpl J. BALL stating that his leave had been extended to 28 Dec.	SM
	22/12/15		Report from A.P.M. reference damage done to farm tools at B sections billet. Damage claimed 18 Francs. Am investigating	SM
			LIEUT A.W. BRETHERTON temporary duty with 8th R.W. KENTS	
	23.12.15.			

2353 Wt. W2544/1454 700,000 5/15 D. D. & L. A.D.S.S./Forms/C. 2118.

72 Field Ambulance

WAR DIARY
or
~~INTELLIGENCE SUMMARY.~~
(Erase heading not required.)

Army Form C. 2118.

Instructions regarding War Diaries and Intelligence Summaries are contained in F. S. Regs., Part II. and the Staff Manual respectively. Title pages will be prepared in manuscript.

(6)

Place	Date	Hour	Summary of Events and Information	Remarks and references to Appendices
NORDAUSQUES	24/12/15	10 AM	Reported at ADMS Office for conference reference move into forward area. Will probably move morning 27th by train (dismounted) Transport by road on 26th to 14 Div area & occupy 43rd F Amb area for a few days before moving up to take over from 2nd West Riding Field Ambulance A 23 a 0.0. sheet 28	
		10.35 AM	Message from 72 I.B. asking numbers of dismounted & mounted party moving with the unit. Replied. Dismounted Officers 9 O.R. 167 Transport Officers 2 ASC 38 Ranks 14. Motor Ambulance Officers 1. ASC 15.	BM.1
			Memo received from 72 I.B. with report by Brigadier on No 52020 Pte J. Jolley Ranks as to his fitness to be employed at his trade & sent home to report to Messrs BRUNNER MOND & Co CHESHIRE. Report states that he would be usefully employed at his trade. Correspondence forwarded to ADMS.	[initials]
"	25/12/15	10.45 AM	Instructions received from ADMS 24 Div. On arrival at L 3 a 6.8. (sheet 27) communicate with OC 2 WR FA & arrange take over Ambulance & outposts on 28th. Motor Cars to be dispatched so as to rejoin at 14 Div rest area. One car to proceed 108 Bde RFA arrange direct with OC Bde.	M.S.107
		11.40 AM	Advance parties units 41 I.B. arrive forenoon 26 accomodate & hand over billets 27th	S.C. 47
		1. P.M.	Baggage wagons will march with 1st line transport	SC 48
		5. P.M.	Received orders & table I for movement. Men to be at station ½ hour before train starts. Billeting parties by 8.19 am train WATTEN on 26.12.15. 40 men per truck. Remainder I.L.T. move early 26.12.15 under orders to be issued by Bde T.O.	72 I.B order 10 copy 10.
			Train No 1. depart 1.59 AM. AUDRUICQ to near POPERINGHE arrive 5.21 AM. 102 men 72 F. Amb. L 3 a 6.8 (27)	Table I.
			" No 4 " 8.9 AM " " " " " 11.47 AM. 47 " " " "	

2353 Wt. W2544/1454 700,000 5/15 D. D. & L. A.D.S.S./Forms/C. 2118.

72 Field Ambulance

Instructions regarding War Diaries and Intelligence Summaries are contained in F. S. Regs., Part II. and the Staff Manual respectively. Title pages will be prepared in manuscript.

WAR DIARY
or
~~INTELLIGENCE SUMMARY.~~
(Erase heading not required.)

Army Form C. 2118.

(7)

Place	Date	Hour	Summary of Events and Information	Remarks and references to Appendices
NORDAUSQUES	25.12/15	5.30PM.	Informed 72 I.B. that they had not given me sufficient accommodation in table 1 & that I required room for 20 more men.	
"	"	7.PM.	20 men may go on NO 3 train brake A1.	BM 12
			Train 3 depart 7.39 AM. AUDRUICQ to near POPERINGHE arrive 11.18 AM.	
"	"		Bde Transport Officer came to the Office & gave verbal order for the Transport to be at Cross roads NORDAUSQUES at 5.35 AM 26.12.15.	
		9.PM.	Order received from 72 I.B. Suspend all orders for move of 24 Division till further notice aaa ack aaa.	BM 15.
			Christmas celebration have been most successful. The Field Ambulance obtained permission to use a large disused mill & fitted it up with tables. At 12.30 the men had a good Christmas dinner. Roast beef, pork, two vegetables, apple, orange & nuts for every man. Christmas pudding, lemonade beer & wine. After dinner at 2.30 'sports' were held until dark & were very good. The Brigadier General put in an appearance. At 6 P.M. prizes were distributed in the hall & the Kings Christmas message read to the men. Afterwards a concert & the evening wound up with a cinema show.	[initials]
"	26/12/15	10.30AM	Message from 72 I.B. G.O.C. will inspect Bde Group marching order tomorrow 10.30 am. All units as strong as possible with Transport. Drafts to parade separately. Details follow. Cancelled	O.S. 2.
"	26.12.15 ~~27.12.15~~	11.6 PM ~~9 AM~~	Message from 72 I.B. begins It is possible that the Commander in Chief may visit you during afternoon of 27.12.15	BM. 16.
"	27.12.15	9 AM	Time table & orders for inspection by G.O.C. 24 Division tomorrow 28.12 at 10.30 AM. received from 72 I.B.	Q 974. 26/12/15

2353 Wt. W2544/1454 700,000 5/15 D. D. & L. A.D.S.S./Forms/C. 2118.

72 Field Ambulance

Instructions regarding War Diaries and Intelligence Summaries are contained in F. S. Regs., Part II. and the Staff Manual respectively. Title pages will be prepared in manuscript.

WAR DIARY
or
~~INTELLIGENCE~~ SUMMARY.
(Erase heading not required.)

Army Form C. 2118.

Place	Date	Hour	Summary of Events and Information	Remarks and references to Appendices
NORDAUSQUES	27.12.15		Reported to ADMS & to APM on return from leave of Dcpe Bell AAC. GOC 24 Div. went round billets & congratulated the Field Ambulance on the good work they had put in in improving billets & in their good sanitary arrangements.	JMh
"	28.12.15	9.50AM.	Field Ambulance 130 strong including 5 Officers marched off for parade ground. Arrived on ground at 10.8 am. & took up position on right of front line. GOC 24 Division arrived at 10.30 AM & inspected the Ambulance. He remarked on the iron ration bag. There is no place on the belt to hang it & it swinging about, looks untidy, wears out rapidly, & breaks up the ration. Parade terminated at 11.30 & the Ambulance marched off. I remained with GOC & at 11.55 the Transport passed. After the parade the GOC congratulated COs on the improvement in the units & suggested that they should now devote more time to night work over open country.	
		12.35PM	Returned to Billets & found the ADMS waiting there. he remained & saw the Transport return. The transport both animals & waggons were in excellent condition.	JMh
"	29.12.15		Received instructions from ADMS to send an officer to report to OC 51. Field Ambulance at POPERINGHE to find out all particulars as to collecting etc with a view to this unit taking over. A report to be rendered on return. Saw ADMS & arranged to go to POPERINGHE myself & take my Quarter Master	

2353 Wt. W2544/1454 700,000 5/15 D. D. & L. A.D.S.S./Forms/C. 2118.

72 Field Ambulance

WAR DIARY

or

~~INTELLIGENCE SUMMARY.~~

(*Erase heading not required.*)

Army Form C. 2118.

Instructions regarding War Diaries and Intelligence Summaries are contained in F. S. Regs., Part II. and the Staff Manual respectively. Title pages will be prepared in manuscript.

(9)

Place	Date	Hour	Summary of Events and Information	Remarks and references to Appendices
NORDAUSQUES	30/12/15	8AM	Left in Car for POPERINGHE. arrived at 10.45. saw OC 51 Field Ambulance & obtained information about collecting, line occupied, dressing station etc. Visited ADMS 17 Div. & arranged that OC 51 F.A. should leave behind a certain number of blankets, stretchers, latrine buckets etc & that I ~~must~~ leave a corresponding number at my billets so that it would save transport. The ADMS 17 Div & OCs Field Ambulances will visit the 24 Div area tomorrow & arrangements will then be completed	
"	"	7PM.	Returned to my unit. Thresh disinfector sent to 8 R.W. Kents No 3801 Pte DYKES. W. returned from leave. No 3077 " KYTE W. proceeded on leave to return on 6th Jan 9.15 am from Victoria	GM.
"	31/12/15	1.30 P.M.	O.Cs 51, 52, 53, Field Ambulances arrived here & were shown round the men's billets. The possibility of exchanging blankets, stretchers etc so that each ambulance changing over would be saved transporting them, was discussed but nothing definite could be decided as up to the present we do not know which ambulances will be taking over from the others. A very wet day, all arrangements made to ~~have~~ practice night collecting over open country, cancelled.	

J. B. Edwards
Capt RAMC
O.C. 72 Field Ambulance

24th Div

72nd Field Amb.
Vol 5

F/16911

24

Jan 1916

72 F.A

S

CONFIDENTIAL

WAR DIARY

OF

(CAPT. G.B.EDWARDS.) OFFICER COMMANDING,

1/2ND FIELD AMBULANCE.

FROM 1st JANUARY 1916 TO 31st JANUARY 1916

72 FIELD AMBULANCE

Instructions regarding War Diaries and Intelligence Summaries are contained in F. S. Regs., Part II. and the Staff Manual respectively. Title pages will be prepared in manuscript.

WAR DIARY
or
~~INTELLIGENCE SUMMARY.~~
(Erase heading not required.)

(1)

Army Form C. 2118.

Place	Date	Hour	Summary of Events and Information	Remarks and references to Appendices
NORDAUSQUES	1.1.16		Forwarded duplicate copy of Diary for September 1915 to O/c Rame Records.	
	"	4 P.M.	Leave of M/2/101449 Le Cpl. BALL extended to 1 January.	O.A.S.C. / 8720 AG Office base ASC Section
"	2.1.16	11.30 AM	Ordered to ADMS office. Informed that Transport would probably move on 4th & that I was to send an advance party of 2 Officers & 16 O.R. on by cars on 5th the remainder by train on 6th.	[illegible] Edmund.
		2.30 PM	Field Ambulance paraded & instructed in use of gas helmets. Rev. FROSSARD returned from leave. Sent N.1537 A to Paymaster i/c Clearing House Base. For December.	S.M.
"	3.1.16	10. am	Received orders from 24 Div. ADMS 24 Div & 72 Bde for transport to move tomorrow & be at X Roads ST MARTIN AU LAERTES at 10-30 am	HQ. Q1735 2/1/16.
		2.30 PM	Attended lecture with lantern slides of the new line to be occupied by 24 Div.	
"	4.1.16.	11. AM.	Received orders ~~HQ~~ for Field Ambulance to move on 6 Jan. Entraining ST. OMER 6 40 AM. arrive POPERINGHE 9-26 AM. Issued orders for advance party to proceed tomorrow at 9.30 am Lt LAING i/c. to take over adv dressing station at BRANHOEK from 51 Field Ambulance. also advanced post at ASYLUM. YPRES & Head Quarters at POPERINGHE. To go in 3 Sunbeam & 1 Ford Cars.	HQ. 24 Div. O/1735 ADMS M 875.
		4 PM.	O.C. 53 Field Ambulance arrived to take over billets	
		6 PM.	One Section of 53 Field Ambulance arrived with one Officer	The personnel of 53 F.A. arrived quite unexpectedly S.M.

2353 Wt. W2544/1454 700,000 5/15 D. D. & L. A.D.S.S./Forms/C. 2118.

Instructions regarding War Diaries and Intelligence Summaries are contained in F. S. Regs., Part II. and the Staff Manual respectively. Title pages will be prepared in manuscript.

72 FIELD AMBULANCE **WAR DIARY** *or* **INTELLIGENCE SUMMARY.** (*Erase heading not required.*)

Army Form C. 2118.

(2)

Place	Date	Hour	Summary of Events and Information	Remarks and references to Appendices
NORDAUSQUES	4-1-16	5 P.M.	Another Sunbeam Ambulance broke down in starting. This leaves me with 2 Sunbeam & 2 unreliable Ford cars. Have written a report to ADMS. These cars are continually breaking down.	
			Lc Cpl. BALL ASC returned from leave to day	
			Lieut J.T. COOKE proceeded on leave to England	
			One case Measles sent to 7. General Hospital from 9th EAST SURREY	
"	5-1-16	5-45AM.	Pte JORDAN on leave to England.	
			S.S. CLARK on leave to England	JM
"		9.20AM.	LIEUT. LAING & LT. GROVES with advanced party left by 3 motor Ambulances (one belonging to 47A.)	
			One Sunbeam Car No 15643 returned from Workshop.	
			One motor Cycle No B.S.A. broke down this morning.	
			No M2 116398 Pte JENKINS H.W. 14 day F.P. No1. for drunkeness	
		2 P.M.	All orders written out & arrangements for the move completed	JM
"	6.1.16	2 AM.	Captain T.W. WEBSTER. LIEUT A.W. BRETHERTON & party move off to entrain at ST OMER. for POPERINGHE.	
		5-30AM	LIEUT R.W. HOGG. & party moved off to entrain at AUDRUCQ for POPERINGHE. I joined this party at 7.30AM train left 7-45AM. changed HAZEBROUCK. No train on had to wait & eventually got a train 12-20 arrived	JM

2353 Wt. W2544/1454 700,000 5/15 D. D. & L. A.D.S.S./Forms/C. 2118.

Instructions regarding War Diaries and Intelligence Summaries are contained in F. S. Regs., Part II. and the Staff Manual respectively. Title pages will be prepared in manuscript.

72 FIELD AMBULANCE

WAR DIARY
or
~~INTELLIGENCE SUMMARY.~~

(Erase heading not required.)

Army Form C. 2118.

(3)

Place	Date	Hour	Summary of Events and Information	Remarks and references to Appendices
POPERINGHE	6-1-16	2.10PM	Arrived POPERINGHE. Found remainder of Ambulance at H^d Q^rs. Sent remainder of C section up to BRANDHOEK to report to Lieut LAING for duty. Took over from Maj. GOWLAND. OC 51 Field Ambulance. Wrote report to ADMS 24 Division also wired completion of move. 7 Cars 17 Div transferred from 51 Field Amb. CAPT. CATHCART reported 1 HD cart by Veterinary Officer on 5-1-16 for lice & itch.	SM
"	7-1-16		Two of my cars broke down obtained loan of two from 73 Field Ambulance. Wrote report to ADMS 24 Div about these cars which are frequently breaking down & are unreliable. Inspected Advanced Dressing Station BRANDHOEK found it dirty & a number of repairs necessary. Stoves, lamps, & many windows required. Sanitary arrangements bad. Report forwarded to ADMS 24 Div. Found Horse lines at POPERINGHE very bad state mud several feet deep. Horse standings brick but had to wade through mud to get to them. No shelter or wind screen. Saw Town Major, found new ground & had permission to use it. Propose building lines & shelters. PTE. KYTE returned from leave.	SM
			CPL. WATTS & PTE 47976 Jones J B detailed for water duties at 5 Corps water tanks G. 7 d 8.5. (sheet 28).	
	8-1-16	11.30AM	Remainder of 51 Field Ambulance left. 49477 Pte McNaughton detailed for duty a signal Office. Indented for Webb equipment for Personnel GRO 1346 4-1-16	SM
	9-1-16		1. Heavy Draught horse received from L 14 b 9.4 (sheet 27). Visited advanced Dressing Station at ~~[illegible]~~ BRANDHOEK & also collecting post at ASYLUM made notes of various things required for these places such as stoves, glass for windows, etc.	SM
	10-1-16		Received new censor stamp No 1668 & destroyed old one sending holder to Base. Visited 5 Corps water tanks & tested water. Each tank holds 2000 gallons & there are 8 tanks. Orderlies are keeping the books correctly showing amount of Chloride of lime used per 100 galls & the names of Units drawing water. Forwarded a report to ADMS 24 Division on bad condition of roads used by cars when collecting. 1 FORD CAR. returned on completion of duty with 108th Battery	SM

2353 Wt. W2544/1454 700,000 5/15 D. D. & L. A.D.S.S./Forms/C. 2118.

72 Field Ambulance

Instructions regarding War Diaries and Intelligence Summaries are contained in F. S. Regs., Part II. and the Staff Manual respectively. Title pages will be prepared in manuscript.

WAR DIARY
or
INTELLIGENCE SUMMARY.
(Erase heading not required.)

Army Form C. 2118.

(4)

Place	Date	Hour	Summary of Events and Information	Remarks and references to Appendices
POPERINGHE	11-1-16	11.30AM	G.O.C. 24 Division inspected the Field Ambulance buildings & horse lines. He remarked on the number of Motor Ambulance cars broken down & said that in future the cars were only to go as far as the Asylum & that horse ambulances were to collect & bring cases back from the aid posts to the Asylum H12 d 6.6. (28). I wrote report to ADMS. pointing out that this meant a 14 mile journey each day for the horses which are temporarily getting 4 lbs hay less than normal ration. The only advantage gained is that the cars are saved. The disadvantages are, that the aid posts can only be cleared twice instead of three times, evacuation is delayed, patients have an extra unloading & loading to undergo before they arrive at CCS. The horses are exposed to shell fire for eight hours & would at present be doing heavy work with a reduced ration. The question of stabling extra horses would be difficult at BRANDHOEK. Horses put on short Hay ration 6 lbs in place of 10 lbs. DRO 35. 9.1.16	
			Six cases Trench foot admitted from 8 R. W. Kent. 1 Case from 9 E. Surrey Regt.	
			1 Car lent by 73 F Amb broke down in YPRES sent for lorrie of 7 A.W.U. back axel of car broken.	
			LIEUT J.T. COOKE returned from leave. 5 Cases Trench feet admitted mostly slight cases	SM
	12.1.16		DADMS 5 Corps visited Field Ambulance. Memo from ADMS 24 Div. that I was to continue using cars in evacuation of casualties as usual & Report on any car damaged at end of week.	
			S.S. CLARKE returned from leave	
			Pte JORDAN	SM
	13.1.16		ADMS 24 Division visited F. Amb. & I then went with him to BRANDHOEK with him to inspect the Advanced Dressing Station.	
			Supplied O.C. 24 Divisional Baths with medical comforts for 40 men. Memo from 72 Infy Bde asking if some arrangement could be made for sick men, coming down by Car at night, to stop at ASYLUM & get their marching boots at present they come down in trench gum boots which are removed at Ambulance & sent back to Unit. the men then being without any boots.	SM

2353 Wt. W2544/1454 700,000 5/15 D. D. & L. A.D.S.S./Forms/C. 2118.

42 FIELD AMBULANCE

Instructions regarding War Diaries and Intelligence Summaries are contained in F. S. Regs., Part II. and the Staff Manual respectively. Title pages will be prepared in manuscript.

WAR DIARY
or
INTELLIGENCE SUMMARY.
(Erase heading not required.)

Army Form C. 2118.

(5)

Place	Date	Hour	Summary of Events and Information	Remarks and references to Appendices
POPERINGHE	14-1-16		CAPT CATHCART & Pte GRIEVESON on leave. Order received to ration two men caretakers of Div. cemetery Hdqrs (20) who will live at ASYLUM. Inspected horses several have mud rash badly. Pte UNDERWOOD 5th NORTHUMBERLAND FUSILIERS wandered in here having lost his way. he was suffering from mental instability Reported case to APM & transferred him to 73 FA for observation. ~~[illegible]~~ Went up to Regt Aid Posts at MILL reported condition of Roads to ADMS. The Roads are very bad & a grave source of danger to patients & the cars in several places the crump holes are very bad indeed & on a dark night it would not be possible to use them.	JMh
	15-1-16		Sgt Maj. ~~[illegible]~~ COGGINS & Sgt Maj BAKER on leave. Received three stoves coal, 5 rolls of felting, two horn troughs, wind screens, & timber for constructional purposes.	JMh
	16-1-16		Sgt. NEWHAM & Sgt. HEDLEY on leave. Inspected horses & mules. Mules in good condition. Horses suffering with lice. Two riders of little use one stumbles badly & is about 12 years old other bad corns always going lame. One heavy D. very debilitated. Two bad workers & won't pull. One rider cracked heel. Memo from ADMS asking if I had supply of ammonia capsules & Atropine in case of Gas attack. Answer yes ample to supply all Regt. MO's & for Field Ambulance use. Memo from DADMS recommending filling sand bags with rubble & clearing holes in road previously reported by me. Am organizing two stretcher squads of handy men as a pioneer section for odd jobs of this sort. ADMS. DADMS & Self went up to Asylum & Regt Aid Posts. Discussed the question of making aid posts near front line. O.C. 1st R. Fusiliers said it was not possible at present as trenches were bad & cases could not be moved during daytime. He also said that new dug-outs were being made & that in two or three weeks time it might be possible to have an aid post closer up. These are at present is about 1½ to 2 hours carry from front line ie about 1 to 1¼ miles. Indented for practice Gas Helmets.	JMh
	17-1-16		Veterinary Officer did Mallein test on 9 H.D & 11 Riders, 8 Mules. ADVS also came round during afternoon & inspected the animals which had been done he left a message for the Veterinary Officer to do two horses	JMh

2353 Wt. W2544/1454 700,000 5/15 D. D. & L. A.D.S.S./Forms/C. 2118.

72 FIELD AMBULANCE

Instructions regarding War Diaries and Intelligence Summaries are contained in F. S. Regs., Part II. and the Staff Manual respectively. Title pages will be prepared in manuscript.

WAR DIARY
or
INTELLIGENCE SUMMARY.
(Erase heading not required.)

Army Form C. 2118.

(6)

Place	Date	Hour	Summary of Events and Information	Remarks and references to Appendices
POPERINGHE	17-1-16		which he had not considered necessary to do on account of their being recently joined remounts bearing marks of having been done before. ADVS advised Cresol solution 3 to 1 bucket of water to be brushed in against the hair for lice.	
		6 P.M.	Sent Lieut Hogg 1 NCO & 18 bearers up to advanced post to stand ready in case of an attack & also if no attack to fill in roads & clean up Asylum. No attack developed & the squad spent the night in filling in & repairing the shell holes along the road between Asylum & Regt aid post about two miles.	
			Received three very good petrol lamps with mantles from the ordnance. Completed reorganization of sections. every man is now detailed by name & as far as possible will be kept in his own section. Cantlies being filled from A & B section as also are men for special work as on water duties at Corps water tanks, Signals, Ration dump Divisional Baths etc.	[illegible]
	18-1-16	12.35 PM	11 Heavy D & 3 Riders Mallein test. No positive result from yesterdays test.	
		3.24 PM	Lieut ILOTT. C.H.T. Rance arrived from 26 General Hospl ETAPLES to report to ADMS 24 Division Lieut PATCH C.T.L. Rance arrived from ROUEN to report to ADMS 24 Division. for me to billet both officers & await instructions. Memo received from ADMS. Visited Advanced Dressing Station at BRANDHOEK.	
	19-1-16	11 AM.	Major LIGERTWOOD RAMC OC 103 Field Ambulance with three Officers arrived for instruction from FERSINGHEIN & returned the same afternoon. Order from ADMS Lieut PATCH to report to OC 8th Queens for duty " " Lieut ILOTT " " " " 24 Divisional Train for duty	[illegible]
			11 Mules & 2 Riders Mallein test. No positive reaction from yesterdays test. AF B113 returned from 8th The Queens saying that it was unnecessary as ruled by the General. Correspondence forwarded to ADMS for authority to discontinue. Report on absorbent qualities of double Cyanide Cotton wool used by Field Ambulance. Report forwarded stating merely ordinary cotton wool used. Cyanide wool not very absorbent. Indent for bricks, timber, Cement & iron roofing again forwarded to CRE as work on buildings is now at a standstill for want of material.	[illegible]

72 FIELD AMBULANCE

Instructions regarding War Diaries and Intelligence Summaries are contained in F. S. Regs., Part II. and the Staff Manual respectively. Title pages will be prepared in manuscript.

WAR DIARY
or
INTELLIGENCE SUMMARY.
(Erase heading not required.)

Army Form C. 2118.

Place	Date	Hour	Summary of Events and Information	Remarks and references to Appendices
POPERINGHE	20-1-16	4 P.M.	B Section relieves C Section at BRANDHOEK & Asylum C Section returning to Head Quarters. Secret memo from ADMS. dealing with after effects of Gas used in recent German attack circulated to all MOs of this unit. Inspected a house which had been demolished by shell fire just at the back of the Head Quarters of this Ambulance. There is a good deal of timber & bricks which would be useful for building approaches to horse lines, cook houses, latrines etc. Saw owner & struck a bargain for 75 Francs the lot as it stands. As wood & bricks are scarce I am not likely to get any from CRE	[initials]
"	21-1-16		Sent in application for permission to purchase above material. CRE. sent out representative to estimate value & he has come to conclusion that the price asked is a very low one so there is some prospect of my being able to start work again tomorrow. Lieut H.S. GROVES goes on leave to return on 28th. Pte ZIFF goes on leave to return on 28th. Pte SMITH & Pte OLIVER 8th Buffs both self inflicted wounds evacuated to 10 CCS by O/C B Section at Advanced dressing Station. I went to 10 CCS & got Private Smith back but Pte OLIVER has a compound fracture L forearm so will be evacuated. Pte SMITH will be ~~——~~ transferred to Special hospital for Self Inflicted wounds at BOESCHAEPE tomorrow. Sent memo to CRE asking for permission to purchase demolished house at back of Field Ambulance the bricks & timber urgently required for constructional purposes. Made bargain for 75 Francs. Lieut SHAW. RE inspected building & said it was very cheap. Indented for 36 Trench stretchers GRO 1372 Indented for 100 doses mixed Typhoid Vaccine	[initials]
	22-1-16		DDMS & DADMS 5th Corps inspected Field Ambulance billets, wards etc & expressed his satisfaction at the work being carried out. I visited adv dressing station Brandhoek & Asylum at YPRES. Made a plan of cellars at ASYLUM & drew up scheme for dealing with sudden increase in casualties. Cellars full of smoke from various fire places used by REs & bearer squad. drew plan for closet in fire place. Inspection gas helmets. Indented for new ones to replace several defective in valves & eye pieces. Town bombed by aircraft at 11.30 P.M little damage done.	[initials]
	23-1-16		Captain W.B CATHCART Sgt Maj. COGGINGS. Sgt Maj BAKER & Pte GRIEVSON returned from leave	[initials]

Army Form C. 2118.

Instructions regarding War Diaries and Intelligence Summaries are contained in F. S. Regs., Part II. and the Staff Manual respectively. Title pages will be prepared in manuscript.

72 Field Ambulance

WAR DIARY
or
INTELLIGENCE SUMMARY.
(Erase heading not required.)

(8)

Place	Date	Hour	Summary of Events and Information	Remarks and references to Appendices
POPERINGHE	24-1-16		Captain WEBSTER & Sgt TOMLINSON ASC MT on leave to 1.2.16.	
			Visited ADMS 24 Div. He told me that GOC was keen on opening a Coffee bar at Asylum for men of night working parties & asked me if it could be run by the Field Ambulance. I told him that it could but first it would be necessary to get a fatigue party to remove the debris clean boilers etc & that as all my men were fully employed I could not do this but could run the place when once filled up	
			A charge against No 15648 Pte Nolan driving without lights Control post 22 12/1/16 at 8PM from APM Canadian Div handed to me by Lt GARNETT OC 7 AMWU	MM
	25-1-16		Received several memos to day from Hd Qrs 24 Div to draw canvas for screening windows at Asylum, mugs drinking, soup rations etc. forwarded the lot to ADMS with a memo that I did not understand what these referred to as I had no previous instruction for what use they were to be put apart from our conversation of yesterday	
			Investigated charge against Pte Noland. dismissed the case & forwarded action taken to APM 24 Div.	
		11.30am	2nd Lt J.A. RENNIE 12 FIELD COY RE sent here by Town Major. This officer had lost his memory & was obviously a mental case. Transferred him to 10 CCS & notified his CO	MM

1577 Wt. W10791/1773 500,000 1/15 D. D. & L. A.D.S.S./Forms/C. 2118.

72 Field Ambulance

Instructions regarding War Diaries and Intelligence Summaries are contained in F. S. Regs., Part II. and the Staff Manual respectively. Title pages will be prepared in manuscript.

WAR DIARY
or
INTELLIGENCE SUMMARY.
(Erase heading not required.)

Army Form C. 2118.

(9)

Place	Date	Hour	Summary of Events and Information	Remarks and references to Appendices
POPERINGHE	25-1-16		Visited BRANDHOEK & ASYLUM YPRES. Instructed Lieut HOGG to collect material for building fire place & to push on the work of cleaning the cellar. Took him my own whitewash & told him to get the walls done as soon as the new fire place was working & all the smoke stopped.	
			MAJOR CONWAY 1st North STAFFORDS came in here & stopped the night. He is to be sent to ARQUES tomorrow for a Board to be held on him for wound pension.	
			Charge against 40794 Dr BUFFHAM by APM NORTHUMBRIAN DIV trotting Mules along road 22-1-16.	
			Received 1 H.D horse from Div Cavalry	JMh
	26-1-16	9 AM	MAJ CONWAY dispatched to ARQUES. Memo from SSO telling me to draw 500 soup cocoa or bovril rations daily.	
			Dealt with charge against 40794 Dr BUFFHAM 10 days F.P. No1 action taken forwarded APM. 24 Division	
			Saw the SSO & arranged with him to draw the 500 rations to day & tomorrow but not after that date & am to let him know when the Coffee bar is ready. Correspondence forwarded to ADMS	
			Requisition to draw 8000 bricks sanctioned by CRE.	
			Received MS 411 from ADMS dealing with arrangement for Coffee bar. A.A.&Q.M.G. to draw & deliver the Coal weekly also arrange storage of water. ADMS asks how many temporary unfit for trench duty men I require to run it. replied six. CRE will board up windows & any minor work.	
			DRO 143 25-1-16. reference this Office No C/126 Paint & Stencils for marking vehicles are now available at Ordnance	JMh
	27-1-16		Reference DRO 143. 27-1-16 no paint is obtainable from store up to the present. Obtained stencil two days ago.	
			Received Q 2285 re coffee bar from A&Q 24 Div	
			No 49488 Pte PORTER sent to HAVRE to report BASE COMMANDANT to be tested for munition worker.	
			DRO. 146 26-1-16 a new pattern gas helmet P.H. HELMETS to be issued shortly.	JMh
	28-1-16		Received 86 trench stretchers. Visited BRANDHOEK & ASYLUM. No paint for marking vehicles can be obtained from Ordnance.	JMh
	29-1-16		Obtained paint from Ordnance. Lieut H.S. GROVES returned from leave. 12 men lent by D.R.S. sent up to	JMh

1577 Wt. W10791/1773 500,000 1/15 D. D. & L. A.D.S.S./Forms/C. 2118.

72 Field Ambulance

Instructions regarding War Diaries and Intelligence Summaries are contained in F. S. Regs., Part II. and the Staff Manual respectively. Title pages will be prepared in manuscript.

WAR DIARY
or
INTELLIGENCE SUMMARY.
(Erase heading not required.)

Army Form C. 2118.

(10)

Place	Date	Hour	Summary of Events and Information	Remarks and references to Appendices
			Continued	
POPERINGHE	29-1-16		ASYLUM YPRES to clear away debris & scrub out rooms for the purpose of making a place to serve hot drinks to working parties coming out of the trenches	GM
"	30-1-16		Nothing to report.	GM
"	31-1-16		Visited Asylum. Coffee bar completed. Took up 1000 rations composed of cocoa & milk tea soup & rum. Will serve hot food to night. Placed Sgt. Martin in charge with six men to run the place. Lieut Hogg to supervise with instructions to keep a record of the number & kind of ration issued each night	
			Received 220 Cape mackintosh.	
			Put up directing board at dressing station at ASYLUM. Cleaning out cellars & whitewashing walls.	
			During the 25 days we have been here the undermentioned work has been completed. A complete set of covered in cook house, latrines, ablution for personnel & for patients, built soap pits grease traps & drainage, at No 2 & at Adv Dressing Station. Latrine bucket pattern, bricked in incinerators to destroy all refuse, wet & dry, Cooking ranges for dixies with chimneys ovens, Slate flooring for cook house, baths, drying rooms, laundry, stand for motor cars, road to horse lines, horse standing & harness sheds, innumerable repairs to roads & approaches, fitting up ward for 100 stretcher cases, pack store with shelves & rifle rack. This work has been done as well as the usual routine work of collecting & treating the sick & wounded of the Division. The men have worked well & shown a keen interest in the progress of the various works they are undertaking. A fuller report & plans will be attached to next month's diary	

J.B. Edwards Capt. [illegible]
O.C. 72 Field Ambulance

1577 Wt. W10791/1773 500,000 1/15 D. D. & L. A.D.S.S./Forms/C. 2118.

S/

Feb 1916
Mar. 1916
April 1916

72nd. Field Ambulance

CONFIDENTIAL

WAR DIARY

OF

(CAPT. G. B. EDWARDS.

OFFICER COMMANDING 72ND FIELD AMBCE.

FROM 1ST FEBRUARY 1916 TO 29TH FEBRUARY 1916

72 FIELD AMBULANCE

WAR DIARY
or
~~INTELLIGENCE SUMMARY.~~
(Erase heading not required.)

Army Form C. 2118.

(1)

Instructions regarding War Diaries and Intelligence Summaries are contained in F. S. Regs., Part II. and the Staff Manual respectively. Title pages will be prepared in manuscript.

Place	Date	Hour	Summary of Events and Information	Remarks and references to Appendices
POPERINGHE	1-2-16		LIEUT EBERTS attends lectures & instruction in gas at OXELAIRE O 17 (Sheet 27 1:40,000) War diary for Jan. forwarded. Visited Asylum YPRES & dressing station BRANDHOEK all satisfactory.	
"	2-2-16		Received from ordnance 3 pr of handle bar muffs for M.T. motor cycle drivers most useful.	
"	3-2-16		CAPT WEBSTER W.J. & Sgt TOMLINSON (M.T.) returns from leave. LIEUT H.O. GOUGH arrived & reported here from 24 GENERAL HOSP.L. sent him onto 8 R.W. KENTS for duty	
"	4-2-16		CAPT. G.B. EDWARDS (CO) on leave to ENGLAND 24 Division Commander & ADMS. inspected Field Ambulance & appeared very pleased with the work that had been done. 1 HD Horse ill with colic	
"	5-2-16		Heavy draft horse still ill sent to 36 M.V.S. Ball race M.Cr. cycle broken. Water proof capes issued to NCOs & men	
"	6-2-16		Message received from 36 M.V.S that HD horse died yesterday peritonitis. Sgt. Tomlinson to Brandhoek for duty with convoy collecting from aid posts in relief of Cpl WILLMOTT	
"	7-2-16		3 full length Baths received from Empress Club as a gift to 72 Field Ambulance. Bath house fitted up & taken into use. A great boon to the patients & men.	
"	8-2-16		Sent 10 men up to Regt Aid Post at MILL in MENIN ROAD to assist R.E.s in building dug-outs for patients in case of heavy casualties. At present the MILL would only hold very few. It is proposed to accommodate at least 100 & to be a place for dumping wounded & for cases to get to possibly in the day time & be treated & cared for until cars could go up under cover of night & bring them in.	
	9-2-16		LIEUT. HOGG. R.W. & Sgt PAGE on leave. 1 Rider handed over to 3rd Rifle Bde. POPERINGHE shelled. no damage of any importance.	
	10-2-16		- - - - - - - - - - - - - - (arrow to 9-2-16 entry)	
	11-2-16		1 Rider handed over to 9 R. Sussex Regt. 1 Rider received from 24 Div Train (a small black pony, & kicker)	
	12-2-16		Hun gas attack between BOESINGHE & STEENSTRAATE. POPERINGHE shelled & 3 Taubes dropped bombs very little damage.	
		10. A.M.	Gas alert & stand to	
		7.30 P.M.	" cancelled Complaint to DMS from 10 C.C.S. stating several wounded from 72 F Amb arrived without blankets & not properly treated	
	13-2-16		Cpl. WILLMOTT (M.T.) & Cpl WITHNELL & Sgt BROWN (ASC) on leave. LIEUT LAING G.F to temporary duty with 2 LEINSTERS in relief of Capt BIDEN wounded. Some heavy gunning at HOOGE. Got in 100 casualties without any hitch. bearers & officers worked well	
	14-2-16	2.45 AM	Returned from leave (CAPT. G.B. EDWARDS). Visited adv. dressing station BRANDHOEK tried to get up to ASYLUM but was stopped as the HUN was shelling the road heavily & all traffic was held up	
		6.40 PM	Received Stand to.	
		7.30 PM	Stand to cancelled but be ready to move at 15 minutes notice. A patient died at Brandhoek no means of identification	
			Cpl. HUNT & Sgt. BLYTHE on leave	

2353 Wt. W2544/1454 700,000 5/15 D. D. & L. A.D.S.S./Forms/C. 2118.

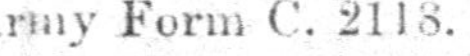

Army Form C. 2118.

72 FIELD AMBULANCE

WAR DIARY
or
INTELLIGENCE SUMMARY.
(Erase heading not required.)

(2)

Instructions regarding War Diaries and Intelligence Summaries are contained in F. S. Regs., Part II. and the Staff Manual respectively. Title pages will be prepared in manuscript.

Place	Date	Hour	Summary of Events and Information	Remarks and references to Appendices
POPERINGHE	15-2-16	3. AM	Stand to received. Memo from REs to 20 at ASYLUM that the REs were too busy to go on with work on dug out at MILL & would my men continue it. Ordered 10 of my men to continue the work. Pump at Asylum blown to pieces by shell bursting under it. Pump repaired. Water supply at Asylum running short. Spoke to ADMS about shortage of Officers he is unable to assist me. 50 extra blankets, supplies & 20 stretchers sent up to Asylum.	
"		7.30 PM	Received message from DDMS 5th Corps to attend any sick from other divisions passing through or staying in POPERINGHE	
"	16-2-16		Saw sick of 2nd ~~Suff~~ SUFFOLKS & 1st GORDONS supplied MOs with dressings.	
"	17-2-16		Pte DYKES sent to ROUEN time expired. Visited BRANDHOEK & ASYLUM. Lieut FOX. RAMC (T.C.) joined for instruction pending posting	
"	18-2-16	1.30 AM	Lieut HOGG returned from leave. POPERINGHE bombed by Taubes. REV. STILL (C of E) joined for duty. Full report in reply to charge brought by 10 CCS against 72 Field Ambulance forwarded to ADMS 24 Division. There were no grounds for the charge which was a gross libel against my officers. Two PB men arrived as caretakers to Cemetery & are attached to me for rations & billets. 15 O.R. reinforcements RAMC for 24 Div arrived & are attached to me pending posting	
"	19-2-16		Sgt PAGE return from leave. Lieut HOGG to Asylum. Sgt PAGE to BRANDHOEK. Sgt BROWN to ASYLUM. Sgt THOMAS, AKERMAN, & SETTERS & 12 men from ASYLUM to No 2 [illegible]. Lieut FOX arrested as a spy & brought here for identification. 1 Cpl & 6 men of reinforcements which arrived yesterday taken on the strength of this unit.	
"	20-2-16	7.30 AM 8.30 AM	POPERINGHE shelled & bombed no damage of any importance. Two new Gas Helmets H.P. pattern issued to all ranks. Old ones withdrawn. Lieut FOX to BRANDHOEK in relief. Lieut GROVES to No 2 [illegible]	
		11.40 PM	POPERINGHE bombed.	
"	21-2-16		Nothing to report.	
"	22-2-16		Cpl WILLMOTT. L/Cpl WITHNELL & Dr BROWN returned from leave. Heavy snow storm. Capt S.M. McLAY RAMC (T.C.) arrived from No 11 G.H. BOULOGNE. Capt H.H. CARTER RAMC (T.C.) from ROUEN & Lieut Y.E. CARTWRIGHT RAMC T.C. from ROUEN, & are attached to this unit for instruction pending posting	

2353 Wt. W2544/1454 700,000 5/15 D. D. & L. A.D.S.S./Forms/C. 2118.

72 FIELD AMBULANCE

Instructions regarding War Diaries and Intelligence Summaries are contained in F. S. Regs., Part II. and the Staff Manual respectively. Title pages will be prepared in manuscript.

WAR DIARY
or
INTELLIGENCE SUMMARY.
(Erase heading not required.)

Army Form C. 2118.

Place	Date	Hour	Summary of Events and Information	Remarks and references to Appendices
POPERINGHE	23-2-16		Sgt BLYTHE ~~Cpl~~ HUNT returned from leave	
		1.–1.30 am	POPERINGHE shelled. Lieut EBERTS. H.F.H. & ~~Cpl~~ CAVANA on leave. Lieut STEWART. A. arrived from BOULOGNE & is attached for instruction pending posting. Visited BRANDHOEK. Lieut de BEAUPRE' E.J. RAMC came down from ASYLUM sick. Received 2 Riders from Glencorse Germany both very good mounts.	
"	24.2.16	1.1 am	Received wire from ADMS to send a M.O. to 8th R.W. Kents for temporary duty. Lieut BRETHERTON. A.W. sent to report to 8 R.W. Kents in the trenches. Lieut de BEAUPRE' sent sick to 12 C.C.S. All leave in 5th Corps stopped. Visited BRANDHOEK. ASYLUM & Regt aid posts at MILL. Capt. CATHCART & Capt CARTWRIGHT to BRANDHOEK Lieut FOX to ASYLUM. 2 Reinforcements arrived for RAMC 24 Division.	
"	25.2.16		2 Reinforcements sent to 74 Field Ambulance. 3 ASC ~~#~~ M.T drivers joined & are taken on the strength of the unit	
	26.2.16		Nothing to report.	
	28.2.16.		Lieut FOX to 2nd ENTRENCHING Battalion for duty. 1. H.D. Horse to 36 M.V. Sect	
	29.2.16		Received instruction from ADMS to prepare to receive casualties of 17 Division at ASYLUM YPRES. There has been nothing of any particular interest to report this month. I still have great trouble with my Sunbeam cars & at the present moment have four in the work shop & one in running order. The other ambulances of this division have the same trouble & it is often difficult to obtain cars from them. The commonest damage is a broken ball race or split chassis. The O.C. work shop says it's due to bad design & that chassis are not long enough. Cars are a long time in the shop as he is unable to obtain spare parts. The same applies to my motor cycles. At the present moment I have 1 motor cycle being used with broken saddle pillar & half of front wheel deficient. The other cycle is in work shop waiting for new spokes & the third cycle has been in order since October 22nd 1915. Reinforcements arriving recently are a poor type of man & of little use. There is a general impression that crocks are ~~thought~~ good enough for RAMC work. This is a great error as the work in a Field Ambulance is of the severest kind & requires strong healthy men. Often bearers have to carry patients three or four miles over rough ground & are working for 24 hours without a rest & under heavy shell fire. When they are not actually out collecting wounded there are a great number of heavy fatigues to be performed. There has been a shortage of forage during the month. The oats are of poor quality & rather a large proportion of maize is being received in lieu of oats. The horses despite this are in good condition. This is in great measure due to good standings & shelters having been erected by the unit.	

G. J. Edwards Capt RAMC
O.C. 72 Field Ambulance

2353 Wt. W2544/1454 700,000 5/15 D. D. & L. A.D.S.S./Forms/C. 2118.

March 1916.

Vol 7

CONFIDENTIAL

WAR DIARY

OF

(Capt. G. B. Edwards)

Commanding 72nd Field Ambulance.

From:- 1-3-16 To:- 31-3-16

VOLUME 7

24DW

72 Field Ambulance.

Instructions regarding War Diaries and Intelligence Summaries are contained in F. S. Regs., Part II. and the Staff Manual respectively. Title pages will be prepared in manuscript.

WAR DIARY
or
INTELLIGENCE SUMMARY.
(*Erase heading not required.*)

Army Form C. 2118.

No 1.

Place	Date	Hour	Summary of Events and Information	Remarks and references to Appendices
POPERINGHE	1-3-16	12 noon	Lieut H.S. Groves. 1 Sgt. 2 Pte Clerks & 3 stretcher squads sent up to Asylum YPRES to reinforce detachment already there as expecting casualties from 3rd & 17th Division who are going to attack the BLUFF I34 (sheet 28)	
			Received 185 sets infantry equipment (leather straps) for personnel	
			Lieut de BEAUPRE returned from 12 CCS for duty. He is still far from fit	
			1. Heavy D. horse evacuated.	JWhitman Capt RAMC
	2-3-16		Duplicate War Diary 1st Nov to 31 Nov. sent to O/c Rame records.	
		4.10 AM	Heavy gunning heard in direction of HOOGE or south	
		10 AM	Drove up to BRANDHOEK & then onto ASYLUM. Active shelling car hung up on road for ½ hour road being shelled. Arrived ASYLUM at 11 AM. found all ranks working hard. walking cases had been arriving since 7 am. 150 cases had been admitted & were being evacuated by 5 MAC no hitch at any time Cases still arriving	JWh
	3-3-16	3 AM	Lieut H.E.M. EBERTS returned from leave	
			POPERINGHE shelled several casualties	
	4.3.16		Number of cases passed through the Field Ambulance from 7 AM. 2-3-16 to 7 AM. 4.3.16 Sick 42 wounded 391 of which 59 sick were 24 Division & 18 wounded 24 Division. The wounded were chiefly 3rd & 17 Division being 258 3rd Div. 113 17th Div. with one or two cases from 20 & 50th Division.	JWh
			Received 1 Triumph & 1 Douglas Cycle. Sent 1 BSA to work shop to be evacuated.	
	5.3.16		Lieut Groves reported that the cellars at Asylum were 3" deep in water & rising owing to heavy rains. Got an old pump from YPRES & managed to pump the cellars & keep them dry.	JWh

2353 Wt. W2544/1454 700,000 5/15 D. D. & L. A.D.S.S./Forms/C. 2118.

72 Field Ambulance

Instructions regarding War Diaries and Intelligence Summaries are contained in F. S. Regs., Part II. and the Staff Manual respectively. Title pages will be prepared in manuscript.

WAR DIARY
or
INTELLIGENCE SUMMARY.
(Erase heading not required.)

Army Form C. 2118.

(2)

Place	Date	Hour	Summary of Events and Information	Remarks and references to Appendices
POPERINGHE	6-3-16		1. H.D. horse sent to M.V. Section severe thrush.	SMh
"	7-3-16		C Section relieved B Section at BRANDHOEK & ASYLUM.	
			Lieut. G.A. McLARTY arrived from No 4 General Hospital & is attached for instructional purposes in work in forward area.	
			Lieut. Cartwright ~~& Carter~~ Capt. Carter rejoined Field Amb H^d Qrs from ASYLUM	
			1. H.D horse evacuated	SMh
"	8-3-16		Lieut Cartwright evacuated to 10 CCS ? T.B. Capt. CARTER posted to 12th Bde R.G.A.	
			Received 300 blankets from Ordnance for use of Regt. M. Os at aid posts	SMh
	9-3-16		No 52020 Pte Jolly to HAVRE for duty at home in munition work (ref	~~Adms~~ ref 771. 8.3.16.
			Lieut. A.W. BRETHERTON RAMC admitted to Field Amb. sick P.U.O.	
			Lieut. E.J. de BEAUPRE to 8 R.W. Kents for temporary duty.	
			Lieut G.A McLARTY to Adv Dressing Station BRANDHOEK	SMh
	10-3-16		Report on arrangements made on morning 2-3-16 to collect & treat casualties of other Division during attack on Bluff, forwarded to ADMS.	
			Six reinforcements arrived.	SMh
	11-3-16		No 74 Field Ambulance brought sick & wounded to BRANDHOEK having taken over the collecting of MAPLE COPS (I. 24 a 2.2. sheet 28)	SMh

2353 Wt. W2544/1454 700,000 5/15 D. D. & L. A.D.S.S./Forms/C. 2118.

72 Field Ambulance

Instructions regarding War Diaries and Intelligence Summaries are contained in F. S. Regs., Part II. and the Staff Manual respectively. Title pages will be prepared in manuscript.

WAR DIARY
or
INTELLIGENCE SUMMARY.
(Erase heading not required.)

Army Form C. 2118.

(3)

Place	Date	Hour	Summary of Events and Information	Remarks and references to Appendices
POPERINGHE	12.3.16		ADMS. 3rd Canadian Division visits the Field Ambulance & was shown round & the arrangements made for collecting & disposal of cases explained to him.	SM
"	13.3.16		Lieut G.A. McCLARTY posted to 8 R.W. Kents in relief Lt. E.J. De BEAUPRÉ. Lieut E.J. De BEAUPRÉ rejoins for duty.	SM
"	14.3.16		Nothing to report.	SM
"	15.3.16		DDMS. 5 Corps & ADMS 1st Canadian Div. went round the Field Ambulance. 1 Rider sent to M.V. Section lacerated wound buttock.	SM
"	16.3.16		1 Cpl & 5 men sent to METEREN (X15 sheet 27) to take over baths.	SM
"	17.3.16		1. H D horse evacuated.	
		9 AM	Operation order No 32 recd from 73 I.B.	
		2 PM	" " No 1 " " ADMS	
			Sent Billeting officer to METEREN he returned later & stated that the 73 I.B. were making no arrangements for the Field Ambulance. 1 Rider evacuated. (the one injured on 15.3.16.	SM

2353 Wt. W2544/1454 700,000 5/15 D. D. & L. A.D.S.S./Forms/C. 2118.

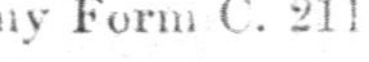

72 Field Ambulance

Army Form C. 2118.

(4)

Instructions regarding War Diaries and Intelligence Summaries are contained in F. S. Regs., Part II. and the Staff Manual respectively. Title pages will be prepared in manuscript.

WAR DIARY
or
INTELLIGENCE SUMMARY.
(Erase heading not required.)

Place	Date	Hour	Summary of Events and Information	Remarks and references to Appendices
POPERINGHE	18/3/16	12 P.M.	Handed over to advance party of 1 Canadian Field Ambulance	
		1. P.M.	Moved off from POPERINGHE. Left C Section at BRANDHOEK with orders to assist the relieving Field Ambulance at night collection & to hand over the advanced dressing station & the Asylum. To join up at METEREN the following day.	SMc
		2. PM	Arrived RENNINGHELST	SMc
		2.17 PM.	Marched off behind 73 I.B. to METEREN (X16 sheet 27)	
METEREN.		6.30 P.M.	Arrived METEREN. Found billets for personnel & transport lines for horses.	
	19.3.16.		Arranged with 142 Field Ambulance, a section of which had taken over the only available building suitable for a hospital, to see & treat any sick of the 73 I.B. & Canadian troops round the locality.	SMc
	20.3.16		Informed that I was to take over from 3rd Canadian Field Ambulance at BAILLEUL on 23.3.16.	SMc
	21.3.16		Went into BAILLEUL & went round the buildings occupied by 3 C.F.A. with the C.O.	SMc
	22.3.16		Received Operation Order No 3 ADMS. 24 Division. & G.G. No 33 of 73 I.B. Am not to take over from 3rd C.F.A. until 30.3.16.	SMc

2353 Wt. W2544/1454 700,000 5/15 D. D. & L. A.D.S.S./Forms/C. 2118.

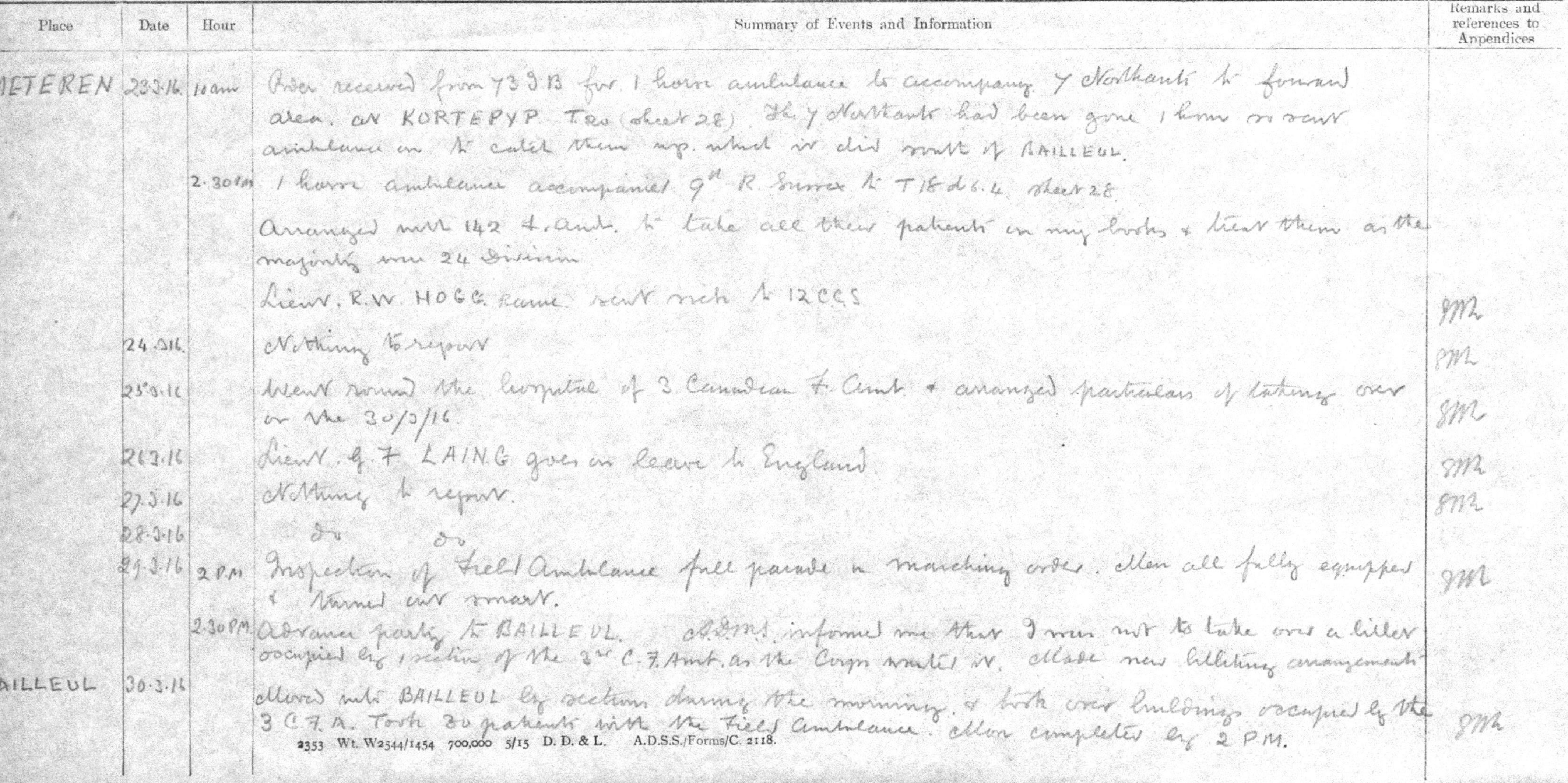

72 Field Ambulance

Instructions regarding War Diaries and Intelligence Summaries are contained in F. S. Regs., Part II. and the Staff Manual respectively. Title pages will be prepared in manuscript.

WAR DIARY
or
INTELLIGENCE SUMMARY.

(Erase heading not required.)

Army Form C. 2118.

(35)

Place	Date	Hour	Summary of Events and Information	Remarks and references to Appendices
METEREN	23.3.16	10am	Order received from 73 I.B for 1 horse ambulance to accompany 7 Northants to forward area at KORTEPYP T20 (sheet 28). The 7 Northants had been gone 1 hour so sent ambulance on to catch them up which it did south of BAILLEUL.	
		2.30PM	1 horse ambulance accompanied 9th R. Sussex to T18 d 6.4 sheet 28	
			Arranged with 142 F. Amb. to take all their patients on my books & treat them as the majority were 24 Division	
			Lieut. R.W. HOGG RAMC sent sick to 12 CCS	SMc
	24.3.16.		Nothing to report	SMc
	25.3.16		Went round the hospital of 3 Canadian F. Amb & arranged particulars of taking over on the 30/3/16.	SMc
	26.3.16		Lieut. G.F. LAING goes on leave to England	SMc
	27.3.16		Nothing to report.	SMc
	28.3.16		do do	
	29.3.16	2 PM	Inspection of Field Ambulance full parade in marching order. Men all fully equipped & turned out smart.	SMc
		2.30PM	Advance party to BAILLEUL. A.D.M.S. informed me that I was not to take over a billet occupied by 1 section of the 3rd C.F. Amb. as the Corps wanted it. Made new billeting arrangements	
BAILLEUL	30.3.16		Moved into BAILLEUL by sections during the morning & took over buildings occupied by the 3 C.F.A. Took 30 patients with the Field Ambulance. Move completed by 2 PM.	SMc

2353 Wt. W2344/1454 700,000 5/15 D. D. & L. A.D.S.S./Forms/C. 2118.

72 Field Ambulance

WAR DIARY
or
INTELLIGENCE SUMMARY.
(Erase heading not required.)

Army Form C. 2118.

(6)

Instructions regarding War Diaries and Intelligence Summaries are contained in F. S. Regs., Part II. and the Staff Manual respectively. Title pages will be prepared in manuscript.

Place	Date	Hour	Summary of Events and Information	Remarks and references to Appendices
BAILLEUL	31/3/16		Day spent in cleaning up buildings, kitchens & arranging wards. Opened as a Divisional Rest Station. All equipment, Medical & Surgical stores etc laid out & checked & being cleaned & rearranged. Very few deficiencies. A good deal of the equipment such as bull's eye lanterns, bed pans, pailliasses, reaping hooks, three out of six scales, weighing etc ~~are~~ never required & take up a lot of room which is wanted for more useful things. These are being sorted out with a view to returning to store.	
			Withdrew personnel from Baths at METEREN.	
			It is doubtful if the Field Ambulance will remain in BAILLEUL but am unable to obtain any definite information.	

G. W. Edmunds.
Commanding
O.C. 72nd Field Ambulance

2353 Wt. W2544/1454 700,000 5/15 D. D. & L. A.D.S.S./Forms/C. 2118.

72 F Amb
Vol 8
24th Div

CONFIDENTIAL

April 1916

WAR DIARY

OF (MAJOR G.B.EDWARDS)

OFFICER COMMANDING 72ND FIELD AMBULANCE

FROM 1ST APRIL 1916 TO 30TH APRIL 1916

72 Field Ambulance

Instructions regarding War Diaries and Intelligence Summaries are contained in F. S. Regs., Part II. and the Staff Manual respectively. Title pages will be prepared in manuscript.

WAR DIARY
or
INTELLIGENCE SUMMARY.
(Erase heading not required.)

Army Form C. 2118.

(1)

Place	Date	Hour	Summary of Events and Information	Remarks and references to Appendices
BAILLEUL	1-4-16.		War Diary for December 1915 forwarded to O/c RAMC Records. Lieut. H S GROVES returned from temporary duty with 107 Bde RFA.	SM
"	2-4-16		Lieut R W Hogg to 12 R. Fusiliers for temporary duty. Commenced overhauling equipment & Surgical & Medical panniers. Applied for authority to return to store a large number of articles which have been found of no use including bulls eye lanterns, bed-pans, Cover tin etc.	SM
"	3-4-16		ADMS visited the Field Ambulance	SM
"	4-4-16		Nothing to report	SM
"	5-4-16		Lieut. G. Laing returned from leave. Informed that 24 Div Hd Qrs would take over our building & billets on 14th.	SM
"	6-4-16		Captain W. B Cathcart to 9th East Surrey Regt for temporary duty.	SM
"	7-4-16		} nothing to report	SM
"	8-4-16			SM
"	9-4-16		G.O.C 24 Division visited the Field Ambulance	SM
"	10-4-16		Nothing to report	SM
"	11-4-16		Finished checking & rearranging panniers. everything complete & in good order Rode into St Janes Cappel & went round Divisional Hd Qrs, estimated accommodation for about 60 patients only.	SM
"	12-4-16		Received orders to detail 1 NCO 14 men & 3 G.S wagons to report R.E. siding STEENWERCK for loading party & assist R.E.	SM
"	13-4-16		All leave stopped. Informed that the Field Ambulance would only be at ST JANES CAPPEL for a short time & that I was to select a site for a DRS East of BAILLEUL.	SM

2353 Wt. W2544/1454 700,000 5/15 D. D. & L. A.D.S.S./Forms/C. 2118.

72 Field Ambulance

Instructions regarding War Diaries and Intelligence Summaries are contained in F. S. Regs., Part II. and the Staff Manual respectively. Title pages will be prepared in manuscript.

WAR DIARY
or
INTELLIGENCE SUMMARY.
(Erase heading not required.)

Army Form C. 2118.

Place	Date	Hour	Summary of Events and Information	Remarks and references to Appendices
BAILLEUL	13.4.16		Rode round area E BAILLEUL found a suitable site at S11a 5. 2. (sheet 28). The A.A.&Q.M.G. 24 Division visited this place & told me to get into communication with the Rents Officer & to decide on the fields I had chosen.	SM
	14.4.16		Nothing to report	SM
	15.4.16		Arranged to clear Field Ambulance of patients prior to moving off on Monday. A.A.Q.M.G. came round later & informed me that the Division would not now be moving on until Tuesday. Had to cancell all arrangements	SM
	16.4.16		Orders to detail 1 N.C.O. & 12 men for loading ambulance trains at BAILLEUL station tomorrow. Order cancelled later. Loaded B & C section wagons & parked them in the square. Evacuated 50 patients.	SM
	17.4.16		Evacuated 50 patients cleaned out building & billets collected all surplus equipment blankets, stretchers etc ready to load on lorries tomorrow.	SM
	18.4.16		24 Divisional Head Qrs took over hospital building & billets & the Field Ambulance moved into St JANES CAPPEL. Received 35 patients 1 hour after moving in. Capt. W.J. WEBSTER returned from temporary duty with 1st North Staffords	SM
	19.4.16 20.4.16		} Spent in cleaning up building & outhouses, erecting baths, latrines, cookhouses etc.	SM SM

2353 Wt. W2544/1454 700,000 5/15 D. D. & L. A.D.S.S./Forms/C. 2118.

72 Field Ambulance

Instructions regarding War Diaries and Intelligence Summaries are contained in F. S. Regs., Part II. and the Staff Manual respectively. Title pages will be prepared in manuscript.

WAR DIARY
or
INTELLIGENCE SUMMARY.
(Erase heading not required.)

Army Form C. 2118.

(3)

Place	Date	Hour	Summary of Events and Information	Remarks and references to Appendices
ST. JANS CAPPEL	21-4-16		Received 3 H.D. Horses & 1 Rider.	JM
	22-4-16	1 AM.	Gas alert. Informed that 50 Division would take over St JANS CAPPEL in a day or so. DDMS & DADMS came round the D.R.S. I am told to find another site as terms cannot be arranged for other ground & RE cannot afford time to repair road	JM
	23-4-16	11 am	Informed today that we are to stay at St JANES CAPPEL so have pushed on the work of drainage. Have erected marquees & put down duck walks & have accommodation for 200 patients. The men have been working hard & well as the ground had to be cleared of large trees which had been felled & were spread all over the field.	JM
	23-4-16	5 P.M.	Informed today that it had now been decided that the Field Ambulance could not stay in St JANS CAPPEL. Chose a new site for D.R.S. S16 d 2.4. (sheet 28)	JM
	24-4-16	4 AM.	BAILLEUL bombed by aircraft large fire appears to be somewhere near Asylum Visited new site for D.R.S. with CRE & DADMS 24 Div. 1 Water Cart 2 mules 1 driver & 1 orderly on loan to No 1 C.C.S.	JM
	25-4-16		Visited new site for D.R.S with CRE drew up plans for huts, tents etc.	JM

2353 Wt. W2544/1454 700,000 5/15 D. D. & L. A.D.S.S./Forms/C. 2118.

72 Field Ambulance

Instructions regarding War Diaries and Intelligence Summaries are contained in F. S. Regs., Part II. and the Staff Manual respectively. Title pages will be prepared in manuscript.

WAR DIARY
or
INTELLIGENCE SUMMARY.
(Erase heading not required.)

Army Form C. 2118.

Place	Date	Hour	Summary of Events and Information	Remarks and references to Appendices
ST JANS CAPPEL	26/4/16		Received 10 PHG Gas helmets with sponge eye protectors ADMS visited new site for DRS. Remission not yet obtained to commence building	SMR
"	27/4/16		Message from 24 Div HQ that huts can now be put up on new site. Visited the site with CRE. Sent 1 NCO & 12 men to assist in unloading huts	SMR SMR
"	28/4/16		Lieut A.W. Bretherton returned from 2 weeks leave Lieut R.W. Hogg returned from temporary duty with 12 R. Fusiliers	SMR
"	29/4/16		Lieut R W HOGG on leave to England	
"	30/4/16	2am	Gas alert received from 24 Div HQ Stand to. Sent 10 oxygen cylinders & 50 stretchers to 73 Field Ambulance who had 251 gassed cases. & 130 wounded. Lieut. E. J. de Beaupré & Lt. Col. & Dr Mr J.T. Cooke on leave to England The Field Ambulance is still at ST JANS CAPPEL. Two huts are part up & the material for remaining 4 is collected at new site.	SMR

1577 Wt. W10791/1773 500,000 1/15 D. D. & L. A.D.S.S./Forms/C. 2118.

24th Div

72 F Amb
Vol. 9

May 1916

S

CONFIDENTIAL

WAR DIARY

OF MAJOR G.B. EDWARDS

O.C. 72ND FIELD AMBULANCE

FROM · 1 · 5 · 16 · TO · 31 · 5 · 16

72 FIELD AMBULANCE

WAR DIARY
or
~~INTELLIGENCE SUMMARY.~~
(Erase heading not required.)

Army Form C. 2118.

(1)

Instructions regarding War Diaries and Intelligence Summaries are contained in F. S. Regs., Part II. and the Staff Manual respectively. Title pages will be prepared in manuscript.

Place	Date	Hour	Summary of Events and Information	Remarks and references to Appendices
ST JANS CAPPEL	1-5-16		Visited new Divisional Rest Station with CRE. Work progressing.	PM
"	2-5-16		Drew 1000 bricks for incinerator & kitchens at DRS.	PM
"	3-5-16		Lieut. G.F. LAING to 2nd Leinsters temporary duty. Lieut. A.W. BRETHERTON 106 Bde R.F.A. temporary duty	
			Drew 12 iron pickets for incinerator grating. 4 Hospital double marquees from 2 C.C.S.	
			Visited DRS. 4 huts 20 x 60 are now up 3 complete without roof. Erected two marquees	
		11.20 AM	Gas alert	PM
	4-5-16		Drew 4 more marquees from No 2 CCS. Well dug at DRS now 11 feet deep 2 ft water	
		3 PM	A driver of a motor ambulance arrived with request for 2 cars to collect some casualties at 30 Div bombing school. Only had one Ford available sent Dr Eberts & an orderly with dressings & 6 stretchers.	PM
	5-5-16		CNOT/12500 Sgt Major BAKER P.E. ASC rejoined for duty after having been away at a training school for a commission. Received 10 Helmets Steel for Officers	PM
	6-5-16		S. Sgt 49520 SETTERS F. RAMC evacuated to No 1 CCS. Drew 1 load of sand & 1 barrel cement. Examined a field for horse lines. Proceeded on leave to ENGLAND	PM
	7-5-16		Lieut. H F H EBERTS sent to 8th Queens temporary duty. Water Cart & mules lent to 1 CCS returned this afternoon	PM
	8-5-16		Drew 5 tons road metal for road outside DRS	PM
	9-5-16		Drew 6 angle iron pickets & 800 bricks from RE Park	PM
	10-5-16		Lieut E J de BEAUPRE & Lieut J.T. COOKE returned from leave	PM
	11-5-16		Nothing to report	PM
	12-5-16	7.30 PM	Gas alert	PM
	13-5-16	3 PM	Gas alert cancelled	

2353 Wt. W2544/1454 700,000 5/15 D. D. & L. A.D.S.S./Forms/C. 2118.

72 FIELD AMBULANCE

WAR DIARY
or
INTELLIGENCE SUMMARY.
(Erase heading not required.)

Army Form C. 2118.

Instructions regarding War Diaries and Intelligence Summaries are contained in F. S. Regs., Part II. and the Staff Manual respectively. Title pages will be prepared in manuscript.

(2)

Place	Date	Hour	Summary of Events and Information	Remarks and references to Appendices
ST JANS CAPPEL	14-5-16		Nothing to report	SM
"	15-5-16		Work at DRS progressing. Proposed to erect huts for personnel as well as for patients.	SM
			Lieut G.F. LAING returned for duty from 2 Leinsters	
"	16-5-16		Lieut. R.W. HOGG returned from leave. 114 Helmets steel indented for bearer division	SM
"	17-5-16		Have been unable to find a suitable site for new horse lines	
"	18-5-16		Lieut H.F.H EBERTS returned to duty from 8th Queens.	SM
"	19-5-16		Returned from leave. Visited DRS. 4 Huts for patients completed 8 Marquees for patients erected. Well 16 ft deep 10 feet water. Skeleton of 6 huts for personnel up. Mess Hut & Hut for Officers billet nearly completed. Two small huts for QrMr Store completed	SM
	20-5-16		Took over transport lines vacated by 24 Div Ammunition Col at S 15 d 1.8 (Sheet 28) Notified Rent Officer. Transport lines in bad repair. Field much cut up. Large pond very foul surroundings left in a very insanitary condition. Detailed working party 1 NCO & 12 men to repair horse standings & clean the place up. Indented for wire & posts to rail off pond which will rest will probably be of great use later on for watering.	SM
			Lieut. G.F. LAING to 1 CCS appendicitis	
	21-5-16		Captain W.B. CATHCART proceeded on leave to IRELAND Lieut. E.J. de BEAUPRÉ to ENGLAND to report W.O. on expiration of contract (24-5-16). Attended ADMS office & was instructed to examine & report on Wells in area marked off on map handed to me. Report to be in by 29th	SM
	22-5-16		Detailed Capt. W.J. WEBSTER Cpl WATTS & Mr LAURENT (interpreter) to carry out Well inspection. Marked off area to be done each day & gave detailed instructions as to form the report was to take	SM
			1 Sgt. 1 Pte 1 HD Horse & 1 Mule sent to CC 24 Div. Train in accordance with instructions received from 24 Div HQ The Field Ambulance establishment to be reduced accordingly.	SM
	23-5-16		Lieut H.F.H EBERTS lectured to the Officers of the Field Ambulance on Anti Gas precautions. An excellent & interesting lecture.	SM

2353 Wt. W2544/1454 700,000 5/15 D. D. & L. A.D.S.S./Forms/C. 2118.

72 FIELD AMBULANCE

Instructions regarding War Diaries and Intelligence Summaries are contained in F. S. Regs., Part II. and the Staff Manual respectively. Title pages will be prepared in manuscript.

WAR DIARY
or
INTELLIGENCE SUMMARY.
(Erase heading not required.)

Army Form C. 2118.

Place	Date	Hour	Summary of Events and Information	Remarks and references to Appendices
ST JANS CAPPEL	24-5-16	11 am	Divisional Commander & A.D.M.S. visited the Ambulance & went round wards etc. The General asked if we had any cases of head eczema due to the caustic soda in Gas helmets. There were none in hospital. The question was is it not advisable to let the mens hair grow a reasonable length instead of close cropping as hitherto or devise some practical method of preventing contact between the helmet & the scalp.	SM
"	"	10 P.M.	Gas alert	
"	25-5-16	5.35 PM	A message arrived asking for a M.O. as 13 men had met with a bombing accident at 50 Div bombing school. Sent 2 M.O.s & 3 cars with dressings & stretchers. 10 cases brought here & transferred to 1 C.C.S.	SM
		7.30 pm	Gas alert cancelled	
	26-5-16		Visited D.R.S. work not progressing so well as R.E.s have had to withdraw eight carpenters for other work. Interviewed C.R.E. & arranged to send 12 of the Field Ambulance men round to assist in the hutting work. Horse Transport inspected by O.C. 24 Divisional Train. Horses, mules, harness & men all in excellent condition. O.C. Train complimented them on the condition of the animals & the amount of work they had put [illegible] their harness which was in very good condition	SM
	27-5-16		Nothing to report	SM
	28-5-16		Lieut H.S. GROVES on two weeks leave to England after 1 years service	SM
	29-5-16		Blankets (240) of personnel returned to Ordnance.	SM
	30-5-16		Captain R.W. HOGG to 1 North Staffs on temporary duty	SM
	31-5-16		Found a large number of small prickly seeds about size of a pea but oval ~~[illegible]~~ amongst oats reported to supply officer who said that they had done no harm & advised mixing with a sack or two of good oats to reduce the proportion in each feed. Visited DRANOUTRE baths & made notes on the method of precipitating & separating the soap from the bath water.	SM

O.C. 72nd Field Ambulance S.M. Edwards Maj. R.A.M.C.

2353 Wt. W2544/1454 700,000 5/15 D. D. & L. A.D.S.S./Forms/C. 2118.

72 F.Amb
Vol 10
June

June 1916

CONFIDENTIAL

WAR DIARY

OF (MAJOR G. B. EDWARDS)

OFFICER COMMANDING 72ND FIELD AMBULANCE

FROM 1ST JUNE 1916 TO 30TH JUNE 1916

72 FIELD AMBULANCE

WAR DIARY
or
~~INTELLIGENCE SUMMARY.~~
(Erase heading not required.)

Army Form C. 2118.

(1)

Instructions regarding War Diaries and Intelligence Summaries are contained in F. S. Regs., Part II. and the Staff Manual respectively. Title pages will be prepared in manuscript.

Place	Date	Hour	Summary of Events and Information	Remarks and references to Appendices
ST JANS CAPPEL	1-6-16.		Forwarded duplicate copy of Feb. War Diary to O/c Rame Records. Captain W. B. CATHCART returned from leave. Visited DRS. The Sgt i/c the party working there complained that the rations they were receiving were not satisfactory, that they received preserved meat every other day. On investigation this has been found to be incorrect & that bully beef has only been issued to them twice in six days. These rations being exactly the same as that issued to the Field Ambulance & of excellent quality. The Divisional General visited the DRS after I had left & stopped putting up any more huts. There is one more hut required for a pack store. The material is already there. Intend seeing ADMS about it in a day or two.	JMR
	2-6-16		Visited DRS. expected DMS 2nd Army but he did not arrive. Measured water in well & found it 2 feet deep. Gave orders for pump to be closed so as to estimate rate at which well fills. Work progressing more rapidly.	JMR
	3-6-16		1 Mule struck off the strength & sent to 73rd I.B. Machine Gun Coy. Detailed Lieut. ?H.? EBERTS to inspect wells & report on their capacity quality etc. Inspection to be carried out over an area inclosed between, on the East the BERTHEN. ST JANS CAPPEL Road from R 22 d 2.0 to R 36 c 6.0. On the South from R 36 c 6 0. to Q 32 d 5 0 & along the CAESTRE ST SYLVESTRE CAPPEL Road to ~~P~~ P 30 a 2.3. On the West by ~~from~~ P. 30 a 2 3 along the road to EECKE & on the north by the EECKE GODEWAERSVELDE Road to where it meets the line at Q 22 c 10.0. & from there straight across to meet the BERTHEN road at R 22 d 2.0. CAPTAIN WEBSTER on leave to SCOTLAND.	Sheet 27. 1/40000
	4.6.16.		Visited DRS. met ADMS CRE & ?Army? ?a4? Division. Arranged to take over the DRS camp on 7th. Lieut W. DIXON. joined for duty	
	5-6-16.		Commenced to send equipment for DRS over in GS wagons from St Jans Cappel. The remainder of the RE workmen left & the completion of huts is to be carried out by the Ambulance.	
	6-6-16		Twelve more GS wagon loads sent over to DRS.	

2353 Wt. W2544/1454 700,000 5/15 D. D. & L. A.D.S.S./Forms/C 2118.

72 FIELD AMBULANCE

Instructions regarding War Diaries and Intelligence Summaries are contained in F. S. Regs., Part II. and the Staff Manual respectively. Title pages will be prepared in manuscript.

WAR DIARY
or
INTELLIGENCE SUMMARY.
(*Erase heading not required.*)

Army Form C. 2118.

Place	Date	Hour	Summary of Events and Information	Remarks and references to Appendices
ST JANS CAPPEL	7/6/16		S.S. Maj P.E. BAKER A.S.C. evacuated Pericarditis	
		3 P.M.	Moved off from St JANS CAPPEL with 60 patients	
BAILLEUL S16c 2.4 (28)		4 PM	Arrived at D.R.S. camp S16c 2.4 sheet 28 1/20000	GM
	8/6/16		All personnel hard at work laying duck boards constructing sludge & soap precipitating tanks, grease traps, completing huts, fitting up wards, building meat store, bath house, boiler, completing cook houses & ablution benches, urinals, urine stands, latrines, making refuse buckets, fire buckets, tables, forms, shelves, cupboards etc etc. D.A.D.M.S. D.D.M.S. 5 Corps & 5th Corps Commander inspected the camp & congratulated the unit on the work they had done. Fatigue party to ST JANS CAPPEL to clean up & stack some bricks for removal tomorrow.	GM
"	9/6/16		A.D.M.S. visited camp & expressed his appreciation of the work being carried out.	GM
	10/6/16		Water in well is used for cooking for personnel & remains at 8 ft deep. Ablution water drawn from pond	GM
	11/6/16		Nothing to report.	GM
	12/6/16		Lieut G.F. LAING on 2 weeks leave to England. Weather set in wet & cold.	GM
	13/6/16		Lieut H.S. GROVES returned from leave. All ranks instructed in new method of wearing gas helmet during gas alarm ie folded in front of chest & fastened by the safety pins.	GM
	14/6/16		Capt W.T. WEBSTER returned from leave. Lieut EBERTS 2 weeks leave to ENGLAND. LIEUT. W. DIXON to 107 Bde RFA temporary duty.	GM
	15/6/16		Orders from A.D.M.S. 24 Division to arrange for ambulance wagon to accompany 73rd I.B. during their move to new part of line	GM
	16/6/16		1 Horse ambulance to meet 13 MIDDLESEX at B1 central (36) at 12.30 noon. 1 Horse ambulance to meet 2nd LEINCESTERS at B1 central (36) at 1.30 P.M.	GM
	17/6/16	10.30 PM	Gas alert. Heavy bombardment which 11.30 PM carried out by our troops in front of PLOEGSTEERT. GAS ALARM. Gongs & hooters heard at 12.30 am & a very heavy bombardment along our line. Gas alarm sounded & all ranks fell in with helmets, inspected & then dismissed. Guards posted along road to warn anyone of approach of gas. 2 AM. sent 2 motor ambulances to assist 73 Field Ambulance. 4.45 am sent 2 more cars to 73 Field Ambulance. 6 am sent 20 stretchers & 40 blankets to 73 F.A.	GM

2353 Wt. W2544/1454 700,000 5/15 D. D. & L. A.D.S.S./Forms/C. 2118.

72 FIELD AMBULANCE

Instructions regarding War Diaries and Intelligence Summaries are contained in F. S. Regs., Part II. and the Staff Manual respectively. Title pages will be prepared in manuscript.

Army Form C. 2118.

WAR DIARY
or
INTELLIGENCE SUMMARY.
(Erase heading not required.)

(3)

Place	Date	Hour	Summary of Events and Information	Remarks and references to Appendices
24 DRS. S14.c2.4 (28)	17/6/		DMS 2 Army inspected the DRS & expressed his appreciation of the work carried out & was particularly pleased with the sanitary arrangements for disposing of refuse & soapy bath water. 1 Horse ambulance sent to accompany 9 R. Sussex & 1 to 7th Northants Regt.	JM
	18/6		DDMS 5 Corps & DDMS Anzacs visited the DRS & were interested in the arrangements made for the treatment of patients & for disposal of refuse	JM
	19/6.		ADMS Sanitation DGC accompanied by a French medical commission. Col Sir William LEISHMAN & others visited the camp & were shown round & appeared to be interested in the various sanitary measures in use. Captain WEBSTER 1 NCO & 2 stretcher squads with 1 ambulance car proceeded to take over an advanced dressing station from 50 Division at N27c9.5 (28 1/20000). They are to be attached to 73rd FIELD AMBULANCE for rations & will be working for them.	JM
	20/6		Nothing to report.	
	21/6.		GOC 24 Division & ADMS inspected camp & expressed himself highly pleased with everything. Patients had just arrived & twenty were being bathed. He was very struck with the dirty soapy water entering the sludge tank at one end & the clean effluent at the other. He was also interested in the destructor where the faeces & refuse are destroyed & urine & sludge evaporated.	JM
	22/6.		1 Horse ambulance sent to accompany 8 Buffs at 2.30 am from trenches to new billets. 1 Horse amb for 1st R Fusiliers at 10 PM. Rode out to advanced dressing station at N27c9.5 (28) everything satisfactory.	JM
	23/6		Lieut R.W. HOGG struck off the strength to report for duty 41 Division. Lieut W DIXON returned from 107 Bde RFA for duty.	JM
	24/6 25/6		Nothing to report.	

72 Field Ambulance

WAR DIARY
or
INTELLIGENCE SUMMARY.
(Erase heading not required.)

Army Form C. 2118.

Instructions regarding War Diaries and Intelligence Summaries are contained in F. S. Regs., Part II. and the Staff Manual respectively. Title pages will be prepared in manuscript.

(4)

Place	Date	Hour	Summary of Events and Information	Remarks and references to Appendices
24th D.R.S. S16 c 2.4 (sheet 28)	26/6.		DADMS 9th Corps & Sanitary Officer 2nd Army visited the DRS & appeared interested in all the sanitary arrangements	SM
	27/6		Lieut KEANE H.T. joined for duty. O.C. 2 C.C.S. Australian Imp. Force visited camp & took copious notes of all the sanitary arrangements. He was given plans of camp & various other plans of soap precipitating chamber, destructor, grease trap etc.	SM
	28/6		Visited Kemmel & looked over Advanced Dressing Station of 3rd Northumbrian Field Ambulance. I remember this place & it was used as a Regt aid post early in 1915 in fact during 1914. It is small & would not be of much value in heavy casualties. Found another place with large cellar which would be very suitable. DDMS 9th Corps & ADMS 24 Div came round camp. The former appeared impressed with the work that had been done.	SM
	29/6		Report on working of 24 DRS & explanation of Sanitary arrangements together with plans forwarded to Army Sanitation [illegible] G.C. in accordance with his request. Visited proposed area for 72 Field Ambulance Head Qrs. A very unsuitable spot. Field too small, swampy & uneven, bad approaches.	SM
	30/6.		Sanitary Officer 2 Army, DADMS 5th Australian Div, DDMS & DADMS 9th Corps & various other Officers visited the Camp. Report on camp attached together with plans	SM

[illegible] Major RAMC
OC 72 Field Ambulance

2353 Wt. W2544/1454 700,000 5/15 D. D. & L. A.D.S.S./Forms/C. 2118.

1

Instructions regarding War Diaries and Intelligence Summaries are contained in F. S. Regs., Part II. and the Staff Manual respectively. Title pages will be prepared in manuscript.

WAR DIARY
or
INTELLIGENCE SUMMARY.

(Erase heading not required.)

Army Form C. 2118.

Place	Date	Hour	Summary of Events and Information	Remarks and references to Appendices
8/16 C.24. (Sheet 28)	28/8/16		Report on the 24th Divnl Rest Station and work carried out by 72nd Field Ambulance	
			Sanitation.	
			The sanitary arrangements at the 24th DRS are worked on a system for the disposal of all refuse, both liquid and solid, by incineration and evaporation. This is carried out by means of a Destructor (plan 4) situated just outside the camp, all refuse being removed at regular intervals from the camp to the destructor. Prior to removal the refuse is deposited in old oil drums, painted white with the particular kind of refuse painted on the side i.e. "Dry refuse", "liquid refuse" only", etc.. These receptacles are placed on concrete stands outside the kitchens and wards. At night the receptacle for dry refuse outside the wards is replaced by a night urine tin (plan 5a). Two large concrete stands are built outside each cookhouse for the purpose of standing the dixies on when serving food. The centre of the stand has a channel running back and draining into an oil drum, lateral channels drain into the central one and serve to carry off any greasy water slopped over in the process of serving meals.	
			Greasy water from the oil drums about the camp and from the dixies is passed through a coke and sand filter placed under a tin-lined bench (plan 5b) situated near the incinerator. All dixies are washed at this bench; the coke and sand from the filter is freed from grease by burning it in the Destructor, after which it is used over again (plan 5c.)	
			Soapy water from the bath house and laundry is precipitated with Chloride of Lime, the precipitate being caught in a sludge tank and the clear effluent collected in a tub sunk in the ground, and used for cleaning the wards. The overflow which is a strong chlorinated water passes down a channel to meet the foul water from the grease trap. In the case of the water from the Ablution Bench, the clear effluent passes into a pond and is used again. The sludge is skimmed off evaporated and burned in the Destructor (Plans 3.a & b and plan 2.)	
			Urine is separated from the excreta by a sloping trough running under the latrine seat, and is collected in an oil drum at the end (plan 5e)	

2

Instructions regarding War Diaries and Intelligence Summaries are contained in F. S. Regs., Part II. and the Staff Manual respectively. Title pages will be prepared in manuscript.

WAR DIARY
or
INTELLIGENCE SUMMARY.
(Erase heading not required.)

Army Form C. 2118.

Place	Date	Hour	Summary of Events and Information	Remarks and references to Appendices

Food is protected by muslin covered frames and a special fly proof meat store (Plan 5a.) A sanitary squad of one corporal and six men carry out the sanitary duties of the camp. One of these men is specially detailed to work the Destructor and one attends to the sludge tanks

Personnel and Routine.

The DRS is built to accomodate 200 patients in addition to patients admitted to the Field Ambulance. The personnel as far as possible are drawn from one section but is reinforced by NCOs and men from other sections if necessary. The personnel of the M.DRS. are detailed into a Day and a Night Staff which varies in number according to the position and number of wards. The present staff consists of 3 officers, one of whom is the section commander., 8 Sgts., 5 Corporals and 48 other ranks. Their duties are as follows:—

Day Duties

1. Clinical & Receiving Room — 1 Sgt, 1 O.R.
2. Surgery — 1 Sgt, 2 O.R.
3. Dispensary — 1 Sgt., 1 O.R.

1 Sgt i/c 4.5 & 6

4. Pack Store — 1 Cpl, *2 O.R.
   *one responsible for rifles
5. Bath House — 1 Cpl, *3 O.R.
   *one boiler man
6. Cleaning Room — Brushers 2 O.R., Ironers 2 O.R., Boots 1 O.R., Packs 2 O.R.
7. Cooks — 2 O.R.
8. Wards — 1 Sgt, 1 Cpl, 4 Nursing orderlies, 5 Gen. Duty "

1 Sgt i/c 9. 10. 11

9. Recreation Room — 1 Cpl, 2 O.R.
10. Barbers — 2 O.R.
11. Sanitary Squad — 1 Cpl, *6 O.R.
   *one - destructor, one - sludge tanks.

Night Duties

Surgery	1 O.R.
Dispensary	1 Sgt
Cooks	2 O.R.
Wards.	1 Sgt. 2 Nursing Ords. 4 Gen. Duty "
Recreation & Dining Rooms	2 O.R.

Tour of Duty

9 a.m. — 6 p.m.
6 p.m. — 9 a.m.

The above personnel are not available for other duties in the camp, but fall in with their sections if called upon to assist other Ambulances in the forward or collecting areas. Camp fatigues, guards, water duties, car orderlies, working parties etc are provided by Headquarters or A Section.

Instructions regarding War Diaries and Intelligence Summaries are contained in F. S. Regs., Part II. and the Staff Manual respectively. Title pages will be prepared in manuscript.

WAR DIARY
or
INTELLIGENCE SUMMARY.
(Erase heading not required.)

Army Form C. 2118.

Place	Date	Hour	Summary of Events and Information	Remarks and references to Appendices
			Patients are transferred to the D.R.S. from Field Ambulances of the same division including the Field Ambulance providing the D.R.S. personnel. No patients are admitted direct to the D.R.S. Cases from any regiment or from Field Ambulances of other divisions are not admitted or transferred to the D.R.S. but are, in the former shewn as admissions and in the latter as transfers to the Field Ambulance. If in the former the patient is from a regiment belonging to the same division as the Field Ambulance admitting the case he is either treated in the Field Ambulance or transferred to the D.R.S. Cases from other divisions, either from regiments or Field Ambulances, are transferred to the D.R.S. of their division, or in the case of regiments to the nearest Field Ambulance of their division. All wounded patients, unless slightly wounded are evacuated to C.C.S.; notifications of the above disposal of patients being forwarded to the unit concerned.	
			Generally from 35 to 40 patients arrive daily, these for the most part being men suffering from minor ailments or slight wounds which incapacitate them for regimental duties for 1 to 3 weeks. They require a little medical or surgical treatment, a thorough rest both bodily and mentally, good and ample diet, light exercise & amusements. To obtain these ends, each patient on admission passes through the following procedure. He is examined at the medical inspection or receiving room by a medical officer (O.C. ½ Section) his particulars taken and a bed allotted to him. He then passes to the pack receiving store where he hands in his rifle, pack, equipment etc, and is issued with clean underclothing, hospital pyjamas, a small linen bag for his personal belongings, socks, slippers, plate, cup, knife, fork etc. From here he passes to the bath house, and hands in all his dirty clothing, including cap and boots. All the above articles are entered in a book and are signed for by the patient and by the Packstore Keeper on admission and on discharge to or from the D.R.S. After having had a hot bath the patient is put to bed, and remains there until marked "up". The whole of his clothing, pack, equipment etc is sent across to the cleaning room where they are brushed, ironed, boots cleaned and greased, rifles cleaned and oiled, and worn out boots and clothing mended or replaced by new. When they have been cleaned they are tied up in bundles and placed in the packstore, the rifle, pack and equipment and clothing all being numbered, which number corresponds with that in the Packstore Book & the number	

Instructions regarding War Diaries and Intelligence Summaries are contained in F. S. Regs., Part II. and the Staff Manual respectively. Title pages will be prepared in manuscript.

WAR DIARY
or
INTELLIGENCE SUMMARY.

(Erase heading not required.)

Army Form C. 2118.

Place	Date	Hour	Summary of Events and Information	Remarks and references to Appendices
			of the bed, when a patient is marked "up" the ward master draws his clothing from the store, and he changes into them, but sleeps in pyjamas each night. Patients marked "up" take all their meals in the Dining Room. Breakfast. 8 a.m Dinner 12 noon, Tea 4 pm Supper 7.30 pm. Rations are drawn for patients and in addition they receive extras drawn from advanced Supply Depot e.g. extra vegetables, fresh fruit, extra milk, stout etc. A well stocked Dispensary is kept at the D.R.S and handed over to the relieving unit. Convalescent patients attend physical drill which is graduated according to the progress in convalescence. The disposal of patients varies. Cases which are not likely to recover in 3 weeks are evacuated to C.C.S. Other cases after 2 wks in the D.R.S. are either discharged to full duty, light duty with their regimental transport or light duty with various divisional units, as temporarily unfit for regimental duty, or they are transferred to a convalescent hospital for further treatment. Infectious or contagious diseases are not treated in the D.R.S.	
			Explanatory Note of Plans.	
			Plan 1.	
			The camp is built in a meadow (S. side 131 yds., E. 72 yds., N. 100 yds., W. 89 yds.) and is on thick blue clay on the slope of a hill, one third from the foot. It has a good road on the northern boundary and is bounded by deep ditches; it is well drained and is surrounded by a thick hedge, and a row of tall trees afford shelter from wind and sun, and act as a screen against aircraft. There are two wide entrances from the road, one at the east or top end of the north boundary, and one at the west or lower end, both opening on to the road across a bridged ditch. Along the N. boundary are accomodated the personnel, in well built huts 30'6" by 16'6", each holding 30 or more men. The cook houses which are similar to those for patients and also the Ablution Bench are situated between these huts and the hedge. At the lower end of the camp, near the entrance	

Instructions regarding War Diaries and Intelligence Summaries are contained in F. S. Regs., Part II. and the Staff Manual respectively. Title pages will be prepared in manuscript.

WAR DIARY
or
INTELLIGENCE SUMMARY.
(Erase heading not required.)

Army Form C. 2118.

Place	Date	Hour	Summary of Events and Information	Remarks and references to Appendices
			is the Quarter Master's Stores 16' by 20', a meat store 10'3" by 10'3", pack store 15'6" by 20'6", rifle store 9'6" by 10'5". Further along the receiving room (marquee) and on the right of this the pack receiving and linen issuing room (marquee) and alongside this the bath house (marquee) with soap precipitating and sludge tanks. Next comes the Cleaning Room (marquee) and behind this at the lower end of the E border, the latrines for patients and personnel. A hedge divides this corner of the camp from the Destructor and Grease Trap. Patients are accomodated in four huts 60' by 30' (40 patients in each) and four marquees (12 to 15 in each) with 2 marquees used as Dining and Recreation Room. These huts together with Cook House, Ablution Bench etc. are situated along the south border. The Orderly Room, Surgery and Dispensary 41' by 10'6" (a hut divided by partitions) is placed at the lower end of this border. All paths in the camp are made of double duckwalks supported and nailed to stakes 6" off the ground, and railed off with posts and wire.	
			The Drainage from the camp runs along the S. border and W. border and is carried away by a deep ditch outside the camp. One third of the way up the S. border the chlorine affluent from the Patients' Ablution Bench runs into this ditch and the effluent from the baths into the west drain both meeting and joining the foul water from the Grease Trap, at the south west corner of the camp.	
			The water for ablution purposes is obtained from a pond at the lower end of W. border, by means of a pump and hose. Bath water from a pond at the west end of camp by similar means and is carried by hand to a boiler (plan 3c). The clear effluent from the Ablution sludge tank runs back into the west pond and is used again. In the case of the effluent from the Bath House, the stream can be diverted either into the pond or ditch, but as the former contains fish the effluent is only run in at intervals.	
			A good supply of cooking water, requiring less than a scoopfull of chloride of lime per 100 gallons is obtained from a well sunk near the lower and middle third of the north border.	
			Drinking water is drawn in water carts from a divisional supply and stored in a 400 gallon tank.	
			A Destructor (plan 4) is built on a piece of ground outside and at the lower end of the camp (plan 1)	

2353 Wt. W2544/1454 700,000 5/15 D. D. & L. A.D.S.S./Forms/C. 2118.

6

Instructions regarding War Diaries and Intelligence Summaries are contained in F. S. Regs., Part II. and the Staff Manual respectively. Title pages will be prepared in manuscript.

WAR DIARY
or
INTELLIGENCE SUMMARY.
(Erase heading not required.)

Army Form C. 2118.

Place	Date	Hour	Summary of Events and Information	Remarks and references to Appendices
			A grease bench and trap (plan 5b) is erected near the Destructor.	

Night urine stands of concrete and brick are built between the huts of both patients and personnel. These stands, during the day are used as stands for dry refuse tins.

A concrete stand is built near each cookhouse for the purpose of standing dixies when food is being served. A tin-lined bench for washing plates, knives etc is erected outside the Dining Rooms.... description page 1

A flyproof meat store (plan 5a) and cutting up room is situated near the main entrance. The meat as soon as removed from the ration cart is cleaned and hung in this store until cut up and issued.

Officers' quarters are situated at the east end of the camp and consist of a mess (40' by 16'6"). A hut 41' by 10'6" divided by canvas partitions into 4 compartments, each accomodating 2 officers. A small hut 16'6" by 20' divided into two compartments, a cook house (plan 8) latrine and an open air bath. Separating the personnel huts from the wards, and the officers' quarters from the bath-house is a grass space 37 yards by 80 yds.

All the sanitary works included in the attached plans have been designed and built by the personnel of the 72nd Field Ambulance during the past month. All cookhouses, latrines, ablution benches, meat stores, rifle and other stores have been constructed and designed by the personnel, who also assisted the R.E.s in erecting 4 large and 6 smaller huts. They have in addition fitted the wards with cupboards, shelves and tables, the dining room with tables and forms, & laid down and railed off 550 yards double, and 220 yds. single duckboards, fitted the pack and rifle store with shelves and rifle racks, made and painted over 100 receptacles for refuse and as fire buckets; painted all the huts; sunk a 16 feet well and completed much work outside the camp such as repairing and painting the Ambulance and G.S. wagons, making roads to the transport field and repairing transport lines. The greater part of the work has been performed by a pioneer squad of 1 Cpl. and 6 men, picked from the sections and posted to A section, on account of their work in civil employment suiting them for this purpose.

2353 Wt. W2544/1454 700,000 5/15 D. D. & L. A.D.S.S./Forms/C. 2118.

Army Form C. 2118.

WAR DIARY
or
INTELLIGENCE SUMMARY.
(Erase heading not required.)

Instructions regarding War Diaries and Intelligence Summaries are contained in F. S. Regs., Part II. and the Staff Manual respectively. Title pages will be prepared in manuscript.

Place	Date	Hour	Summary of Events and Information	Remarks and references to Appendices

They have proved invaluable in every area in which the Field Ambulance has worked both in the building of sanitary contrivances & in erecting shell proof dug-outs at advanced dressing stations and in making approaches to the Field Ambulance.

Plan 2.

Precipitating and sludge box constructed of wood and rendered watertight. It is divided into ten compartments, (1.) a reservoir into which the soapy water flows from the ablution bench; from this it passes through three holes at the bottom of the dividing plate, into (2.) in which is dropped a wire cage containing a mixture of chloride of lime and coke. The water flows up through this and over a weir into a lock (3.) which carries it to the bottom and then up through (4.) which is similar to 2. — the water level in 3 and 4 being below that in 1 and 2. The precipitated sludge is carried over a weir from 4 into (5.) and thence through a hole at the bottom into (6.) and similarly through (7) (8.) (9) & (10). the holes being on alternate sides of the plates dividing these chambers. The clear effluent in 10. is carried by a trough to the pond and used over again. The water level in 5 to 10 is below that in 4. The partitions between 5 & 6, 6 & 7, 7 & 8, 8 & 9, 9 & 10 are three or four inches above the water level and act as baffle plates to hold up the precipitated soap, which, rising to the surface, slides over the side, which is cut away and rounded off 1/2" above water level, into a trough which carries it to an oil drum, and is taken to the Destructor and evaporated and burnt.

Plan 3 a & b.

Is somewhat similar to plan 2, excepting the precipitating chamber which is separate to the sludge box & is divided into 5 compartments, the 3 middle compartments being precipitating chambers. The water level in the first and last compartments is higher than that in the 3 middle compartments which is under pressure and covered with a watertight lid, clamped and screwed down with four bolts and thumb screws. The water passes up through 1st precipitating chamber, down 2nd and up the 3rd. The sludge box is a large watertight box holding 400 gallons & divided into 7 compartments. The sludge which comes to the surface in the first 4 or 5 compartments is scooped out at intervals by a tin spade

Army Form C. 2118.

WAR DIARY
or
INTELLIGENCE SUMMARY.
(Erase heading not required.)

Instructions regarding War Diaries and Intelligence Summaries are contained in F. S. Regs., Part II. and the Staff Manual respectively. Title pages will be prepared in manuscript.

Place	Date	Hour	Summary of Events and Information	Remarks and references to Appendices
			bent over at the end to form a trough. The chlorine effluent flows along a channel into a tub sunk in the ground, and is used for scrubbing out wards. The overflow from this runs into a ditch and mixes with the foul water from the grease trap, or it may be diverted into the pond and used again.	
			Note The baffle plates are now fixed and the cock bar dispensed with, as it was found necessary to make the joints between the plates and sides of the box absolutely watertight.	
			A difficulty is experienced in judging the soap concentration of the water and the amount of chloride of lime required to precipitate it. For this reason the tanks need very careful supervision and constant attention to prevent the addition of too much lime or too little. It would probably be an easier and better plan to collect the supply of bath water for the day in a large graduated tank. At the end of the day the soap concentration of the whole supply could be tested by removing a known quantity and testing it. The required amount of chloride of lime could then be added and the water allowed to run into the sludge box during the night.	
			Plan 3.c. explains itself. The boiler is an iron barrel and is easily obtained from a brewery & can often be found in ruined villages.	
			Plan 4.	
			A Refuse Destructor built of brick, iron bars & cement and constructed to deal with all solid and liquid refuse. The top is made with concrete reinforced with cross pieces of old iron bars & pieces of railings obtained from wrecked buildings. In it are made five or as many circular holes as are required according to the size and the no. of personnel in the camp. Oil drums are suspended through these holes by means of an iron bar passed through the drum near the top rim, & hang down into the fire. These are used to evaporate urine, sludge or if necessary, to boil water. The sludge is evaporated down to a thick paste and then spread on the top of the incinerator, where it dries into a dirty grey powder, and is scraped into the fire and burnt. At the side and in front of the Destructor is a concrete platform for mixing the refuse prior to its being burnt. It is a great advantage to build a roof over this platform to keep the refuse as dry as possible.	

2353 Wt. W2544/1454 700,000 5/15 D. D. & L. A.D.S.S./Forms/C. 2118.

9

Instructions regarding War Diaries and Intelligence Summaries are contained in F. S. Regs., Part II. and the Staff Manual respectively. Title pages will be prepared in manuscript.

WAR DIARY
or
INTELLIGENCE SUMMARY.
(Erase heading not required.)

Army Form C. 2118.

Place	Date	Hour	Summary of Events and Information	Remarks and references to Appendices

The Destructor in use deals easily with the refuse of 400 and could probably deal with a larger number. Nothing but refuse from the camp is used, coal and wood being unnecessary. All tins, after incineration are separated and used in making standings for water carts etc. A wire cage (Plan 5 c) is suspended in the fire, in a similar manner to the urine chambers, and is used to burn the grease & clean the coke from the grease trap, after which it can be used again. An important detail in the construction is the arch over the front opening, as without this, the front wall tends to split and collapse onto the bars.

In a previous type built, the tops of the urine evaporating tins were covered & and a small slit made in the side of the drum & opening into the incinerator, the steam passing up the chimney. The only advantage was that, in the confined space at our disposal i.e. a small yard, the smell was carried up the chimney & into our neighbours yard. The disadvantage, a serious one, was that it considerably reduced the capacity of the tins. The advantage gained by this type is seldom necessary if the Destructor is in the open, and due consideration given to the position and the prevailing wind. At its worst the smell has never been sufficient to cause any annoyance when the wind has been blowing from it across the camp.

<u>Plan 5.</u>

A. Meat Store. A small hut, divided by a muslin partition and a door into a fly proof store, & a cutting up room. The meat is suspended by hooks and the floor is covered with tin, & sprinkled with sawdust.

B. Grease trap. An ordinary ablution bench erected near the Destructor. The bench slopes towards a central V shaped gutter running along its whole length. A beading is added round the edge and the whole covered with tin. A small tray of wire mesh at one end, and a perforated plate in the gutter catch suspended matter. All greasy water is poured down the gutter and greasy dixies washed on the bench. The foul water passes into a drum, cut like a urine tin (E) & perforated at the bottom, and then filters down through two oil drums half filled with coke. At the bottom of these, it runs into a 10 ft channel lined with oildrums cut in half lengthways, the joints being sealed with puddled clay and the channel filled with sand and coke, the coke and sand being removed every 3 days and cleaned by burning it in a cage suspended into the fire of the

2353 Wt. W2544/1454 700,000 5/15 D. D. & L. A.D.S.S./Forms/C. 2118.

Instructions regarding War Diaries and Intelligence Summaries are contained in F. S. Regs., Part II. and the Staff Manual respectively. Title pages will be prepared in manuscript.

WAR DIARY
or
INTELLIGENCE SUMMARY.
(Erase heading not required.)

Army Form C. 2118.

Place	Date	Hour	Summary of Events and Information	Remarks and references to Appendices
			Incinerator. The grease-free water runs into a ditch and mixes with the chlorine stream from the bath-house.	
			Plan 5c Coke cage. A cage made by removing the top and bottom rims of an oil drum, and replacing the body and bottom of the drum by a cage of wire netting. An iron bar run through the top rim, supports the cage when let down into the fire through one of the circular holes in the top of the Destructor.	
			D. Urine tin. Two ordinary oil drums one of which has been divided lengthwise and in which lateral slits are cut in the edge to fit it over the back half of the other drum. The tins are painted white, and the inner surface is coated with tar.	
			E. Latrine. As shewn in plan, a tin gutter is fitted under the front edge of the seat and projects towards the bucket so as to almost touch its front rim. The gutter slopes gently towards a tin, at the end of the seats, where the urine collects and is removed for evaporation. The gutter needs careful adjustment so as not to be too far from the bucket or too close up to the under surface of the seat	
			Plan 6.	
			Manure Destructor, constructed of 5 pieces of corrugated iron and fitted together in a similar manner to a cheap tin toy. The chimney is made of oil drums. Iron bars form a flooring to the fire. Manure, mixed with tins to help ventilation, is thrown in on top of a fire to start its destruction. When once working, the damp manure is placed on the top & around the sides where it dries, and is then burnt.	
			Plan 7.	
			Cook House. Is built of corrugated iron on three sides, and is open on the fourth. Roof of corrugated iron 8' at the front & 7'3" at the back. Dimensions:- Side 10', front 12', height 8' in front and 7'3" behind. Floor of hard, firm clay. The fire place is built of brick cement & iron bars, and will take 10 dixies. The tin ovens of an ordinary Congo	

2353 Wt. W2544/1454 700,000 5/15 D. D. & L. A.D.S.S./Forms/C. 2118.

N

Instructions regarding War Diaries and Intelligence Summaries are contained in F. S. Regs., Part II. and the Staff Manual respectively. Title pages will be prepared in manuscript.

WAR DIARY
or
INTELLIGENCE SUMMARY.
(Erase heading not required.)

Army Form C. 2118.

Place	Date	Hour	Summary of Events and Information	Remarks and references to Appendices
			stove are fitted into a brick fire place so that a flue runs under, around one side, & over the top of the oven, the floor, of the oven not being directly over but a little to the left of the fire in the L. oven and to the R. in the R. oven. These fire places will cook for 300 patients; the water in the dixies boils in 20 minutes, using the normal amount of fuel. One side of the fire can be used by closing a damper at the end of the other. When dixies are not on the fire, an oval shaped piece of tin is placed over the hole.	
			Plan 8.	
			Varies from plan 7 in the space between the ovens being utilized to boil a dixie, and that the flue runs under, up the side, and round the back of the oven, the top of the oven being used to keep dishes hot. The chimney is common to the oven and the fire for the 3 dixies.	
			28 – VI – 16.	
			G. J. S. Emmons [?] Major. R.A.M.C. O.C. 72nd Field Ambulance.	

2353 Wt. W2544/1454 700,000 5/15 D. D. & L. A.D.S.S./Forms/C. 2118.

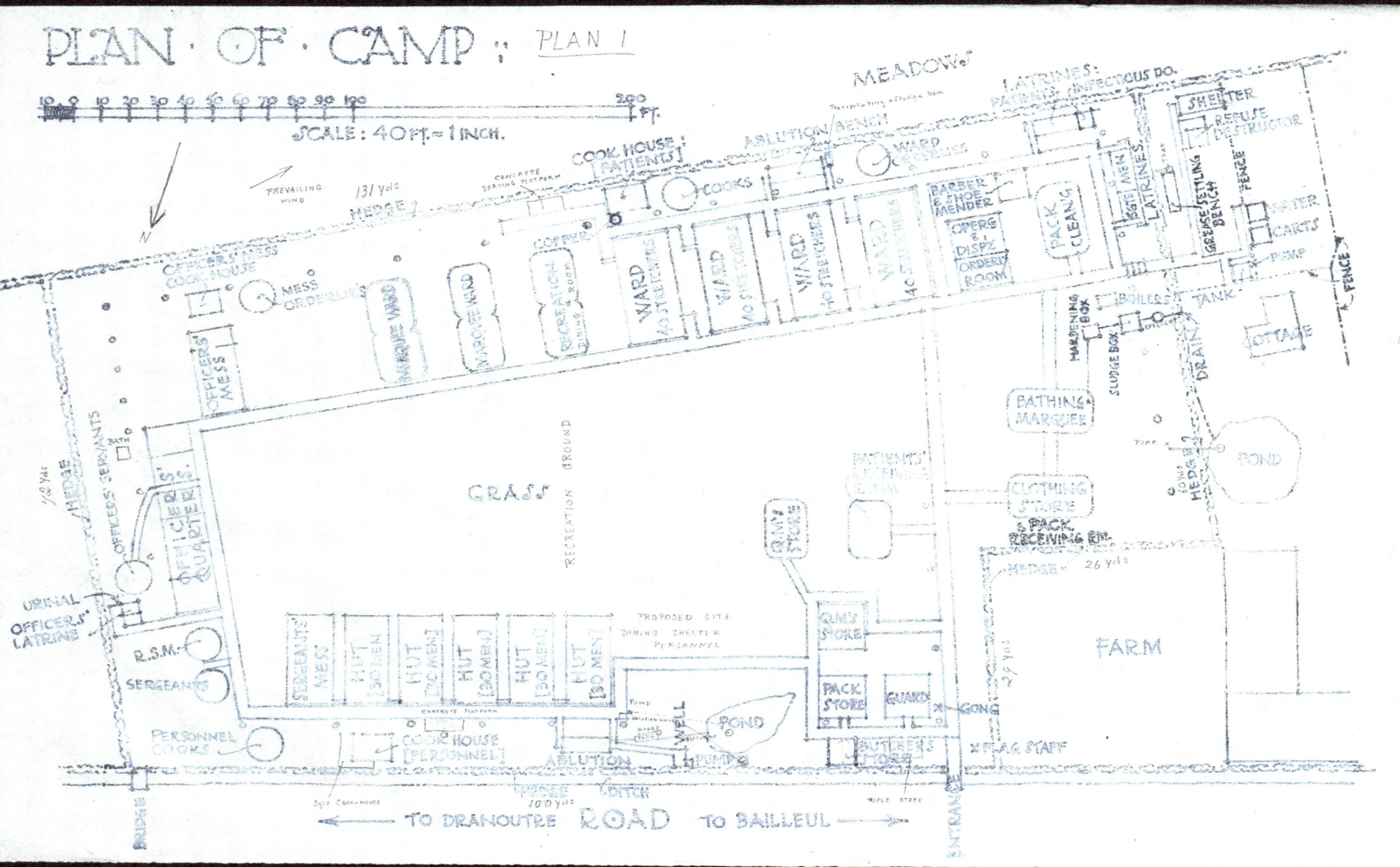

PLAN · OF · CAMP : PLAN I
10 0 10 20 30 40 50 60 70 80 90 100 200 FT.
SCALE: 40 FT. = 1 INCH.
N
PREVAILING WIND
131 yds
HEDGE
MEADOWS
LATRINES: PATIENTS' INFECTIOUS DO.
SHELTER
REFUSE DESTRUCTOR
ABLUTION BENCH
COOK HOUSE [PATIENTS]
CONCRETE SERVING PLATFORM
COOKS
WARD ORDERLIES
BARBER & SHOE MENDER
OPERG & DISPY
ORDERLY ROOM
PACK CLEANG
SGTS MEN
LATRINES
GREASE SETTLING BENCH
FENCE
WATER CARTS
PUMP
FENCE
OFFICERS' MESS COOK HOUSE
MESS ORDERLIES
MARQUEE WARD
MARQUEE WARD
RECREATION DINING ROOM
COPPER
WARD 40 STRETCHERS
WARD 40 STRETCHERS
WARD 40 STRETCHERS
WARD 40 STRETCHERS
HARDENING BOX
SLUDGE BOX
BOILERS
TANK
DRAIN
COTTAGE
OFFICERS' MESS
BATHING MARQUEE
BATH
OFFICERS' SERVANTS
72 yds
HEDGE
OFFICERS' QUARTERS
GRASS
RECREATION GROUND
PATIENTS' RECEIVING ROOM
CLOTHING STORE
& PACK RECEIVING RM.
PUMP
60 yds
HEDGE
POND
QMS STORE
HEDGE
26 yds
URINAL
OFFICERS' LATRINE
PROPOSED SITE DINING SHELTER PERSONNEL
QM'S STORE
R.S.M.
SERGEANTS
SERGEANTS' MESS
HUT [30 MEN]
HUT [30 MEN]
HUT [30 MEN]
HUT [30 MEN]
HUT [30 MEN]
29 yds
FARM
PACK STORE
GUARD
GONG
CONCRETE PLATFORM
PUMP
WELL
POND
PERSONNEL COOKS
COOK HOUSE [PERSONNEL]
ABLUTION
PUMP
BUTLERS STORE
FLAG STAFF
Sgts Cook-house
HEDGE
100 yds
DITCH
RIFLE STORE
BRIDGE
TO DRANOUTRE ROAD TO BAILLEUL
ENTRANCE

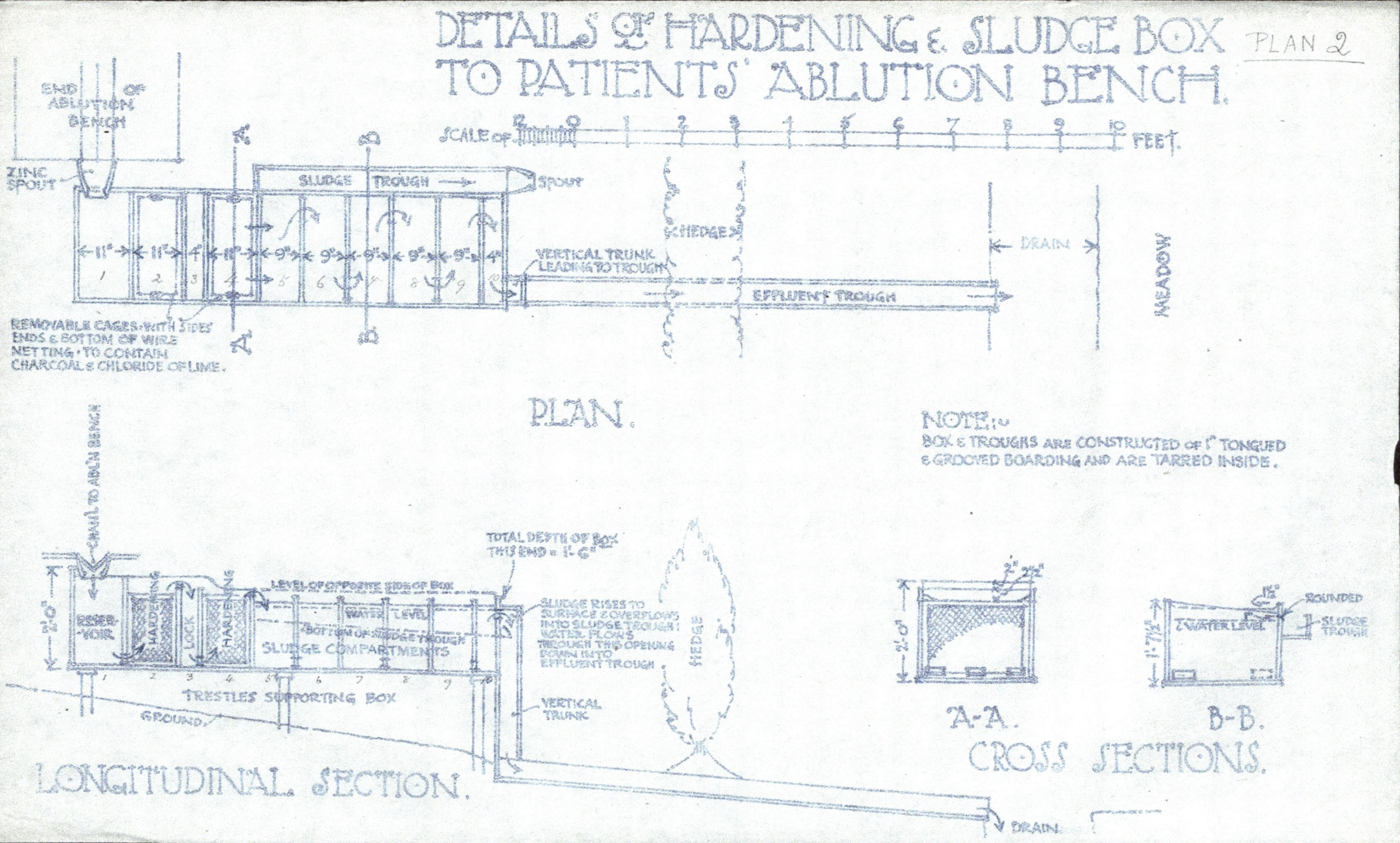

DETAILS OF HARDENING & SLUDGE BOX TO PATIENTS' ABLUTION BENCH.

PLAN 2

SCALE OF 12 [inches] 0 1 2 3 4 5 6 7 8 9 10 FEET.

END OF ABLUTION BENCH

ZINC SPOUT

SLUDGE TROUGH →

SPOUT

11" 11" 4" 11" 9" 9" 9" 9" 9" 4"

1 2 3 4 5 6 7 8 9 10

A A B B

HEDGE

VERTICAL TRUNK LEADING TO TROUGH

EFFLUENT TROUGH

DRAIN

MEADOW

REMOVABLE CAGES, WITH SIDES, ENDS & BOTTOM OF WIRE NETTING, TO CONTAIN CHARCOAL & CHLORIDE OF LIME.

PLAN.

NOTE:—
BOX & TROUGHS ARE CONSTRUCTED OF 1" TONGUED & GROOVED BOARDING AND ARE TARRED INSIDE.

CHANNEL TO ABL'N BENCH

2'-0"

RESERVOIR

HARDENING

LOCK

HARDENING

LEVEL OF OPPOSITE SIDE OF BOX

WATER LEVEL

BOTTOM OF SLUDGE TROUGH

SLUDGE COMPARTMENTS

TOTAL DEPTH OF BOX THIS END = 1'-6"

SLUDGE RISES TO SURFACE & OVERFLOWS INTO SLUDGE TROUGH: WATER FLOWS THROUGH THIS OPENING DOWN INTO EFFLUENT TROUGH.

1 2 3 4 5 6 7 8 9 10

TRESTLES SUPPORTING BOX

GROUND

VERTICAL TRUNK

HEDGE

DRAIN

LONGITUDINAL SECTION.

2" 2½"

2'-0"

A-A.

1½"

ROUNDED

WATER LEVEL

SLUDGE TROUGH

1'-7½"

B-B.

CROSS SECTIONS.

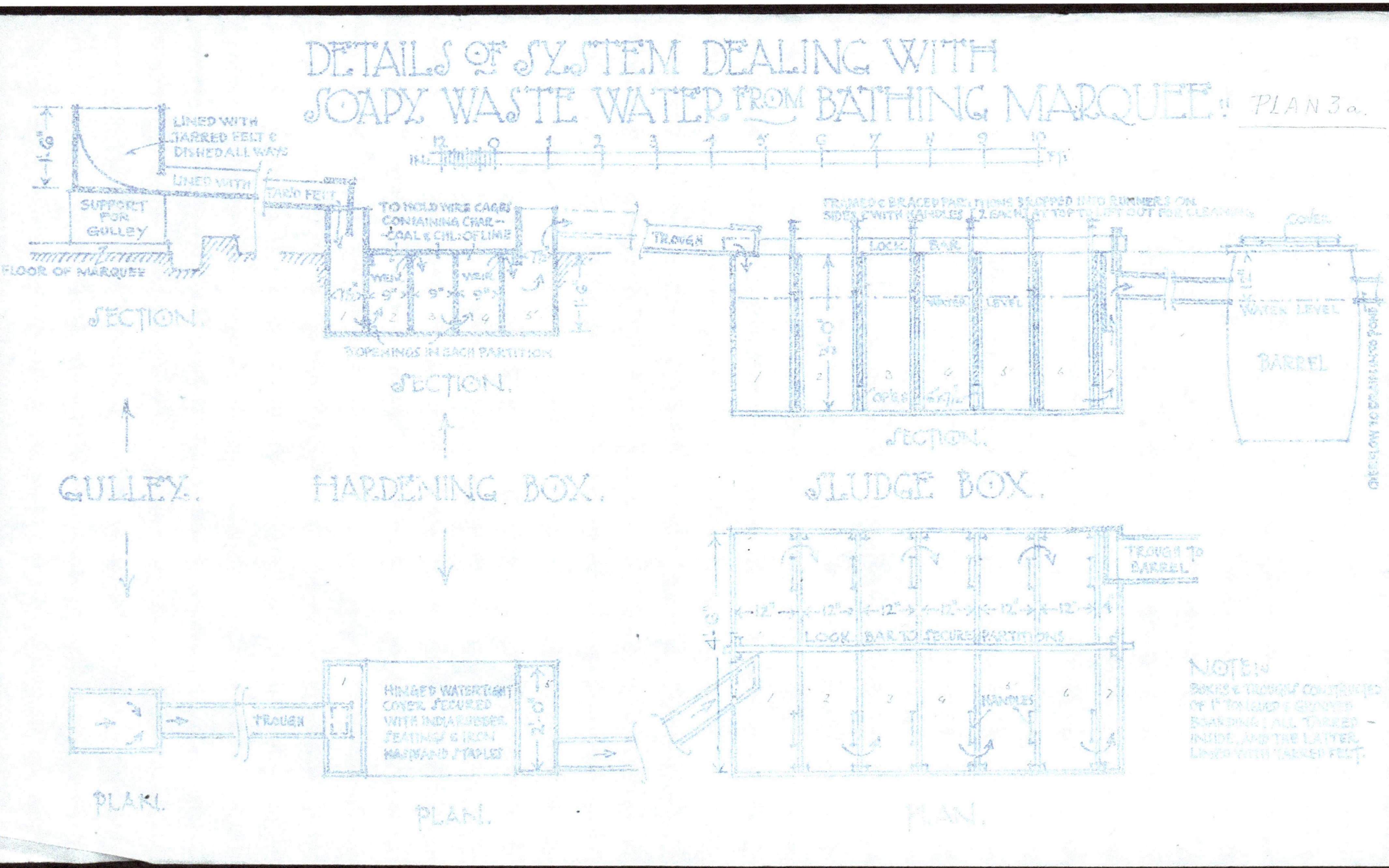
DETAILS OF SYSTEM DEALING WITH
SOAPY WASTE WATER FROM BATHING MARQUEE!!
PLAN 3a.
LINED WITH TARRED FELT & DISHED ALL WAYS
LINED WITH TAR'D FELT
SUPPORT FOR GULLEY
FLOOR OF MARQUEE
SECTION.
TO HOLD WIRE CAGES CONTAINING CHAR-COAL & CHL: OF LIME
WEIR
OPENINGS IN EACH PARTITION
SECTION.
TROUGH
FRAMED & BRACED PARTITIONS SLOPPED INTO RUNNERS ON SIDES, WITH HANDLES (2 EACH) AT TOP TO LIFT OUT FOR CLEANING
LOCK BAR
WATER LEVEL
SECTION.
COVER
BARREL
GULLEY.
HARDENING BOX.
SLUDGE BOX.
TROUGH TO BARREL
LOCK BAR TO SECURE PARTITIONS
HANDLES
TROUGH
HINGED WATERTIGHT COVER SECURED WITH INDIARUBBER SEATINGS & IRON HASPS AND STAPLES
NOTE:
BOXES & TROUGHS CONSTRUCTED OF 1" TONGUED & GROOVED BOARDING; ALL TARRED INSIDE, AND THE LATTER LINED WITH TARRED FELT.
PLAN.
PLAN.
PLAN.

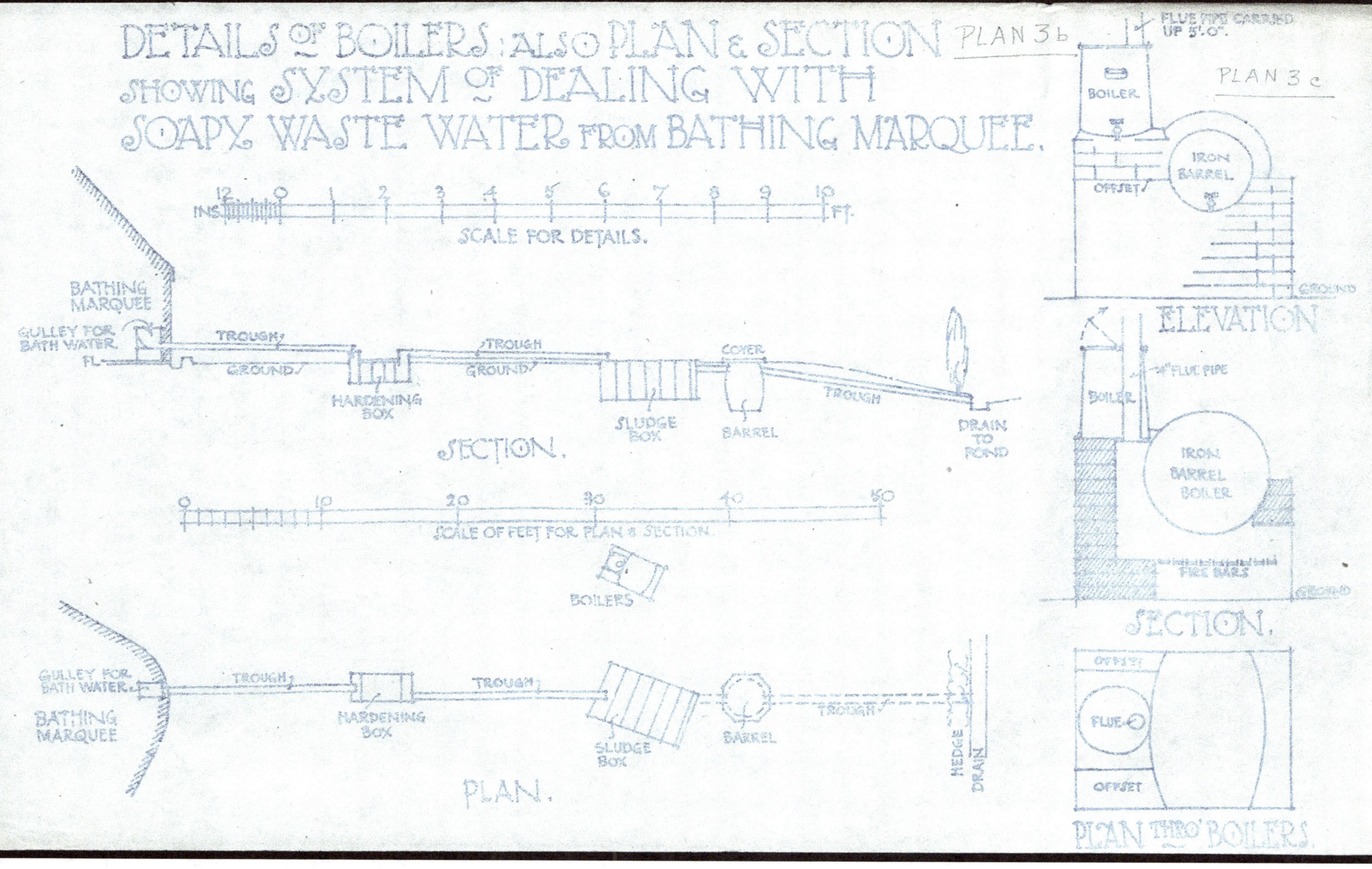
DETAILS OF BOILERS: ALSO PLAN & SECTION
SHOWING SYSTEM OF DEALING WITH
SOAPY WASTE WATER FROM BATHING MARQUEE.
PLAN 3b
PLAN 3c
FLUE PIPE CARRIED UP 5'.0".
BOILER
IRON BARREL
OFFSET
GROUND
ELEVATION
4" FLUE PIPE
BOILER
IRON BARREL BOILER
FIRE BARS
GROUND
SECTION.
OFFSET
FLUE
OFFSET
PLAN THRO' BOILERS.
12 INS 0 1 2 3 4 5 6 7 8 9 10 FT.
SCALE FOR DETAILS.
BATHING MARQUEE
GULLEY FOR BATH WATER
FL.
TROUGH
GROUND
HARDENING BOX
TROUGH
GROUND
SLUDGE BOX
COVER
BARREL
TROUGH
DRAIN TO POND
SECTION.
0 10 20 30 40 50
SCALE OF FEET FOR PLAN & SECTION.
BOILERS
GULLEY FOR BATH WATER.
BATHING MARQUEE
TROUGH
HARDENING BOX
TROUGH
SLUDGE BOX
BARREL
TROUGH
HEDGE
DRAIN
PLAN.

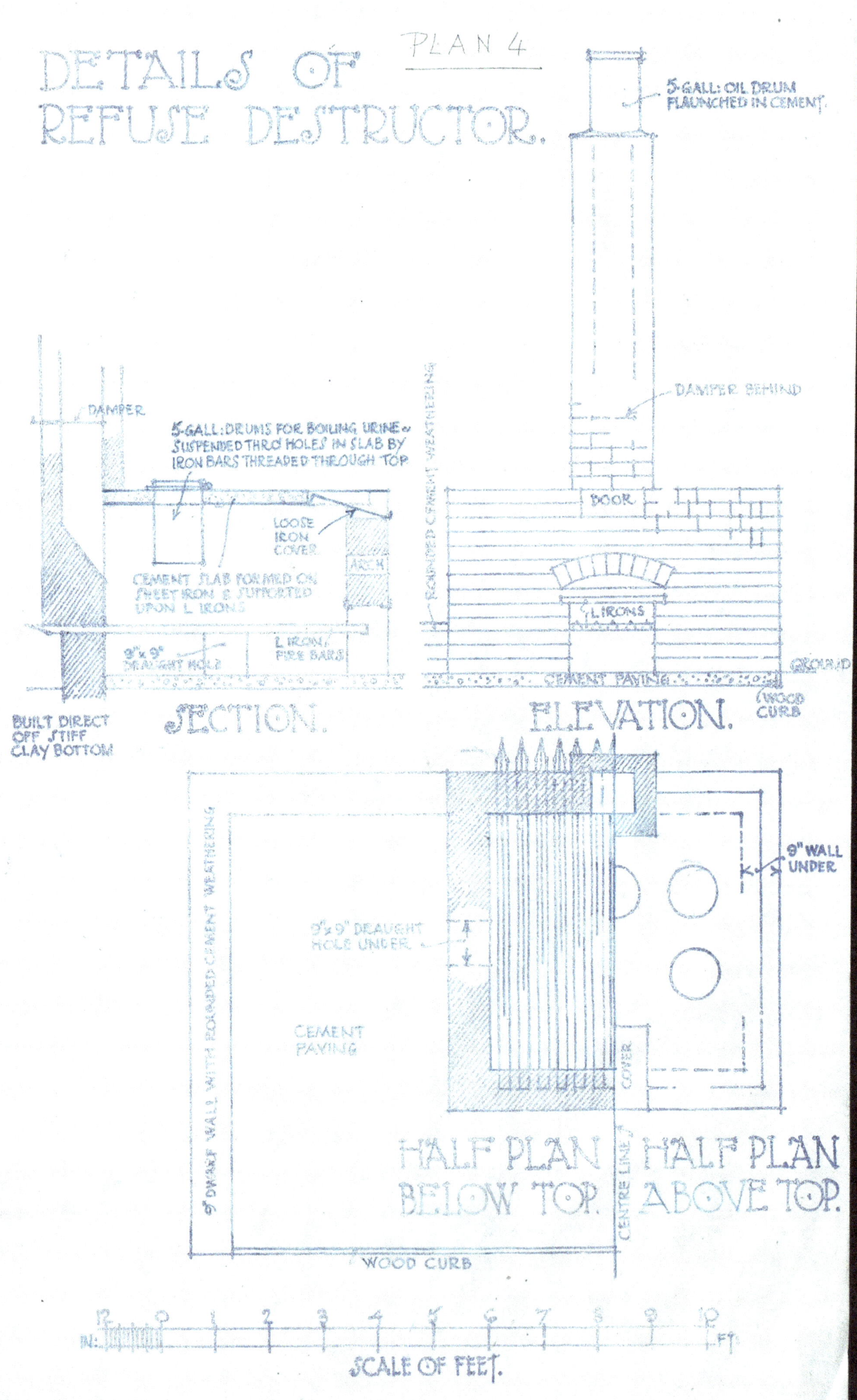
PLAN 4
DETAILS OF REFUSE DESTRUCTOR.
5-GALL: OIL DRUM FLAUNCHED IN CEMENT.
DAMPER
5-GALL: DRUMS FOR BOILING URINE ~ SUSPENDED THRO' HOLES IN SLAB BY IRON BARS THREADED THROUGH TOP
LOOSE IRON COVER
ARCH
CEMENT SLAB FORMED ON SHEET IRON & SUPPORTED UPON L IRONS
9" x 9" DRAUGHT HOLE
L IRON FIRE BARS
BUILT DIRECT OFF STIFF CLAY BOTTOM
SECTION.
ROUNDED CEMENT WEATHERING
DAMPER BEHIND
DOOR
L IRONS
CEMENT PAVING
GROUND
WOOD CURB
ELEVATION.
9" WALL UNDER
9" x 9" DRAUGHT HOLE UNDER
CEMENT PAVING
COVER
9" DWARF WALL WITH ROUNDED CEMENT WEATHERING
HALF PLAN BELOW TOP.
CENTRE LINE
HALF PLAN ABOVE TOP.
WOOD CURB
12 0 1 2 3 4 5 6 7 8 9 10
IN: FT.
SCALE OF FEET.

PLAN 5

PLANS OF WARD BUTCHERS' STORE AND MISCELLANEOUS DETAILS

SCALE OF FEET FOR PLANS.

SCALE FOR DETAILS.

SECTION.

MEAT SAFE

CANVAS

BUTCHERS' STORE. A

PLAN.

BENCH

CANVAS DOOR

SAFE 10'x4' WITH 3 BEARERS OVER TO TAKE 6 CARCASES

WINDOW: WIRE NETTING

GREASE BENCH. B

BEADED EDGE

TO FALL TOWARDS CHANNEL

CHANNEL

STRAINER ARE ZINC COVERED

PERFORATED ZINC STRAINER

TOP EDGES CHAMFERED

10"x10" REMOVABLE TRAY WITH 1/2" MESH WIRE BOTTOM TO CATCH LARGE SOLIDS

PERFORATED BOTTOM

5-GALL: OIL DRUMS

10'-0"

DUCK BOARDS

TO DRAIN

BASKETS FOR BURNING C FOULED COKE INDESTRUCTOR

TOP AND BOTTOM (PERFORATED) MADE FROM 5-GALL: OIL DRUM

4-GALL PETROL CAN PAINTED RED WITH WHITE LETTERS

FIRE BUCKETS.

5-GALL: DRUM PAINTED WHITE WITH 2" LETTERING "URINAL"

SHIELD CLIPPED OVER BACK OF DRUM

CEMENT RENDERED

URINE PAILS. D

ZINC GUTTER TO CATCH URINE

E

SUPPORTS 4 FEET APART

BOARDED SUPPORT FOR LAT: BUCKETS OR DRUMS

TYPICAL PLAN OF WARD.

TABLE

RUBBISH

CANVAS SCREEN

SHELVING

PRINCIPALS

BEDPANS ETC.

BROOMS

CORNER CUPBOARD A. [WITH FOLDING DOORS]

PRINCIPAL

20 STRETCHERS

DIMENSIONS:-
60'-0" LONG x 20'-0" WIDE.
ROOF SEGMENTAL:
HT. AT SPRINGING = 8'-0"
" " CENTRE = 10'-0"

FOLDING DOORS

TABLE

DUCK BDS.

WINDOWS CILL 3'-6" FROM FLOOR, IN 2 HEIGHTS WITH SASHES HUNG AT TOP TO OPEN OUT

STAND FOR NIGHT URINE & DRY REFUSE PAILS

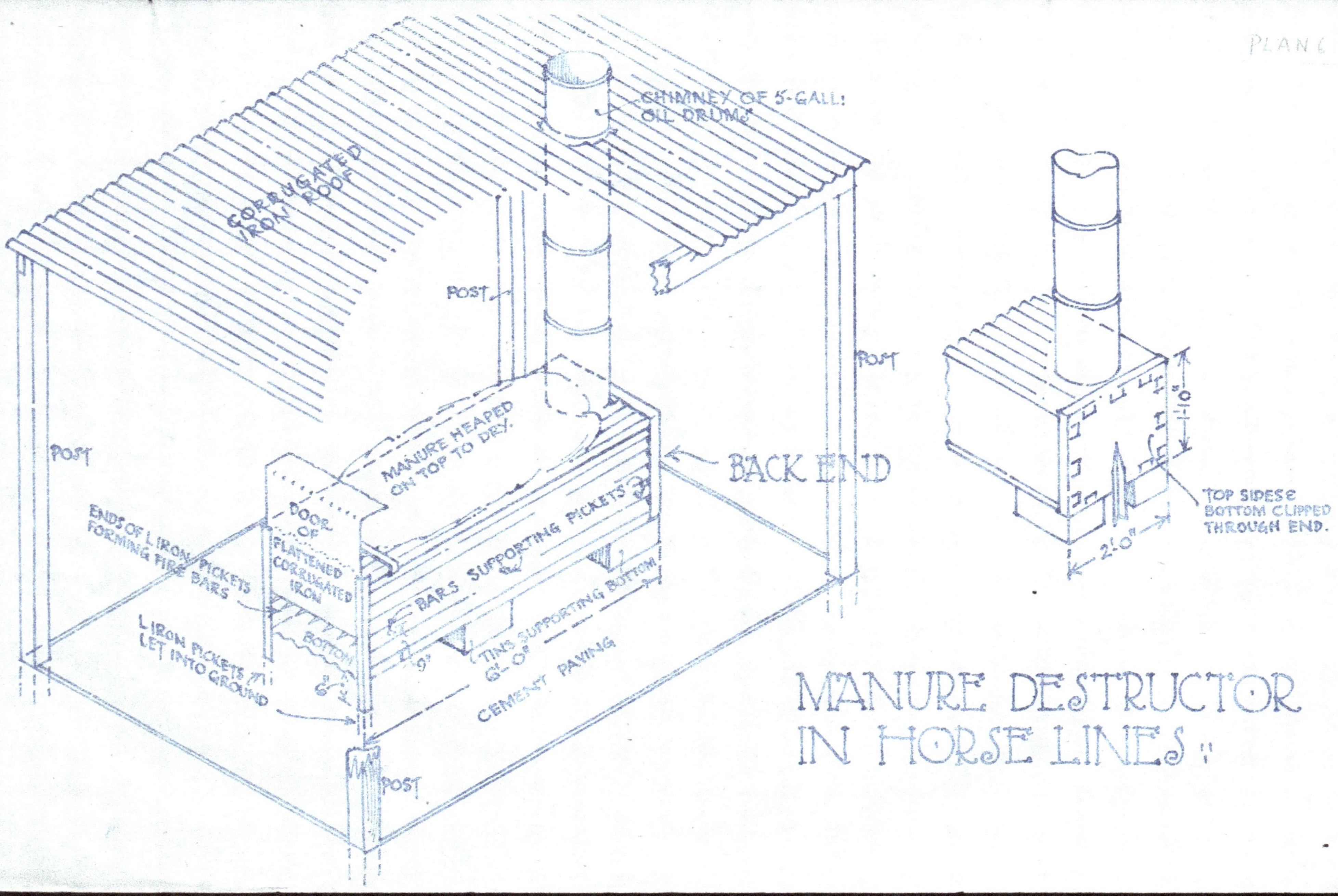
PLAN 6
CORRUGATED IRON ROOF
CHIMNEY OF 5-GALL: OIL DRUMS
POST
POST
POST
POST
MANURE HEAPED ON TOP TO DRY.
BACK END
DOOR OF FLATTENED CORRUGATED IRON
ENDS OF L IRON PICKETS FORMING FIRE BARS
BARS SUPPORTING PICKETS
TINS SUPPORTING BOTTOM
L IRON PICKETS LET INTO GROUND
BOTTOM
9"
6'-0"
6"
CEMENT PAVING
1'-10"
2'-0"
TOP SIDES & BOTTOM CLIPPED THROUGH END.
MANURE DESTRUCTOR IN HORSE LINES

DETAILS OF COOK HOUSES FOR PATIENTS & PERSONNEL.

PLAN 7

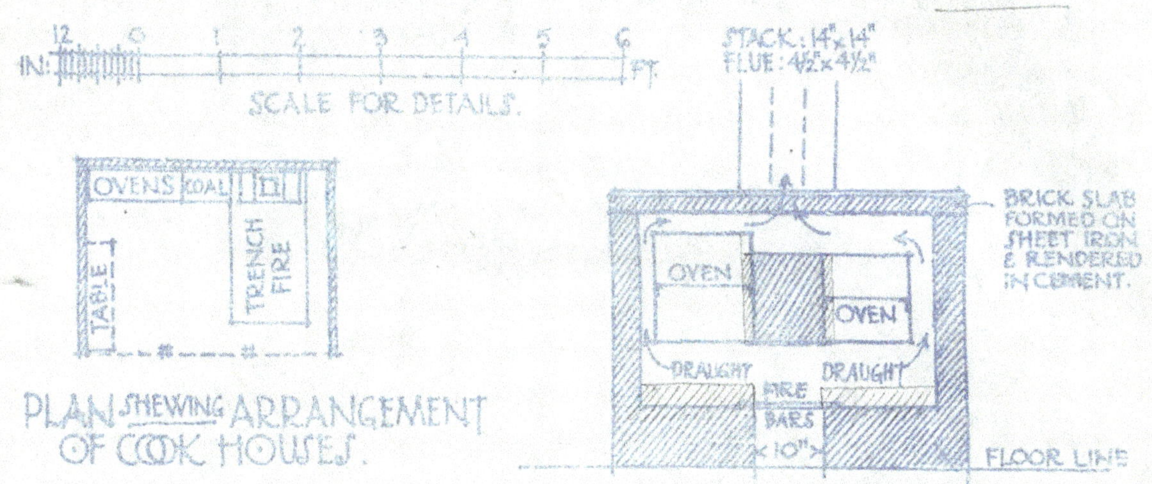

CROSS SECTION THRO' OVENS.

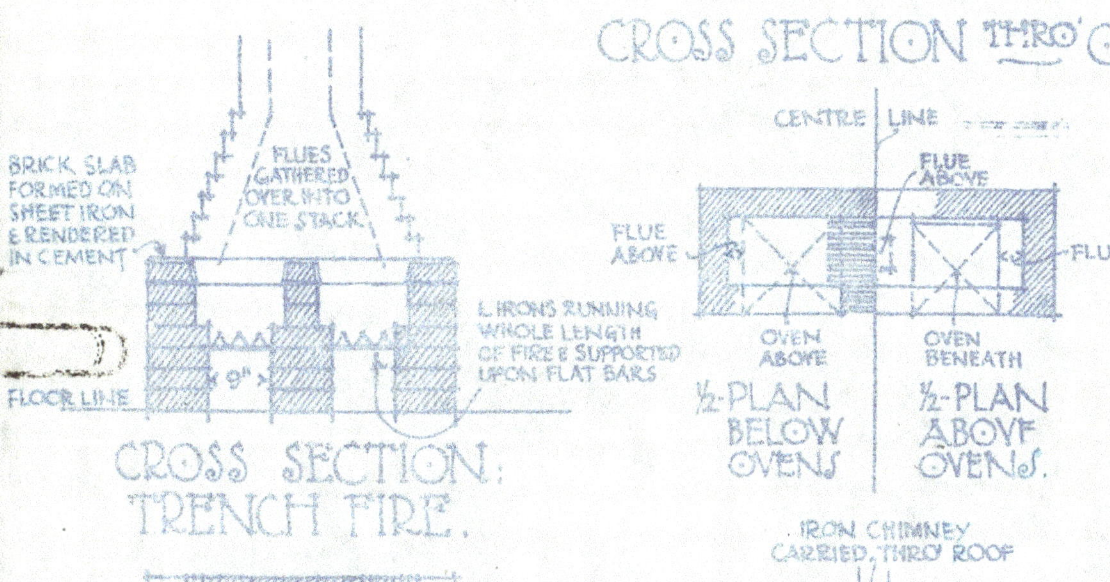

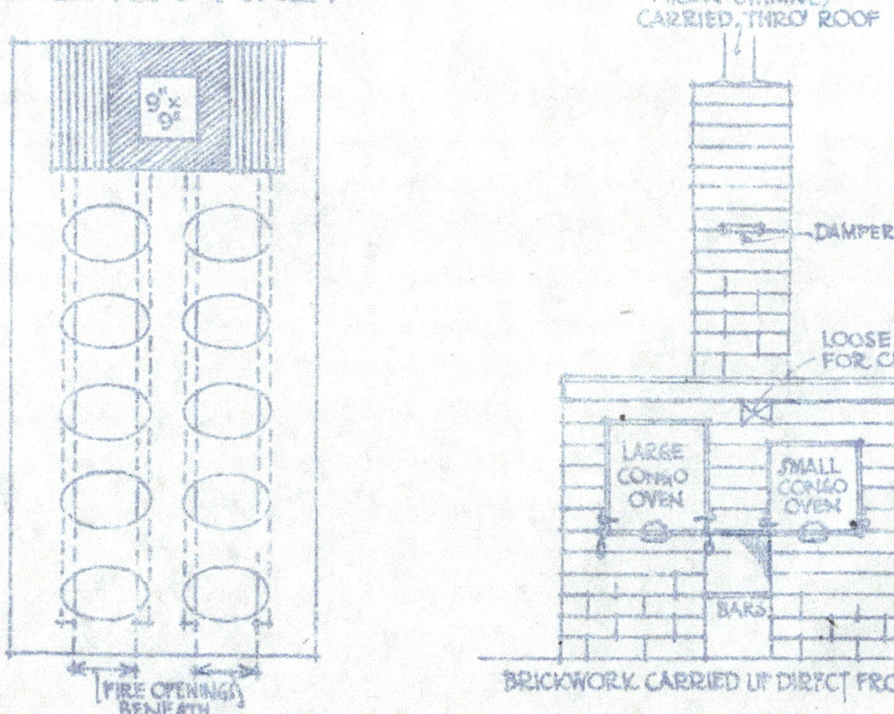

PLAN OF TRENCH FIRE. ELEVATION OF OVENS.

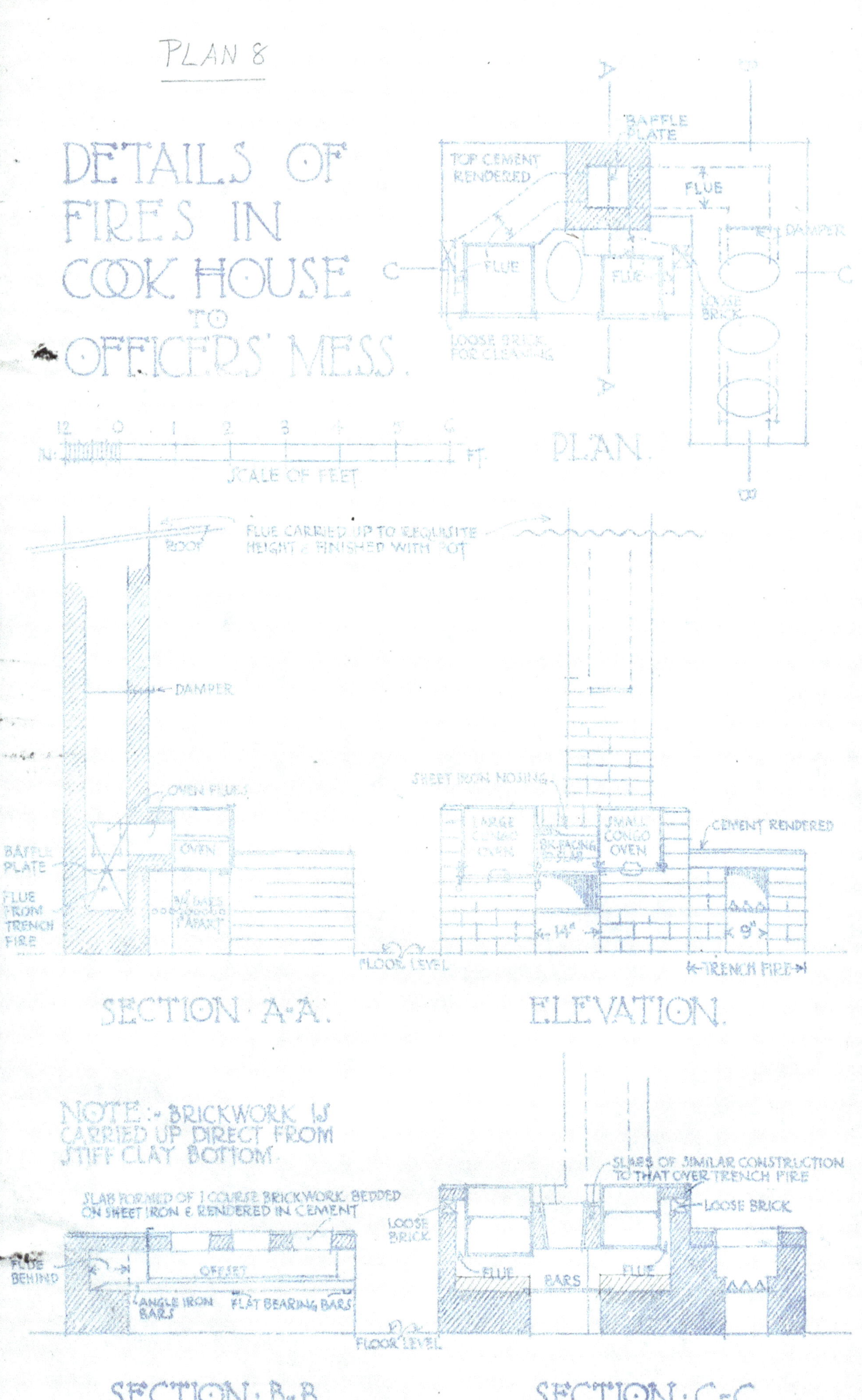

PLAN 8
DETAILS OF FIRES IN COOK HOUSE TO OFFICERS' MESS.
BAFFLE PLATE
TOP CEMENT RENDERED
FLUE
DAMPER
FLUE
FLUE
LOOSE BRICK
LOOSE BRICK FOR CLEANING
SCALE OF FEET
PLAN.
FLUE CARRIED UP TO REQUISITE HEIGHT & FINISHED WITH POT
ROOF
DAMPER
OVEN FLUES
BAFFLE PLATE
OVEN
FLUE FROM TRENCH FIRE
1" APART
FLOOR LEVEL
SECTION A-A.
SHEET IRON NOSING
LARGE CONGO OVEN
SMALL CONGO OVEN
CEMENT RENDERED
14"
9"
TRENCH FIRE
ELEVATION.
NOTE:- BRICKWORK IS CARRIED UP DIRECT FROM STIFF CLAY BOTTOM.
SLAB FORMED OF 1 COURSE BRICKWORK BEDDED ON SHEET IRON & RENDERED IN CEMENT
FLUE BEHIND
OFFSET
ANGLE IRON BARS
FLAT BEARING BARS
FLOOR LEVEL
SECTION B-B.
SLABS OF SIMILAR CONSTRUCTION TO THAT OVER TRENCH FIRE
LOOSE BRICK
LOOSE BRICK
FLUE
BARS
FLUE
SECTION C-C.

MEDICAL

24 July
72 F. Amb
Vol. 11

July 1/16

S

CONFIDENTIAL

WAR DIARY

OF

(MAJOR G.B. EDWARDS) OFFICER COMMANDING 72 FIELD AMBULANCE

FROM 1ST JULY 1916 TO 31ST JULY 1916

72 FIELD AMBULANCE **WAR DIARY** *or* **INTELLIGENCE SUMMARY.** (1).

(Erase heading not required.)

Army Form C. 2118.

Instructions regarding War Diaries and Intelligence Summaries are contained in F. S. Regs., Part II. and the Staff Manual respectively. Title pages will be prepared in manuscript.

Place	Date	Hour	Summary of Events and Information	Remarks and references to Appendices
BAILLEUL S16 c 2.4 (28) 24th D.R.S.	1-7-16.	10 AM.	1 NCO & No 4, & 5, bearer squads C section to KEMMEL N.21 d 4.4. (28) Advanced Dressing Station 3rd NORTHUMBRIAN F.A. on advance party to learn position of trenches.	
		10 AM.	LIEUT H.F.H. EBERTS, one NCO, 9 1 6 O.R., to a field at M23 d 7.9. (28) as advance party to drain field & clear ground for field ambulance encampment.	
		11 AM.	Visited Kemmel Adv Dressing Station of 3rd NORTHUMBRIAN F.A. & also village in search of cellar for advanced dressing station. A large BRASSERIE at N 21 C 7.6 with a little alteration & strutting up of cellar would make an excellent spot for stretcher cases & would accommodate 40 to 50 stretcher cases & could be made to hold about 80 stretcher cases & numerous sitting cases. There is a good approach & good exit both for bearers & cars.	
		7. P.M.	Cars No 1543, & 1547 lent to 73 F Amb.	SMK
"	2-7-16.		O.C 7th AUSTRALIAN FIELD AMB. visited D.R.S. & was shown round the camp & the sanitary arrangements explained to him.	
			1 Case of measles of 1st NORTHANTS REGT transferred from 3rd NORTHUMBRIAN FIELD AMB.	
			Duplicate war diary for MARCH forwarded to O/c RAMC Records.	
"	3-7-16.	10 AM	Officers from No 1 AUSTRALIAN F AMB. 15 A.F. Amb. & 5th AUSTRALIAN DIVISION visited & were shown round the D.R.S. The Sanitary Officer of 5th DIV. left an NCO to make plans of the sanitary arrangements & general working of the D.R.S.	SMK
		4.40 PM	Lectured all officers of the Unit on the working of an Advanced Dressing Station particularly in reference to special cases, clerical work, & returns.	
"	4-7-16		Visited M23 d 7.9. (28) Drainage work completed	SMK
			2 NCOs & 3 O.R from 5th Sam. Section reported for instruction	
			Notification received from ADMS 24 Div. that 6 Australian F. Amb. would take over DRS on 6th	M S 1433 4/7/16. SMK

1577 Wt. W10791/1773 500,000 1/15 D. D. & L. A.D.S.S./Forms/C. 2118.

72 FIELD AMBULANCE.

Instructions regarding War Diaries and Intelligence Summaries are contained in F. S. Regs., Part II. and the Staff Manual respectively. Title pages will be prepared in manuscript.

WAR DIARY
or
INTELLIGENCE SUMMARY.
(Erase heading not required.)

Army Form C. 2118.

Place	Date	Hour	Summary of Events and Information	Remarks and references to Appendices
BAILLEUL S16 c 2.4. Sheet 28 1/20,000. 24th D.R.S	5-7-16		LIEUT H.S. GROVES to KEMMEL to Adv. Dressing Stn. 3rd NORTHUMBRIAN F.A. to take over.	
	6-7-16	12. Noon.	6th AUSTRALIAN F. Amb took over D.R.S Marched off at 3PM. for M 23 d 7.9 (28)	
M23 d 7.9 Sheet 28/20000		4. P.M.	Arrived at a Field M23 d. 7.9 & pitched all tents of Field Ambulance & prepared to receive patients from advanced Dressing Station at Kemmel.	
		6. P.M.	Lieut W. DIXON & Lt. H.T. KEANE with tent sub div & remainder of C Section bearers to KEMMEL with ~~[illegible]~~ equipment of section.	
			Took over Adv Dressing Station from 3rd NORTHUMBRIAN F. Amb.	
"	7-7-16		Visited Adv. Dressing Station & arranged for a party to clean out cellars of BRASSERIE & ~~[illegible]~~ improve exits.	
"	8-7-16.		Received orders to hand over KEMMEL to a Field Amb. of 50 DIVISION. Ascertained from ADMS 50th Div. that the 3rd NORTHUMBRIAN F. Amb would relieve me at 10 AM tomorrow. Received orders to send an adv party to S16.c 2.4 to take over from 6th Australian F. Amb. Sent 1 officer 1 Cpl 16 O.R.	
		11. P.M.	Lt. W DIXON & 3 bearer squads C Section returned to M23 d 7.9 (28)	
"	9-7-16	10 AM	1 Officer & 2 squads B section to S16 c 2.4 (28)	
		12 noon	Remainder C Section rejoined from KEMMEL	
		3 P.M.	Marched off for S16. c 2.4 (28) Found 6 Australian F Amb. still there & that they had received no orders to move	

1577 Wt. W10791/1773 500,000 1/15 D. D. & L. A.D.S.S./Forms/C. 2118.

72 FIELD AMBULANCE

Instructions regarding War Diaries and Intelligence Summaries are contained in F. S. Regs., Part II. and the Staff Manual respectively. Title pages will be prepared in manuscript.

WAR DIARY
or
INTELLIGENCE SUMMARY.
(Erase heading not required.)

Army Form C. 2118.

(3)

Place	Date	Hour	Summary of Events and Information	Remarks and references to Appendices
BAILLEUL S16 c 2.4 (sheet 28 1/20000)	9-7-16	4 P.M.	Arrived at S16 c 2.4 (28) Found 6 Australian F. Amb still in possession	SM
"	10-7-16	10 AM	Took over from 6th Australian F Amb. &	
		12 Noon	6th Australian F Amb marched off	
			3 Officers 3 NCOs & 6 O.R. of Dental personnel of Australian Field Ambulances left with me by order DMS 2nd Army for rations & accommodation.	
			1 Officer 1 NCO 6 O.R. to T20 c (sheet 28) Collecting post for sick in neighbourhood & RED LODGE 1 motor ambulance car to T20 c (28) Post taken over from 1st AUSTRALIAN F Amb.	
			All ranks busy cleaning up camp & ponds which have become fouled during the three days the ground was occupied by the 6 Australian F. Amb.	SM
"	11-7-16		Visited T20 c (28) Found everything working satisfactorily. Australians had left a large accumulation of stores of all kinds which were not handed over to me and dumped under tarpaulin.	SM
"	12-7-16		4 Stretcher Cases Gunners collected at RED LODGE 41 Div & brought to the DRS (now opened as a Field Ambulance) A civilian boy brought in with grenade wounds right hand severe	SM
"	13-7-16		Report on Pork & Bean ration forwarded to ADMS.	SM
"	14-7-16		1 NCO & 1 man sent to S16 a 2.3 (28) as guard over stores for HdQrs 24 Div	
		3 P.M.	1 NCO & 12 O.R. " " " to strike camp & load lorries	
			No 40812 Pte Pitts B joined for duty from 5th Corps	
			No 40774 Pte Islam L " " " " 4 Field Ambulance	SM

1577 Wt. W10791/1773 500,000 1/15 D. D. & L. A.D.S.S./Forms/C. 2118.

72 FIELD AMBULANCE

Instructions regarding War Diaries and Intelligence Summaries are contained in F. S. Regs., Part II. and the Staff Manual respectively. Title pages will be prepared in manuscript.

WAR DIARY
or
INTELLIGENCE SUMMARY.
(Erase heading not required.)

Army Form C. 2118.

Place	Date	Hour	Summary of Events and Information	Remarks and references to Appendices
S16 C 2.4 (28)	15-7-16	10 AM	Visited cellar at BRASSERIE KEMMEL with O.C. 104 Field Coy R.E. & discussed method of strutting up cellars & making rests for stretcher cases.	SM
"	16-7-16		Party 1 NCO. 24 O.R. to KEMMEL to work under REs at BRASSERIE	SM
"	17-7-16		Opened again as 24th D.R.S.	SM
"	18-7-16		Working party of 25 men to KEMMEL to reinforce party already there.	SM
"	19-7-16		Whole of working party returned from KEMMEL. Orders to hand over Post at T20C (28) on 20th to a Field Amb of 20 Division & the DRS on 21st	ADMS OO 11.
			Party of 15 Officers various units were conducted round the camp & instructed in the sanitary methods adopted.	
			Advance party 1 Officer + 15 OR of 60th Field Ambulance arrived.	SM
"	20-7-16		Post at T20C (28) handed over to 60 F Amb. Lt H.S. KEANE & party returned	
			CAPT. H.F.H. EBERTS & party rejoined HQrs from Adv Dressing Station at N27C 9.5 (28) LINDENHOEK	
			O.C. 60 F. Amb. & arrived with the 60th Field Ambulance. Capt W.T. WEBSTER with C Section to METEREN X 15d 6.8 (27) to take over from 74 Field Ambulance	SM

72 FIELD AMBULANCE

WAR DIARY
or
INTELLIGENCE SUMMARY.
(Erase heading not required.)

Army Form C. 2118.

(5)

Instructions regarding War Diaries and Intelligence Summaries are contained in F. S. Regs., Part II. and the Staff Manual respectively. Title pages will be prepared in manuscript.

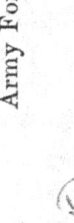

Place	Date	Hour	Summary of Events and Information	Remarks and references to Appendices
S16 c 2.4 (Sheet 28)	21/7/16	10 AM	Handed over to 60th Field Ambulance & marched to METEREN X15 d 6.8 (sheet 27)	SMc
	22/7/16		Nothing to report.	SMc
	23/7/16	3 PM	No Bde or Divisional orders yet received for 22nd or 23rd. ADMS OO 19 & OO 20 received.	
		7 PM	Divisional Routine orders for 22 received. An order for me to draw 1 rider from 106 Coy ASC at 12 noon sharp to day. No Bde movement order received.	SMc
	24/7/16		Sent to 72 I. Bde for orders & found they had left. Applied to ADMS for orders. Received orders from ADMS to entrain at BAILLEUL WEST at 11-28 P.M. Arrived at entrainment platform at 8 & commenced entraining 8-30 P.M. All entrained by 9.30 P.M. Flat trucks very difficult to load as high sides about 2 feet & only small cutting in centre so that wheels had to be lifted onto truck. Saw a movement order of 72 I. Bde but no mention of my unit. Reported fact to ADMS	SMc
	25/7/16		Arrived LONGUEAU ~~...~~ (Sheet AMIENS 17) at 9 am detrained & marched off at 9.40 am for OISSY via AMIENS – DREUIL – AILLY BREILLY – FOURDRINOY – CAVILLON arrived OISSY 6-15 P.M. Men marched well & were quite fresh on arrival. Two fell out	SMc
	26/7		Erected three marquees & opened for sick. Sent car round to Regt. MOs at 2 P.M. Men practised in working with loaded stretchers over rough ground. Bathing parade. Arranged for Bde to police drinking supply & hours for water carts to fill	SMc
	27/7 + 28/7	29/7	Nothing to report. Men exercised daily by drill & sports. Kits inspected, foot inspection parades carried out.	SMc
	30/7/		Recd Bde orders for Transport to move at 9 P.M. Transport started at 11 PM for J 24 b sheet 62D.	SMc
	31/7/	10 am	Field Ambulance marched to entrain at AILLY at 2 P.M. Train did not leave until 5 P.M. Men kept waiting in hot sun. Detrained at MERICOURT & marched to J24 b (62D) Men very fatigued when they arrived at 10.30 P.M. Transport arrived at 5 PM. A cooker would have been invaluable, however all received hot tea before turning in. Orders to send whole of Bearer Division with Bde to MORLANCOURT.	SMc SMc

S M Edwards Maj RAMC.

1577 Wt. W10791/1773 500,000 1/15 D. D. & L. A.D.S.S./Forms/C. 2118.

Aug 1916

5

CONFIDENTIAL

140/1949

WAR DIARY

OF

MAJOR G. B. EDWARDS

OFFICER COMMANDING 1/2ND FIELD AMBULANCE

FROM 1ST AUGUST 1916 TO 31ST AUGUST 1916

72 FIELD AMBULANCE

Instructions regarding War Diaries and Intelligence Summaries are contained in F. S. Regs., Part II. and the Staff Manual respectively. Title pages will be prepared in manuscript.

WAR DIARY
or
INTELLIGENCE SUMMARY.
(Erase heading not required.)

Army Form C. 2118.

(1)

Place	Date	Hour	Summary of Events and Information	Remarks and references to Appendices
DIVE COPSE (62D) T24b8.6.	1.8.16.		Bearer Division under Capt. W.J. WEBSTER attached to 72 I. Bde at MORLANCOURT K9a4.2 62D also Capt. H.B. GROVES. & Capt. H.F.H. EBERTS. Transport 1 GS wr with stretchers, haversacks, etc. 1 Water Cart 1 Motor Cycle 3 Horse ambulances. Total Rank. Officers 8 NCOs 6. O.R. 108 Wagon orderlies 4 = 121 ASC Sgt 1. Drivers 5 1 Cyclist MT = 7. Transport Heavy Draught 8 mules 2.	
		5 PM	72 Bde OO 66 received. Bde moved to MEAULTE E17b	8M
"	2.8.16		1 Motor Cyclist to report to O.C. MAC. Sappers Corner for duty L9d8.0. 62D	
		8 30am	Active Operation Order ADMS No 473/2/16 received	
			ADMS Office closes at CORBIE & opens at 3 PM to day at HAPPY VALLEY L2b2.8.	
			Weather hot & dry very dusty.	
			Visited Bearer Division which have moved to Sand Pits E18d5.5.62D also OC 106 & 107 Field Ambulances & obtained information from them about Advanced Dressing Station etc.	8M
"	3.8.16		Visited SAPPERS CORNER & then went onto ADMS at HAPPY VALLEY & to bearers at SAND PITS. discussed arrangements for clearing the wounded.	8M
"	4.8.16		Visited Advanced Dressing Stations of several Field Ambulances of 55 Division	8M
"	5.8.16.		Request received from ADMS for masks to be used by burial parties in Bernafay & Trones wood. Made several hundred camphor masks & forwarded to Q 24 Division	
			Two Clerks sent to Walking Wounded Post at BRONFAY FARM F29b9.0 62D.	8M
			Message from ADMS asking me to inspect bathing arrangements at CHIPILLY Q3d8.6.62D. Found all available accommodation being used by French Troops.	8M

72 FIELD AMBULANCE

Instructions regarding War Diaries and Intelligence Summaries are contained in F. S. Regs., Part II. and the Staff Manual respectively. Title pages will be prepared in manuscript.

WAR DIARY
or
INTELLIGENCE SUMMARY.
(Erase heading not required.)

Army Form C. 2118.

Place	Date	Hour	Summary of Events and Information	Remarks and references to Appendices
DIVE COPSE 62D J24b8.6.	6.8.16		Ambulance Car 47 badly split near chassis. Visited the A.D.S. of 5th Field Ambulance at CARNOY A13d5.9 62c. Good accommodation good road plentiful water supply, evacuation simple. Protection from shell fire good in places sandbags keep out splinters.	SM
"	7.8.16		Received orders to take over SAPPERS CORNER & CARNOY from 5th Field Ambulance relief to be completed by 2PM 8th	SM
"	8.8.16		Bearer Division moved to BRONFAY FARM F29b9.0 62D Bearer Divisions from 74 73 will also be at BRONFAY + all bearers will be under orders of DADMS.	
			Capt G. LAING 2 NCOs & 6 O.R. to CARNOY ads.	
		8 am.	Order to take over from 5th Field Ambulance cancelled. Have not recalled ads party at CARNOY	
		9.30am	Received message from ADMS to visit him tomorrow at 9.30 am.	SM
	9.8.16	9.30	Visited ADMS at HAPPY VALLEY told to take over from 55 Div Field Amb at ads WEST PERONNE A20b5.9. 62c Visited ads at W PERONNE + BILLON FARM F30a6.6. 62D	
			Orders for move published, detailed 2 Officers 20 OR to W. PERONNE* 1 Officer & 10 OR to BILLON Transport to be at BRONFAY FARM at present they are as under wagons at DIVE COPSE Horses at X roads K14d 2.2 62D * Capt LAING & party at CARNOY to complete the personnel at W. PERONNE.	
		4PM	Advance parties as above left DIVE COPSE.	
		4.30PM	Message from ADMS cancelling relief of 55 Div.	
		8PM.	O.O. 38 ADMS To relieve 5th Field Ambulance as on 7th relief to be complete by 12 noon of 10th message sent to ads party to halt at Sappers Corner & await further orders.	SMB

2353 Wt. W2544/1454 700,000 5/15 D. D. & L. A.D.S.S./Forms/C. 2118.

72 FIELD AMBULANCE

WAR DIARY
or
INTELLIGENCE SUMMARY.
(*Erase heading not required.*)

Army Form C. 2118.

(3)

Instructions regarding War Diaries and Intelligence Summaries are contained in F. S. Regs., Part II. and the Staff Manual respectively. Title pages will be prepared in manuscript.

Place	Date	Hour	Summary of Events and Information	Remarks and references to Appendices
DIVE COPSE 62D J 24 b 8.6.	10.8.16	7.45am	Ambulance moved out from Dive Copse. C Section Transport to Carnoy to pick up adv party at Sappers Corner & W. Peronne. Unload & rejoin H.Q. at Sappers Corner. B Section Transport to proceed to Transport lines at K14d 22 62D & park with wagons loaded. Remainder of Field Ambulance & Transport to Sappers Corner.	
		11 am	Relief of 5 Field Ambulance Completed but O.C. waiting orders to move. Ground round Sappers Corner very foul. open pits of decomposing refuse human excreta. also a corn field close by used as an open latrine by French Transport who were at this place. Ground a mass of fly larvae. Flies everywhere. Wrote report to ADMS & asked for permission to interview French Town Major at BRAY to try & arrange to have corn cut & ground burnt. Forwarded 200 camphor respirators to Q 24 Div. ADMS moved to Citadel. F 21 b 3.2. 62D	SM.
SAPPERS CORNER. L9d80 62D	11.8.16		Visited ADMS. & Town Major at BRAY. Commenced clearing ground of refuse, burning manure etc. Visited Bearers at BRONFAY FARM. All clerical work is done by personnel at Walking Wounded Post & Corps main dressing Station at Dive Copse. No A & D Books are kept by Field Ambulance. Bearer Post at BERNAFAY WOOD S 22 d 9.0. 57c. The arrangement for all bearers to be under DADMS is unsatisfactory & is likely to lead to confusion in their receiving orders. I am not kept informed of their movements & find difficulty in keeping in touch with plans etc. Bearers are rationed by their own Field Ambulances & this is leading to a good deal of confusion as they (the bearers) are constantly changed between Bronfay Farm & Bernafay Wood. All bearers should come under the Field Amb working the forward area. The original plan of Bearers being	

2353 Wt. W2544/1454 700,000 5/15 D. D. & L. A.D.S.S./Forms/C. 2118.

72 FIELD AMBULANCE

WAR DIARY
or
INTELLIGENCE SUMMARY.
(*Erase heading not required.*)

Army Form C. 2118.

Instructions regarding War Diaries and Intelligence Summaries are contained in F. S. Regs., Part II. and the Staff Manual respectively. Title pages will be prepared in manuscript.

Place	Date	Hour	Summary of Events and Information	Remarks and references to Appendices
SAPPERS CORNER L9d8.0 62D			attached to Bdes is not satisfactory & has fallen through. Sappers Corner is too far back for H.Q. of Field Ambulance which should be at Bronfay Farm from which place we could keep in touch with bearers & the A.D.S. A small staff could remain at Sappers Corner to see local sick & issue dressings etc to Regt Aid Posts. A large stock of dressings have been brought up to Sappers Corner & are issued to A.D.S. & Regt Aid Posts. This is more satisfactory than the previous arrangement when A.D.S had to send back to Div Corps for dressings.	SMB
"	12.8.16		1 Cpl reported for duty. 1 Pte sent to XIII Corps for temporary duty. No 72464 Pte Andrews C.H. wounded in leg. Visited Bronfay & Carnoy	SMB
"	13.8.16		Corn at Sappers Corner being cut. Visited Bearer Post at BERNAFAY WOOD. Sanitation bad. Arranged to send up a sanitary squad from Sappers Corner. Lighting of dug out bad. Am sending up acetylene stand lamps. Regulation pattern leak & as they would have to be inside the dug out, the distance for tubing to outside being too long, they cannot be used. 3rd Division making an Ammunition Dump outside the A.D.S at Carnoy & blocking road for cars. Report to A.D.M.S.	SMB
	14.8.16		Casualties 49153 Pte Thompson W. Killed. 50032 " Gibson A. wounded 65161 " Cutting C.H. "	SMB

2353 Wt. W2544/1454 700,000 5/15 D. D. & L. A.D.S.S./Forms/C. 2118.

72 FIELD AMBULANCE

WAR DIARY
or
INTELLIGENCE SUMMARY.
(Erase heading not required.)

Army Form C. 2118.

Instructions regarding War Diaries and Intelligence Summaries are contained in F. S. Regs., Part II. and the Staff Manual respectively. Title pages will be prepared in manuscript.

(5)

Place	Date	Hour	Summary of Events and Information	Remarks and references to Appendices
L 9 d.8.0 62D	15.8.16			
		10 30 pm	Received memo MS 1590 ~~ADMS~~ ADMS. additional ex Bearers Bernafay Farm Detail working party 1 NCO 24 OR to make new dug-out at BRIQUETERIE to report to 72 Bde H.Q at 5 am 16-8-16. Drew 25 picks & 25 shovels from RE also Trench guides & sent up to Bearers Casualties No 63529 Pte Davison E wounded.	SM
	16.8.16		Arranged with ADMS that the Transport of the Field Ambulance should be parked at Bernafay Farm. Also that I should have two motor cycles at my disposal as one was not sufficient to keep up communication between the Bearer Post HQ of the Field Ambulance & ADMS.	SM
	17.8.16		Capt C.A. BRISCO 73rd Field Ambulance Capt J.V.O. ANDREWS 74 Field Ambulance reported for duty with 72 Field Ambulance	SM
	18.8.16	11 am	Left Sapper Corner & went to Carnoy Lt Andrews remaining at Sapper Corner with Qr Mr 2 cars & 5 OR. Tent Division at Carnoy opened another clearing Station Lieut KEANE to 1 North Staffords for duty to replace Capt WAUGH Killed	
		4 PM	Heavy rush of wounded mostly walking cases, evacuated to walking wounded post by 9 horse Ambulance wagons Motor Ambulance Service bad. Frequently there are no cars here & intervals of an hour to two hours between the departure & arrival of a car.	
		6 PM	Batches of German wounded coming in 9, 3, 2, 5,	
		7 PM	Cases coming in fairly steadily.	
		9 30 PM	All clear	
		12 PM	Reported to ADMS distribution of bearers 100 cases passed through during the night	SM

72 FIELD AMBULANCE **WAR DIARY** *or* **INTELLIGENCE SUMMARY.**

(Erase heading not required.)

Instructions regarding War Diaries and Intelligence Summaries are contained in F. S. Regs., Part II. and the Staff Manual respectively. Title pages will be prepared in manuscript.

Army Form C. 2118.

Place	Date	Hour	Summary of Events and Information	Remarks and references to Appendices
BRONFAY 8.22 d 9.0. 57C	21.8.16	1 P.M.	Issued instructions to Bearer Officers at Bernafay Wood & Briqueterie with reference to distribution of bearers & working of reliefs.	
		2.20 P.M.	Received memo from Bearer Officer at Bernafay Wood saying that Bdes & Regts. 3 R.Bs were making absurd demands for bearers. asking for a 100 bearers for 1 place 70 for another & that altogether demands for over 300 bearers had been received.	
		6 P.M.	Reliefs working satisfactorily. The demands mentioned above were found to be quite unnecessary. 1 N.C.O. & 8 bearers cleared all the casualties	SMR
"	22.8.16	12.10 A.M.	Visited the Walking wounded post & found that only 56 cases of 24 Division had passed through during last 24 hours mostly 8 Queens, 1st Fusiliers & 3 R.Bs	
		9. A.M.	Two Officers from 61 F Amb. came to my dug-out & stated that their unit was going to take over.	
		10 A.M.	OC 60 F Amb arrived & said he was going to relieve me.	
		12.30 P.M. / 12.40 P.M.	OO 51 ADMS / OO 52 ADMS } re relief received. Visited Carnoy	
		7 P.M.	62 Field Amb relieved personnel at Carnoy. 62nd F Amb personnel relieved Sappers Corner 60 F Amb relieved personnel at Bronfay Farm	
		10 P.M.	Bearers relieved at Bearer posts by the bearers of above units.	SMR

2353 Wt. W2544/1454 700,000 5/15 D. D. & L. A.D.S.S./Forms/C. 2118.

72 FIELD AMBULANCE

WAR DIARY
or
INTELLIGENCE SUMMARY.
(Erase heading not required.)

Army Form C. 2118.

(7)

Instructions regarding War Diaries and Intelligence Summaries are contained in F. S. Regs., Part II. and the Staff Manual respectively. Title pages will be prepared in manuscript.

Place	Date	Hour	Summary of Events and Information	Remarks and references to Appendices
BRONFAY FARM S 22 d 9.0. 47c		1 P.m	I have moved across to BRONFAY FARM & notified ADMS of the muddle in which the bearers were involved & that I had taken them in hand. Also requesting that no further relief took place or orders were issued to bearers excepting by me or through me so that I might keep in touch with them & if possible get some system working as under present arrangements the bearers were being overworked & worn out for no purpose. Sent motor cyclist to Bearer posts asking O/C for numbers of bearers of each Field Amb at each Post.	
		3.50 P.	Am now in possession of full information as to distribution of bearers & am withdrawing as many as possible from bearer posts to get them back for a rest & feeding at Bronfay farm. Am also sorting them out into their respective Field ambulances. Am withdrawing the whole of 74 from posts for 24 hours rest. Have written to ADMS & asked him to inform Brigades & through them their Regt M.Os that all available bearers are working & that it only leads to confusion to wire to Div. H.Q. for 100, 50, 80 etc bearers as was done recently when there were already 300 bearers working in the line. The O/C of bearers at each of the bearer posts will distribute the bearers under him to the best advantage, & any application for more bearers at a certain place should be made to him when if possible he will supply them. It is imperative that a reserve of bearers should be kept at Bronfay to relieve those that have been working & also in case of great necessity one must have rested men to undertake the work. I propose having 2 divisions in the line & 1 resting	
		6.20 p.m	Order from ADMS to detail an MO for duty with 2 Leinsters Capt BRETHERTON detailed. Casualties Pte IRLAM seriously wounded abdomen	SMc

2353 Wt. W2544/1454 700,000 5/15 D. D. & L. A.D.S.S./Forms/C. 2118

72 FIELD AMBULANCE

Instructions regarding War Diaries and Intelligence Summaries are contained in F. S. Regs., Part II. and the Staff Manual respectively. Title pages will be prepared in manuscript.

WAR DIARY
or
INTELLIGENCE SUMMARY.
(Erase heading not required.)

Army Form C. 2118.

(6)

Place	Date	Hour	Summary of Events and Information	Remarks and references to Appendices
CARNOY A 13 d 5·9 62c	19·8·16	3·30am	Rations sent up to bearers at Bernafay Wood	
			1 Officer 3 NCOs & 16 bearers 70 stretchers & 3 horse Ambulances sent up to BRIQUETERIE	
		11·30am	1 NCO & 30 bearers returned from BRIQUETERIE.	
		12 noon	Capt WEBSTER returned from BRIQUETERIE. 20 bearers of 73 Field Amb arrived at Bernafay from the line.	
		12·10 noon	No cases coming in at Carnoy. Visited bearer posts. No information at Briqueterie of any casualties.	
		12·30 noon	All the bearers now up the line with the exception of 9 at Bernafay. ADMS forwarded message from BDE asking for more bearers. Not understood as line is clear & no casualties. Also bearers are being sent back from bearer posts as they are not required at present. Casualties	
		7 p.m.	do 48 ADMS re relief of bearers received from ADMS.	
		10·30pm	Capt Webster & Capt Eberts & 30 bearers sent up to Briqueterie	
		9 p.m.	72 bearers relieved at Bernafay wood by bearers of 74? Amb.	SM
	20·8·16		Bearers all very fagged, Relief badly worked, & men have no sooner arrived back after a 3½ mile march than they have been sent off again. Up to the present the DADMS has had to work the bearer relief & disposition which with his other duties is a futile undertaking	SM
	"			

2353 Wt. W2544/1454 700,000 5/15 D. D. & L. A.D.S.S./Forms/C. 2118.

Army Form C. 2118.

Instructions regarding War Diaries and Intelligence Summaries are contained in F. S. Regs., Part II. and the Staff Manual respectively. Title pages will be prepared in manuscript.

72 FIELD AMBULANCE WAR DIARY
or
INTELLIGENCE SUMMARY.

(*Erase heading not required.*)

Place	Date	Hour	Summary of Events and Information	Remarks and references to Appendices
SAPPERS CORNER	23/8/16		Tent Division of 72 Field Ambulance moved to Sappers Corner last night. Bearer Division of 72, 73, 74 F Amb assembled at Bronfay Farm last night & are to join their Brigades to day	
"	"	9.30am	The 72 F Amb less Bearer Division marched off from Sappers Corner for Dive Copse	
DIVE COPSE		11.40am	Arrived Dive Copse unloaded wagons. Transport parked at X roads K14 c 2.1. 62[d] Equipped F Block ready to open at 12 noon tomorrow. O/c Bearers informed me that he had received orders from ADMS to detail 30 bearers as car orderlies to report to MAC* at Div Copse. The Bearers would now appear to receive orders direct from ADMS. Has not had to alter ration state as all bearers are rationed from this unit. * When the Division went into the line all Field Ambulance Cars & Cycles joined MAC at Div Copse & came under the orders of the OC MAC. My personal experience & that of OC other Field Ambulances whom I have discussed this. Is that on the whole it is not a satisfactory arrangement.	SM.
"	24/8/16	12 noon	Opened F Block	
		6 PM	Closed F Block	
"	25/8/16	9am	Came under XV Corps. Bearer Division reported to be a march. Also refilling point has moved. The Division would appear to be moving but have received no orders as yet.	SM
		12.55PM	The Commandant Main Dressing Station Div Copse informed me that the 5 Division had relieved the 24th Div	

2353 Wt. W2544/1454 700,000 5/15 D. D. & L. A.D.S.S./Forms/C. 2118.

72 FIELD AMBULANCE

WAR DIARY
or
INTELLIGENCE SUMMARY.
(Erase heading not required.)

Army Form C. 2118.

Instructions regarding War Diaries and Intelligence Summaries are contained in F. S. Regs., Part II. and the Staff Manual respectively. Title pages will be prepared in manuscript.

(10)

Place	Date	Hour	Summary of Events and Information	Remarks and references to Appendices
DIVE COPSE	25/8/16		Messenger sent to ADMS returned unable to find him as he had moved.	
		1 PM	Got in touch with Bearers now at E 13.14 62D. also found refilling point	
		6.30 PM	DADMS arrived at Div Corps & gave me location of ADMS & information about the move.	SMB
"	26/8/16	6 am	Opened F Block.	
		11.30 am	Closed F Block. Commandant Div Corps informed me that I was to move to S 28 d 8.5 62D & that MAC would return Cars & orderlies by 6 PM to night	
		2 PM	OO 56 ADMS received order to move to S 30 b 3.7. 62D & that Bearers would join me there.	
			Moved off from Div Corps	
S 30 b 3.7 62D		8 PM	Move completed & Bearers joined up. Pitched tents built incinerator, dug latrines, Rained heavily soon after getting into camp.	SMB
	27/8/16	9 am	Opened to receive sick of 72 Bde	
		11.10 am	OO 57 ADMS. Orders to relieve 44 F Amb at F 6 a 1.0. 62D on 30/8/16 Went up to see OC 44 F Amb. Visited main Dressing Station & Bearer Posts. at S 22 c 0.4 57c S 23 a 1.8. 57c S 16 d 6.8 57c	SMB
			Rained heavily. Very bad ground & long carries. Stretcher parties worked by relays between the bearer posts	

72 FIELD AMBULANCE

WAR DIARY
or
INTELLIGENCE SUMMARY.
(*Erase heading not required.*)

Army Form C. 2118.

Instructions regarding War Diaries and Intelligence Summaries are contained in F. S. Regs., Part II. and the Staff Manual respectively. Title pages will be prepared in manuscript.

(11)

Place	Date	Hour	Summary of Events and Information	Remarks and references to Appendices
D 30 b 3.7 62D	27/8/16		Lieut H. J. KEANE posted for duty with 141 Indian Cav. Field Amb	ADMS 393/16 27/8/16. SM
"	28/8/16		Capt EBERTS to 2nd Leinsters to relieve Capt BRETHERTON	
			Capt BRETHERTON & Capt ANDREWS with tent subdivision & equipment to XV Corps main Dressing Station	
			Raining heavily all day	SM
"	29/8/16	10am	Still Raining. Recd OO 59 ADMS.	
		8Pm	Advance Party 2 NCOs & 8 OR to 44 7 Amb at F6.1.0 62D	
			Lieut. E EVANS attached for temporary duty.	
"	30/8/16	7am	Capt WEBSTER, Capt GROVES & 18 bearers advance party to Bearer Post at S22c 0.4 57c	
	"	10Pm	Moved off to relieve 44 7 Amb. Heavy Rain. Roads very bad. Road between main Dressing Station at F6.1.0 62D & Bearer Post S22c 0.4 57c impassable for Motor Cars. Am taking all horses & mules up to F6.1.0 62D & using horse Ambulances to clear from Bearer post at S22c 0.4 57c.	
		8P.M	Relief of 44 7 Amb at all Posts Completed.	
			Capt Andrews returned to 74 7 Amb. Lt Evans sent to XV C.M.D.S. for duty.	SM

2353 Wt. W2544/1454 700,000 5/15 D. D. & L. A.D.S.S./Forms/C. 2118.

Army Form C. 2118.

Instructions regarding War Diaries and Intelligence Summaries are contained in F. S. Regs., Part II. and the Staff Manual respectively. Title pages will be prepared in manuscript.

72 FIELD AMBULANCE WAR DIARY
or
INTELLIGENCE SUMMARY.

(Erase heading not required.)

(12)

Place	Date	Hour	Summary of Events and Information	Remarks and references to Appendices
F6a1.0 62D MAMETZ	31/8/16	11.15am	3 NCOs + 36 OR bearers arrived from 74 F Amb as reinforcements	
		12 Noon	2 NCOs + 30 OR " " 73 " "	
		1.30 PM.	Above parties sent up to Bearer Posts to assist 72nd Bearers Enemy putting over large number of gas shells affecting ambulance horses at S22 c 0.4 57c Casualties arriving in steady stream. Horse ambulances working well under great difficulties. 6 horses required to each wagon. The Dressing Station at F6a1.0. is cleared by open Motor Buses holding 30 sitting cases. Stretcher cases are cleared by Cars of the Field Ambulance. The evacuation are being carried out satisfactorily	SM

S H Simmons
Maj RAMC.
OC 72nd Field Ambulance

2353 Wt. W2544/1454 700,000 5/15 D. D. & L. A.D.S.S. Forms/C 2118.

24th Div

24

140/1124

Sept. 1916

S/

CONFIDENTIAL

72 F. Amb. V. 13
73 " 13
74 " 12

WAR DIARY

OF

MAJOR G.B. EDWARDS Officer Commanding 72 FIELD AMBULANCE

FROM 1-9-16 To. 30-9-16

72 FIELD AMBULANCE

WAR DIARY
or
INTELLIGENCE SUMMARY.
(*Erase heading not required.*)

Army Form C. 2118.

Instructions regarding War Diaries and Intelligence Summaries are contained in F. S. Regs., Part II. and the Staff Manual respectively. Title pages will be prepared in manuscript.

Place	Date	Hour	Summary of Events and Information	Remarks and references to Appendices
MAMETZ F6a 2.2 sheet 62 D/40000	1-9-16.	3 am.	Raining hard, roads & tracks in very bad condition. Evacuation of wounded from Quarries S22c 0.4 sheet 57c being carried out with difficulty by horse ambulances with 6 horses to each & working with nine ambulance wagons	
	"	3.15 am	Driver of A section wagon reports wagon stuck in shell hole on MONTAUBAN Quarry road unable to be got out. Bearers working well under exceedingly difficult circumstances. Long carries over tracks knee deep in mud & pitted with shell holes unable to use wheeled stretchers	SM
		2.45 PM	66 bearers sent up to Quarries to reinforce bearers at various bearer posts & regt. aid posts.	
	2.9.16	7 am.	2 Officers 2 NCOs & 41 bearers from 74 Field Ambulance arrived at A.D.S. F6a 2.2, (62D)	
		7.30 am	Above party sent up to relieve similar number of 72 bearers now in the line.	
		5 P.M.	72 bearers relieved as above & returned to A.D.S. received hot stew & are now resting.	
		7.30 PM	20 stretchers supplied to 3rd Rifle Bde. 50 stretchers & various dressings supplied to bearer posts. Casualties coming in in a steady stream weather improving. Another wagon unable to remove from shell hole. D.A.D.M.S. 55 Div was up here & taking notes on arrangements for evacuation etc.	SM
		8.30 PM	Another (making third) Amb wagon stuck in shell hole & smashed unable to remove	
	3.9.16.	9.10 am	Bearer reinforcements sent up to bearer posts 200 bearers & four officers now up the line Nothing of importance to report. Roads still very bad. A party now trying to get Amb wagons out of shell holes.	SM
		12 noon	Capt Cathcart reports that two ambulance wagons have been pulled out & now returning to A.D.S.	

2353 Wt. W2544/1454 700,000 5/15 D. D. & L. A.D.S.S./Forms/C. 2118.

72 FIELD AMBULANCE.

WAR DIARY
or
INTELLIGENCE SUMMARY.

(Erase heading not required.)

Army Form C. 2118.

(2)

Instructions regarding War Diaries and Intelligence Summaries are contained in F. S. Regs., Part II. and the Staff Manual respectively. Title pages will be prepared in manuscript.

Place	Date	Hour	Summary of Events and Information	Remarks and references to Appendices
MAMETZ	4/9/16	12 to 5PM.	Relieved all 73rd & 74th Field Ambulance bearers in the line by remainder of 72 & adv party of 2/1 WESSEX F. Amb 55 Div.	
F6a 2.2 Sheet 62D 1/40000			Quiet day slight rain fall, roads slippery but not too bad. A certain amount of repair done	JM
		12Pm	O.C. ADMS 65 recd.	
	5/9/16	12 noon	Relieved 72nd Personnel at bearer posts & aid posts by personnel of 2/1 Wessex F Amb.	
		"	Personnel of 73 & 74 F Amb returned to their units.	JM
		7-15PM	Relief complete.	
		7.20Pm	Recd O.C. ADMS 66 & 67. We move out of the line tomorrow. Have had a busy time & the bearers have worked splendidly. Received the usual number of memos & wires from Bdes Regts etc for more bearers at a time when all bearers were fully employed & working as hard as any mortal possibly could. In almost all cases the requests for more bearers as usual were far in excess of the numbers required & in one case where 50 bearers were asked for two squads cleared the place with ease. Medical Officers of the Field Ambulances at the Quarries & bearer posts were at all times in touch with each other & arranged bearer reliefs & reinforcements between their posts & Regt aid posts. This was explained to Bdes, Regt. MOs & others in reply to their urgent messages. Worked well & effectively & kept the line clear. Without exception the officers & bearers & I have received messages from Regt MOs, who are able to appreciate the difficulties, praising the strength & fearless manner in which my men have carried out their work.	
	6/9/16	11am	Moved out & handed over ADS. Personnel moved in motor buses to D30 b 2.8 (sheet 62D) Transport following	
		12noon.	Recd orders that I would be O.C. Divisional Transport moving by road to new area tomorrow	JM

72 FIELD AMBULANCE

Instructions regarding War Diaries and Intelligence Summaries are contained in F. S. Regs., Part II. and the Staff Manual respectively. Title pages will be prepared in manuscript.

WAR DIARY
or
INTELLIGENCE SUMMARY.
(Erase heading not required.)

Army Form C. 2118.

(3)

Place	Date	Hour	Summary of Events and Information	Remarks and references to Appendices
BUIRE D30b2.8 (62D)	6/9/16	8 PM	Received order that time of starting for Transport altered. Issued orders to various units Starting point BUIRE x Roads 3 am. To be clear of VECQUEMONT 8.30 am.	
on march	7/9/16	3 am	Transport left BUIRE. Personnel are to proceed to EAUCOURT (abbeville sheet 14) by train at 12 & 2 PM.	SM
		8.15am	Clear of VECQUEMONT. Halted watered & fed horses.	
		10-45Pm	Moved off from VECQUEMONT.	
		3. P.m	Arrived LONGPRE & ARGOEUVES halted for night.	SM
	8/9/16	7.30am	Left ARGOEUVES	
		12 Noon	Arrived FLEXICOURT. met by O.C 24 Div Train. Transport split up into various units. I proceeded with Transport of my own unit	
EAUCOURT (abbeville 14)		6 PM.	Arrived EAUCOURT. & found Personnel had arrived previous night. & were all billeted	SM
	9/9/16.		Day spent in arranging the billets, working out sanitary arrangements, bathing personnel. Capt W.B CATHCART to 106 Bde R.F.A. for temporary duty at K18a (62D)	SM
	10/9/16		Lieut EVANS rejoined from XV Corps main Dressing Station Reported sick & evacuated with Corneal ulcer. 1 NCO rejoined from XV C.M.D.S. Equipment unpacked & cleaned checked & made up to scale.	SM

2353 . Wt. W2544/1454 700,000 5/15 D. D. & L. A.D.S.S./Forms/C. 2118.

72 FIELD AMBULANCE.

Army Form C. 2118.

WAR DIARY
or
INTELLIGENCE SUMMARY.
(*Erase heading not required.*)

Instructions regarding War Diaries and Intelligence Summaries are contained in F. S. Regs., Part II. and the Staff Manual respectively. Title pages will be prepared in manuscript.

Place	Date	Hour	Summary of Events and Information	Remarks and references to Appendices
EAUCORT	11/9/16		Capt. A.W. BRETHERTON & remainder of party rejoined from XV Corps M.D.S. Ambulance wagons & G.S. wagons inspected cleaned & notes on repairs required taken	SM
	12/9/16		Nothing of importance to report.	SM
	13/9/16	4 ~~PM~~	G.O.C. 24 Div & A.D.M.S. inspected Camp. 1 Rider evacuated An old lame horse drawn at METEREN & never been fit to ride. 3 Ambulance wagons sent to work shop Abbeville for repairs.	SM
	14/9/16 15/9/16		General Routine work cleaning & repairing. Capt Ebets & Lt Dixon 48 hrs Paris	SM
	16/9/	8 am	A.D.M.S. M.S. 1694 be ready to entrain at short notice. Capt McLEOD (temporary duty with 1 N Staffs) to be permanently posted to 1 N. Staffs. Struck off ~~strength~~ of this unit. Lieut EVANS taken on strength. (but sick at base).	SM
	17/9/16		Capt Ebets & Lt Dixon returned from 48 leave.	SM

2353 Wt. W2544/1454 700,000 5/15 D. D. & L. A.D.S.S./Forms/C. 2118.

72 FIELD AMBULANCE

WAR DIARY
or
INTELLIGENCE SUMMARY.
(Erase heading not required.)

Army Form C. 2118.

Instructions regarding War Diaries and Intelligence Summaries are contained in F. S. Regs., Part II. and the Staff Manual respectively. Title pages will be prepared in manuscript.

Place	Date	Hour	Summary of Events and Information	Remarks and references to Appendices
EAUCOURT	18/9/.	1.30 PM	Adms OO 71. Recd	
		4 PM	Adms OO 72 "	
			Lieut D. M. Brown RAMC joined for temporary duty	
		5.30 PM	Entraining order received from 72nd I. Bde	SM
	19/9		Five Sunbeam motor Ambulances, Two Ford Ambulances, & Two motor cycles, with personnel handed over to 24 Div. Supply Col.	
		4 PM.	Marched off from EAUCOURT.	
		7.45 PM	Entrained with Transport & personnel at ABBEVILLE.	SM
VALHUON	20/9	2 AM	arrived BRYAS N 26. sheet 36B 1/40000. Marched to VALHUON N 8 (36B) & went into billets at 3 A.M.	
N 8 sheet 36 B 1/40000.		4.30 PM	Advance party of 1 Officer 2 NCO + 4 O.R. to report to 27 Field Ambulance at LES 4 VENTS W. 9 (36 B).	
			Three maps sheet 36B & 36C received.	
		8 P.M.	Five Sunbeam Ambulances 2 Fords. 1 Sgt + 10 drivers reported from 30 Div Supply Col.	
			S/Sgt Setter evacuated to C.C.S.	SM
	21/9. 22/9.		Nothing to report.	SM
	23/9.		Visited LES 4 VENTS & went round the various wards & grounds with the OC 27 F Amb. Good accommodation but badly arranged owing to the way the huts have been put up without method. Sanitary arrangements superficial appearance look alright. but on closer inspection are very crude & will require a good deal of work done on them.	SM

2353 Wt. W2544/1454 700,000 5/15 D. D. & L. A.D.S.S./Forms/C. 2118.

72 FIELD AMBULANCE

Instructions regarding War Diaries and Intelligence Summaries are contained in F. S. Regs., Part II. and the Staff Manual respectively. Title pages will be prepared in manuscript.

WAR DIARY
or
INTELLIGENCE SUMMARY.
(Erase heading not required.)

Army Form C. 2118.

(6)

Place	Date	Hour	Summary of Events and Information	Remarks and references to Appendices
HOUDAIN.	24/9	10-15 AM.	Ambulance moved off from VALHUON	
		3.30 PM	Arrived HOUDAIN T33c (36B) & went into billets	
		5 PM.	Two motor cycles & cyclists reported for duty from 30 Div. Supply Col.	SM
	25/9	7 AM	Marched off from HOUDAIN	
LES 4 VENTS W9 (36B)		10 AM	Arrived Les 4 VENTS. W9 (36B) Took over from 27 Field Ambulance Hd Qrs. also Posts at Hospital Corner. X 17 c 0.3. (36B) A.D.S. at CABARET ROUGE. & two bearer posts further up.	
			1. Heavy & Horse injury to eye severe. Took over baths at CAMBLAIN L'ABBE W22 (36B).	
			Capt W. J. WEBSTER to 1 North Stafford Regt. for Temporary duty. ~~Took over~~	SM
	26/9		Took over Soup Kitchen at CARENCY X 15 d (36B). Arranged to obtain lines for soup from refilling point of the 3 sides of the Division.	
			Have now 5 medical Officers only for duty. Remainder on Temporary duty with Regiments.	
			Have reduced the men in forward area by 1 & now have Two at CABARET ROUGE & one at HOSPITAL CORNER.	
			Went round the Field Ambulance & mapped out drainage system. made plans for cleaning out soap & grease pits etc which are all very foul & drew up diagrams for grease & soap precipitating & filtering traps etc. Indented on REs for materials for the above & wood for latrines. A great deal of work to be done both here & up the line.	SM
	27/9		Went up to Hospital Corner all quiet there	SM

3353 Wt. W2544/1454 700,000 5/15 D. D. & L. A.D.S.S./Forms/C. 2118.

72 FIELD AMBULANCE.

Instructions regarding War Diaries and Intelligence Summaries are contained in F. S. Regs., Part II. and the Staff Manual respectively. Title pages will be prepared in manuscript.

WAR DIARY
or
INTELLIGENCE SUMMARY.
(Erase heading not required.)

(7)

Army Form C. 2118.

Place	Date	Hour	Summary of Events and Information	Remarks and references to Appendices
LES 4 VENTS W 9 (36b)	28/9		Went up to CABARET ROUGE A.D.S. Left instructions with Capt Laing to convert the Miller James Stretcher carriers into a narrower gauge by closing the frame & placing cross pieces at ends so that they can be used down the trench as roads are exposed to enemy view & can only be used at night.	SM
	29/9		Nothing to report.	SM
	30/9		Went round all Regt Aid Posts, Bearer Posts etc held by the Division. All good but trenches & roads in places require repair to allow stretcher carriers to be used to best advantage. Called in at CABARET ROUGE on my back. Stretcher carriers have been converted as above & are very useful. Very few casualties. LIEUT. S. M. BROWN to 37th Labour Bn. This leaves me with 4 Med Officers. Have had to reduce the personnel in the line by 2 MOs & now have 1 at CABARET ROUGE only. Have been informed that my strength will be reduced permanently while in this army* by 2 medical Officers. At present it is reduced by 4.	*1st Army SM

S. B. Edwards.
Maj. RAMC
OC 72 Field Ambulance

2353 Wt. W2544/1454 700,000 5/15 D. D. & L. A.D.S.S./Forms/C. 2118.

Oct. 1916 24th Div 140/187 MEDICAL.

24

CONFIDENTIAL

WAR DIARY

OF LIEUT: COL: G. B. EDWARDS

COMMANDING 72nd FIELD AMBULANCE

FROM 1 - 10 - 16 TO 31 - 10 - 16

72 FIELD AMBULANCE

Instructions regarding War Diaries and Intelligence Summaries are contained in F. S. Regs., Part II. and the Staff Manual respectively. Title pages will be prepared in manuscript.

WAR DIARY
or
INTELLIGENCE SUMMARY.
(Erase heading not required.)

(1)

Army Form C. 2118.

Place	Date	Hour	Summary of Events and Information	Remarks and references to Appendices
LES 4 VENTS W.9 (36B) 1/40000	1-10-16		One H D horse evacuated necrosis off hind. Sanitary work well in hand. Concrete grease precipitating chamber completed with concrete drain & sand filter bed. Drew 3000 bricks, 3 barrels cement, 2 loads sand & various amounts of timber. Classes of instruction in foot massage for troops in the trenches commenced at main dressing station A.D.S. & Bearer Posts.	GMK
"	2-10-16		Pte Scott sent to ADMS office to assist in office work. At present the number of men employed outside the unit is as follows. Divisional Soup kitchen 3 Baths 1 NCO 4 men Divisional H^d Qrs 1 man. The latter man lent to Div H.Q. nine months ago. I have never been able to get back as he is a good draughtsman. Received a memo from a medical officer asking me to send him a horse & servant to 4th Corps H^d Qrs as he has been posted to me for duty but will be retained at Corps H^d Qrs for duty!! Servant & horse not despatched, this officer has been transferred to 74th Field Ambulance. Very wet day. Promotion to acting rank. L^c Sgt Simpson to Sgt. Cpl Walsh to L^c Sgt. L^c Cpl Kyle to Cpl.	GMK
"	3-10-16		Very wet & stormy day. Visited baths at CAMBLIAN L'ABBE W21b 5.0. (36B). Present bathing arrangements very inadequate drew up plans for improvements & forwarded to ADMS. Work completed at Main Dressing Station W9 (36B) fly proof latrine 12 seats. 75 yds guttering made from corrugated iron sheeting & fitted round roof of officers ward. Shelves in surgical & medical wards. 8 prs of tressels. Two red cross & two Union Jack flags painted on tin in accordance with 1st Army order. Work on soap precipitating chamber, baffle chamber & effluent reservoir well under way. Work on fly proof meat store & cutting up room commenced. Captain Eberts to Cabaret Rouge. A.D.S. S14 c 5.5 (36 c) Lieut C. L. WITTINGHAM RAMC joined for temporary duty from 109th Bde R.F.A.	GMK
"	4-10-16		Wet stormy day. Nine reinforcements joined.	
"	5-10-16		Drew 200 yards duck boards from R E dump.	GMK
		5.30 PM	Received orders from ADMS to detail 9 men for loading slag to report to 17th Corps H^d Qrs to night	
		6. P.M.	Nine men left in accordance with above order	GMK

2353 Wt. W2544/1454 700,000 5/15 D. D. & L. A.D.S.S./Forms/C. 2118.

72 FIELD AMBULANCE

WAR DIARY
or
INTELLIGENCE SUMMARY.
(Erase heading not required.)

Army Form C. 2118.

Instructions regarding War Diaries and Intelligence Summaries are contained in F. S. Regs., Part II. and the Staff Manual respectively. Title pages will be prepared in manuscript.

Place	Date	Hour	Summary of Events and Information	Remarks and references to Appendices
LES 4 VENTS W9 (36 B.)	6.10.16		Lieut WHITTINGHAM. struck off action strength & posted to 12 ROYAL FUSILIERS for duty 32 men at ADS, Hope Corner, & Valley aid posts, relieved by similar number from Main Dressing Station	G.W.E.
"	7.10.16		Five men sent to report to R.E. at NIEPPE FOREST to assist in felling trees. Designed an improved type of incinerator to burn refuse, excreta, evaporate urine, & sludge & heat water for baths work commenced on this to day	G.W.E.
"	8.10.16.		Lieut W. DIXON struck off the strength & posted for duty with 106 Bde R.F.A. from temporary duty with 8th Queens Captain W.B. CATHCART rejoined from temporary duty with 106 Bde R.F.A.	G.W.E.
"	9.10.16			
"	10.10.16		Proceeded on leave to England. Captain H.B. GROVES to 7th North Hants for temporary duty. 1 O.R. evacuated to 18 C.C.S.	G.W.E.
"	11.10.16		Dr BELL & Dr HANLIN returned from F.P. No 1 with A.P.M. Dr BELL to 195 Coy ASC. Dr HUGHES joined in relief of Dr BELL Pte SEYMOUR returned from leave.	G.W.E.
"	12.10.16		Pte DALBY returned from leave. Sgt. KING ASC. M.T. admitted to 7 Amb fracture L patella due to cycle accident	G.W.E.
"	13.10.16		Capt CATHCART & Sgt MARTIN to gas class for instruction. Sgt KING evacuated.	G.W.E.
"	14.10.16		Officers charger drawn from Div Train a poor animal appears to have had lung trouble. 1 H.D horse struck off strength. Pte Ash ASC admitted to 7 Amb.	G.W.E.

2353 Wt. W2544/1454 700,000 5/15 D. D. & L. A.D.S.S./Forms/C. 2118.

72 FIELD AMBULACE

WAR DIARY
or
INTELLIGENCE SUMMARY.
(Erase heading not required.)

Army Form C. 2118.

(3)

Instructions regarding War Diaries and Intelligence Summaries are contained in F. S. Regs., Part II. and the Staff Manual respectively. Title pages will be prepared in manuscript.

Place	Date	Hour	Summary of Events and Information	Remarks and references to Appendices
LES 4 VENTS W 9 (36 B)	15-10-16		1 L^c Cpl & 5 men with 1 Sunbeam car, driver, & orderly to PERNES for duty at IV Corps school of instruction	SMR
"	16-10-16		1. H D horse drawn from Div Train. Are now one H D surplus. S.S. Maj TATTERSAL ASC joined for duty. Cpl Kyte 1 month leave to England on expiration of time service.	SMR
"	17-10-16			SMR
"	18-10-16		Cpl GALLACHER R ASC M.T. joined for duty from 30 Div Supply Col.	SMR
"	19-10-16		Pte SUTHERLAND returned from leave.	SMR
"	20-10-16		S S SETTERS & Pte RUSH awarded Military Medal.	SMR
"	21-10-16		Returned from leave having been delayed at BOULOGNE. Capt Cathcart visited 40 Div area & reported on work of 135 Field Ambulance to be relieved by 72nd shortly	SMR
"	22-10-16		DADMS Canadian Corps visited the ambulance & was shown round & work explained to him.	SMR.
"	23-10-16		Order of relief received. 2nd Canadian Field Ambulance to relieve 72nd F Amb on 26th. 72nd to relieve 135th F A. on 27th. Application for special leave Pte Murdoch forwarded to ADMS.	SMR

2353 Wt. W2544/1454 700,000 5/15 D. D. & L. A.D.S.S./Forms/C. 2118.

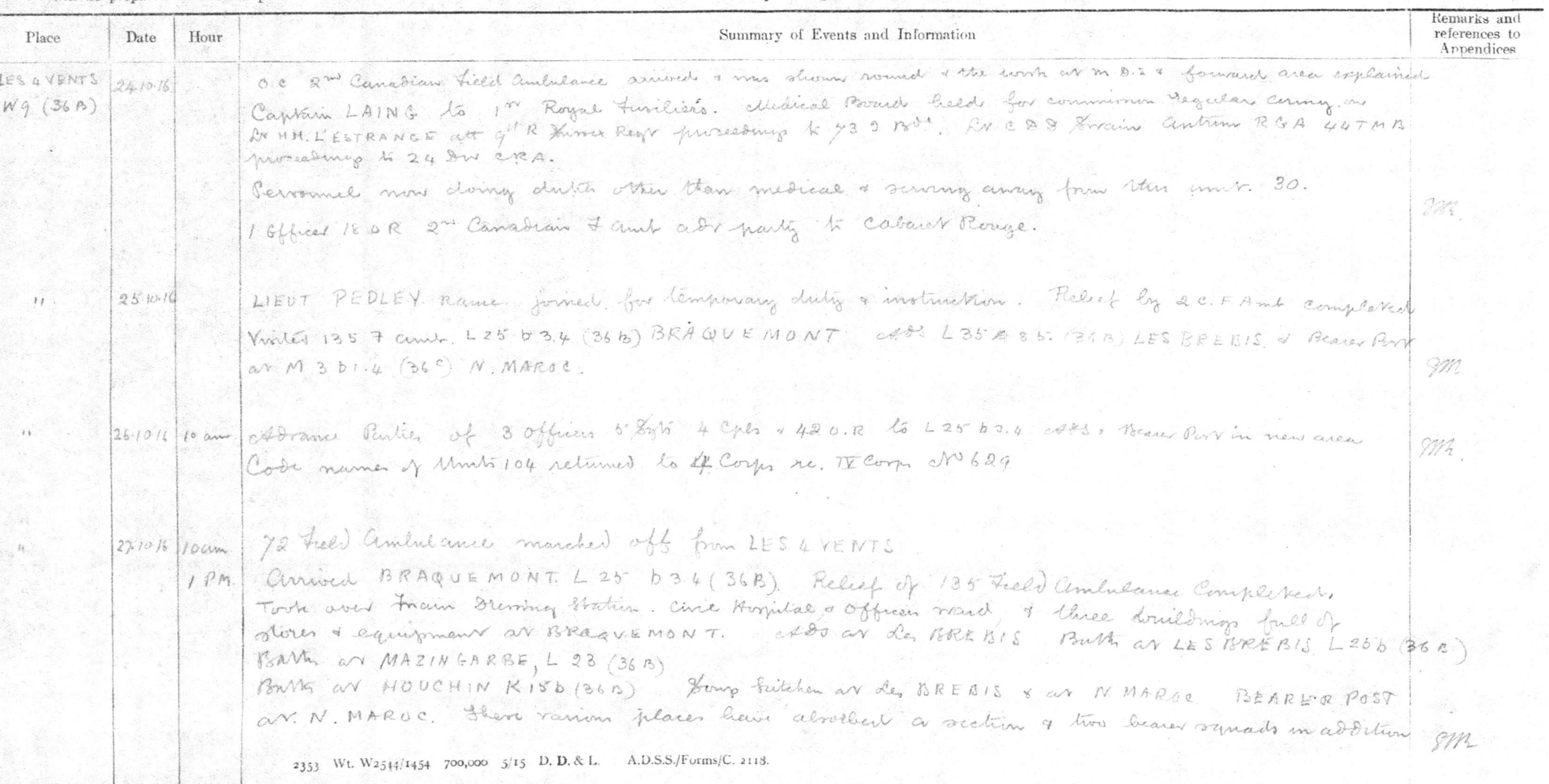

72 Field Ambulance

Instructions regarding War Diaries and Intelligence Summaries are contained in F. S. Regs., Part II. and the Staff Manual respectively. Title pages will be prepared in manuscript.

WAR DIARY
or
INTELLIGENCE SUMMARY.
(Erase heading not required.)

Army Form C. 2118.

(4)

Place	Date	Hour	Summary of Events and Information	Remarks and references to Appendices
LES 4 VENTS W9 (36B)	24.10.16		O.C. 2nd Canadian Field Ambulance arrived & was shown round & the work at M.D.S. & forward area explained. Captain LAING to 1st Royal Fusiliers. Medical Board held for commission regular army on Lt H.H. L'ESTRANGE att 9th R Sussex Regt proceeding to 73 I Bde. Lt C D I Swain Antrim RGA 44 TMB proceeding to 24 Div CRA.	
			Personnel now doing duties other than medical & serving away from this unit. 30.	
			1 Officer 18 OR 2nd Canadian F Amb ADS party to Cabaret Rouge.	JM
"	25.10.16		LIEUT PEDLEY RAMC joined for temporary duty & instruction. Relief by 2 C.F.Amb completed. Visited 135 F Amb. L25 b3.4 (36B) BRAQUEMONT ADS L35 a 8.5. (36B) LES BREBIS & Bearer Post at M3 b1.4 (36C) N. MAROC.	JM
"	26.10.16	10 am	Advance Parties of 3 Officers 5 Sgts 4 Cpls & 42 O.R to L25 b3.4 ADS & Bearer Post in new area. Code names of Units 104 returned to IV Corps re. IV Corps No 629	JM
"	27.10.16	10 am	72 Field Ambulance marched off from LES 4 VENTS	
		1 PM	Arrived BRAQUEMONT L25 b3.4 (36B). Relief of 135 Field Ambulance Completed. Took over Main Dressing Station. Civic Hospital & Officers ward & three buildings full of stores & equipment at BRAQUEMONT. ADS at Les BREBIS Bath at LES BREBIS L25 b (36B) Bath at MAZINGARBE, L23 (36B) Bath at HOUCHIN K15 b (36B) Soup Kitchen at Les BREBIS & at N MAROC BEARER POST at N. MAROC. These various places have allotted a section & two bearer squads in addition	JM

2353 Wt. W2544/1454 700,000 5/15 D. D. & L. A.D.S.S./Forms/C. 2118.

72 FIELD AMBULANCE

Instructions regarding War Diaries and Intelligence Summaries are contained in F. S. Regs., Part II. and the Staff Manual respectively. Title pages will be prepared in manuscript.

WAR DIARY
or
INTELLIGENCE SUMMARY.
(Erase heading not required.)

Army Form C. 2118.

Place	Date	Hour	Summary of Events and Information	Remarks and references to Appendices
BRAQUEMONT L25b3.4 (36B)	28-10-16		Made a tour of inspection of all the buildings taken over in BRAQUEMONT. These are now unoccupied having been vacated by Field Ambulances which were not relieved. They contain a large quantity of stores both medical, ordnance & Red Cross & medical comforts. Report forwarded to ADMS suggesting that these be put into circulation or else stored in one central place to avoid deterioration & also to save personnel who are now being used as caretakers in four different places.	GBE
"	29-10-16		Visited baths at MAZINGARBE & Les BREBIS also ADS at Les Brebis. Pte Goodwin & Pte Howard awarded 7 days F.P. No 1. Pte Ingram 1 North Staffs sent in with memo for examination under suspicion of malingering man examined & found genuine he is suffering from anaemia & marked debility report to 72 I Bde.	GBE
"	30-10-16		24 Divisional Rest Stn opened at BRAQUEMONT to day.	GBE

G.B. Edwards. Lt Col RAMC.
OC 72 Field Ambulance

72 Field Ambulance

Instructions regarding War Diaries and Intelligence Summaries are contained in F. S. Regs., Part II. and the Staff Manual respectively. Title pages will be prepared in manuscript.

WAR DIARY
or
INTELLIGENCE SUMMARY.
(Erase heading not required.)

Army Form C. 2118.

(6)

Place	Date	Hour	Summary of Events and Information	Remarks and references to Appendices
			Report on work completed by this unit while at LES 4 VENTS between 25/9/16 & 25/10/16. Diagrams & plans attached	

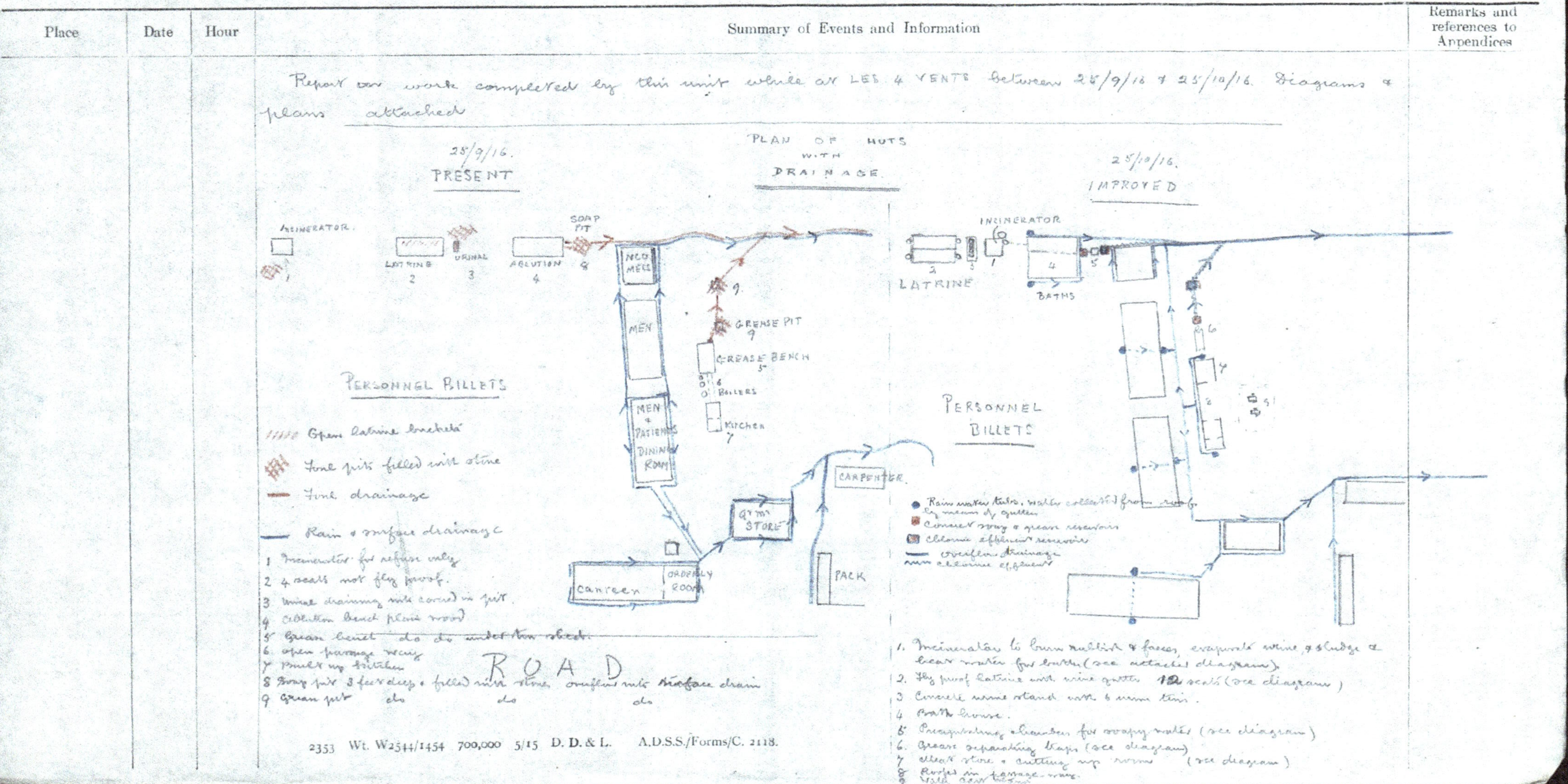

2353 Wt. W2544/1454 700,000 5/15 D. D. & L. A.D.S.S./Forms/C. 2118.

72 Field Ambulance

Instructions regarding War Diaries and Intelligence Summaries are contained in F. S. Regs., Part II. and the Staff Manual respectively. Title pages will be prepared in manuscript.

WAR DIARY
or
INTELLIGENCE SUMMARY.

(Erase heading not required.)

Army Form C. 2118.

Place	Date	Hour	Summary of Events and Information	Remarks and references to Appendices
			PLAN OF HUTS WITH DRAINAGE	
			PATIENTS PRESENT 25/9/16. — ROAD — PATIENTS IMPROVED 25/10/16.	
			PATIENTS LATRINE; URINAL; OFFICERS LATRINE; PANTRY; MESS; OFFICERS WARD; OPEN SPACE; SURGICAL; ABLUTION; MEDICAL; BARBER; BATH; BATH; DISPENSARY; Highwalk; RAIL; ROAD; PRIVATE GARDEN; OPERATING THEATRE; MESS + OFFICERS BILLETS; OFFICERS COOK HOUSE. Duck walk; Foul Pits; Foul drainage; Rain & surface. Bath water; Rain Tubs.	1 Officers Latrine 2 Patients' Cook house 3 Officers Mess Cookhouse 4 Patients' Latrine 5 Ablution Room 6 Changing " 7 Bath " 8 Dressing 9 Dirty Linen 10 Cleansing Room 11 Clean Linen 12 Drying Room 13 Boilers 14 Soap trap 15 Covered in passage 3a Tank for greasy water removed daily to trap
			Note. Drainage completed, Latrines & Ablution room complete. Soap trap (see diagram) completed. Remainder of work in various stages when unit left for new area.	
			[signature] Lt Col Rame	

2353 Wt. W2544/1454 700,000 5/15 D. D. & L. A.D.S.S./Forms/C. 2118.

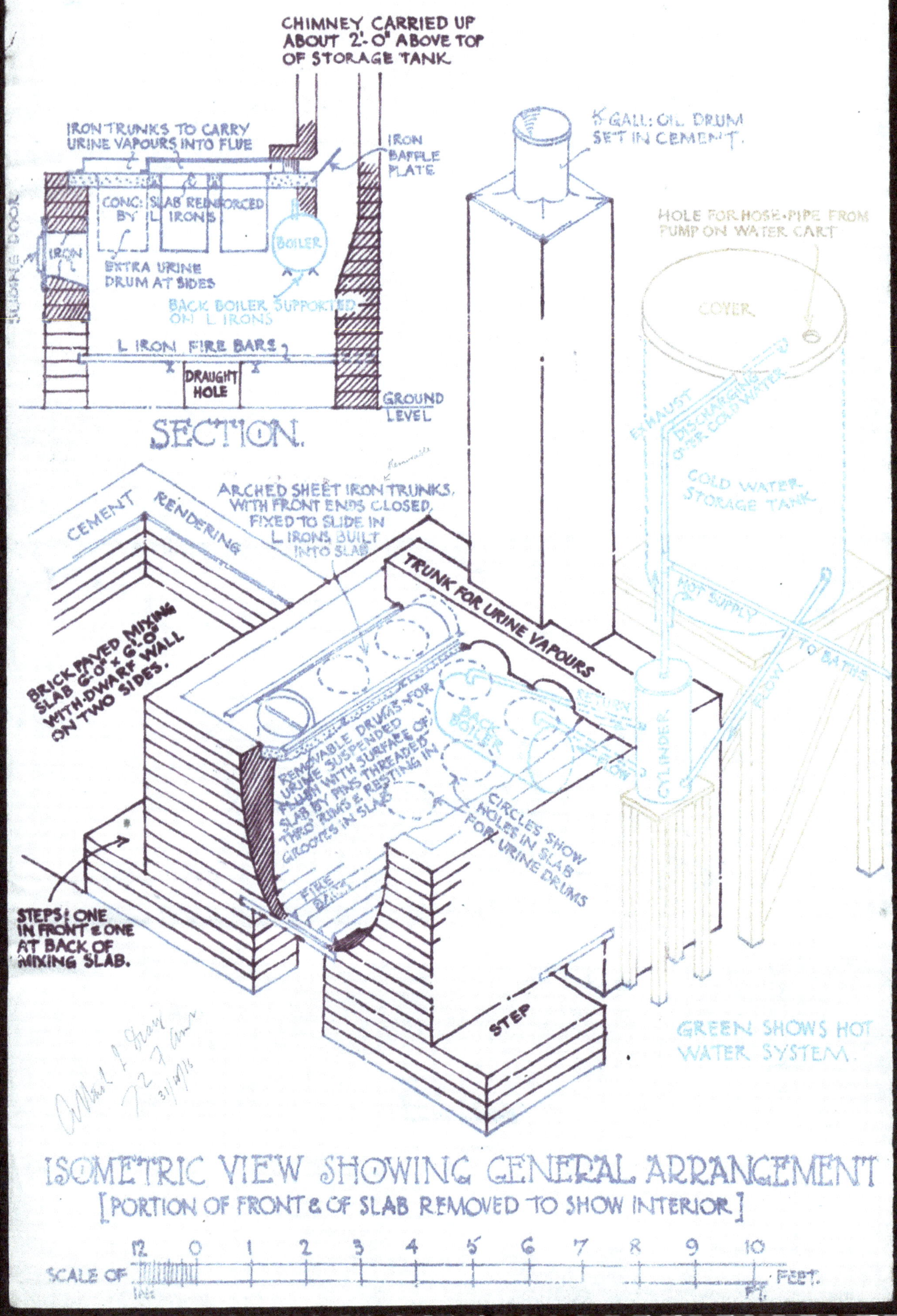
REFUSE DESTRUCTOR WITH SYSTEM FOR HEATING WATER & EVAPORATING URINE.
CHIMNEY CARRIED UP ABOUT 2'-0" ABOVE TOP OF STORAGE TANK
IRON TRUNKS TO CARRY URINE VAPOURS INTO FLUE
IRON BAFFLE PLATE
CONC: SLAB REINFORCED BY L IRONS
IRON
BOILER
EXTRA URINE DRUM AT SIDES
BACK BOILER SUPPORTED ON L IRONS
L IRON FIRE BARS
DRAUGHT HOLE
GROUND LEVEL
SECTION.
5 GALL: OIL DRUM SET IN CEMENT.
HOLE FOR HOSE-PIPE FROM PUMP ON WATER CART
COVER
EXHAUST
DISCHARGING OVER COLD WATER
COLD WATER STORAGE TANK
CEMENT RENDERING
ARCHED SHEET IRON TRUNKS, WITH FRONT ENDS CLOSED, FIXED TO SLIDE IN L IRONS BUILT INTO SLAB
TRUNK FOR URINE VAPOURS
HOT SUPPLY
TO BATHS
FLOW
CYLINDER
BRICK PAVED MIXING SLAB 6'-0" x 6'-0" WITH DWARF WALL ON TWO SIDES.
BACK BOILER
REMOVABLE DRUMS FOR URINE SUSPENDED FLUSH WITH SURFACE OF SLAB BY PINS THREADED THRO' RIMS & RESTING IN GROOVES IN SLAB
CIRCLES SHOW HOLES IN SLAB FOR URINE DRUMS
FIRE BARS
STEPS: ONE IN FRONT & ONE AT BACK OF MIXING SLAB.
STEP
GREEN SHOWS HOT WATER SYSTEM.
ISOMETRIC VIEW SHOWING GENERAL ARRANGEMENT
[PORTION OF FRONT & OF SLAB REMOVED TO SHOW INTERIOR]
12 0 1 2 3 4 5 6 7 8 9 10
SCALE OF INS. FEET.

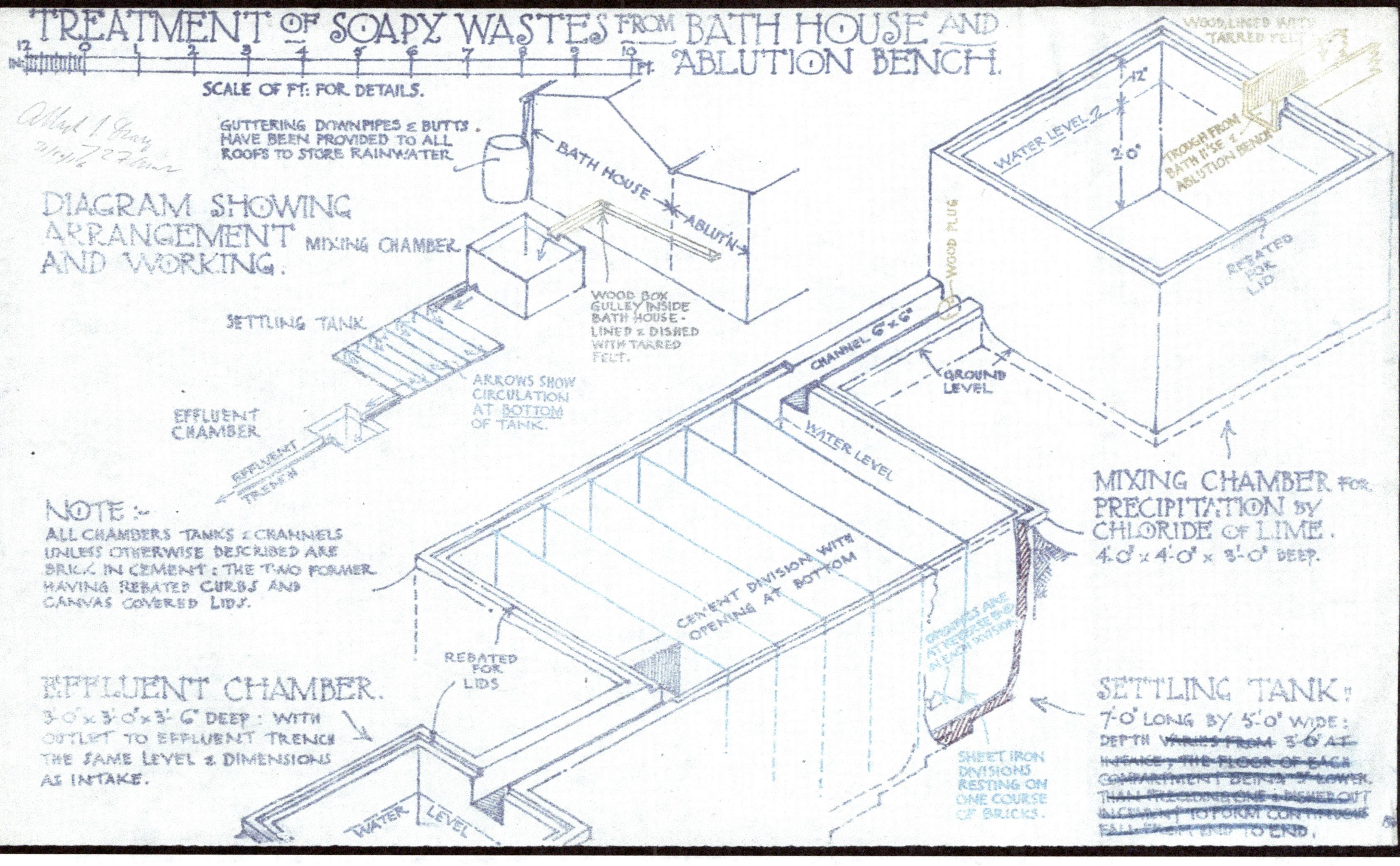
TREATMENT OF SOAPY WASTES FROM BATH HOUSE AND ABLUTION BENCH.
12 IN. 0 1 2 3 4 5 6 7 8 9 10 FT.
SCALE OF FT: FOR DETAILS.
GUTTERING DOWNPIPES & BUTTS. HAVE BEEN PROVIDED TO ALL ROOFS TO STORE RAINWATER
BATH HOUSE
ABLUT'N
DIAGRAM SHOWING ARRANGEMENT AND WORKING.
MIXING CHAMBER
SETTLING TANK
EFFLUENT CHAMBER
EFFLUENT TRENCH
WOOD BOX GULLEY INSIDE BATH HOUSE - LINED & DISHED WITH TARRED FELT.
ARROWS SHOW CIRCULATION AT BOTTOM OF TANK.
NOTE:- ALL CHAMBERS TANKS & CHANNELS UNLESS OTHERWISE DESCRIBED ARE BRICK IN CEMENT: THE TWO FORMER HAVING REBATED CURBS AND CANVAS COVERED LIDS.
EFFLUENT CHAMBER. 3'-0" x 3'-0" x 3'-6" DEEP: WITH OUTLET TO EFFLUENT TRENCH THE SAME LEVEL & DIMENSIONS AS INTAKE.
REBATED FOR LIDS
WATER LEVEL
CEMENT DIVISION WITH OPENING AT BOTTOM
CHANNEL 6" x 6"
WOOD PLUG
GROUND LEVEL
WATER LEVEL
OPENINGS ARE AT REVERSE ENDS IN EACH DIVISION
SHEET IRON DIVISIONS RESTING ON ONE COURSE OF BRICKS.
WOOD, LINED WITH TARRED FELT
12"
2'-0"
WATER LEVEL
TROUGH FROM BATH H'SE & ABLUTION BENCH
REBATED FOR LID
MIXING CHAMBER FOR PRECIPITATION BY CHLORIDE OF LIME. 4'-0" x 4'-0" x 3'-0" DEEP.
SETTLING TANK: 7'-0" LONG BY 5'-0" WIDE: DEPTH 3'-6"

SYSTEM FOR PURIFICATION OF WATER FROM GREASE BENCH.

END OF GREASE BENCH: TOP & TROUGH COVERED WITH TIN.

TIN SPOUT OVER END OF TROUGH

5-GALL: DRUM CONTAINING REMOVABLE WIRE NET CAGE TO CATCH TEA LEAVES ETC:

CEMENT BLOCK FOR DRUM

PERFORATIONS FOR OUTLET

MIXING CHAMBER FOR PRECIPITATION BY CHLORIDE OF LIME: 4'-0" x 4'-0" x 3'-0" DEEP WITH CANVAS COVERED LID.

6"

LEVEL OF LIQUID

2'-6"

SLOPING WEIR

12"

COKE

18"

2"

12"

GROUND LEVEL

CHAMBERS & CHANNELS FORMED IN BRICK, CEMENT RENDERED.

COKE TRENCH 12'-0" LONG WITH 3 CEMENT BAFFLERS TO DEVIATE FLOW

BAFFLERS

PERFORATED IRON GRID

9"

A

A

DETAILS.

LEVEL OF WATER ON TOP OF SAND

GROUND LEVEL

SAND FILTER: 3'-0" x 3'-0" x 3'-0" DEEP

5"

4"

18"

EFFLUENT TRENCH

GRID

COKE

WEIR

12"

LEVEL OF WATER ON TOP OF SAND & OF OUTLET

SAND

CEMENT

2'-0"

SECTION·A-A.

SCALE OF FEET 12 0 1 2 3 4 5 6 7 8 9 10 FT. FOR DETAILS.

DIAGRAM SHOWING ARRANGEMENT AND WORKING.

GREASE BENCH

DRUM

SLOPING WEIR.

MIXING CHAMBER [PRECIPITATION]

COKE TRENCH

THRO' GRID OVER WEIR & UP THRO' SAND FILTER

SAND FILTER

EFFLUENT TRENCH TO DITCH

FLY-PROOF LATRINE AND MEAT SAFE.

Attach to Diary R.J. Ca
7/11/16.

FLY-PROOF LATRINE.

NOTE:- BUCKETS ARE REMOVED THROUGH CLOSE-FITTING DOORS AT BACK OF ENCLOSURE.

BATTEN FIXED TO CLOSE LIDS AUTOMATICALLY.

ENCLOSURE BROKEN TO SHOW INTERIOR

BRICK PAVING

IRON CHANNEL TO CATCH URINE FIXED TO FALL TOWARDS DRUM

CEMENT RENDERED ENCLOSURE FOR URINE DRUM, WITH REBATED LID COVERED WITH CANVAS.

TOP OF SAFE · ALSO SPANDRELS BETWEEN SAME & ROOF ARE LINED WITH FLY-PROOF MUSLIN

VENTILATING SPANDREL

SKELETON DOORS COVERED WITH FLY-PROOF MUSLIN & MOVING IN RUNNERS FIXED TO FLOOR, END WALLS & BEAM ABOVE

FIXED

INTERIOR OF SAFE LIME WHITED

THIS HALF TO SLIDE BACK

HANDLE

POST BEHIND

TIN TRAYS BENEATH HOOKS

CONCRETE FLOOR

END WALL REMOVED TO SHOW INTERIOR

FLY-PROOF MEAT SAFE.

SCALE OF 12 0 1 2 3 4 5 6 7 8 9 10 FEET.
IN: FT:

Nov 1916 24th Div 140/1562 94

CONFIDENTIAL

Vol 15

WAR DIARY

OF (LIEUT COL G. B. EDWARDS)

OFFICER COMMANDING 72ND FIELD AMBULANCE.

FROM. 1ST NOVEMBER 1916.

TO 30TH NOVEMBER 1916.

72 FIELD AMBULANCE

Instructions regarding War Diaries and Intelligence Summaries are contained in F. S. Regs., Part II. and the Staff Manual respectively. Title pages will be prepared in manuscript.

WAR DIARY
or
INTELLIGENCE SUMMARY.
(Erase heading not required.)

(1)

Army Form C. 2118.

Place	Date	Hour	Summary of Events and Information	Remarks and references to Appendices
BRAQUEMONT L25 b.4.4 (36B)	1/11/16		Lieut F. G PEDLEY to 106 Bde R.F.A for duty. Lieut W DIXON joined for duty from 106 RFA. Inspected Baths at L 22 central & forwarded report to ADMS 24 Div. 1 HD Horse handed over to 12 R. Fusiliers	GME
"	2.11.16		DDMS. 1st Corps inspected to day.	GME
"	3.11.16		Lieut. BLYTHE to ADS Les BREBIS	GME
"	4.11.16	6.30PM	Gas Alert.	GME
"	6.11.16		1 NCO & 5 OR. lent to CRE. Officers instructed in use of Novita apparatus lent by MO 255 Tunneling Coy	GME
"	7.11.16		Lieut EBERTS returned to Hd Qrs from ADS. Instructions received from ADMS 24 Div to assist 6 Division who are providing working parties. MS 1834. Small box respirators received	GME
"	8.11.16		Lieut GOODING 17 Field Ambulance to ADS. Inspected baths at MAZINGARBE. Capt BRETHERTON on leave " EBERTS to 24 DAC. temp duty	GME
"	9.11.16		New Baths at L'Abattoir opened Box respirators issued to personnel. Arranged with Q to close baths tomorrow.	GME

2353 Wt. W2544/1454 700,000 5/15 D. D. & L. A.D.S.S./Forms/C. 2118.

42 FIELD AMBULANCE

Instructions regarding War Diaries and Intelligence Summaries are contained in F. S. Regs., Part II, and the Staff Manual respectively. Title pages will be prepared in manuscript.

WAR DIARY
or
INTELLIGENCE SUMMARY.
(Erase heading not required.)

(2)

Army Form C. 2118.

Place	Date	Hour	Summary of Events and Information	Remarks and references to Appendices
L25 b 44. (36 B)	10.11.16		Inspected Baths, ADS & Bearer Post at N. Maroc.	SM
"	13.11.16		Lt & QrMr J. T. COOKE on leave.	
			Drew up plans for reconstruction of Baths at Les Brebis forwarded to GOC & approved.	SM
"	14.11.16		New horse in replacement taken over.	SM
"	16.11.16		Inspection by 1st Corps Commander. Two reinforcements joined.	SM.
"	19.11.16		Capt Cathcart on leave.	SM
		5 Pm	Cancel Gas alert.	
"	21.11.16		Capt. Bretherton returned from leave.	
			Sgt Earle ASC joined for duty from 195 Coy ASC Sgt Halliday to 195 Coy for duty	SM
			Report on health of No 3 Australian Tunneling Coy forwarded to ADMS	SM
"	22.11.16		Sgt Major Coggins on leave.	
			Bought chaff cutter for Transport lines 135 Francs.	
	"		Capt Laing to ADS. Lieut Blythe to 1N. Staffs for duty	SM
			Capt Webster rejoined from temp duty with 1st N. Staffs.	

2353 Wt. W2544/1454 700,000 5/15 D. D. & L. A.D.S.S./Forms/C. 2118.

72 FIELD AMBULANCE

WAR DIARY
or
INTELLIGENCE SUMMARY.
(Erase heading not required.)

Army Form C. 2118.

(3)

Instructions regarding War Diaries and Intelligence Summaries are contained in F. S. Regs., Part II. and the Staff Manual respectively. Title pages will be prepared in manuscript.

Place	Date	Hour	Summary of Events and Information	Remarks and references to Appendices
L25b44 (36B)	23.11.16		Lt & Qr. Mr. Cooke returned from leave	SM
	24.11.16		Dr EBERTS from 24 DAC to 107 Bde RFA for temp duty	SM
			Capt Groves on sick list.	SM
			5 T W men reported for duty from 1st C.R.S	SM
	25.11.		5 T U to Houchin baths for duty.	
			DDMS I Corps inspected billets of 3 Australian Tunnelling Coy	SM
	26.11.		Inspected baths. R.E. workmen have commenced work on reconstruction.	
			1 Cpl to 1 N. Staffs for duty vice Cpl Querney who has joined this unit.	SM
	28.11		New dressing room completed for dressing septic cases.	SM
	29.11		Capt Groves on leave. Inspected Field Ambulance Transport with the Div Train	SM
	30.11.	12.40 am	Gas alert.	
			Distribution of personnel	

		Officers	WO	NCO	OR
Main Dressing Stn	Rame	5	1	18	74
	ASC		1	4	36
A D Station		2		1	16
Bearer Post.				1	8
Baths Les Brebis				1	16
" Abattoir				1	19.
" Houchin					4.

Soup Kitchen	OR	2
detached	Officer	1
	NCO	2
	O.R	1
Leave	NCO	4
	O.R.	17
	Officer	1

2353 Wt. W2544/1454 700,000 5/15 D. D. & L. A.D.S.S./Forms/C. 2118.

92 Field Ambulance

Instructions regarding War Diaries and Intelligence Summaries are contained in F. S. Regs., Part II. and the Staff Manual respectively. Title pages will be prepared in manuscript.

WAR DIARY
or
INTELLIGENCE SUMMARY.
(Erase heading not required.)

(4)

Army Form C. 2118.

Place	Date	Hour	Summary of Events and Information	Remarks and references to Appendices
			During the month work has been carried out in improving horse lines & e.s.s.c. billets, enlarging accommodation for patients making spring beds bed side lockers, Tables & shelves fitting up electric light. repairing & painting wagons, making cellar at bearer post gas proof. A good deal of carpenters work has been put in at the baths making ironing benches, shelves, latrines, notice boards etc. Numerous directing boards have been made & posted at various places.	
			A new drying room is under construction whereby the heat from the incinerator is to be utilised in drying clothes.	
			Average number of patients remaining in Field Ambulance Daily 70	
			Prevailing disease. Pyrexia	
			S. V. Edmunds. Lt. Col. R.A.M.C. O.C. 92 Field Ambulance.	

Dec 1916

24th Div

24

CONFIDENTIAL

Vol 16

WAR DIARY

140/1905

OF (LIEUT COL G.B. EDWARDS. D.S.O.)

OFFICER COMMANDING 72ND FIELD AMBULANCE

FROM 1. 12. 16 TO 31 - 12 - 16

72 Field Ambulance

Instructions regarding War Diaries and Intelligence Summaries are contained in F. S. Regs., Part II. and the Staff Manual respectively. Title pages will be prepared in manuscript.

WAR DIARY
or
INTELLIGENCE SUMMARY.
(Erase heading not required.)

(1)

Army Form C. 2118.

Place	Date	Hour	Summary of Events and Information	Remarks and references to Appendices
BRACQUEMONT	1.12.16		Nil.	SM
L 25 B	2.12.16		"	SM
(36 B)	3.12.16		Inspected A.D.S. + Bearer Post. all correct.	
		5 P.M.	Cancel Gas Alert.	SM
	4.12.16		Visited Divisional Baths all in working order	SM
	5.12.16		Report to A.D.M.S. reference coal consumption & shortage. Request for 3½ tons per week coal + also ration allowance	SM
		2.40 P.M.	Gas Alert. 1 German prisoner admitted sick from prisoners camp.	SM
	6.12.16		Captain W.R. Webster on sick list. Visited A.D.S.	SM
	7.12.16		Bearer Squads changed at Bearer Post & A.D.S. Shelf fitted in Q.M. Store	SM
	8.12.16		Conducted a class of officers from 24 Division round Divisional Baths & Field Ambulance	SM
		12 mn	Cancel Gas Alert.	
	9.12.16		Visited Baths at Houchin. Sent recommendations for improvements to 24th Division. Received 3 new hoods for Horse Ambulance wagons. Lieut F.K MARRIOTT RAMC. attached for instruction.	SM
	10.12.16		Capt H.X GROVES returned from leave.	
		6 P.M.	Gas Alert. Order for stores resubmitted to C.R.E.	SM

2353 Wt. W2544/1454 700,000 5/15 D. D. & L. A.D.S.S./Forms/C. 2118.

72 FIELD AMBULANCE **WAR DIARY** *or* **INTELLIGENCE SUMMARY.** Army Form C. 2118.

Instructions regarding War Diaries and Intelligence Summaries are contained in F. S. Regs., Part II. and the Staff Manual respectively. Title pages will be prepared in manuscript.

(*Erase heading not required.*)

(2)

Place	Date	Hour	Summary of Events and Information	Remarks and references to Appendices
BRACQUEMONT	11-12-16		Acting Sgt Simpson & L'Cpl Withnell recommended for commissioned rank.	SM
L 25 B	12-12-16		Capt W B Webster discharged to duty.	SM
(36 B)	13-12-16	9am	Cancel Gas Alert. Visited Baths & ADS.	SM
	14-12-16		Visited new Reinforcement Training Camp at Noeux les Mines. Arranged to detail MO to see morning sick.	SM
		5.15pm	Gas Alert. Visited Baths at [illegible]. 200 blankets lent to O.C. Reinforcement Camp.	
	15-12-16		Lieut W. Dixon on leave to NICE. Took over Baths at Noeux les Mines. 3 GS wagons to report RE dump for purpose of conveying road metal for repair of roads at LOOSE. Two hospital beds handed over to MO 3 Australian Tunneling Coy.	SM
	16-12-16	9.20am	Cancel Gas Alert. Visited Soup Kitchens & Baths all correct. G.O.C. inspected Field Ambulance	SM
	17-12-16		Inspected H.T. harness all in very good shape. 1 GS Wagon broken down & left at LOOSE. Plans of field ovens in use by this unit forwarded to G.O.C.	SM
	18-12-16	4.20pm	Gas Alert. 18 Temporary unfit men reported for duty at Baths. 1 GS wagon returned from Loose. Capt. WEBSTER on leave.	SM
	19-12-16		Visited Officers Rest Station at Aire	SM
	20-12-16		Arranged to draw 1 ton of coal for Div Laundry at 2 PM on Tuesdays. Training Camp removed to ALLOUAGNE 1 MO & Ambulance to accompany on march. Reminded ADMS re shortage of coal. 1 ambulance car detailed for duty with O.C. S African Labour Corps for 10 days at VAUDRICOURT	SM

2353 Wt. W2544/1454 700,000 5/15 D. D. & L. A.D.S.S./Forms/C. 2118.

72 FIELD AMBULANCE

Instructions regarding War Diaries and Intelligence Summaries are contained in F. S. Regs., Part II. and the Staff Manual respectively. Title pages will be prepared in manuscript.

WAR DIARY
or
INTELLIGENCE SUMMARY.
(Erase heading not required.)

Army Form C. 2118.

(3)

Place	Date	Hour	Summary of Events and Information	Remarks and references to Appendices
BRACQUEMONT	21-12-16		1 Rider drawn from Div Train, badly groomed, poor condition.	SM
L25B	22.12.16		Squads at Bearer Post & ADS changed.	SM
(36B)	23.12.16		Nil	SM
	24.12.16		Nil	SM
	25.12.16		Nil	SM
	26.12.16	2.10am	Gas Alert. Pump at L'Abattoir baths broken down. Lt. Dixon returned from leave	SM
	27.12.16		Visited baths & ADS. 1 ton coal dust received at Les Brebis baths instead of 3 tons. Report to Q 24 Div.	SM
	28-12-16		Capt Webster returned from leave. Shortage of socks at baths 3000 asked for 900 received, 2000 obtained from DADOS.	SM
			Pump at L'Abattoir baths repaired but broke down immediately afterwards	SM
	29.12.16	10am	Cancel Gas Alert. Capt LAING Capt EBERTS on leave	SM
	30.12.16		Inspection of all box respirators	SM
	31.12.16		One Sunbeam Car returned from duty with S. African Labour Corps	SM

S. W. Edwards.
Lt. Col. RAMC.
OC 72 Field Ambulance

24th Div. 140/1997 24

Jan. 1917

CONFIDENTIAL

Vol 17

WAR DIARY

OF

LIEUT: COL: G.B. EDWARDS, D.S.O.

OFFICER COMDG: 72ND FIELD AMBULANCE

FROM 1ST JANUARY 1917 TO 31ST JANUARY 1917

Instructions regarding War Diaries and Intelligence Summaries are contained in F. S. Regs., Part II. and the Staff Manual respectively. Title pages will be prepared in manuscript.

72 FIELD AMBULANCE **WAR DIARY** *or* **INTELLIGENCE SUMMARY.**

(Erase heading not required.)

(1)

Army Form C. 2118.

Place	Date	Hour	Summary of Events and Information	Remarks and references to Appendices
BRACQUEMONT L25b (36B)	1-1-17		—	
	2.1.17		—	
	3.1.17		1 Case Cerebro Spinal Meningitis admitted from 9th Royal Sussex	SM
	4.1.17		—	
	5.1.17		Inspected Transport all in good condition, clean & smart turn out 3 G.S. Wagon & 3 Limber Wagon covers required to replace old ones worn out.	SM
	6.1.17		—	
	7.1.17		—	
	8.1.17		8 Contacts with C.S.M. of 8 Royal West Kents, returned to duty from isolation	SM
	9.1.17		Inspection by D.M.S. 1st Army. He appeared pleased with the unit & condition of the Field Ambulance & has asked for models & sketches of new drying room & incinerator combined, to be forwarded to Hd Qrs also a sketch of bench for dressings	SM
			Capt. A.W. Bretherton on special leave 10 days	
	10-1-17		Capt. S.H.T. Eberts & Capt G. Lainey returned from leave. Trench Raid by 2nd Leinsters. 1 Sgt Ranie & 2 Bearers Squad went up to assist at 1 P.M. returned at 11 P.M. 17 wounded Leinsters admitted.	SM
	11-1-17		G.O.C. 24 Div visited the wounded & congratulated them on their very fine performance in last night raid.	SM
	12-1-17		—	
	13-1-17		—	

72 FIELD AMBULANCE **WAR DIARY** *or* **INTELLIGENCE SUMMARY.**

(Erase heading not required.)

Army Form C. 2118.

Instructions regarding War Diaries and Intelligence Summaries are contained in F. S. Regs., Part II. and the Staff Manual respectively. Title pages will be prepared in manuscript.

Place	Date	Hour	Summary of Events and Information	Remarks and references to Appendices
L25b (36B)	14.1.17		G.O.C. 24 Division inspected new drying room & incinerator & asked for plans.	SMR
		7.40	~~am~~ Gas alert.	
"	15.1.17		All T.U men employed by Field Ambulance at Baths & Soup Kitchen handed over to O.C. 24 Div. Coy for discipline. Lieut. F.R. Marriott on leave 10 days.	SMR
"	16.1.17	3.50	P.m. Cancel Gas alert.	
"	17.1.17		Capt Parkinson DADMS Sanitation 1st Army came round to see various sanitary contrivances made by unit.	SMR
"	18.1.17		——	SMR
"	19.1.17	7.30am	Gas alert.	
	20.1.17		Report from Baths that stock of clean linen running short & that there is difficulty in replenishing from Clean Linen Stn. Saw Q 24 Div about it & arranged to draw extra from DADOS.	SMR

2353 Wt. W2544/1454 700,000 5/15 D. D. & L. A.D.S.S./Forms/C. 2118.

72 FIELD AMBULANCE **WAR DIARY** *or* **INTELLIGENCE SUMMARY.**

(Erase heading not required.)

Army Form C. 2118.

Instructions regarding War Diaries and Intelligence Summaries are contained in F. S. Regs., Part II. and the Staff Manual respectively. Title pages will be prepared in manuscript.

(3)

Place	Date	Hour	Summary of Events and Information	Remarks and references to Appendices
L25 b (36B)	21-1-17		1 Car detailed for 24 hours duty from MAC to convey odd cases of wounded to CCS. This is to be a permanent duty in future.	SM
"	22.1.17		ADMS 21 Division, DADMS 1st Army, OC 22 CCS & OC 13 MAC taken round the Field Ambulance & the various sanitary arrangements demonstrated. OC 65 Field Ambulance & his QM came round prior to taking over	SM
"	23.1.17		Visited 65 F Amb at Allouagne ALLOUAGNE D7a 2.5 (36B/40000.) Lieut. SHORE RAMC ~~attached~~ for temporary duty	SM
"	24.1.17		Sgt CRASKE evacuated to CCS.	SM
"	25.1.17		Inspected Divisional Baths	
"	26.1.17	10am	Advance party from 65 Field Ambulance sent up to ADS & Bearer Posts to take over.	SM
		4pm	OO 101. ADMS received	
		8pm	All OOs cancelled. All reliefs cancelled & advance parties returned to their units.	SM
	27-1-17		——	

Instructions regarding War Diaries and Intelligence Summaries are contained in F. S. Regs., Part II. and the Staff Manual respectively. Title pages will be prepared in manuscript.

72 FIELD AMBULANCE

WAR DIARY
or
INTELLIGENCE SUMMARY.
(Erase heading not required.)

Army Form C. 2118.

Place	Date	Hour	Summary of Events and Information	Remarks and references to Appendices
L25b (36B)	28.1.17		Visited Baths, Redistribution of Personnel at ADS, Baths, & Bearer Posts.	SM
				SM
"	29.1.17		——	SM
"	30.1.17		——	
"	31.1.17		Baths out of order due to frost. Capt MARRIOTT returned from leave	SM

S M Emmons Lt Col RAMC
OC 72 Field Ambulance

2353 Wt. W2544/1454 700,000 5/15 D. D. & L. A.D.S.S./Forms/C. 2118.

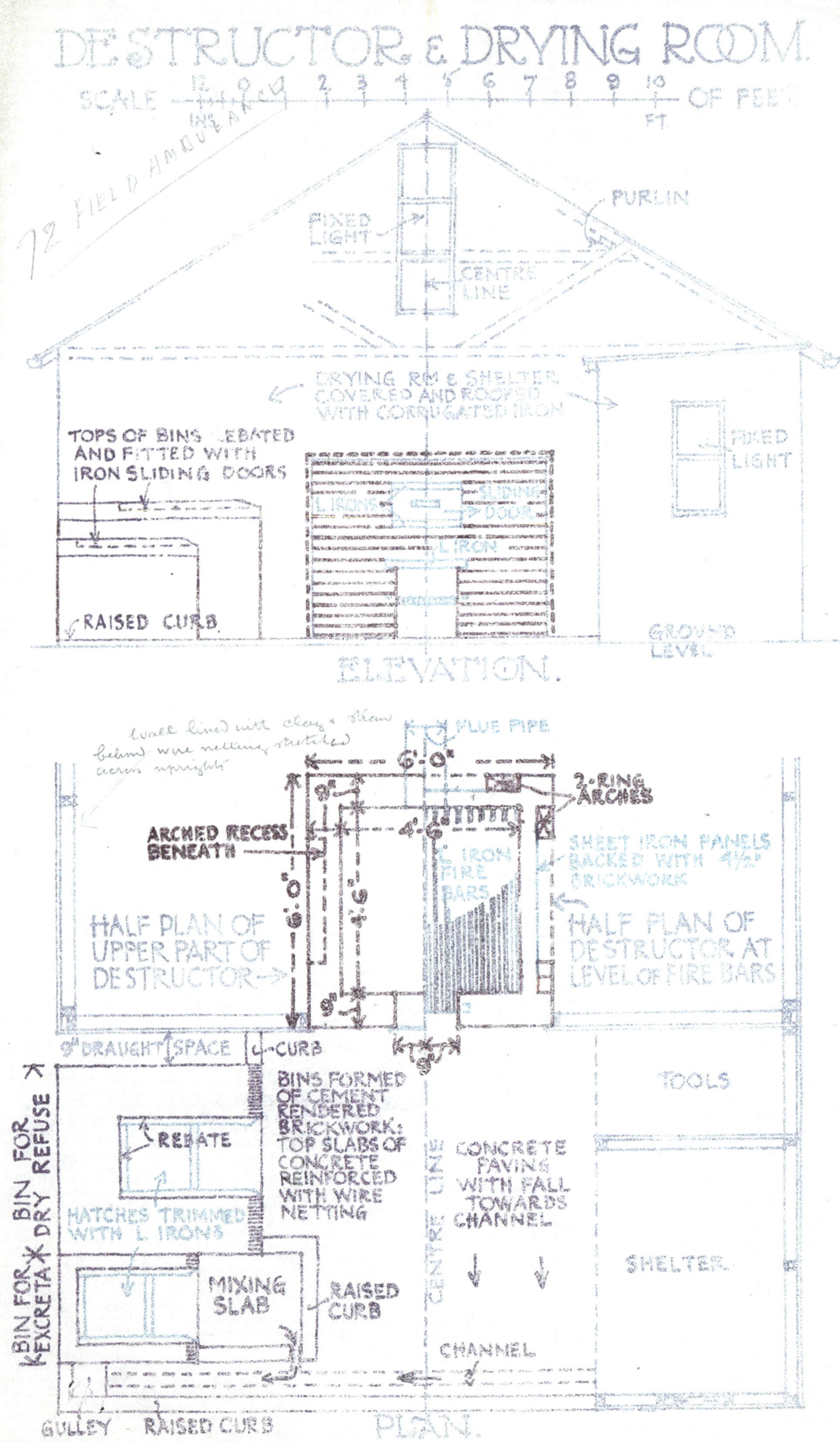
DESTRUCTOR & DRYING ROOM.
SCALE
OF FEET
FT.
72 FIELD AMBULANCE
PURLIN
FIXED LIGHT
CENTRE LINE
DRYING RM & SHELTER COVERED AND ROOFED WITH CORRUGATED IRON
TOPS OF BINS REBATED AND FITTED WITH IRON SLIDING DOORS
L IRONS
SLIDING DOOR
L IRON
FIXED LIGHT
RAISED CURB
GROUND LEVEL
ELEVATION.
Wall lined with clay & straw behind wire netting stretched across uprights
FLUE PIPE
6'.0"
2-RING ARCHES
ARCHED RECESS BENEATH
4'.6"
L IRON FIRE BARS
SHEET IRON PANELS BACKED WITH 4½" BRICKWORK
6'.0"
4'.6"
HALF PLAN OF UPPER PART OF DESTRUCTOR
HALF PLAN OF DESTRUCTOR AT LEVEL OF FIRE BARS
9" DRAUGHT SPACE
L-CURB
TOOLS
BIN FOR DRY REFUSE
BINS FORMED OF CEMENT RENDERED BRICKWORK: TOP SLABS OF CONCRETE REINFORCED WITH WIRE NETTING
REBATE
CENTRE LINE
CONCRETE PAVING WITH FALL TOWARDS CHANNEL
HATCHES TRIMMED WITH L IRONS
SHELTER
BIN FOR EXCRETA
MIXING SLAB
RAISED CURB
CHANNEL
GULLEY
RAISED CURB
PLAN.

DESTRUCTOR & DRYING ROOM.

SCALE 12 0 1 2 3 4 5 6 7 8 9 10 OF FEET.
INS. FT.

72 FIELD AMB

PURLIN
TIE BEAM
CENTRE LINE
HALF SECTION
HALF ELEVATION
IRON FLUE PIPE AND CONE TOP FROM OLD DESTRUCTOR
CEMENT FLAUNCHING
BINS FITTED WITH IRON DOORS SLIDING IN L IRONS
SHEET IRON SUPPORTED ON 3 L IRONS
FLUE PIPE [OIL DRUMS]
DOOR IN CORNER
BRICK BASE 2'-6" x 2'-6" CEMENT RENDERED
4'-6"
4'-0"
STAY
CURB
CHANNEL
CURB
L IRON FIRE BARS
IRON PANEL
GR'D LINE
GR'D LINE
CEMENT RENDERED CONCRETE

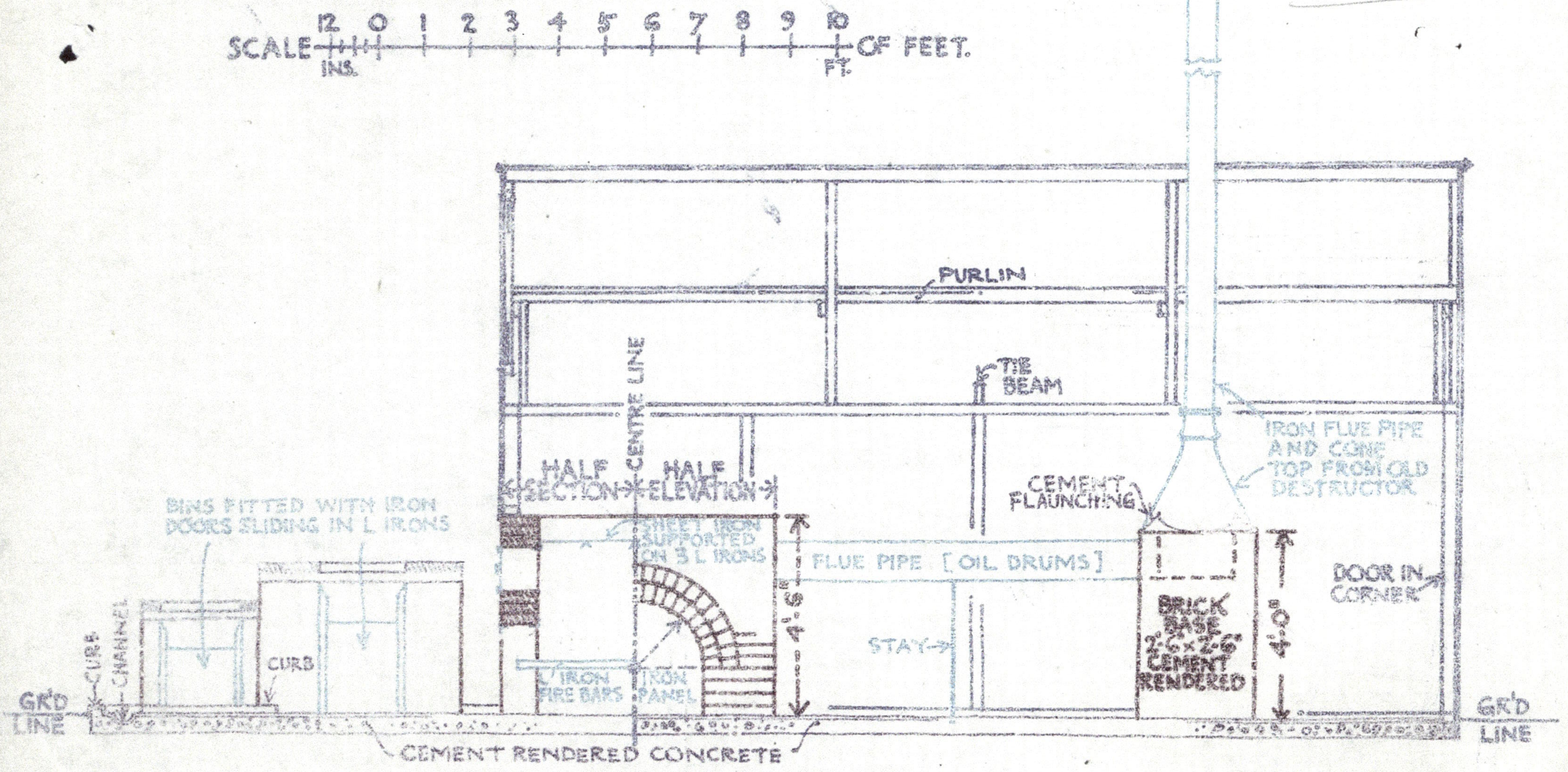

SECTION.

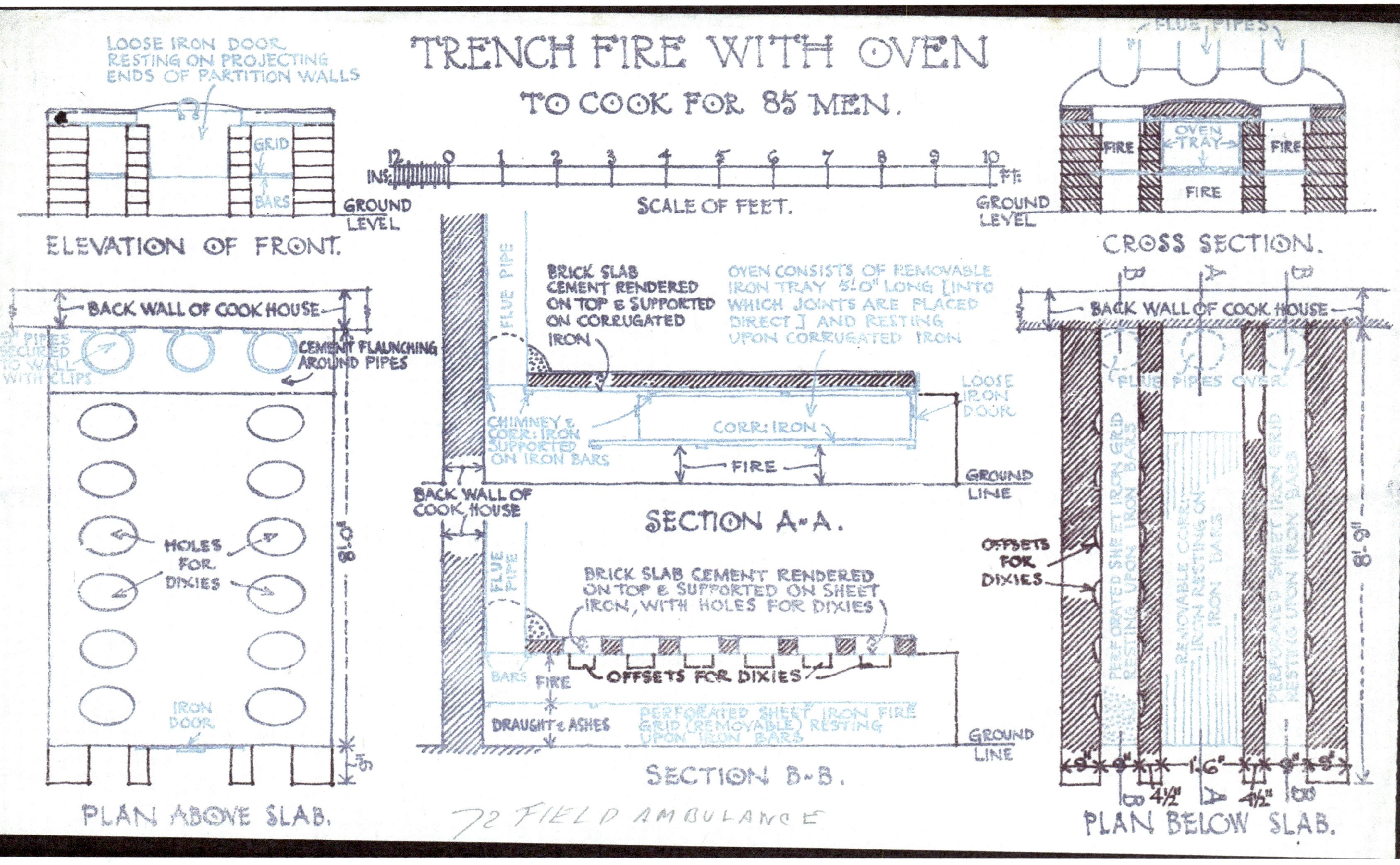

TRENCH FIRE WITH OVEN
TO COOK FOR 85 MEN.
LOOSE IRON DOOR RESTING ON PROJECTING ENDS OF PARTITION WALLS
GRID
BARS
GROUND LEVEL
ELEVATION OF FRONT.
SCALE OF FEET.
INS.
FT.
FLUE PIPES
FIRE
OVEN TRAY
CROSS SECTION.
BACK WALL OF COOK HOUSE
9" PIPES SECURED TO WALL WITH CLIPS
CEMENT FLAUNCHING AROUND PIPES
HOLES FOR DIXIES
IRON DOOR
8'.0"
9"
PLAN ABOVE SLAB.
FLUE PIPE
BRICK SLAB CEMENT RENDERED ON TOP & SUPPORTED ON CORRUGATED IRON
OVEN CONSISTS OF REMOVABLE IRON TRAY 5'.0" LONG [INTO WHICH JOINTS ARE PLACED DIRECT] AND RESTING UPON CORRUGATED IRON
LOOSE IRON DOOR
CHIMNEY & CORR: IRON SUPPORTED ON IRON BARS
CORR: IRON
FIRE
GROUND LINE
BACK WALL OF COOK HOUSE
SECTION A-A.
BRICK SLAB CEMENT RENDERED ON TOP & SUPPORTED ON SHEET IRON, WITH HOLES FOR DIXIES
OFFSETS FOR DIXIES
BARS
DRAUGHT & ASHES
PERFORATED SHEET IRON FIRE GRID (REMOVABLE) RESTING UPON IRON BARS
SECTION B-B.
72 FIELD AMBULANCE
FLUE PIPES OVER
PERFORATED SHEET IRON GRID RESTING UPON IRON BARS
REMOVABLE CORR: IRON RESTING ON IRON BARS
OFFSETS FOR DIXIES
8'.9"
9" 9" 1'.6" 9" 9"
4½" 4½"
A B
PLAN BELOW SLAB.

Feb. 1917 24th Div Medical ·24

CONFIDENTIAL

140/1997
Vol 18

WAR DIARY

OF

LIEUT: COL: G. B. EDWARDS D.S.O

OFFICER COMDG: 72ND FIELD AMBULANCE

FROM 1ST FEBRUARY 1917 TO 28TH FEBRUARY 1917

72 FIELD AMBULANCE

Instructions regarding War Diaries and Intelligence Summaries are contained in F. S. Regs., Part II. and the Staff Manual respectively. Title pages will be prepared in manuscript.

WAR DIARY
or
INTELLIGENCE SUMMARY.
(Erase heading not required.)

(1)

Army Form C. 2118.

Place	Date	Hour	Summary of Events and Information	Remarks and references to Appendices
L25b (36B)	1-2-17		One case of mumps from unit sent to infectious hospital	BMR
"	2.2.17		DDMS 1st Corps inspected the Field Ambulance.	BMR
"	3.2.17		Capt Marriott taken on strength of unit. Capt Marriott to 24 Div Training Btn for temporary duty	BMR
"	4.2.17		Capt A.S Groves returned from temporary duty with 8 Buffs.	BMR
"	5.2.17		S. Maj Tattersal ASC attached Evacuated to 33 CCS	BMR
"	6.2.17		—	
"	7.2.17		—	
"	8.2.17		ADMS 37th Div came round.	BMR
"	9.2.17		Capt Laing temporary duty 9 E. Surrey Regt. O.C 50th Field Ambulance came round & was shown ACs ADS, Baths etc. Probably be relieving this unit on 12th Capt Laing returned from 9 E Surrey Regt.	BMR

2353 Wt. W2544/1454 700,000 5/15 D. D. & L. A.D.S.S./Forms/C. 2118.

72 FIELD AMBULANCE

Instructions regarding War Diaries and Intelligence Summaries are contained in F. S. Regs., Part II. and the Staff Manual respectively. Title pages will be prepared in manuscript.

WAR DIARY
or
INTELLIGENCE SUMMARY.
(*Erase heading not required.*)

Army Form C. 2118.

Place	Date	Hour	Summary of Events and Information	Remarks and references to Appendices
L28b (36B)	10-2-17	11.45 AM	OO 101 ADMS received. 1 Case measles from unit sent to Infection Hospl	SMR
"	11-2-17		Advance party to ALLOUVAGNE D7a 2.6. (36B)	
		11 AM	Advance party from 50 F.A. arrived	
	12-2-17		Handed over to 50 F Amb. Marched off at 1 PM. arrived ALLOUVAGNE 5 PM. G.O.C. in C. inspected unit on the march.	SMR.
ALLOUVAGNE D7a 2.5 (36B)	13-2-17		Cars detailed to follow units on the march to Rest Area. Three men of unit struck off strength for duties at Rouen No 4 Base depot.	SMR
"	14-2-17		Visited LILLERS, BUSNES, to find suitable place for Baths. Obtained a Brewery at LILLERS. Made arrangements for collecting morning sick from units in rest area. 1 Car detailed for duty 1 Corps ~~Scabies~~ Scabies hospital. Inspected men billets & found them in good condition, dry & comfortable.	SMR SMR

72 FIELD AMBULANCE

Instructions regarding War Diaries and Intelligence Summaries are contained in F. S. Regs., Part II. and the Staff Manual respectively. Title pages will be prepared in manuscript.

WAR DIARY
or
INTELLIGENCE SUMMARY.
(Erase heading not required.)

Army Form C. 2118.

(3)

Place	Date	Hour	Summary of Events and Information	Remarks and references to Appendices
D7.a 2.5' (36B)	15/2/17		—	
"	16.2.17		Handed over model of drying room to DMS 1st Army. Visited 1st Army Sanitary models. Inspection of Section equipment.	SM
"	17.2.17		Training	SM
"	18.2.17		Training	SM
"	19.2.17		Training	SM
"	20.2.17		ALLOUAGNE placed out of Bounds.	SM
"	21.2.17		ALLOUAGNE in Bounds. 19th Sherwood Foresters & 24th Div Train there placed in isolation.	SM
"	22.2.17		—	
	23.2.17		1 Case of Measles from Unit sent to Infectious Hospl	SM

2353 Wt. W2544/1454 700,000 5/15 D. D. & L. A.D.S.S./Forms/C. 2118.

Instructions regarding War Diaries and Intelligence Summaries are contained in F. S. Regs., Part II. and the Staff Manual respectively. Title pages will be prepared in manuscript.

72 FIELD AMBULANCE **WAR DIARY** *or* **INTELLIGENCE SUMMARY.** (4)

(Erase heading not required.)

Army Form C. 2118.

Place	Date	Hour	Summary of Events and Information	Remarks and references to Appendices
~~[illegible]~~ D 7 a 2 5 (36B)	24/2/17		Capt. L. S. Kidd RAMC attached for duty temporarily	
	25/2/17		1 Case measles from Unit to Infection Hosp.	SM
"	26/2/17		Advance Party 1 NCO 5 OR to Officers Rest Station Aire.	SM
"	27/2/17		Advance Party 1 NCO 5 OR do do	SM
			Pte Jones struck off ~~strength~~ to Boulogne Transport Depot	
			L Cpl Lumsden " " " " 1st Army School Sanitary Course	SM
			1 Case returned from 1st Corps Scabies Hosp.	
			Capt R. B. ROBSON RAMC attached for temporary duty	SM
			Interpreter on leave.	SM.
	28/2/17		Pte Booth struck off ~~strength~~ duty at Transport Depot.	
			To take over Officers Rest Station at Aire on 1st/3/17 & 1st Corps Rest Station on 4/3/17	

S. J. S. Simmons

2353 Wt. W2544/1454 700,000 5/15 D. D. & L. A.D.S.S./Forms/C. 2118.

24th Div

140/2042

MEDICAL 24

Vol ~~19~~ 20

CONFIDENTIAL

WAR DIARY

OF

LIEUT COLONEL G. B. EDWARDS D.S.O.

OFFICER COMMANDING 72ND FIELD AMBULANCE

FROM 1ST MARCH 1917 — TO 31ST MARCH 1917

72 FIELD AMBULANCE.

Instructions regarding War Diaries and Intelligence Summaries are contained in F. S. Regs., Part II. and the Staff Manual respectively. Title pages will be prepared in manuscript.

WAR DIARY
or
INTELLIGENCE SUMMARY.
(Erase heading not required.)

Army Form C. 2118.

(1)

Place	Date	Hour	Summary of Events and Information	Remarks and references to Appendices
ALLOUAGNE	1-3-17		Five reinforcements joined for duty. All a good class of men who have served before & been down	
D7a 3.7. 36B			to the base sick. Officers Rest Station Area taken over from 74 Field Amb. Staff 1 Officer 20 O.R.	SRE
"	2-3-17		Visited 1st Corps Rest Station A section	SRE
"	3.3.17		Advance party to 1st Corps R. Station	SRE
"	4.3.17	9.30AM	Marched out of ALLOUAGNE to ~~[illegible]~~ LABEUVRIERE D17a.4.4 36B	SRE
LABEUVRIERE	4.3.17	11 AM	Took over 1st Corps Rest Station A section from 74 Field Ambulance 300 patients. The wards & surroundings	
D17a 4.4.36B			were dirty & billets very dirty & untidy. Forwarded report to OC 74 Field Ambulance.	SRE
"	5.3.17		ADMS. moves from LABEUVRIERE to BARLIN 1st CANADIAN DIV. H.Q. move into LABEUVRIERE	SRE
"	6.3.17		Duplicate war diary for Gov'nt forwarded to Records. War diary for Jan. Feb 17 to Base.	
			Sgt Tennas to Staff Sgt from 1-2-17. 1 Corps order No 5.	SRE
"	7.3-17.		Capt KIDD RAMC struck off strength & posted to 3 Australian Tunnelling Coy for duty.	SRE
"	8.3.17		Drew up plans for ploughing & cultivating land around C.R.Station.	SRE
"	9.3.17		DDMS I Corps inspected C.R.S. Capt LAING returned from duty with 2nd Leinsters	SRE
"	10.3.17		1st Corps Commander inspected C.R.Station.	SRE
"	11.3.17		Capt Bretherton returned from duty with 8 Queen's	
"	"		Capt. N.R MATHEWS A.A.M.C. attached for duty from 3rd Australian Tunnelling Coy	SRE

2353 Wt. W2544/1454 700,000 5/15 D. D. & L. A.D.S.S./Forms/C. 2118.

72 FIELD AMBULANCE

Instructions regarding War Diaries and Intelligence Summaries are contained in F. S. Regs., Part II. and the Staff Manual respectively. Title pages will be prepared in manuscript.

WAR DIARY
or
INTELLIGENCE SUMMARY.
(Erase heading not required.)

Army Form C. 2118.

Place	Date	Hour	Summary of Events and Information	Remarks and references to Appendices
LABEUVRIERE	12-3-17		—	
D17a 4.4.36b	13-3-17		—	
"	14-3-17		—	
"	15-3-17		—	
"	16-3-17		Inspected Officers Rest Station at AIRE & found everything satisfactory. Capt Mathews to 13 Middlesex temp duty. 8 Reinforcements O R joined for duty all men who have been down to Base sick fairly good physique. Capt Bretherton for duty with 24 Div. Training Btn.	BBR
"	17-3-17		Pte Wood F.A.V. to England for a commission	BBR
"	18-3-17	3. PM.	Attended ADMS I Corps conference at Noeux les Mines Nothing of any interest.	BBR
"	19-3-17		13 Corps billeted in Labeuvriere Tried to jump several of our billets, unsuccessfully;	BBR
"	20-3-17		Lieut W.A WILDBLOOD ASC joined from 24 Div Train for temporary duty as Transport Officer	BBR.
"	21-3-17		Forwarded a report to ADMS 24 Division pointing out the unsatisfactory manner in which the 24 S. S. Col carried out repairs to Ambulance Cars	BBR
			Arranged to see sick of 13 Corps at 10 am daily	BBR
	22-3-17		B Corps requested use of patients baths Regretted unable to meet their wishes	BBR

72 FIELD AMBULANCE

Instructions regarding War Diaries and Intelligence Summaries are contained in F. S. Regs., Part II. and the Staff Manual respectively. Title pages will be prepared in manuscript.

WAR DIARY
or
INTELLIGENCE SUMMARY.
(Erase heading not required.)

Army Form C. 2118.

(3)

Place	Date	Hour	Summary of Events and Information	Remarks and references to Appendices
LABEUVRIERE D17a44.36	23-3-17		Memo from DDMS pointing out that Diary for Aug 1916 had not been received. The Diary which covered active operation on Somme found & forwarded.	SBR
"	24-3-17		—	
"	25-3-17		—	
"	26-3-17		Report from OC 24 Div S. Col on Sgt Hatchell MT ASC my transport Sgt. Have asked OC 3rd S Col for a report on this NCO.	SBR
"	27-3-17		—	
"	28-3-17	10 am	Called at ADMS Office. He told me that I would be taking over an ADS at ABLAIN ST NAZAIRE X10b7.9 from 12 Canadian Field Ambulance on 1st. 1 Officer charger evacuated ruptured eye ball.	SBR
	29-3-17		Visited ADS ABLAIN ST NAZAIRE. Good accommodation in cellars requires cleaning up & repairing & proper fitting for Gas curtains. Can clear Aid Post at night only as the ADS & road (duck walk) up to Post are under direct observation from VIMY ridge. Captain C.S. McCONKEY RAMC SR. joined for duty from Rouen. Pte. Shields joined for duty from ADMS.	SBR SBR

72 FIELD AMBULANCE

Instructions regarding War Diaries and Intelligence Summaries are contained in F. S. Regs., Part II. and the Staff Manual respectively. Title pages will be prepared in manuscript.

WAR DIARY
or
INTELLIGENCE SUMMARY.
(Erase heading not required.)

Army Form C. 2118.

(4)

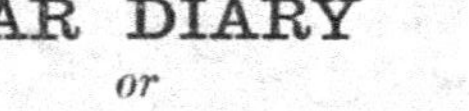

Place	Date	Hour	Summary of Events and Information	Remarks and references to Appendices
LABEUVRIERE D17a44 36B	30/3/17		Memo from DDMS 1st Corps to get in touch with 1st Corps agricultural expert 1st Corps Lieut C P MAC AULEY.	
			Met Lieut. MAC AULEY & discussed the question of suitable plants cabbage etc to be put in now. Arranged to supply two more animals for ploughing ground at LAPUGNOY. DADMS 1st Corps called to ask about arrangements made for disinfecting blankets.	
			Car No 7 returned from Aire. Ford No 1 sent to Aire to replace it.	
			Saw ADMS about rationing my party of 2 officers & 58 OR at ABLAIN ST NAZAIRE. They are too far for me to ration. Received memo from ADMS that the party were to be rationed by Btn occupying the area. This is most unsatisfactory as the Btn is constantly changing. Have arranged to ration the party up to & including the 2 April after which they will draw rations from 74 F Amb at Fosse 10 R8 central 36.B.	
			Capt Matthews returned from duty with 13th Middlesex Regt	[initials]

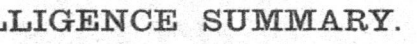

Army Form C. 2118.

72 FIELD AMBULANCE

WAR DIARY
or
INTELLIGENCE SUMMARY.
(Erase heading not required.)

(5)

Instructions regarding War Diaries and Intelligence Summaries are contained in F. S. Regs., Part II. and the Staff Manual respectively. Title pages will be prepared in manuscript.

Place	Date	Hour	Summary of Events and Information	Remarks and references to Appendices
LABEUVRIERE D17a 44 36 B	31-3-17		Capt Laing + Capt Eberts. 50 O.R proceeded to ADS ABLAIN ST NAZAIRE To be distributed as under. ABLAIN { 2 Officers 1 Car 1 Motor Cycle { 44 OR RAMC 2 OR MT ASC.	
			Grand Servins 12 Canadian F. Amb. 1 Car 1 Water Cart 1 OR RAMC 2 OR ~~MT~~ (1 HT. 1 MT) ASC	2 Mules
			Fosse × 74 Field Amb. { 1 Limber. 2 Mules 1 OR MT ASC { 1 OR RAMC	
			ADMS came round Corps Rest Station. An advance party from 16 Field Ambulance proceeded to Aire to take over Officers Rest Station on 1st. Capt Fuller (17 F Amb) in charge. Pte Lewis detailed for duty with 12 Labour Btn (Kings Liverpools) & struck off strength of this unit.	SJE
			S. J. S. Edwards Lt Col RAMC	

2353 Wt. W2544/1454 700,000 5/15 D. D. & L. A.D.S.S. Forms/C. 2118.

24th Div. 140/2086 MEDICAL 2·4

Apl. 1917 S Vol. 20

CONFIDENTIAL

WAR DIARY

OF

LIEUT COLONEL G.B. EDWARDS D.S.O.

OFFICER COMMANDING 72ND FIELD AMBULANCE.

FROM 1ST APRIL 1917 TO 30TH APRIL 1917

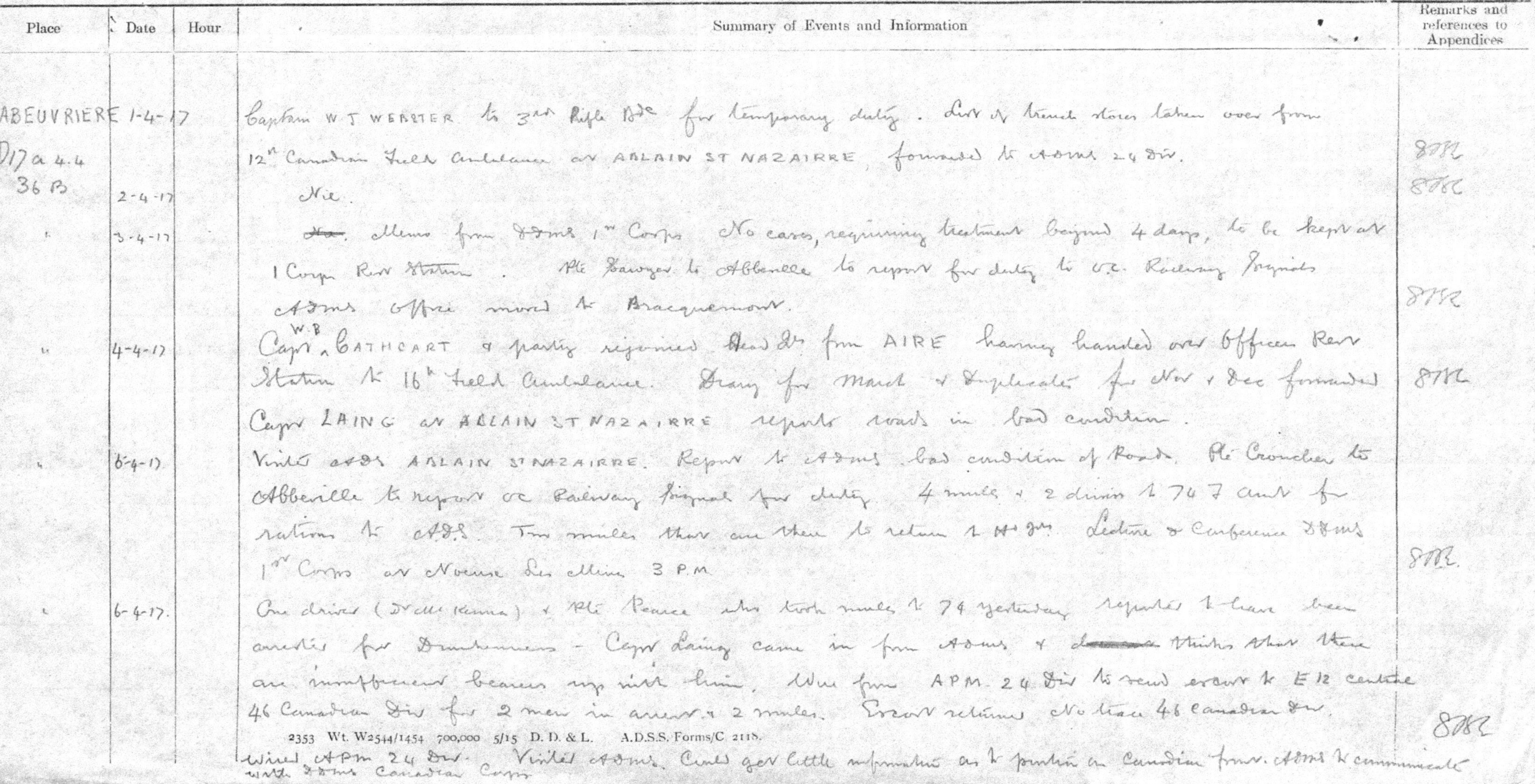

Army Form C. 2118.

Instructions regarding War Diaries and Intelligence Summaries are contained in F. S. Regs., Part II. and the Staff Manual respectively. Title pages will be prepared in manuscript.

72 FIELD AMBULANCE (Attd. 1st Corps Rest Stn) WAR DIARY or INTELLIGENCE SUMMARY. (1)

(Erase heading not required.)

Place	Date	Hour	Summary of Events and Information	Remarks and references to Appendices
LABEUVRIERE D17 a 4.4 36 B	1-4-17		Captain W. J. WEBSTER to 3rd Rifle Bde for temporary duty. List of trench stores taken over from 12th Canadian Field Ambulance at ABLAIN ST NAZAIRRE, forwarded to ADMS 24 Div.	SMR
	2-4-17		Nil.	SMR
"	3-4-17		Memo from DDMS 1st Corps No cases, requiring treatment beyond 4 days, to be kept at 1 Corps Rest Station. Pte Sawyer to Abbeville to report for duty to O.C. Railway Signals. ADMS Office moved to Bracquemont.	SMR
"	4-4-17		Capt W.B. CATHCART & party rejoined Head Qrs from AIRE having handed over Officers Rest Station to 16th Field Ambulance. Diary for March & Duplicate for Nov & Dec forwarded. Capt LAING at ABLAIN ST NAZAIRRE reports roads in bad condition.	SMR
"	5-4-17		Visited ADS ABLAIN ST NAZAIRRE. Report to ADMS bad condition of Roads. Pte Croucher to Abbeville to report OC Railway Signals for duty. 4 mules & 2 drivers to 74 F Amb for rations to ADS. Two mules that are there to return to H Qrs. Lecture & Conference DDMS 1st Corps at Noeux les Mines 3 P.M.	SMR
"	6-4-17		One driver (Dr McKenna) & Pte Pearce who took mules to 74 yesterday reported to have been arrested for Drunkenness – Capt Laing came in from ADMS & thinks that there are insufficient bearers up with him. Wire from APM 24 Div to send escort to E 12 central 46 Canadian Div for 2 men in arrest. 2 miles. Escort returned. No trace 46 Canadian Div. Wired APM 24 Div. Visited ADMS. Could get little information as to position in Canadian front. ADMS to communicate with DDMS Canadian Corps	SMR

2353 Wt. W2544/1454 700,000 5/15 D. D. & L. A.D.S.S. Forms/C 2118.

72 FIELD AMBULANCE

WAR DIARY
or
INTELLIGENCE SUMMARY.
(Erase heading not required.)

Army Form C. 2118.

Instructions regarding War Diaries and Intelligence Summaries are contained in F. S. Regs., Part II. and the Staff Manual respectively. Title pages will be prepared in manuscript.

(2)

Place	Date	Hour	Summary of Events and Information	Remarks and references to Appendices
D17a.4.4.	7-4-17		Capt H.S. GROVES 1 Sgt & 3 men to ADS ABLAIN ST NAZAIRE	SM
36B	8-4-17		Memo to APM 4 Canadian Div. re Pte Pearce asking for evidence of the men on Guard at time of his arrest. No evidence yet received re Dr McKenna. Both the above men brought here by Transport Officer who found them at BARLEM with APM. 4 C. Div.	SM
	9-4-17		Charge against Dr McKenna recd. Wishes to be tried by CM. Canadian Attack on Vimy Ridge successful. Evacuation of wounded very satisfactory.	SM
	10-4-17		Examined metallic poison testing apparatus & tried the various tests. Found in good condition	SM
	10-4-17		Pte Pearce 21 days FP No1. Dr McKenna 28 days FP No1.	
			Received No 9380 Napier car to replace 1 Sunbeam evacuated. Napier car bad construction for F.A. work front axle only 6" from ground also differential only 6" from ground. Report to OC 24 Div Supply Col.	SM
	11-4-17		Another Field Cashier 13 Corps found shot through head in dug-out. Brought to Corps Rest Station & report to 13th Corps.	SM
			Capt A.W. BRETHERTON struck off the ~~strength~~ to England. Contract expired	SM

2353 Wt. W2544/1454 700,000 5/15 D. D. & L. A.D.S.S. Forms/C 2118.

Instructions regarding War Diaries and Intelligence Summaries are contained in F. S. Regs., Part II. and the Staff Manual respectively. Title pages will be prepared in manuscript.

72 FIELD AMBULANCE **WAR DIARY** *or* **INTELLIGENCE SUMMARY.**

(Erase heading not required.)

Army Form C. 2118.

(3)

Place	Date	Hour	Summary of Events and Information	Remarks and references to Appendices
D17a 4.4 36B	12-4-17		Conference ADMS 24 Division 72 I. Bde attack	SM
"	13-4-17		13 Corps leave Labeuvrière.	
"	14-4-17	11.10AM	ADMS No 362/16 Send 1 Section to Girls school Bracquemont. B section under Capt Cathcart with Capt Matthews marched to Bracquemont at 11-20 am	SM
			Visited ADMS 4 Canadian Div to find out about relief of my Section at ADS ABLAIN. To be relieved by 12 Canadian F Amb this evening	
"	15-4-17		ADS ABLAIN relief completed & C Section rejoined Hd Qrs.	
			B. Section moved to Bully Grenay & took over bearer posts at Pt Grenay & S. Maroc & ADS Bully Grenay from 73 F Amb. Visited bearer posts & ADS. 73 not in touch with 72 Bde or regimental aid posts.	SM
			Capt Webster rejoined from 3rd R Bde.	
"	16-4-17		C. Section Capt McConkey, Capt Laing, Capt Sheit, Capt Grove, to Bracquemont	
			Pte Bignold wounded chest. Pte Athance wounded buttock.	SM
			1 Rides evacuated. In touch with 72 Bde & all regt aid posts. Evacuation satisfactory	
	17-4-17		C bearers to Cité St Pierre & ~~Calonne~~ Calonne. Pte Rust reported died of wounds received on 11th. Pte Durham wounded.	

2353 Wt. W2544/1454 700,000 5/15 D. D. & L. A.D.S.S. Forms/C. 2118.

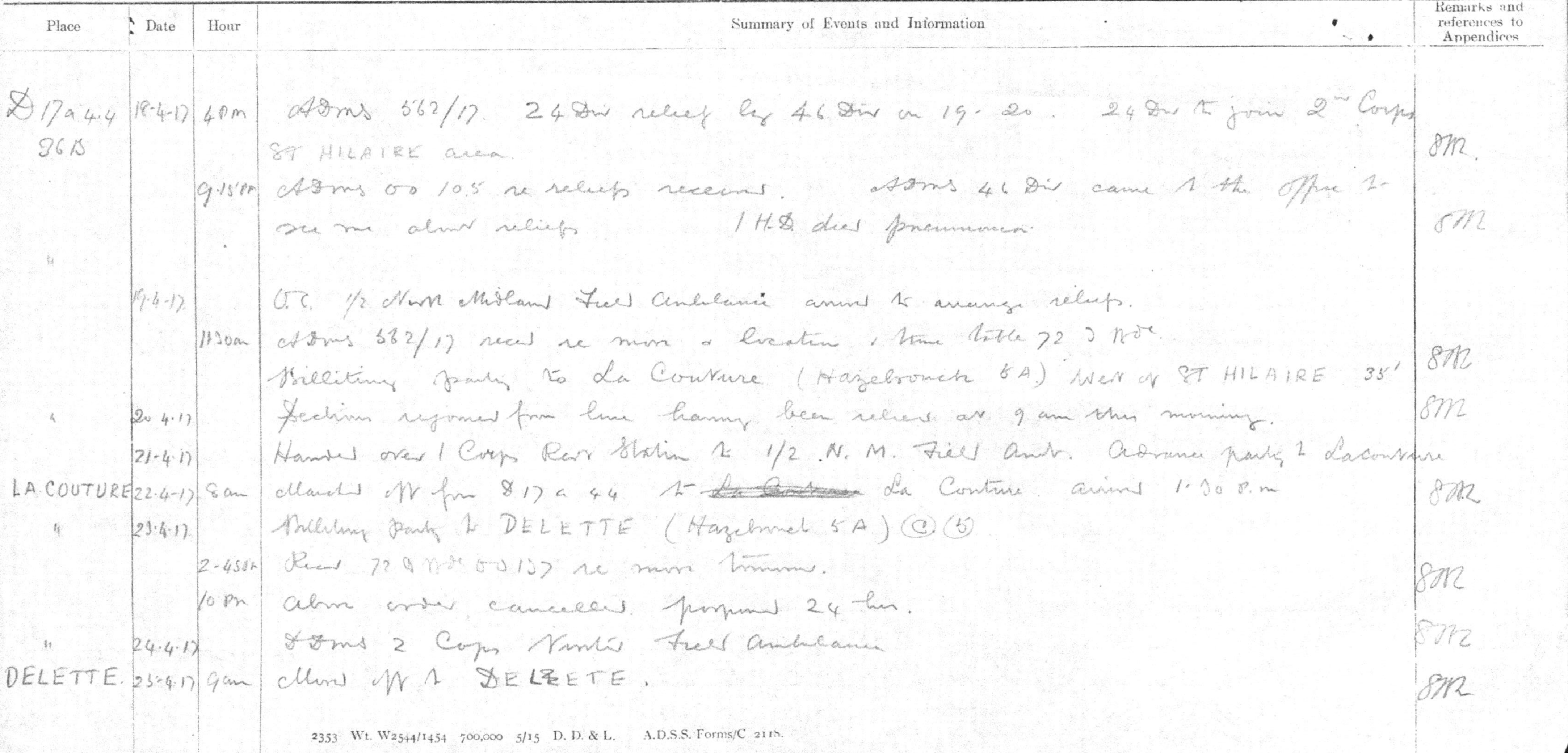

72 FIELD AMBULANCE **WAR DIARY** *or* **INTELLIGENCE SUMMARY.** (*Erase heading not required.*)

Army Form C. 2118.

Instructions regarding War Diaries and Intelligence Summaries are contained in F. S. Regs., Part II. and the Staff Manual respectively. Title pages will be prepared in manuscript.

(4)

Place	Date	Hour	Summary of Events and Information	Remarks and references to Appendices
S17a4.4 96B	18-4-17	4 PM	ADMS 562/17. 24 Div relief by 46 Div on 19-20. 24 Div to join 2nd Corps ST HILAIRE area.	SM.
		9.15 PM	ADMS OO 105 re relief received. ADMS 46 Div came to the Office to see me about relief. 1 H.D. died pneumonia.	SM
"	19-4-17		O.C. 1/2 North Midland Field Ambulance arrived to arrange relief.	
		11.30am	ADMS 562/17 recd re move & location & time table 72 I Bde. Billeting party to La Couture (Hazebrouck 5A) West of ST HILAIRE 35'	SM
"	20-4-17		Section rejoined from line having been relieved at 9 am this morning.	SM
	21-4-17		Handed over 1 Corps Rest Station to 1/2 N.M. Field Amb. Advance party to Lacouture	
LA COUTURE	22-4-17	8am	Marched off from S17a44 to ~~La Couture~~ La Couture arrived 1.30 p.m	SM
"	23-4-17		Billeting party to DELETTE (Hazebrouck 5A) (C)(5)	
		2-45pm	Recd 72 I Bde OO 137 re move tomorrow.	SM
		10 PM	Above order cancelled postponed 24 hrs.	
"	24-4-17		ADMS 2 Corps Visited Field Ambulance	SM
DELETTE.	25-4-17	9am	Moved off to DELETTE.	SM

72 FIELD AMBULANCE

Army Form C. 2118.

Instructions regarding War Diaries and Intelligence Summaries are contained in F. S. Regs., Part II. and the Staff Manual respectively. Title pages will be prepared in manuscript.

WAR DIARY
or
INTELLIGENCE SUMMARY.
(*Erase heading not required.*)

(5)

Place	Date	Hour	Summary of Events and Information	Remarks and references to Appendices
DELETTE	26.4.17		Nil	SM
"	27.4.17		Commenced course of training Programme [illegible]. Took over Scabies Hospital at MALANOY FARM NE of ST HILAIRE Capt Groves & 1 NCO 14 OR.	
			Capt Mathews to 24 Divisional Signal Coy for temporary duty.	SM
"	28/4/17		Nil	
"	29/4/17		Nil	
"	30/4/17		Capt. G.F. Lamey [?] struck off strength to 1st North Staffordshire Regt for duty. Capt. H. Blyth from 1 N Staffs taken on strength & temporary attached to 2 Corps D.D.M.S. Nine O.R. sent to Heavy Artillery Group for duty & struck off the ~~strength~~ T/3/029311 C. S. Mays [?] R. Bagshaw ASC taken on strength	SM

S.J. Edwards [?]
Lt Col RAMC
OC 72 Field Ambulance

May 1917

No 72 F a

140/2161

Medical

May 1917

S

CONFIDENTIAL

Vol 21

WAR DIARY

Vol VI

OF (LIEUT: COL: G.B. EDWARDS. D.S.O.)

OFFICER COMMANDING 1/2ND FIELD AMBULANCE

FROM 1st MAY 1917 TO 31st MAY 1917.

COPY.

5.

B.E.F.

SUMMARY OF MEDICAL WAR DIARIES of

72nd Field Ambulance,

24th Division,

1st Corps, 1st Army, till 21.4.17.,
2nd Corps, 1st Army, from 21.4.17-10.5.17.
2nd Corps, 2nd Army, from 10.5.17.

WESTERN FRONT, APRIL - MAY, 1917.

O.C. Lt.Colonel S. B. Edwards.

SUMMARISED UNDER THE FOLLOWING HEADINGS:-

Phase "B" - Battle of Arras. "April - May, 1917."

1st Period, April 1917. Attack on Vimy Ridge.

2nd Period, May 1917. Capture of Siegfried Line.

72nd F.A., 24th Division B.E.F. Western Front.

O.C. Lt.Col. S. B. Edwards. April 1917.

1st Corps, 1st Army, till 21.4.17. 1.
2nd Corps, from 21.4.17.

Phase "B" - Battle of Arras. "April - May, 1917."

1st Period, April 1917. Attack on Vimy Ridge.

April	H.Q. at Labeuvriere D.17.a.4.4. (36b) C.R.S.
4th	Med. Arr. Officers R.S. Aire handed over to 16th F.A.
15th	Moves det. & Med. Arr.
	C. section at A.D.S. Ablain relieved.
	B. section to Bully Grenay and took over Br. P. at Pr. Grenay, and S. Maroc and A.D.S. Bully Grenay from 75th F.A.
16th	Casualties R.A.M.C. 0 & 2 W.
	Moves det. "C" Brs. to Cite St. Pierre and Calonne.
17th	Casualties R.A.M.C. 0 & 1 D. of wounds. 0 & 1 wounded.
21st	Moves & Transfer To La Couture, 2nd Corps Area, on relief by 1/2nd N. Mid. F.A.

72nd F.A., 24th Division, B.E.F. Western Front.

O.C. Lt.Col. S. B. Edwards. April 1917.

2nd Corps, 1st Army. 2.

Phase "B" - Battle of Arras. "April - May, 1917."

1st Period, April 1917. Attack on Vimy Ridge.

April H.Q. at La Couture.

21st Moves & Transfer To La Couture, 2nd Corps Area.

25th Moves To Delette.

25th-30th Routine.

72nd F.A., 24th Division B.E.F. Western Front.

O.C. Lt.Col. S. B. Edwards. April 1917.

1st Corps, 1st Army, till 21.4.17. 1.
2nd Corps, from 21.4.17.

Phase "B" - Battle of Arras. "April - May, 1917."

1st Period, April 1917. Attack on Vimy Ridge.

April H.Q. at Labeuvriere D.17.a.4.4. (36b) C.R.S.

4th Med. Arr. Officers R.S. Aire handed over to 16th F.A.

15th Moves det. & Med. Arr.

C. section at A.D.S. Ablain relieved.

B. section to Bully Grenay and took over Br. P. at Pr. Grenay, and S. Maroc and A.D.S. Bully Grenay from 75th F.A.

16th Casualties R.A.M.C. 0 & 2 W.

Moves det. "C" Brs. to Cite St. Pierre and Calonne.

17th Casualties R.A.M.C. 0 & 1 D. of wounds. 0 & 1 wounded.

21st Moves & Transfer To La Couture, 2nd Corps Area, on relief by 1/2nd N. Mid. F.A.

72 FIELD AMBULANCE

Vol VI

WAR DIARY
or
INTELLIGENCE SUMMARY.
(Erase heading not required.)

Army Form C. 2118.

Instructions regarding War Diaries and Intelligence Summaries are contained in F. S. Regs., Part II. and the Staff Manual respectively. Title pages will be prepared in manuscript.

Place	Date	Hour	Summary of Events and Information	Remarks and references to Appendices
	1917			
DELETTE Sheet 5A 1/100,000	1 MAY		One rider received from 36 M.V.S. poor condition.	SSE
	2 "		Nil.	
"	3 "		Annual Field Amb Sports held. Men very keen & in excellent condition. Transport competition judged by O.C. 24 Divisional Train who complimented the men on their excellent turn out & good condition of all animals. Pte Holt rejoined unit not being required at HA Group.	SSE.
"	4 "		Nil	
"	5 "		Received 4 H.D. 1 Ride remounts for ADMS 24 Div. & 1 Mule 1 H.D. for 12 Sherwoods. Received a motor cycle from Div Supply Col after lengthy correspondence. Cycle is an old one with leaky petrol tank & repaired frame. Report to O.C. D.S. Col.	SSE.
"	6 "	10 am	ADMS OO 106 received. Handed over MALANOY Frm. Scabie Hosp to 74 Field Amb.	SSE

72 FIELD AMBULANCE

Vol VI

WAR DIARY
or
INTELLIGENCE SUMMARY.

(Erase heading not required.)

Army Form C. 2118.

Instructions regarding War Diaries and Intelligence Summaries are contained in F. S. Regs., Part II. and the Staff Manual respectively. Title pages will be prepared in manuscript.

(2)

Place	Date	Hour	Summary of Events and Information	Remarks and references to Appendices
DELETTE. 5.A. 1/100.000	1917 7th May		Capt. MATHEWS rejoined unit. Capt. GROVES to 24th Div. Signal Coy temp. duty.	SMR
"	8th "		Capt MATHEWS & 6 O.R. to rest camp at Seaside for 10 days. 3 H.D handed over to 74 F. Amb. 24 Div Band 25 strong reported to this unit without	
		3.50PM	rations Report forwarded to 24. Div H.Q. ADMS 582/19 Be ready to move off immediately	SMR
"		5 PM	ADMS OO 107. recd.	
"	9th		9 E Surreys to LIGNY 1 N. Staffs to RILY.	SMR
"	10th	10AM	Moved off from DELETTE	
BOESEGHEM		4.30PM	Arrived BOESEGHEM N.E. of AIRE. a long hot & dusty march. Men all in good condition two only fell out one sore feet, one exhaustion, GOC Div. watched unit march into camp. 8 RW. Kents DELETTE to WITTES. 72 Bde WANDONNE to BOESEGHEM 8 QUEENS ERNY to WITTES 9 E SURREYS LIGNY to BOESEGHEM. 1 N STAFFORDS RILY to BOESEGHEM. Visited Regt MOs & Bde H.Q. in new area arranged for stragglers on march ~~[illegible]~~ on 12th	SMR

2353 Wt. W2544/1454 700,000 5/15 D. D. & L. A.D.S.S. Forms/C 2118.

72 FIELD AMBULANCE

Vol VI

WAR DIARY
or
INTELLIGENCE SUMMARY.
(Erase heading not required.)

Army Form C. 2118.

(3)

Instructions regarding War Diaries and Intelligence Summaries are contained in F. S. Regs., Part II. and the Staff Manual respectively. Title pages will be prepared in manuscript.

Place	Date	Hour	Summary of Events and Information	Remarks and references to Appendices
BOESEGHEM 5A 1/100.000 NE. AIRE	1917 MAY 11th		Claim certificate & report on claim for 80 Francs damage at DELETTE forwarded to 72 I. Bde Claim disputed by me Estimate of actual damage 5 to 10 Francs.	[illegible]
	12	8 AM	Marched off from BOESEGHEM. to GODEWAERSVELDE arriving at 4 P.M. Carried 150 Stragglers of 72 I. Bde to new area	[illegible]
GODEWAERSVELDE Sheet 27 1/40.000. Q 12 b 1.4.	13th		Visited O.C. 69 F.A. 23rd Div at his M.D.S. VLAMERTINGHE "The MILL" H 2. c. 4 1. (28). Arranged to send advance party to night to ADS. "The Bund" I 15 d 1.1 (28) [illegible] Post "Cow Farm" I 22 b. 4. 2. R.A.Ps "Halfway house" I 17. c 6. 8. & Stafford Trench. I 24 c. 5.6 Some misunderstanding at first I was told to take over from 69 FA. now it appears that they are to retain the Bund & part of Stafford Trench. I am to form a new ADS alongside them. Main Dressing Station to be a hut at Brandhoek G 12 b 5.9. (28) I am also to form a X Corps M.D.S for lightly wounded in field where hut is situated. 71 Field Amb have a working party in this field. Several Field Ambs have been in & out & although the plans were drawn up some time ago practically nothing has been done & very little material is at hand. Took over plans etc from O.C. 71 F Amb	

2353 Wt. W2544/1454 700,000 5/15 D. D. & L. A.D.S.S. Forms/C. 2118.

72 FIELD AMBULANCE

Vol VI

WAR DIARY
or
INTELLIGENCE SUMMARY.
(Erase heading not required.)

Army Form C. 2118.

Instructions regarding War Diaries and Intelligence Summaries are contained in F. S. Regs., Part II. and the Staff Manual respectively. Title pages will be prepared in manuscript.

(4)

Place	Date	Hour	Summary of Events and Information	Remarks and references to Appendices
BRANDHOCK	1917 May			
G12 b 5.9 Sheet 28 1/40 000.	13th	5 PM	Marched off from GODEWAERSVELDE arrived Brandhock at 5 P.M. Personnel bivouac in field	SM
"	14th		72 I Bde now in the line & 1 Section of Field Ambulance Capt ROBSON & Lt WINDSOR joined for duty. The latter only attached Indents for material submitted to X Corps DDMS for approval	
"	15th		Went round ADS. Bearer posts & RAPs & visited Bde HQ. at YPRES.	SM
			New plan of camp drawn up & submitted to DDMS X Corps.	
"	16th	6 PM	Gas alert. Drawing material for Camp. Tents, marquees, timber, cement, lamps etc etc.	SM
	17		Nil.	SM
"	18th		DDMS X Corps visited camp.	SM
	19		Good progress being made in construction of X C M D S. L. Wounded	SM
	20		Some difficulty in obtaining material	SM
	21		Nil.	SM
	22		do	SM
	23		2nd Army Commander & DMS 2 Army DDMS 14 Corps DDMS X Corps inspected camp	SM

72 Field Ambulance

WAR DIARY

Vol VI

or

INTELLIGENCE SUMMARY.

(Erase heading not required.)

(5)

Army Form C. 2118.

Instructions regarding War Diaries and Intelligence Summaries are contained in F. S. Regs., Part II. and the Staff Manual respectively. Title pages will be prepared in manuscript.

Place	Date	Hour	Summary of Events and Information	Remarks and references to Appendices
	1917 May			
C 12 b 5.9. Sheet 28	24.		Capt McCONKEY on leave to England. Capt MATHEWS rejoined with 6 O.R. from Seaside Rest Camp	SM
"	25		Capt MATHEWS to 12 Australian F. Ambulance. 9 Marquees received from X Corps R.E. dump with wrong poles etc. Reported to DDMS X Corps	SM
"	26.		Heard that when completed that 67 F. Amb will probably take over	SM
"	27		Work on camp being pushed on but a great deal of delay being caused by difficulty in obtaining supplies & tent poles.	SM
"	~~28~~	2am	Gas alarm O.O. 72 Bde 144 recd O.O. ADMS 111 recd.	SM
"	~~28~~.		Adv party 97 F Amb arrived. Adv party of 96 F Amb arrived & detailed to relieve similar number of my men in the forward posts. Recd 1 Triumph Cycle in good condition.	
"	29.		Camp nearly completed a few more tents to erect. Kitchens, latrines, Offices, Ablution benches & shelters, duck walks etc completed. 97 F Amb arrived	SM
"	~~30~~.		Adv Party of 72 F Amb to Camp at R 5 a 5.0 Sheet 27. 96 FA relieved bearers in the line	SM SM
	30		Handed over to 97 F Amb & moved Ambulance to R 5 a 5.0. Sheet 27.	SM
"	31		Kit Inspection, Equipment overhauled, SM	

S J J Evans Lt Col RAMC
O.C. 72. Field Ambulance.

2353 Wt. W2544/1454 700,000 5/15 D. D. & L. A.D.S.S. Forms/C 2118.

Carbons.

B.E.F.

SUMMARY OF MEDICAL WAR DIARIES of

72nd Field Ambulance,

24th Division,

1st Corps, 1st Army, till 21.4.17.,
2nd Corps, 1st Army, from 21.4.17-10.5.17
2nd Corps, 2nd Army, from 10.5.17.

WESTERN FRONT, APRIL - MAY, 1917.

O.C. Lt.Colonel S. B. Edwards.

SUMMARISED UNDER THE FOLLOWING HEADINGS:-

Phase "B" - Battle of Arras. "April - May, 1917."

1st Period, April 1917. Attack on Vimy Ridge.

2nd Period, May 1917. Capture of Siegfried Line.

72nd F.A., 24th Division B.E.F. Western Front.

O.C. Lt.Col. S. B. Edwards. May 1917.

2nd Corps, 1st Army, till 10.5.17. 1.
2nd Corps, 2nd Army, from 10.5.17.

Phase "B" - Battle of Arras . "April - Mat 1917."

May H.Q. at Delette.

6th Med. Arr. Scabies Hospital Malanoy Farm handed over to 74th F.A.

10th Moves & Transfer To Boeseghem, 2nd Army Area.

72nd F.A., 24th Division B.E.F. Western Front.

O.C. Lt.Col. S. B. Edwards. May 1917.

2nd Corps, 1st Army, till 10.5.17. 1.
2nd Corps, 2nd Army, from 10.5.17.

Phase "B" - Battle of Arras . "April - Mat 1917."

May H.Q. at Delette.

6th Med. Arr. Scabies Hospital Malancy Farm handed over to 74th F.A

10th Moves & Transfer To Boeseghem, 2nd Army Area.

(6339) Wt. W160/M3016 1,500,000 10/17 McA & W Ltd (E 1898) Forms W3091. Army Form W.3091.

Cover for Documents.

Nature of Enclosures.

S U R G E R Y.

20. Eyes.

Notes, or Letters written.

Vol 22

CONFIDENTIAL.

June 1917

5

140/2230

War Diary

of

Lieut-Col. G.B. EDWARDS. D.S.O.,

72nd Field Ambulance.

from 1 June 1917 to 30 June 1917

(Volume VII)

Army Form C. 2118.

72 Field Ambulance

Vol VII

Instructions regarding War Diaries and Intelligence Summaries are contained in F. S. Regs., Part II. and the Staff Manual respectively. Title pages will be prepared in manuscript.

WAR DIARY
or
INTELLIGENCE SUMMARY.
(Erase heading not required.)

(1)

Place	Date	Hour	Summary of Events and Information	Remarks and references to Appendices
R5a 5.0. Sheet 27 1/40 000	1 June 1917		Capt Eberts struck off strength on expiration of contract & proceeding to England	8MK
do	2/6/17		Lieut. Windrow posted to 8th R.W. Kents. Lieut H. Blythe rejoined from leave	8MK
do	4/6/17		One rider evacuated for continued lameness. Went round forward area with Brigadier 72 I. Bde visited 41 Div H.Q & studied model of ground over which coming offensive is to take place	8MK
M.3 a 5 2. Sheet 28 1/40,000	5/6/17		Capt. McConkey rejoined from leave. Moved to M. 3a. 5.2 sheet 28	
"	6/6/17		Drew from DADOS. 40 waterbottles for Div Band. 12 men of Div Band to 73 FA 12 to 74 F Amb. Five O.R. reported for temporary duty from 139 Field Ambulance. Drew 12 stretchers & 20 blankets from 73 F Amb. 1 Officer 1 NCO & 11 OR to Wellington Post. G 24 d 3.4. to form collecting post for wounded arriving by light railway. Visited Bde H.Q 72 I Bde	8MK
"	7/6/17	3.10am	Attack on Messines Ridge opened. Visited 72 I Bde at H. 34 central (28).	
		3 PM.	1 Officer 18 OR. to assist 74 FA at Voormezeele I 31 c central (28)	
		4 PM.	Bearer Division & 3 Officers to field near 72 I Bde HQ at H 34 central	
			Visited Wellington Post no patients appear to be coming that way. Visited ADMS	8MK
	8/6/17.		Took over ADS. at Dickebusch H 33 b 6.9. (sheet 28) & ADS Voormezeele I 31 c central (28) from 138 F. Amb & bearer posts in front of Voormezeele from 74 & 73 F Amb ~~with~~ the Bearer Division at H 34 central moved to occupy these stations	8MK

2353 Wt. W2544/1454 700,000 5/15 D. D. & L. A.D.S.S. Forms/C. 2118.

Army Form C. 2118.

Instructions regarding War Diaries and Intelligence Summaries are contained in F. S. Regs., Part II. and the Staff Manual respectively. Title pages will be prepared in manuscript.

42 Field Ambulance
Vol VII

WAR DIARY
or
INTELLIGENCE SUMMARY.
(Erase heading not required.)

(2)

Place	Date	Hour	Summary of Events and Information	Remarks and references to Appendices
M 3 a 5.2 sheet 28 1/40000	9-6-17		H.Q & Transport Lines at M 3 a 5.2. sheet 28 Ambulance remaining closed A.D.S. Dickebusch H 33 b 6.9 (28) evacuating through Corps main Dressing Station ~~at~~ at BRANDHOEK Collecting Post at Voormezeele I 31 c central Bearer Posts in front to Trolley Head The area in front of this being cleared by 73 & 74 F Amb bearers Visited A.D.S. Collecting Post & Bearer Posts wounded being got away ~~satisfactorily~~	SBR
do.	10-6-17		1 Officer & 10 O.R. 131 F Amb handed over to me by 138 F Amb now returned to their unit. also 5 O.R. 134 F Amb returned to their unit	
	11-6-17		Visited 69 Field Amb at Vlamertinghe Mill H. 8. a 3.9 sheet 28 & made arrangements preparatory to taking over tomorrow but it doubtful if I will take over as have received three orders to day which have been cancelled. Cases now being sent from A.D.S to M.D.S. 140 F. Amb. at M 6 a. 88	SBR
		6 PM	Capt McConkey & Adv party of 2 NCOs & 10 O.R. to 69 F Amb. Arr to take over tomorrow	
	12-6-17.		Orders to take over from 69 F.A. cancelled. 138 F Amb are to relieve me at A.D.S. Collecting Post & Bearer Posts Relief complete at 1 P.M. & Personnel returned to H.Q at M 3 a 5.2 sheet 28. Visited ADMS who told me to get into communication with O.Cs F. Ambs who had ADS's etc in part of line which 24 Div would be holding shortly. Visited OC 69 F.A. at Vlamertinghe. also OC 96 F.A.	SBR

2353 Wt. W2544/1454 700,000 5/15 D. D. & L. A.D.S.S./Forms/C 2118.

Instructions regarding War Diaries and Intelligence Summaries are contained in F. S. Regs., Part II. and the Staff Manual respectively. Title pages will be prepared in manuscript.

72 Field Ambulance

WAR DIARY
or
INTELLIGENCE SUMMARY.
(Erase heading not required.)

Vol VII

Army Form C. 2118.

(3)

Place	Date	Hour	Summary of Events and Information	Remarks and references to Appendices
M3 a 5.2 Sheet 28 1/40000	12.6.17		Visited OC 5 London FA at Brandhoek G 12 b 6.9. Sheet 28 also X Corps Collecting post at KRUISSTRAAT. H24 a 6 9. Sheet 28. 1 Officer 1 NCO & 17 OR sent to report to Capt. McConkey who has now formed ADS at The Bund I 15 d 1.0. Sheet 28 with a collecting post at Kruisstraat G24 a 6.9 (28) & I 13 a 6.2. (28)	
"	13.6.17		Went round line visiting ADS Woodcot house I 20 c 5.2 (28) The Bluff. Hedgerow. Lovers Lane Sunset Subway. Have posted bearers of 74 F Amb in this part of the line. Have not taken over any of these posts as the Divisions have holding parties in them from various Field Ambulances as although we are in the line which has to evacuate via these posts the posts themselves are not in our area. Pte Young Pte Grits evacuated Gassed (shell) All bearer posts ADS etc staffed for attack tomorrow. Personnel distributed as under	
"	~~14/17~~		N. Sector 72 Field Amb Car stand at H24 a 6.9 2 cars. 1 NCO & 5 OR. Railway Germans cases unloaded from ADS at I 13 a 6 2. 1 Officer 1 NCO 6 OR. ADS The Bund. I 15 d 1 0. Bearer relay Posts at Cow Farm I 22 b 4 2. Shaftord Street I 24 c 5.3 ADS Railway Dugouts I 21 c. 5 4. Bearer Posts The Halt. I 22 c.7.3. Larch wood I 33 c. 3.5. 4 bearers with each Regt Aid Post & 2 runners also 2 runners at 72 Inf Bde S Sector. ADS Woodcot house. I 20 d 5.2. Collecting Post The Bluff. I 33 c. 2.8. Bearer Posts at Sunset Subway I 34 c 1.2. Hedge Row. I 34 a 7.5. Lovers Lane I 34 b 6.2. Bearers with Regt Aid Posts	878

2353 Wt. W2544/1454 700,000 5/15 D. D. & L. A.D.S.S. Forms/C. 2118.

72 Field Ambulance

Vol VII

Instructions regarding War Diaries and Intelligence Summaries are contained in F. S. Regs., Part II. and the Staff Manual respectively. Title pages will be prepared in manuscript.

WAR DIARY
or
INTELLIGENCE SUMMARY.
(Erase heading not required.)

Army Form C. 2118.

4

Place	Date	Hour	Summary of Events and Information	Remarks and references to Appendices
M 3a 5.2 Sheet 28	13/6/17	Continued	Horse Amb 6 at H24 a 6.9 also 2 cars. Horse Amb 3 at Car regulating post at H32 d 9.4. also 8 cars. 2 Cars at I 20 d 5.2. All cases to be evacuated to 140 F Amb at M 6 a 8.8	SMR
	14/6/17		Arrange to Ration 95 OR Salvage Coy. Visited Bund & Railway Dugouts. 17 Reinforcements reported for duty. Pte Armitage evacuated Shell Shock. Attack by 17 & 72 Bde carried out successfully at 7.30 am.	SMR
	15/6/17		Selected site at H24 a 7.9 (25) for A.D.S.	SMR
H24 a 7.9 (Sheet 28)	16/6/17		Moved H.Q & Transport to H24 a 7.9. 1 Officer 12 OR 74 F Amb attached for duty at the Bund.	SMR
	17/6/17		Visited ADS Railway Dugouts & Bde H.Q at Larch wood & all bearer Posts. Very heavy shelling railways almost impossible nearly all cases have to be hand carried. Bearers very exhausted. ADMS asked to supply a relief all my bearers being in the line. Casualties to day Killed O.R. 6 Wounded 16.	SMR
	18/6/17		1st Lt Kellogg U.S.A. medical Reserve Corps sent to me for duty. 12 OR 74 F Amb attached for duty.	SMR

2353 Wt. W2544/1454 700,000 5/15 D. D. & L. A.D.S.S./Forms/C. 2118.

Instructions regarding War Diaries and Intelligence Summaries are contained in F. S. Regs., Part II. and the Staff Manual respectively. Title pages will be prepared in manuscript.

72 Field Ambulance
Vol VII

WAR DIARY
or
INTELLIGENCE SUMMARY.
(*Erase heading not required.*)

Army Form C. 2118.

(5)

Place	Date	Hour	Summary of Events and Information	Remarks and references to Appendices
H24a7.9 Sheet 28	19/7/17		Motor Car got up as far as Transport Farm I 21 a 6.2 (sheet 28) early this morning & cleared 4 stretcher cases as the railway across the Knollstraat has been too badly damaged to use by day.	SRR
"	20/6/17		Enemy shelling this camp 1 mule wounded 2 officers & several OR of 10 N Fusiliers killed. DDMS X Corps visited unit this morning. Tried to persuade him to leave a couple of MAC cars here as mine are fully worked & it throws a great strain on them evacuating urgent cases to CCS as well as clearing the line. DDMS does not think it safe for MAC cars !! G.O.C. 24 Div visited the unit this afternoon. MAC have arranged to clear three times a day 5 am. 2 p.m. 10 p.m.	SRR
"	21/6/17		Hun still shelling fields round about	SRR
"	22/6/17		O.C. 70 F Amb came up to find out medical arrangements	SRR
"	23/6/17		Shelling more marked last two days several 8" round about dressing station & cellars.	SRR

2353 Wt. W2544/1454 700,000 5/15 D. D. & L. A.D.S.S./Forms/C. 2118.

Instructions regarding War Diaries and Intelligence Summaries are contained in F. S. Regs., Part II. and the Staff Manual respectively. Title pages will be prepared in manuscript.

72 F Ambulance

Vol VII

WAR DIARY
or
INTELLIGENCE SUMMARY.

(Erase heading not required.)

(6)

Army Form C. 2118.

Place	Date	Hour	Summary of Events and Information	Remarks and references to Appendices
H24a79 Sheet 28	23/7/17		Capt Cathcart, Capt Webster, Capt Allen (73 F.A.) to relieve Capt McCartney, Capt Webster, Lt Pedley. Capt Robson from Kruisstaat to 73 F.A. 1 H.D. horse killed shell	
"	24/7/17		Relieved 33 bearers + 2 NCOs by similar number of 73 F Amb. ADS at Bund blown away. Railway unable to be used. Evacuation very difficult but am running cars as far up as possible although roads are bad & heavily shelled so far have escaped any serious damage. Visited ADS Railway Dugout. Found new ADS in small dug out at Bund.	SBE
	25/7/17		Post at Kruisstaat blown in unable to hold it any longer. 1 Motor Cycle smashed to pieces. Have stopped stretcher cars coming via Kruisstaat now come via Shrapnel corner & Café Belge.	
	26/7/17		Adv Party 70 F Amb arrived	SBE
	27/7/17		Capt Briggs joined for duty	
	28/7/17		Relieved by 70 Field Ambulance.	
	30/7/17		Entrained for Rest Area.	

S B Emmons Lt Col Comdg
O.C. 72 Field Ambulance

2353 Wt. W2544/1454 700,000 5/15 D. D. & L. A.D.S.S./Forms/C. 2118.

July 1917

Vol 23

140/2289

CONFIDENTIAL

WAR DIARY

OF (Lt. Col. G. B. EDWARDS D.S.O.)

OFFICER COMMANDING 1/2nd FIELD AMBULANCE

FROM 1st JULY 1917 TO 31st JULY 1917.

72 Field Ambulance

Instructions regarding War Diaries and Intelligence Summaries are contained in F. S. Regs., Part II. and the Staff Manual respectively. Title pages will be prepared in manuscript.

WAR DIARY
or
~~INTELLIGENCE SUMMARY.~~
(Erase heading not required.)

Vol. VIII

Army Form C. 2118.

(1)

Place	Date	Hour	Summary of Events and Information	Remarks and references to Appendices
LUMBRES Sheet A B. B. 4. 4.	July 1.		Erected tents & opened for patients. Indents for equipment to complete forwarded. Reinforcements examined [illegible]	8MR
"	2		Cases for evacuation Sitting to 10 CCS Stretcher 58 CCS [illegible] 10 CCS.	8MR
"	3.		Nil	8MR
	4		ADMS on leave. Took over duties ADMS Attended conference DAQ Examined P.B. men	8MR
"	5		Nil.	8MR
"	6.		1 H.D & 1 Ride received. Capt Briggs to 8 Queens temp duty. 11 Reinforcements arrived.	8MR
"	7		Nil	8MR
	8		Capt Lodge Patch from 8 Queens reported for duty	8MR
	9		Nil	8MR
	10		Nil	8MR
	11		Nil.	8MR
	12		Nil [illegible] on leave.	8MR
	13.		Two reinforcements reported for duty	8MR
	14		Nil	8MR
	15		Pte Howard to 1 N. Staffs for water duties.	8MR

2353 Wt. W2544/1454 700,000 5/15 D. D. & L. A.D.S.S. Forms/C. 2118.

72 Field Ambulance

Instructions regarding War Diaries and Intelligence Summaries are contained in F. S. Regs., Part II. and the Staff Manual respectively. Title pages will be prepared in manuscript.

WAR DIARY
or
INTELLIGENCE SUMMARY.
(Erase heading not required.)

Vol VIII (2)

Army Form C. 2118.

Place	Date	Hour	Summary of Events and Information	Remarks and references to Appendices
LUMBRES	July			
"	16		Capt. Robson to 13 Middlesex temp duty. Lieut Pedley 8 R. W. Kents temp duty	BBL
"	17		Unit moved off at 5 am to RENESCURE area E 8. 0. (5A.) with composite Bde of 2 Btns 72nd Bde & 1 of 17th & 73rd Bde. Returned from leave	BBL
RENESCURE ~~Foot~~ T5c1.0 Sheet 27.	18		Moved off at 5.30 am to march to CAESTRE area. Advance party found that billets were already occupied eventually obtained billets at V 11. c. 3.6. Sheet 28 instead of W. 3 central arrived at destination at 10 am.	BBL.
V11.c.3.6 Sheet 28.	19.		Moved off at 8 am arrived Q 19. c. 3.6. Sheet 27 at 9.30 am. Capt Lodge Patch to Queens. Capt Briggs rejoined unit.	BBL.
Q19.c.3.6 Sheet 27.	20.		Moved off at 5.30 am to G 26 d 0.1. Sheet 28 arrived at 9.30 am. Capt Pedley rejoined unit.	BBL.
	21.		Visited OC 70 F. Amb at DICKEBUSCH & went round the line LOCK 8. LARCH WOOD COMPTON CORNER CANADA ST TUNNELS visited all the Regt aid Posts & discussed plans with OC 70 FA. II Corps Z scheme medical arrangements received	BBL
	22		Advance Party 1 Officer & 28 O.R. to 70 F. Amb at DICKEBUSH to take over ADS. etc at Railway Dugouts, Manor Farm Larch wood I 21, 22, 29 (Sheet 28)	BBL
	23.		Took over Main Dressing Station at DICKEBUSCH H 34 a. 6.9. Sheet 28 from OC 70 F. Amb. Relief completed at 10.30 am.	BBL

2353 Wt. W2544/1454 700,000 5/15 D. D. & L. A.D.S.S. Forms/C. 2118.

Instructions regarding War Diaries and Intelligence Summaries are contained in F. S. Regs., Part II. and the Staff Manual respectively. Title pages will be prepared in manuscript.

72 Field Ambulance **WAR DIARY** *or* **INTELLIGENCE SUMMARY.** Vol VIII (3)

(Erase heading not required.)

Army Form C. 2118.

Place	Date	Hour	Summary of Events and Information	Remarks and references to Appendices
DICKEBUSCH	July			
H34a69	24.		Visited Lock 8 at 4 am. Place very heavily gassed with gas shells had to keep box respirator	
sheet 28			on all the time. 1 NCO + 4 men holding this place as an ADS later on.	SMR
	24		Visited Lock 8 at 3 pm arranged to send up working party of six men to-night.	
			1 Lt Walker USA attached for temporary duty. Capt Pore MO 9 E Surreys killed	SMR
	25.		1 Officer 20 OR 74 F Amb reported for duty at Larch Wood	
			1 Officer 20 OR 73 " " " " "	
			1 Officer & remainder of Bearer Division 74 F Amb reported for duty.	
			1 Officer & 46 OR 73 F Amb reported for duty.	
			Lt Stephens USA reported for duty.	
			Dr Higgins + Pte Sanderson wounded Dr Higgins died shortly afterwards	
			1 Sgt Clerk sent to II C Main Dressing Station for duty	SMR.
			Corps Main Dressing Station Opened. All records to be taken there. Field Amb books closed at 12 noon	
	26.		Visited Lock 8 & Larch Wood	
			Capt Selby attached for duty.	
			Capt Robson + Capt Stephens to Corps Main Dressing Station for duty	SMR

2353 Wt. W2544/1454 700,000 5/15 D. D. & L. A.D.S.S. Forms/C. 2118.

72 Field Ambulance **WAR DIARY** *or* **INTELLIGENCE SUMMARY.** Vol VIII

(4)

Army Form C. 2118.

Instructions regarding War Diaries and Intelligence Summaries are contained in F. S. Regs., Part II. and the Staff Manual respectively. Title pages will be prepared in manuscript.

(Erase heading not required.)

Place	Date	Hour	Summary of Events and Information	Remarks and references to Appendices
DICKEBUSCH	July			
H34a6.9 Sheet 28	27.		Holding party of 1 Officer Capt Price 73 F.A & 6 OR withdrawn from Woodcote house.	SBR
"	28.		Capt Briggs to England to Report to India Office Struck off strength	
			Sgt Hatchell ASC MT recommended for D.C.M. for action in saving a car on 25/7/17	
			Enemy shelled Dickebusch with gas shells at 1.30 am whole camp sneezing.	SBR
"	29		Capt Robson & Capt Stephens evacuated sick	
"	30		All bearers now in line Collecting Post at Larch Wood ADS at Lock 8 evacuation by trolleys from Larch Wood to Lock 8 & thence by Cars, MDS I 11 c in. D.S. H 27 a. 0.0 Sheet 28. Pioneers detailed to keep line in repair.	SBR
			Divisional Band 2 NCOs + 22 OR reported for duty as bearers also Div Concert Party 1 NCO 7 OR	SBR
"	31		Established a Loading Post to load W. wounded on trams at I 31. a 6.0. Sheet 28. 2 Officers & 66 OR 24 TMB & 4 Officers & 100 OR 247 MGC reported at 4 am for duty as stretcher bearers All sent to Lock 8 & from thence to Larch Wood.	
		3.50am	Attack opened. 4.30 am went up to Lock 8 & Larch Wood. Evacuation working satisfactorily Tram line blown up in many places but repaired & in working order at 6.10 am.	

S B Edmunds
Lt Col RAMC
OC 72 F. Amb.

16 140/2364 MEDICAL.

Aug 1917

S

Vol 24

CONFIDENTIAL

WAR DIARY

OF

LIEUT COLONEL G.B. EDWARDS. D.S.O.

OFFICER COMMANDING 72ND FIELD AMBULANCE

FROM 1 Aug 1917 TO 31 Aug 1917

42 Field Ambulance . **WAR DIARY** *or* **INTELLIGENCE SUMMARY.** (*Erase heading not required.*)

Vol IX

(1).

Army Form C. 2118.

Instructions regarding War Diaries and Intelligence Summaries are contained in F. S. Regs., Part II. and the Staff Manual respectively. Title pages will be prepared in manuscript.

Place	Date	Hour	Summary of Events and Information	Remarks and references to Appendices
DICKEBUSCH H34a6.9 Sheet 28.	Aug 1917 1st		Very bad weather has been raining all night & continues	
		9-15 AM	Memo from ADMS instructing me to detail 50 bearers to report to 14 D. Bde as they are asking for them. There is a large reserve of Bearers at Larch Wood next door to the Bde & altogether there are over 300 bearers in the line	
		11 am	Wire from 14 D Bde saying more bearers required large number of wounded to be collected. Later this was proved to be incorrect. This Bde has in every action wired for bearers when they were not required. Have reported to ADMS.	
		11 am	39 O.R. (Infantry) arrived from reinforcement camp to act as bearers No nominal roll & fully equipped Them have been sent to Larch Wood under Capt Russell to report to Capt McCurkey. Personnel of T.M.B.s sent up yesterday to assist bearers have been relieved to day They were not of the great assistance & their heart did not appear to be in the work	8MR
	2nd		Visited ADS Lock 8 & Larch Wood. Country in very bad condition & ground so soft & muddy that it takes six to eight bearers to manage one stretcher case from front line. Gone to run for men in forward area	8MR
	3rd		~~Four reliefs~~ reliefs of Rame Personnel carried out to day. 1 Sgt & 21 O.R. of 74 7 [illegible] being relieved	8MR

2353 Wt. W2544/1454 700,000 5/15 D. D. & L. A.D.S.S. Forms/C. 2118.

Instructions regarding War Diaries and Intelligence Summaries are contained in F. S. Regs., Part II. and the Staff Manual respectively. Title pages will be prepared in manuscript.

72 Field Ambulance

WAR DIARY
or
INTELLIGENCE SUMMARY.
(Erase heading not required.)

Vol. IX

(2)

Army Form C. 2118.

Place	Date	Hour	Summary of Events and Information	Remarks and references to Appendices
H34 a & 9 Sheet 28	Aug. 1917			
	3	Continued	1 Sgt. 2 Cpls + 35 O.R. 73 F Amb relieved. Sgt Richardson & Pte Dicker killed on the way down	
			12 O.R. 72 F Amb relieved. 1 NCO 17 O.R. Divisional Concert party withdrawn from W.W. loading point	SRR
	4		Investigated case of C.S.M. at 104 F Coy R.E. H34 (sheet 28). Report forwarded to ADMS	SRR.
	5		Contacts of above case 2 sent to 74 F Amb for isolation	SRR
	6.		Two rides handed over to 179 Bde. 24 Div Band & reinforcements withdrawn from the line.	
			Ranee bearers only now working the evacuations.	SRR.
	7		Capt J VANDANDAIGUE R.A.M.C. attached to this unit for temporary duty.	
			1 Ride handed over to 72 I. Bde. This now reduces my establishment to 8 rides	SRR
			Cpl Franklin recommended D.C.M. Pte ... Naughton for M.M.	
			Cpl Franklin admitted to 74 F Amb & evacuated to 3 Canadian C.C.S.	SRR
	8		Sgt Hatchell A.S.C. attached to this unit awarded D.C.M.	
	9.		Visited ADS Loch 8 & Larch Wood. Bearers having a hard time on account of the bad weather & long carry but all appear cheerful under exceptionally trying conditions. It has been found necessary to employ bearers in front of RAPs as the carry to the RAP is too great for the Regt Bearers & there is no place for a RAP further forward so that was done.	SRR

2353 Wt. W2544/1454 700,000 5/15 D. D. & L. A.D.S.S. Forms/C. 2118.

Army Form C. 2118.

WAR DIARY
or
INTELLIGENCE SUMMARY.
(Erase heading not required.)

Instructions regarding War Diaries and Intelligence Summaries are contained in F. S. Regs., Part II. and the Staff Manual respectively. Title pages will be prepared in manuscript.

72 Field Amb. Vol IX

3

Place	Date	Hour	Summary of Events and Information	Remarks and references to Appendices
H34a.3.9. (28)	Aug 1917			
	9 Continued.		established Advanced Posts where the Regt bearers carry cases & our men act as relays	SMR
	10		Nil	
	11		1 H.D & 1 Ride evacuated	
	12.		14 ORs joined for duty. A good lot of men	SMR
	13		Nil	SMR
	14		Nil.	SMR
	15		~~Cap~~ Camps around Dickebusch bombed by enemy planes 42 cases brought here 25 serious stretcher cases, 14 sitting & 3 dead. There are a large number of troops of various divisions in camps around here indent on me for medical supplies also all their sick come here. I have 1 M.O. who is kept busy night & day. Report to ADMS. There appear to be no Field Ambulances of these divisions round here & some of the units are without M.O's.	SMR
	16		ADMS F 266 ordered me to detail two large cars to report for duty with 20 MAC Cars detailed. Leaves 5 here all fully engaged & no cars in at time of writing	SMR
	17		Capt Webster & Capt Cathcart to DRS with Pyrexia. This leaves me with 3 M.O's 2 in the line & one here. The shortage of M.O's has been badly felt during recent active operations & I have had to keep M.O's in most unhealthy positions for 14 days without relief	SMR

2353 Wt. W2544/1454 700,000 5/15 D. D. & L. A.D.S.S. Forms/C. 2118.

Instructions regarding War Diaries and Intelligence Summaries are contained in F. S. Regs., Part II. and the Staff Manual respectively. Title pages will be prepared in manuscript.

72 Field Ambulance

WAR DIARY
or
INTELLIGENCE SUMMARY.
(Erase heading not required.)

Vol IX

4

Army Form C. 2118.

Place	Date	Hour	Summary of Events and Information	Remarks and references to Appendices
H 34 a 6.9 (28)	Aug 1917 19		Pte Rose recommended for M M	SMR
"	20		ADMS 5'32/1 18/8/17 recd to day. Lt Pedley posted from 72 F Amb. to 9th East Surrey Regt for permanent duty.	SMR.
"	21.		1 Cpl joined for duty. Cards with particulars of service of Officers forwarded to DDMS. Corps	SMR
"	22.		Capt Billing posted to this unit for duty 21-8-17.	SMR
	23		11 O.R. reported for duty. A good lot of men	SMR.
	24.	11-30 PM	Wire from ADMS telling me to get in touch with 17 & 72 D Mds & arrange for evacuation of wounded if they move. Got in touch with Mds & find that they are under orders to support the 14 Div infantry of Stirling Castle. Saw DADMS 14 Div & made arrangements through him with OC 43 F Amb to supply bearers when Bns move into the line.	SMR.
	25.		Above move cancelled. Capt. Cathcart returned to Duty from DRS. Examined ASC for Class A	SMR
	26.		2nd Lt. Walker M.O.R.C. U.S.A. attached for duty	SMR
	27		Pte Shone, Pte Sand 14 days F.P. No 1. Not complying with an order. Cpl Duerney awarded allied Medal.	SMR

2353 Wt. W2544/1454 700,000 5/15 D. D. & L. A.D.S.S. Forms/C. 2118.

Army Form C. 2118.

Instructions regarding War Diaries and Intelligence Summaries are contained in F. S. Regs., Part II. and the Staff Manual respectively. Title pages will be prepared in manuscript.

72 Field Ambulance **WAR DIARY** *or* **INTELLIGENCE SUMMARY.** Vol. IX

(Erase heading not required.)

5

Place	Date	Hour	Summary of Events and Information	Remarks and references to Appendices
H34a.6.9 Sheet 28	1917 Aug. 28		Capt Webster discharged from Hospital + proceeded on leave	
		12 noon	Opened as M.D.S. + transferred from 2 Corps 5 Army to X Corps 2 Army	
			Capt. W. C. F. Harland TF posted for duty with this unit	SDE
	29th		Nil	SDE
	30th		Rennie from 2 Corps M.D.S. rejoined for duty	SDE
	31st		Nil	SDE

S D Edwards Lt Col RAMC
OC 72 Field Amb.

16.

140/2438

MEDICAL.

Vol 25

Sep 1.1917

CONFIDENTIAL

WAR DIARY

OF

LIEUT COLONEL G.B. EDWARDS. D.S.O.

OFFICER COMMANDING 72ND FIELD AMBULANCE.

FROM 1 Sept 1917 TO 30 Sept 1917

Instructions regarding War Diaries and Intelligence Summaries are contained in F. S. Regs., Part II. and the Staff Manual respectively. Title pages will be prepared in manuscript.

72 Field Ambulance

WAR DIARY
or
INTELLIGENCE SUMMARY.

(Erase heading not required.)

Vol X

(1)

Army Form C. 2118.

Place	Date	Hour	Summary of Events and Information	Remarks and references to Appendices
DICKEBUSCH H34a6.9 Sheet 28	1917 Sept. 1		ADMS informed me that 39th Div will relieve 24 Div tomorrow & that 24 Div will take over the line now held by 23 Div on our left. I am to hand over LARCH WOOD & LOCKS to 134 7 Amb. but will retain the MDS at DICKEBUSCH I am not to take over any ADS etc from 23rd who are handing them over to 25 Div but will take them over later from 25 Div.	BMR
	2.		Handed over LARCH WOOD & LOCKS to 1347 Amb.	BMR
	3.		Took over ADS at WOODCOT HOUSE & have arranged with OC 767A 25 Div to clear his cases from the BUND, COW FRM & HALFWAY HOUSE through WOODCOT to Corps MDS at Dickebusch. 24 Div have only 1 Bn at RAILWAY DUGOUTS which clear through woodcot. The remainder will be cleared via Menin Road through YPRES to my MDS at Dickebusch. Arranged with OC 767A for him to treat my cases at his ADS on Menin Road. I have personnel at HOOGE TUNNELS CLAPHAM JUNCTION & STIRLING CASTLE with cars at the ADS of 767 Amb.	BMR
	5.		LT. H.E. MARTIN reported for duty. He is 43 years old, suffers from rheumatism, & has had 13 years experience in lunacy being assistant MO to a lunatic asylum for past 13 years. He has 5 weeks service 5 days at Blackpool & just over 4 weeks at a base hospital. Have reported the above facts to ADMS & told him that officers of above type are useless to me	BMR
	6.		Six B.R men arrived to replace 6 ASC Batmen.	BMR

Instructions regarding War Diaries and Intelligence Summaries are contained in F. S. Regs., Part II. and the Staff Manual respectively. Title pages will be prepared in manuscript.

'Army Form C. 2118.

WAR DIARY
or
INTELLIGENCE SUMMARY.
(Erase heading not required.)

72 FIELD AMBULANCE VOL X (2)

Place	Date	Hour	Summary of Events and Information	Remarks and references to Appendices
H84 a.6.9 (Sheet 28)	1917 Sept 6.		A.D.M.S. conference to discuss preparation of ADS, Relay Posts, RAPs etc for an offensive by 23 Div.	SMR
"	7.9.17		Work to be carried out. W.W. post to be built at I 28 b 2.4 Bearer Post I 24 d 25.4. RAP J19 a 55.4. J 13 c 65.15. J13 d 4.0. (Zillebeke map 1/10,000.) Material to be ordered & medical & surgical indents to be submitted. Pioneer Officer 24 Div to meet me & arrange for working parties.	SMR
	8-9-17	4-15pm	Working party sent up to I 28 b 24 to build dugouts for w. wounded post. O.C. 6 London F. Amb (47 Div) is to take over from OC 76 F Amb. Have arranged to carry on same system of evacuation as I had with 76 F.A.	SMR
			LT de BRAY USA attached for duty. Captain VANDANDAIGUE rejoined from duty with 13 Middlesex	
	9-9-17		No 4 Car smashed by shell fire. Driver wounded & evacuated. Car orderly wounded at duty. Working Parties sent up to push on work at RAPs & Relay Posts.	SMR
	11-9-17		Dressings etc for equipping above stations now complete at M.D.S. Dickebusch ready for distribution	SMR
	12-9-17		Adv Party of 69th F.A. arrived at Woodcot house.	SMR
	13-9-17		Adv Party 70 F A arrived at M.D.S. Dickebusch. Handed over Dickebusch to 70 F.A. & Woodcot house & forward area to 69 F.A. including ADS on Menin Road	SMR

2353 Wt. W2544/1454 700,000 5/15 D. D. & L. A.D.S.S./Forms/C. 2118.

Instructions regarding War Diaries and Intelligence Summaries are contained in F. S. Regs., Part II. and the Staff Manual respectively. Title pages will be prepared in manuscript.

72 Field Ambulance

WAR DIARY
or
INTELLIGENCE SUMMARY.
(Erase heading not required.)

Army Form C. 2118.

Vol X

Place	Date	Hour	Summary of Events and Information	Remarks and references to Appendices
	1917 Sept			
FLÊTRE W17d 3.9. Sheet 27.	14		Moved off from Dickebusch by bus at 7.30 am for FLÊTRE	SMR
	15		Kit inspection B Section brought up to strength.	SMR
	~~19~~ 20		All cars left at 10 am for BAPAUME. ~~Lieut~~ Capt Martin to 12 Royal Fusiliers Temp duty	SMR
	21	5am	F. Amb entrained at CAESTRE together with transport at ~~[illegible]~~ 8-53 am	SMR
BEAULENCOURT N11 c 7.3. Sheet 57c.		12 PM	Arrived at Camp N11 c 7.3 (Sheet 57 C) BEAULENCOURT after 8 mile march from station.	
	22		Captain HARLAND rejoined from 106 Bde RFA	SMR
	23.		Visited III Corps Scabies Hospl & 34 DRS former 104 F Amb latter 102 F Amb	SMR
	24		Adv Parties to DOINGT I 36a 2 0 sheet 62C to 34 DRS	SMR
DOINGT I 36 a 2.0. Sheet 62C	25		F Amb moved by route march to DOINGT.	SMR
	26		Took over DRS from 104 F Amb.	SMR
	27		Took over III Corps Scabies Station from 103 F Amb. Lt. Martin posted by ADMS to 12 R. Fusiliers for duty. Lieut du Bray for duty to 24 DAC. Capt Wallace posted to me for duty from 24 R. E.	SMR

2353 Wt. W2544/1454 700,000 5/15 D. D. & L. A.D.S.S. Forms/C. 2118.

Instructions regarding War Diaries and Intelligence Summaries are contained in F. S. Regs., Part II. and the Staff Manual respectively. Title pages will be prepared in manuscript.

72 Field Ambulance

WAR DIARY
or
INTELLIGENCE SUMMARY.

(Erase heading not required.)

Vol X

Army Form C. 2118.

Place	Date	Hour	Summary of Events and Information	Remarks and references to Appendices
DOINGT I36a.2.0 Sheet 62C.	1917 Sept. 28th		ADMS 24 Div came round 24 DRS. There is a good deal of work to be carried out in preparation for the winter. At present all roofs leak there are no fire places, rooms very cold & draughty. Personnel under canvas. Sanitary arrangements poor.	
			E. S. Edmunds Lt Col RAMC OC 72 Field Ambulance	SSR

2353 Wt. W2544/1454 700,000 5/15 D. D. & L. A.D.S.S. Forms/C. 2118.

16

MEDICAL.

VII 26

CONFIDENTIAL

WAR DIARY

OF

LIEUT COLONEL G.B. EDWARDS. D.S.O.

OFFICER COMMANDING 72ND FIELD AMBULANCE.

FROM 1 October 1917 TO 31 October 1917

Instructions regarding War Diaries and Intelligence Summaries are contained in F. S. Regs., Part II. and the Staff Manual respectively. Title pages will be prepared in manuscript.

WAR DIARY or INTELLIGENCE SUMMARY.

72 FIELD AMBULANCE VOL XI

(Erase heading not required.)

Army Form C. 2118.

(1)

Place	Date	Hour	Summary of Events and Information	Remarks and references to Appendices
DOINGT.	1917 October			
T36a 2.0	1		Nil	SMR
62c.	2		DDMS III Corps Inspected Corps Scabies Station	
			1 H.S evacuated	SMR
	3		Nil	SMR
	4		do	
	5		do	
	6-11		do	
	12		Nil	SMR
	13		DDMS came round DRS & CSS 1 other evacuated	SMR
	14-16		Nil	SMR
	17.		DMS III Army inspected DRS & CSS	SMR
	18	12 PM	7 Corps take over from III Corps Now under 7 Corps	SMR
20th	19 ~~19-23~~		Nil ~~Nil~~ Lt W A KELLOGG MORE USA joined for duty	
	21-23 24		Nil Corps Commander Inspected DRS & CSS	SMR
	25-28		Nil	SMR

D. D. & L., London, E.C. (A7883) Wt. W807/M1672 350,000 4/17 Sch. 52a Forms/C/2118/14

Instructions regarding War Diaries and Intelligence Summaries are contained in F. S. Regs., Part II. and the Staff Manual respectively. Title pages will be prepared in manuscript.

72 FIELD AMBULANCE

WAR DIARY
or
INTELLIGENCE SUMMARY.
(Erase heading not required.)

VOL XI

(2)

Army Form C. 2118.

Place	Date	Hour	Summary of Events and Information	Remarks and references to Appendices
DOINGT I 36 a 2 0 sheet 62c	October 29.		Inspection of whole Field Ambulance Box Respirators.	EBE
do	30		Lt. T E WALKER MO.R.C USA to 8th Buffs Temp duty.	EBE
do	31.		Nil.	EBE

E B Edmunds
Lt Col R.A.M.C.
OC 72nd Field Ambulance

D. D. & L., London, E.C. (A7883) Wt. W807/M1672 350,000 4/17 Sch. 52a Forms/C/2118/14

15

14/2578

MEDICAL.

9B 27

CONFIDENTIAL

WAR DIARY

OF

LIEUT COLONEL G.B. EDWARDS. D.S.O.

OFFICER COMMANDING 72ND FIELD AMBULANCE.

FROM Nov 1st 1917 TO Nov 30th 1917

Instructions regarding War Diaries and Intelligence Summaries are contained in F. S. Regs., Part II. and the Staff Manual respectively. Title pages will be prepared in manuscript.

Army Form C. 2118.

72 FIELD AMBULANCE WAR DIARY or INTELLIGENCE SUMMARY.

(Erase heading not required.)

VOL XII

(1)

Place	Date 1917	Hour	Summary of Events and Information	Remarks and references to Appendices
DOINGT I 36 a. 20 sheet 62c	November 1.		1st Lt. T B KERN M.O.R.C USA reported for duty	SME
	3.		Working party of 1 NCO 10 OR to 73 F Amb.	SME
	5.		No 98156 Pte Pratt struck off strength to 1 N. Staff for water duties	SME
	7.		Lt & Qr Mr Cooke on leave 15 days to England	SME
	9.		1st Lt KELLOGG MORC USA to 8 R.W. Kents for duty in relief of Capt McCarthy to England. No 52023 Sgt Cavanagh C joined for duty from 24 Div Concert Party	SME
	10		No 9854 S.S. WISE A.W. to 60 Field Ambulance Struck off Strength	SME
	17.		Working party 1 NCO + 10 OR returned from 73 Field Ambulance	SME
	18.		1st Lt T.B. KERN. 2 NCOs + 22 O.R. to 5 CCS for temp. duty. 1st Lt WALKER MORC USA returned from 8 R.W. Kents	SME

D. D. & L., London, E.C.
(A7883) Wt. W803/M1672 350,000 4/17 Sch. 52a Forms C/2118/14

72 FIELD AMBULANCE

WAR DIARY
or
INTELLIGENCE SUMMARY.
(*Erase heading not required.*)

Vol. XII

(2)

Army Form C. 2118.

Instructions regarding War Diaries and Intelligence Summaries are contained in F. S. Regs., Part II. and the Staff Manual respectively. Title pages will be prepared in manuscript.

Place	Date	Hour	Summary of Events and Information	Remarks and references to Appendices
DOINGT	1917 November			
I36 a. 2. 0. Sheet 62c	19.		1st Lt WALKER to 5 CCS for temp duty. Two motor Amb to 73 F Amb for temp duty	8RR
"	24		ADMS 24 Div inspected the DRS Lt Cooke returned from leave	8RR
"	29		Two motor Amb returned from 73 F Amb	8RR
"	30		2 NCOs + 22 OR returned from 5 CCS	8RR

S. D. S. Edwards
Lt Col RAMC
O.C. 72 Field Ambulance

D. D. & L., London, E.C. (A7883) Wt. W2093/M1672 350,000 4/17 Sch. 52a Forms/C/2118/14

6

MEDICAL.

140/2696 Vol 28

CONFIDENTIAL

WAR DIARY

OF

LIEUT COLONEL G.B. EDWARDS. D.S.O.

OFFICER COMMANDING 12ND FIELD AMBULANCE

FROM Dec. 1st 1917 TO Dec. 31st 1917

72 FIELD AMBULANCE **WAR DIARY** or **INTELLIGENCE SUMMARY.** Vol XVI

(Erase heading not required.)

Army Form C. 2118.

Instructions regarding War Diaries and Intelligence Summaries are contained in F. S. Regs., Part II. and the Staff Manual respectively. Title pages will be prepared in manuscript.

(1)

Place	Date	Hour	Summary of Events and Information	Remarks and references to Appendices
	1917 December			
DOINGT I 36 a 2.0	1st		Received order from Town Major to allow five civilians to occupy a ruined house in grounds of Div Rest Stn.	
Sheet 62c			There is only one small room & no sanitary arrangements. Have pointed this out & in the mean time	
			have a party of men constructing a kitchen & latrine	SMR
do	2		ADMS 2nd Cav Division called to ask if I could accommodate patients of his Div at 24 Rest Stn. Yes	SMR
do	4		Visited No 5 CCS & went round with the O.C.	SMR
do	5		Instructions from ADMS to relieve Lt Kerr at 5 CCS. Cancelled later	SMR
do	6		Lt Kerr & Lt Stalker rejoined from 5 CCS. Lieut Kerr to 1 North Staffs for instruction under Capt	
			Cathcart	SMR
do	7		New containers of Box Respirators issued to personnel	SMR
"	8		24 Division now administered by Cavalry Corps having relieved 7th Corps.	SMR
"	9		4 H.D. horses & 2 G.S. wagons to 73 F.Amb for duty at Div Baths & Laundry	SMR
			Capt Cathcart rejoined from 1st N. Staffs. Lt Kerr posted to 1 N Staffs & struck off strength	SMR
			DDMS Cavalry Corps called but did not inspect	SMR
"	10		Cpl Walsh rejoined with reinforcements from Base Details	SMR
"	11		Six Reinforcements joined for duty. Pte Turner 21 F.P. No 1.	SMR
	13		ADMS 24 Div inspected DRS.	SMR

D. D. & L., London, E.C. (A5883) Wt. W503/M1672 350,000 4/17 Sch. 52a Forms/C/2118/14

Instructions regarding War Diaries and Intelligence Summaries are contained in F. S. Regs., Part II. and the Staff Manual respectively. Title pages will be prepared in manuscript.

72 Field Ambulance **WAR DIARY** *or* **INTELLIGENCE SUMMARY.** *(Erase heading not required.)* Vol XIII (2)

Army Form C. 2118.

Place	Date 1917	Hour	Summary of Events and Information	Remarks and references to Appendices
DOINGT	December			
I 36 a 2.0			Baths more fencing cut & a large bath stolen from DRS. Reports to Town Major. Later bath	
Sheet 62c	15		traced to some Australian Gunners & returned. 1st Lt J. T. H. HOGAN. M.O.R.C. U.S.A reported for duty	SMR
	17		ADMS 24 Div visits the 24 DRS	SMR
	18		Transferred from 3rd Army to 5th Army.	SMR
	19		Recd. 330 Francs from Div Canteen to be spent on mens Christmas Dinner	SMR
	20		Lecture & instruction to Cox orderlies in their duties	SMR
	22		Lt Hogan to 55 CCS for temporary duty	SMR
	24		ADMS 4 Australian Div called to enquire as to method adopted in the treatment of Scabies.	SMR
	26		Cpl Walsh evacuated to CCS Pyrexia	SMR
	27		Capt H. F. H. EBERTS. reported for duty. OC 647 Amb. called to enquire if I could	SMR
			oblige him by taking some Scabies cases. Yes.	SMR
	28		Lt Kellogg returned from Paris leave & rejoined the 8 R. W. Kents.	SMR
	29		Surg Gen Brown inspected DRS & Scabies Station. Lt Walker returned from 8 R W Kents &	
			proceeded on 10 days leave to Paris.	SMR
	30		No 88102 Pte Lumsden G. remanded for trial by F.G.C.M.	
	31		Capt Cathcart on 15 days leave to Ireland. Application for F.G.C.M. on Pte Lumsden forwarded.	SMR

G. B. Edmunds Lt Col RAMC
OC 72 Field Ambulance

D. D. & L., London, E.C. (A7883) Wt. W807/M1672 350,000 4/17 Sch. 52a Forms/C/2118/14

Jan 1918 11

16.0/2754

MEDICAL. Vol XIV

Vol 29

24

CONFIDENTIAL

WAR DIARY

OF

LIEUT COLONEL G.B. EDWARDS. D.S.O.

OFFICER COMMANDING 72ND FIELD AMBULANCE

FROM 1 Jan 1918 TO 31 Jan 1918

72 FIELD AMBULANCE

Instructions regarding War Diaries and Intelligence Summaries are contained in F. S. Regs., Part II, and the Staff Manual respectively. Title pages will be prepared in manuscript.

WAR DIARY or INTELLIGENCE SUMMARY.

(Erase heading not required.)

Vol XIV

(1)

Army Form C. 2118.

Place	Date	Hour	Summary of Events and Information	Remarks and references to Appendices
DOINGT. I36a 2.0 Sheet 32c	1918 Jan.			
	1st		Took over duties ADMS during his absence on leave. Capt McCONKEY returned from leave 31-12-17	SMR
	2nd		Attended conference at DDMS. Cavalry Corps	SMR
	4		DDMS inspected the DRS + Corps Scabies Station here to day. Capt Ebert to CCS sick	SMR
	6		Pte Conlon FP No 1. 7 days Pte Donnelly FP No 1 21 days. Application for transfer of Pte Donnelly to infantry forwarded	SMR
	8		No evacuations to day roads too slippery for car or horses. Lt Walker returned from leave. Lt Walker MORC USA promoted grade of Captain.	SMR
	9		Attended Conference DDMS Cav. Corps. Supplied Capt Archer M.O/c 24 Div Training Btn with medical stores + equipment	SMR
	11		Capt Ebert rejoined from CCS	SMR
	13		Pte Linnsden sentenced to FP No 1 by FGCM Promulgated to day	SMR
	14		Capt Harland on leave from to day. Attended conference of Consult Surg 5 Army.	SMR
	15		Capt Cathcart returned from leave.	SMR
	16		Attended Conference DDMS Cavalry Corps. Drew 1 H.D horse. Rec'd mid ...	SMR

D. D. & L., London, E.C. (A7833) Wt. W593/M1672 350,000 4/17 Sch. 52a Forms/C/2118/14

Instructions regarding War Diaries and Intelligence Summaries are contained in F. S. Regs., Part II. and the Staff Manual respectively. Title pages will be prepared in manuscript.

72 Field Ambulance

WAR DIARY or INTELLIGENCE SUMMARY.

(Erase heading not required.)

Vol XIV

(2)

Army Form C. 2118.

Place	Date	Hour	Summary of Events and Information	Remarks and references to Appendices
DOINGT I 36a 2.0. Sheet 32c	1918 Jan			
	19th		Capt McConkey to 1 N Staffs temp duty. Lt Kerr on leave.	SDR
	20		ADMS returned from leave. Handed over to him this morning. Report on Scabies forwarded to DDMS Cav Corps.	SDR
	21		Indented for 45 Carbine buckets. DMS 5 Army visited DRS & Scabies Stn to-day.	SDR
	23		Conference at ADMS	SDR
	26		Inspection of DRS by ADMS	SDR
	27		ADMS 1 Cav Div came round to get plans of disinfector. Pte Hilborne transferred from 2 Cav F Amb to rejoin this unit.	
	28		Capt Webster to 8 The Queens temp duty. Capt Patch on leave. OC 9 Cav FA & OC 1 Cav F Amb came over to be shown round the DRS & Corps Scabies Station.	SDR
	29		Capt Harland returned from leave	SDR
	30		Capt Ebert to temp duty with ADMS. Capt Selby on leave. 1 Officer & 2 NCOs from 1 Cav F Amb were shown round DRS & CSS to-day	SDR
	31		DDMS Cavalry Corps & ADMS 1 Cav Div came round.	

S.D. Edwards
Lt Col RAMC
OC 72 Field Ambulance

D. D. & L., London, E.C. (A7883) Wt. W5o7/M1672 350,000 4/17 Sch. 52a Forms/C/2118/14

Feb. 1918. 24

MEDICAL.

Vol 30

CONFIDENTIAL.

140/2849

WAR DIARY

OF

LIEUT COLONEL G.B. EDWARDS. D.S.O.

OFFICER COMMANDING 72ND FIELD AMBULANCE.

FROM February 1st 1918 TO February 28th 1918

72 FIELD AMBULANCE

Instructions regarding War Diaries and Intelligence Summaries are contained in F. S. Regs., Part II, and the Staff Manual respectively. Title pages will be prepared in manuscript.

WAR DIARY or INTELLIGENCE SUMMARY.

(Erase heading not required.)

Army Form C. 2118.

Vol. XV

(1)

Place	Date	Hour	Summary of Events and Information	Remarks and references to Appendices
DOINGT I 36a. 2.0. Sheet 32c	1918 FEB			
	1		Electric light out of order. Repaired	SM
	3		Capt. WALKER to 9 E Surrey Regt temp duty. G.O.C. 24 Division inspected the D.R.S	SM
	4		Capt WEBSTER rejoined from temp duty 8 The Queens Regt	SM
	7		Report on Scabies Stn forwarded to DDMS Cav Corps	SM
	8		1 Mental Case & 6 Italians evacuated to 5 CCS & 34 CCS respectively.	SM
	9		Report to DDMS & to OC 353 E&M Coy RE re the unsatisfactory working of Electric light	SM
	10		Report to Area Commandant Insanitary practice of Italian Troops. Visited Bde HQ	SM
			S M Knowles ASC (attached Transport) admitted 5 CCS accident	SM
	11		Visited Sanitary School Peronne & 41 S. Hyg Section. visited 5 CCS	SM
	12		Electric light cut off during repairs. Capt Webster on leave. Took over Scabies Station	SM
			from him. MO i/c 6 USA Engineers called & was shown round. Arranged to deal with	
			his sick	SM
	13		ADMS called.	SM
	14		Recreation Room refitted & improved. Water supply connected by pipe with bath	SM
	15		Electric lighting repaired & now in working order	SM

D. D. & L., London, E.C. (A7883) Wt. W809/M1672 350,000 4/17 Sch. 52a Forms/C/2118/14

72 Field Ambulance

Army Form C. 2118.

Instructions regarding War Diaries and Intelligence Summaries are contained in F. S. Regs., Part II. and the Staff Manual respectively. Title pages will be prepared in manuscript.

WAR DIARY
or
INTELLIGENCE SUMMARY.
(*Erase heading not required.*)

Vol XV

(2)

Place	Date	Hour	Summary of Events and Information	Remarks and references to Appendices
DOINGT I 36 a 2.0 Sheet 32c	1918 FEB			
	18		Rev Hanlon on leave to NICE	SM
	19		Col NIXON Consulting Phys 5th Army called & was shown round.	SM
	21		Drove to CORBIE to arrange billets for Unit on 27th	SM
	22		Capt KELLOGG MORC USA struck off strength & posted to 8 R. W. Kents	SM
	23	11am	ADMS O.O. 127 Re move [illegible]	SM
	24		1 Cpl Reinforcement joined from Base Depot	SM
	25		Field Amb 2/1 E Lancs F Amb 66 Div arrived & camped in Transport field. Officers & men being instructed in the work in DRS & Scabies Stn. Recd orders to report 41 CCS for instruction	SM
	26		Handing over of DRS & Scabies Stn to 2/1 E Lancs F Amb completed	SM
	"		Visited ADMS. Transport left at 1 pm by Road for Corbie. Adv Party 1 Officer 8 OR left at 3 pm	SM
	27		Destination altered to Aubigny. F Amb left by train to Villers Bretonneux. By road from there to Aubigny. Transport rejoined unit. C.O. left to join 41 C.C.S.	[illegible]
	28		Received orders to move to [illegible] on morning of March 1st	[illegible]

[illegible signature]
Capt RAMC for O.C. 72nd F. Amb.

D. D. & L., London, E.C. (A7883) Wt. W609/M1672 350,000 4/17 Sch. 52a Forms/C/2118/14

17 Mar. 1918

MEDICAL. VOL.

140/2849 Vol 31

CONFIDENTIAL

WAR DIARY

OF

LIEUT COLONEL G.B. EDWARDS. D.S.O.

OFFICER COMMANDING 72ND FIELD AMBULANCE.

FROM March 1st. 1918 TO March 31st 1918

Instructions regarding War Diaries and Intelligence Summaries are contained in F. S. Regs., Part II. and the Staff Manual respectively. Title pages will be prepared in manuscript.

WAR DIARY

or

~~INTELLIGENCE SUMMARY.~~

(*Erase heading not required.*)

Army Form C. 2118.

Place	Date	Hour	Summary of Events and Information	Remarks and references to Appendices
AUBIGNY	1/3/18		CAPT. H.G. HARLAND (Ten.) RAMC took over the Tempy Command of the Unit from	
MAP 62c.			Lt Col. G.B. EDWARDS RAMC. The Unit trained this day from AUBIGNY, CORBIE	
O2 d. 6.0.			AREA to BRIE. & marched to DEVISE neighborhood at V 3. a. 6. 3. MAP 62c.	HD
DEVISE	2/3/18		Settled into huts - weather bad. Lt & Q.M. J.T. COOKE. proceeded on 14 days	Lt Col RAMC
V3 a 6 3 62c			leave to United Kingdom.	HD
"	4/3/18		ADMS (Col. BUSWELL) visited Camp. Route march morning. Stretcher bearer	
			drill afternoon.	HD
"	6/3/18		Training Programme.	
"	8/3/18		CAPT. C.N. COAD MC. RAMC. proceeded to XIX Corps H.Q. for Tempy. Duty.	HD
"	9/3/18		Training Programme. Summer time comes into force at 11 pm.	HD
"	10/3/18		Kit Inspection - Orders to relieve Cav. Fld Ambce at POEUILLY & VERMAND	HD.
"			To be completed by 6.0 am 13th. Advance party proceeded.	
"	11/3/18		B Section details to take over ADS VERMAND R 32. a. 7. 6 MAP 62c &	
			RAP.s at MUGUET WOOD M.15.C. VADENCOURT CHATEAU R.17.a.2.8 & COOKER	
			QUARRY R.11.c.8.10. relieving No 2 Cav. Fld. Ambce ~~(also RAP at LEVERGUIER) L.28.c.5.~~	HD.

D. D. & L., London, E.C.
(A7883) Wt. W803/M1672 350,000 4/17 Sch. 52a Forms/C/2118/14

Army Form C. 2118.

Instructions regarding War Diaries and Intelligence Summaries are contained in F. S. Regs., Part II. and the Staff Manual respectively. Title pages will be prepared in manuscript.

WAR DIARY
or
~~INTELLIGENCE SUMMARY~~.
(*Erase heading not required.*)

Place	Date	Hour	Summary of Events and Information	Remarks and references to Appendices
DEVISE	12/3/18		H.Q. & C Section with transport proceeded to POEUILLY Q 28 b. 9. 0 & relieved No 3 Cav. Fd. Ambce.	MD.
POEUILLY Q28.b.9.0 Map 62c	13/3/18		Capt. FRANKLIN RAMC & 8 Stretcher Bearers C Section proceeded to LE VERGUIER Relay Bearer Post L. 33. b. 8. 8 & RAP L 28. c. 5. 2.	MD.
"	15/3/18		Additional 4 Bearers sent to LE VERGUIER. CAPT MACCONKEY & 2 Lance Cpls to GAS Course VILLERS CARBONNET. Lt. HOGAN J.T.H. – U.S.A. M.O.R.C. evac. accidental injury to CCS. TINCOURT. Lt BUXTON RAMC 74 Fd Ambce reported for Tempy Duty.	MD.
"	16/3/18		2 Bearers relieved at LE VERGUIER.	
"	17/3/18		Arrived at POEUILLY from leave, after reporting to ADMS at BOUVINCOURT & took over Command of the unit from 1st March. 1918. from CAPT HARLAND RAMC (Ten)	MD.
"	18/3/18		Remanded Pte TAGO RAMC & Pte PRICE RAMC for Trial by Court Martial. Visited ADS VERMAND also 1st Relay Post. R 18. c. 8. 5. & 2nd Relay Post Essling Redoubt. M14c.5.2. & RAP MEURGAT Wood. M. 15. cent. Two marquees erected for GAS Sub-Centre. Sgt. CAVENAGH returned from 5 Army School of Instruction.	MD.

D. D. & L., London, E.C. (A7893) Wt. W803/M1672 350,000 4/17 Sch. 52a Forms/C/2118/14

Army Form C. 2118.

Instructions regarding War Diaries and Intelligence Summaries are contained in F. S. Regs., Part II. and the Staff Manual respectively. Title pages will be prepared in manuscript.

WAR DIARY
or
~~INTELLIGENCE SUMMARY.~~
(Erase heading not required.)

Place	Date	Hour	Summary of Events and Information	Remarks and references to Appendices
POEUILLY MAP 62c.	19/3/18	Tues.	ADMS. inspected men for reclassification.	
			Reinforcement - Sgt. STIRZAKER 9317 - General duty Section. Visited ADS. VERMAND	
			making good progress with building of dugout for Dressing Room etc.	AD.
			Visited RAP at VANDENCOURT. R17. a. 2.8. + COOKER QUARRY R11.a.8.0	
			CAPT. MacConkey returned from Gas Course at VILLERS CARBONNET.	DDMS Col Pocock XIX Corps inspected GAS arrangements.
"	20/3/18	Wed.	CAPT CART ~~WRIGHT~~ HCART MICKYCAT RAMC returned from course Sanitary Course Peronne.	
			Lt+QM. T.T. Cooke returned from leave Lt BUXTON RAMC rejoined	
			1st. Fd. Ambce. TREFCON. W.10.a. 2 wheeled stretcher loaned to	AD.
			CAPT LODGE-PATCH 8 Bn QUEENS Regt. Lt.Col. G.B. EDWARDS handed over	
			Imprest account of the unit.	
"	21/3/18	Thurs.	Order from ADMS (Col. BUSWELL) 6.30 am. to "Man Battle Station" enemy bombardment	
			commenced 4. am. "Walking wounded" arrived at ADS. VERMAND 5.30 am.	
			This was moved into partly built "Dug Out" in the tumulus. As there was some	
			Congestion of the "Dressing Room" with wounded it was decided that "Lying Cases"	AD.
			Should be dressed in the "Elephant Dug-Outs" & the former Dressing Room in	
			a Nissen Box Hut used for dressing the walking wounded. This	

D. D. & L., London, E.C. (A7883) Wt. W803/M1672 350,000 4/17 Sch. 52a Forms/C/2118/14

Instructions regarding War Diaries and Intelligence Summaries are contained in F. S. Regs., Part II. and the Staff Manual respectively. Title pages will be prepared in manuscript.

WAR DIARY
or
~~INTELLIGENCE SUMMARY.~~
(Erase heading not required.)

Army Form C. 2118.

Place	Date	Hour	Summary of Events and Information	Remarks and references to Appendices
POEUILLY	21/3/18	Thurs	Completely eased the temporary Congestion. CAPT W.J. WEBSTER RAMC. Showed great Gallantry in going up with Extra Stretcher bearers to the "Collecting Post" MAISSEMY thro' a heavy barrage between VILLECHOLLES & MAISSEMY & cleared the Collecting Post of wounded.	
			Dr. GRIFFIHS ASC. MT. Showed great devotion to duty & courage in driving his car whose body was mostly blown away leaving a Skeleton Frame & the radiator was perforated in spite of which he brought back 8 sitting wounded 4 of whom were unable to walk.	
			The following NCO's & men are missing from the following posts which were in the line. on the morning of the German attack 21.3.18	
			RAP. Muguet Wood. M.15c. — Sgt. MARTIN RAME 1; Pte MARTIN " 1; " AMOS " 1; " BRYANT " 1; " REED " 1; " McCASKIE " 1; Total 6	MAP Ref. 62c. 1.20,000
			ESSLING REDOUBT M.14c52 (1st RELAY POST) — CORL. DOCKRILL 1; Pte RIDDICK 1; " BLACKWELL 1; RIXON 1; " THOMPSON 1; Total 5	
			1st RELAY POST (R.18.c.52) — Pte PENMAN 1; " MOLE. 1; Total 2 = 13.	HD

D. D. & L., London, E.C. (A7883) Wt. W593/M1672 350,000 4/17 Sch. 52a Forms/C/2118/14

Army Form C. 2118.

Instructions regarding War Diaries and Intelligence Summaries are contained in F. S. Regs., Part II. and the Staff Manual respectively. Title pages will be prepared in manuscript.

WAR DIARY
or
INTELLIGENCE SUMMARY.
(Erase heading not required.)

Place	Date	Hour	Summary of Events and Information	Remarks and references to Appendices
			While the 24th Division were holding the Front Line the following were the positions of.	
POEUVILLY	21/3/18	Thurs	① RAP. MUGUET WOOD M15 cent.	MAP Ref.
			VEDANCOURT Chn R17 a. 2. 8. also Ambce Car Stand.	BELLENGLISE. 1. 10,000.
			COOKER QUARRY R11. a. 8. 6	
			LeVERGUIER. L29. d 8. 7. Car Stand	
			VENDELLES R8. a. 5. 8.	
			② ADS. VERMAND consisting of Nissen Bows & Elephant dug outs in course of erection.	
			(JAENCOURT ADS in 66 Div. Area run by 2/3 East Lancs F.A. took wounded of 24 Div.n from LE VERQUIER. Personnel & Car supplied by 72 F.A.)	
			③ MDS POEUVILLY	
			Transport – Arrangements made by 10 MAC. for Ambulances & Lorries of 19th CORPS. Following personnel 72 Fd Ambce wounded & evac'd C.C.S. 65192 Sgt. HARVEY at VERMAND – 44876 Pte REVIE Beaucourt Rd } RAMC 49716 Pte COOPER at VEDANCOURT	[initials]
ST CREN	22/3/18	Fri.	ADS VERMAND moved to POEUVILLY. HdQrs of FA. from POEUVILLY to ST. CREN	
			ADS. POEUVILLY moved the same day from POEUVILLY to ST CREN. At 11. pm. orders received from ADMS for whole unit to proceed to St CHRIST sur SOMME	[initials]
MACHELEPOT	23/3/18	Sat.	At 6am. unit moved across St Christ Bridge (SOMME) with the 14th Cavalry Divn to MARCHELEPOT. At about 11pm. moved from MACHELEPOT to CHAULNES	[initials]

D. D. & L., London, E.C. (A7883) Wt. W803/M1672 350,000 4/17 Sch. 52a Forms/C/2118/14

Army Form C. 2118.

Instructions regarding War Diaries and Intelligence Summaries are contained in F. S. Regs., Part II, and the Staff Manual respectively. Title pages will be prepared in manuscript.

WAR DIARY
or
INTELLIGENCE SUMMARY.

(Erase heading not required.)

Place	Date	Hour	Summary of Events and Information	Remarks and references to Appendices
CHAULNES	24/3/18	Sun.	The whole of 24th Divn arrived in CHAULNES AREA. Moved from CHAULNES to ROSIERES at 2 pm. as the Division was turned out to man a line HYENCOURT le-Grand - OMIECOURT - HYENCOURT-le-PETIT FONCHETTE-FOUCHES - HATTENCOURT 17 Infy Bde 73 IB. 72 IB. from left to right. Brigade Hdqrs of 72nd IB. at HALLU	
			Medical Positions - ADS (left) LIHONS 74 Fd Ambce; ADS. (Right) CHILLY 73 Fd Ambce	
			MDS ROSIERES. 72 Fd Ambce	
			Cases evacuated to 47 CCS. ROSIERES. Borrowed 20 Stretchers from Lt Col. L'Estrange (OC. 5 CCS ROSIERES) also 25 Stretchers from 47 CCS.	[initials]
ROSIERES I 3. AMIENS 17	25/3/18	Mon.	5.15 pm. Transport of Fd Ambces moved to CAYEUX. forthwith Bearer Divn to retire along ROSIERES-CAIX - CAYEUX Rd. Keeping in touch with 72. Infy Bde & functioning to VILLERS BRETONNEUX G2 AMIENS 17. ADMS office DEMUIN G3 AMIENS 17	[initials]

D. D. & L., London, E.C. (A7853) Wt. W803/M1672 350,000 4/17 Sch. 52a Forms/C/2118/14

Instructions regarding War Diaries and Intelligence Summaries are contained in F. S. Regs., Part II. and the Staff Manual respectively. Title pages will be prepared in manuscript.

WAR DIARY
or
~~INTELLIGENCE SUMMARY.~~
(*Erase heading not required.*)

Army Form C. 2118.

Place	Date	Hour	Summary of Events and Information	Remarks and references to Appendices
ROSIERES	25-3/18	Mon.	Contd - Composite Bn. formed by. Lt Col. MACKENZIE GSO 1 24 Divn	
I 3 AMIENS 17			CAPT McCONKEY RAMC 72 FA. detailed to form an ADS. with 48 Bearers	
			with two Ambce Cars at the Quarry CAIX H3 Amiens 17 Med Equipment	
			Stretchers 20	
			Shell Dressings 200	
			Med Comforts - Tea & Cocoa.	[initials]
CAYEUX	26-3/18	Tues	Visited 72 Infy Bde Hdqrs at WARVILLERS Detailed 2 Bearers as Runners	
H3 AMIENS 17			to Keep in touch c Brigade. Made following Medl. Arrangements	
			for evacuation sick & wounded of Brigade	
			RAP. WARVILLERS.	
			Car Stand " 1 NCO 4 Other ranks posted to Composite Bn of	
			8 Roy. West Kent's 9 East Surreys & 1 North Staff	[initials]
			under MO. Capt. Ebert's 72 FA. Tempy attached	
			ADS. Le QUESNOY 1 MO. 1 NCO 8 OR	
			Car Stand 2 Mot. Ambces	
			MDS CAYEUX Chn.	

D. D. & L., London, E.C. (A7883) Wt. W89/M1672 350,000 4/17 Sch. 52a Forms/C/2118/14

Instructions regarding War Diaries and Intelligence Summaries are contained in F. S. Regs., Part II, and the Staff Manual respectively. Title pages will be prepared in manuscript.

WAR DIARY
or
INTELLIGENCE SUMMARY.
(Erase heading not required.)

Army Form C. 2118.

Place	Date	Hour	Summary of Events and Information	Remarks and references to Appendices
CAYEUX	27/3/18	Wed	Large number of casualties about lying 35 & sitting 165. Great difficulty in evacuating wounded eventually evacuated sitting by Ammunition Lorries to Villers Bretonneux & ~~Amiens~~ from there by Ammunition Train to AMIENS.	ADJ
			Following personnel of 72 Fld Amblce wounded & evacuated to CCS this day. (at BEAUFORT W. Le QUESNOY) Capt H. F.H. Clarke, Pte Robert 1458, " Smith 65188, Pte Ansell 65357, " COLLYER 68872	} Remr.
CAYEUX to DUMUIN	28/3/18	Thurs	Left for DUMUIN & evacuated rapidly lying & sitting cases to THENNES owing to German advance. Dressing Station formed at DUMUIN. Sick & wounded transferred from DUMUIN & THENNES to DRESSING STATION at ROUVREL. Sick & wounded evacuated by MAC Cars & Lorries to 41 CCS. NAMPS. Dressing Station Cleared.	ADJ
ROUVREL St. SAUFLIEU	29/3/18	Fri.	MDS. ROUVREL transferred to ST. SAUFLIEU ADS formed at COTTENCHY Collecting Post ROUVREL Bearer Post at DOMMARTEN Formed MDS ST SAUFLIEU.	
ST SAUFLIEU	30/3/18	Satd	ADS COTTENCHY Bearer & RAP. handed over to 74 Field Amblce	
ST SAUFLIEU	31/3/18	Sund	Over flow of Sick & wounded of 74 F.A. at SAINS en AMIENNOIS evacuated to 41 CCS NAMPS au VAL.	ADJ [illegible] Lt Col. RAMC OC. 72 Fd Amblce.

D. D. & L., London, E.C. (A7883) Wt. W803/M1672 350,000 4/17 Sch. 52a Forms/C/2118/14

Army Form C. 2118.

Instructions regarding War Diaries and Intelligence Summaries are contained in F. S. Regs., Part II. and the Staff Manual respectively. Title pages will be prepared in manuscript.

WAR DIARY
or
INTELLIGENCE SUMMARY.
(Erase heading not required.)

Place	Date	Hour	Summary of Events and Information	Remarks and references to Appendices
ST. SAUFLIEU	31/3/18	Sunday	The following Officers Nco's + men's of 72nd Fd. Ambce names were forwarded for distinction (Immediate Reward) for gallantry + devotion to duty during the German attack from the 21.3.18 to 27.3.18. on the LE VERGUIER - VERMAND FRONT.	
			CAPT. WILLIAM BLACKER CATHCART RAMC. recommended for Military Cross	
			CAPT WILLIAM JOSEPH WEBSTER RAMC " " Bar to Military Cross.	
			No. 52008 Acting Corpl. STANLEY ARTHUR GRIMES RAMC for DCM	
			" 53486 Pte JAMES WILLIAM PARTIS RAMC for DCM.	
			" M/2 131231 Pte CHARLES PAUL GRIFFITH ASC MT. for DCM.	
			" M/2 081536 Pte HARRY WHITEHOUSE ASC. MT (10 MAC attd 72 FA.) for DCM.	
			Lt + Qmstr J.J. COOKE RAMC for Mention in Despatches	
			Adjudant HENRI BOISSY Interpreter to 24 Divl. Service attached 72 Fd Ambce for MC.	
			[signature] Lt Col. RAMC. O.C. 72 Fd Ambce.	

D. D. & L., London, E.C. (A7883) Wt. W80/M1672 350,000 4/17 Sch. 52a Forms/C/2118/14

19 MEDICAL.

Vol 32

CONFIDENTIAL

WAR DIARY

140/2902.

OF

C.H. DENYER. M.C.

LIEUT COLONEL ~~C.B. EDWARDS. D.S.O.~~

OFFICER COMMANDING 72ND FIELD AMBULANCE

FROM April 1st 1918 TO April 30th 1918

Army Form C. 2118.

WAR DIARY
or
INTELLIGENCE SUMMARY.
(*Erase heading not required.*)

Instructions regarding War Diaries and Intelligence Summaries are contained in F. S. Regs., Part II. and the Staff Manual respectively. Title pages will be prepared in manuscript.

Place	Date	Hour	Summary of Events and Information	Remarks and references to Appendices
ST. SAUFLIEU B3 AMIENS 17 1-100,000	1/3/18	Mon.	Received memo from ADMS last evening requiring number of personnel which would proceed by road & train in event of a move. Horse Transport would proceed by road & RAMC personnel by train. Sick & wounded evacuated to 41 CCS NAMPS au VAL. B3. AMIENS. 1-100,000.	[signature]
			CAPT C.N. COAD MC. RAMC for duty with 15 & 19 Entrenching Bn. To report to 72nd Infy Bde. COTTENCHY	[initials]
"	2/3/18	Tues.	Central Record Office established by 72 Fd Amblce at St. SAUFLIEU	
"	3/3/18	Wed.	Visited ADMS. Div. Hdqrs COTTENCHY. Received orders from ADMS to proceed to VERS South of AMIENS on 4.3.18 & to remain for two (73 FA also) 74 FA to move to BOVES. Latter order cancelled.	[initials]
ST. SAUFLIEU AMIENS Ecole de Jeunes Filles Rue Porte de PARIS	4/3/18	Thurs.	Order received from ADMS 24 Divn to proceed to AMIENS & take over a Walking Wounded Dressing Station XIX Corps at RUE PORTE de PARIS (a girls school) from 111 F.A. 16th Divn. Marched off 10 am. Arrived AMIENS 1.45 pm. Transport lines at farm near Rifle Range about 3 Kilometres W of Amiens	[initials]

D. D. & L., London, E.C. (A7883) Wt. W803/M1672 350,000 4/17 Sch. 52a Forms/C/2118/14

Instructions regarding War Diaries and Intelligence Summaries are contained in F. S. Regs., Part II. and the Staff Manual respectively. Title pages will be prepared in manuscript.

WAR DIARY
or
~~INTELLIGENCE SUMMARY.~~
(Erase heading not required.)

Army Form C. 2118.

Place	Date	Hour	Summary of Events and Information	Remarks and references to Appendices
St SAUFLIEU & AMIENS	4/4/18	Thurs	Cleared 600 wounded between 2 pm 4/4/18 & 3 am 5/4/18 from various division	
			73 Fd Amb & 72 Fd Ambce occupying same building former in reserve.	AD
AMIENS	5/4/18	Fri.	DDMS XIX Corps inspected XIX Corps W.W. Post. Arranged with X MAC to supply 1 lorrie for	
			evacuating wounded. 24 MAC of III Corps cleared 40 walking wounded. 58th Fd Amble	
			supplied 1 lorrie. DDMS III Corps (Col MACDONALD) inspected III Corps W.W. POST at	
			old 41 Stationary Hosp. ~~[illegible]~~ He arranged for 24 MAC to clear wounded. Handed	AD
			over III Corps W.W. Post AMIENS Rue Porte de Paris to 73rd Fd Amblce	
			Orders from DDMS 3rd Corps to select an alternative W.W. D Station Selected Girls School RUE du HEM West End of AMIENS.	
AMIENS	5th/18	Fri	Orders from ADMS 24 Divn. prepare to move at short notice	
AMIENS	6/4/18	Sat	Orders received for Ambulance to move ~~from~~ to St VALERY-SUR-SOMME. H. Transport move by	
			Bdges. 2.30 pm M.T. moves off at 1.15 pm Personnel by train from SALEUX 7.30 pm	
			Proceeded with Motor Transport. Arrived ST VALERY at 5 pm Established a Hosp. at	AD
			CASINO. 1 Ford Car lent to 73 FA. 1 Motor Cyclist lent to ADMS.	
			Arranged for Amblce Cars to proceed with each Bdge as they marched off.	

D. D. & L., London, E.C. (A7883) Wt. W809/M1672 350,000 4/17 Sch. 52a Forms/C/2118/14

Instructions regarding War Diaries and Intelligence Summaries are contained in F. S. Regs., Part II. and the Staff Manual respectively. Title pages will be prepared in manuscript.

WAR DIARY
or
INTELLIGENCE SUMMARY.
(Erase heading not required.)

Army Form C. 2118.

Place	Date	Hour	Summary of Events and Information	Remarks and references to Appendices
St VALERY	7/4/18	Sund	Personnel of the Field Ambulance arrived at 3 a.m. this morning from CAYEUX.	
Sur SOMME			Brigade Areas 72 Area around ARREST 73 Area around FREVILLE 17 Area	
			area around CAYEUX. Arranged with AA + QMG thro' ADMS to take over	
			a room in the CASINO for Hosp.	
"	8/4/18	Mon	Arrived sick of 72 Infy Bde Sherwood Foresters PEAUVILLE + M.G. Mach. Gun Coy	
			St VALERY. Orders from ADMS for Ambulance to clear their own Bdes. Posted Capt	
			GRAHAM came under instructions from ADMS to 8 R W Kents. Horse Transport	
			of Amblce arrived from AMIENS under CAPT CATHCART with CAPT WEBSTER	
			Otherwise [illegible] in St VALERY Rue St MARTIN & billets for Officers	
"	9/4/18	Tues	Ordered inspection of Kit & Clothing of Unit. Unit [illegible] out.	
"	10/4/18	Wed	Inspected Box Respirators of Unit. Ordered complete new Equipment for	
			8 RW Kents, 9 East Surreys, 1st North Staffords.	
"	11/4/18	Thurs	Visited 72 Bde Hdqrs. Arrived. Arranged for Capt COAD RAMC to take over duties of	
			MO i/c 1 North Staffords from today. Visited 8 RW Kents Capt Walker MORC & 9 East Surreys Capt Walker ORMC	

D. D. & L., London, E.C. (A7883) Wt. W6o3/M1672 350,000 4/17 Sch. 52a Forms/C/2118/14

Instructions regarding War Diaries and Intelligence Summaries are contained in F. S. Regs., Part II. and the Staff Manual respectively. Title pages will be prepared in manuscript.

WAR DIARY
or
INTELLIGENCE SUMMARY.
(*Erase heading not required.*)

Army Form C. 2118.

Place	Date	Hour	Summary of Events and Information	Remarks and references to Appendices
ST VALERY Sur Somme	12/4/18	Friday	Arrangements for Collection of Sick of 24 Div. Artillery at SOREL North of ABBEVILLE. Evacuation to [illegible] to LONGPRE. Returning car broken by Shell fire at MASSEMY [illegible] 24 DSC ST VALERY CAPT S.A. WILKINSON CAMC. joined this day for duty from No 7 [illegible] Hosp. ETAPLES.	[initials]
"	13/4/18	Sat	DDMS 18th Corps (Col Prynne) inspected 72 F.A. ST. VALERY sur Somme.	
	15/4/18	Mon	Received order to draw 1 [illegible] from 24 Div Train FRESSENVILLE.	
PINCHVALISE	16/4/18	Tues	[illegible] State rendered. Orders from ADMS to be prepared to move at Short notice. [illegible] by Train & [illegible] Transport by road. Moved Personnel from CASINO (Hotel) St Valery to PINCHVALISE with exception of CAPT HALLIDAY & [illegible] & M. BOISSY [illegible] + 12 O.R. who proceed as Advance Party to BRYAS tomorrow, with Ambulance Motor Cars (Includes [illegible] & 2 [illegible]). Cars to be detailed to follow Bus on arrival at BRYAS.	[initials]
"	17/4/18	Wed	Unit moved [illegible] at 5 am & marched to Entrainment at FEUQUIERES [illegible] informed by R.T.O. [illegible] Train departed FEUQUIERES [illegible]	[initials]
VALHUON	18/4/18	Thurs	Arrived BRYAS [illegible] marched to billets in VALHUON. [illegible] CAPT F.S. HARLAND — [illegible] for a Base Hospl. or [illegible]	
LENS 1/100,000				

D. D. & L., London, E.C.
(A7883) Wt. W203/M1672 350,000 4/17 Sch. 52a Forms/C/2118/14

Army Form C. 2118.

Instructions regarding War Diaries and Intelligence Summaries are contained in F. S. Regs., Part II. and the Staff Manual respectively. Title pages will be prepared in manuscript.

WAR DIARY
or
INTELLIGENCE SUMMARY.
(Erase heading not required.)

Place	Date	Hour	Summary of Events and Information	Remarks and references to Appendices
VALHUON LENS E.I. 1:100,000	18/4/18	Thurs	Also CAPT McCONKEY'S application for transfer to India. Detailed CAPT HARLAND for temporary duty with XVIII (Shee Reserve) Corps. H.Qrs. Arranged for clearing sick of 72nd Infy Bde. at following locations 72 Bde H.Qs. DIEVAL	A.D.
		Map Ref	(F.I LENS. II) 8th Bn R.W. KENTS OURTON 1st Bn. NORTH STAFFORDS HUCLIER (E.I. LENS II) (F.I LENS II.) 9 Bn E. SURREYS DIEVAL 72 TMB. 103 Coy RE. OURTON. (F.I LENS II.) 101 Coy ASC. 72 FIELD AMBLCE } VALHUON E.I. LENS II. 1:100.000.	
			Obtained Complete new Med. Equipment for "Bus" of 72 Infy Bde after considerable difficulty.	A.D.
"	19/4/18	Fri.	Arranged for clearing sick of 24 Bn Machine Guns. H.Q. TROISVAUX 2 Coys " BETHONVILLE BELVAL 1 Coy CONTEVILLE	
VALHUON DIVION 11 Lens G.1.	20/4/18	Sat.	Orders from 'Q' 24 Divn for unit to move to DIVION. Unit marched off at 11.15 am & arrived at DIVION at 2.15 pm. Distance 12 Kilometres.	
DIVION	21/4/18	Sun.	Conference at ADMS Office THIEULOYE ref formation of a Divisional Collecting Station in Case of a retirement. To be situated between MDS & CCS. This would keep extra supplies of Blankets Stretchers & Medical Comforts. Distributed 150 Shell dressings to 9 East Surreys, 1st North Staffords. 8 R. West Kents.	A.D.

2353 Wt. W2544/1454 700,000 5/15 D. D. & L. A.D.S.S. Forms/C 2118.

Instructions regarding War Diaries and Intelligence Summaries are contained in F. S. Regs., Part II. and the Staff Manual respectively. Title pages will be prepared in manuscript.

WAR DIARY
or
INTELLIGENCE SUMMARY.

(*Erase heading not required.*)

Army Form C. 2118.

Place	Date	Hour	Summary of Events and Information	Remarks and references to Appendices
DIVION Hdm. A. 1	22/4/18	Mon	Filled Ordnance Panniers with Shell dressings & ordinary dressings. c ATS.	
"	23/4/18	Tues	Obtained from ADMS Stomach warmers 20 endeavour to be made to keep 50.	AD
"	24/4/18	Wed.	Inspection of Ambulance by GOC 24th Divn (Br Genl Howre Naine) Resubmitted a/Sgt Davidson (Pte) No. 65323 for promotion to permanent rank of Cpl. Training – Physical exercise in morning with Stretcher drill – Route march in afternoon	AD
"	26/4/18	Thurs	Unit proceeds to HOUDAIN for Bathing & change of Clothes under Capt McConkey. Rame	
"	27/4/18	Ind.	Visited Town Major DIVION & arranged to move Horse Lines to Stables at I 24. d. a. 5. Sheet 36B FRANCE 1.40.000 Evacuated 3 Pte Mitchell, Prentice, James of recent reinforcements with Malaria they have had several attacks of Malaria in Salonica Malta & Italy.	AD.
"	28/4/18	Satur	Routine. Physical Drill in morning. Route march afternoon	
"	30/4/18	Sun	Parade – Marching Order when received from ADMS that the unit will move to AIX NOULETTE on the 1st May.	A. D. Murphy Lt Col Rame OC. 72 Fd Amb.

T2134. Wt. W708–776. 500000. 4/15. Sir J. C. & S.

71

May 1918

MEDICAL.

Vol 33

140/2983.

CONFIDENTIAL

WAR DIARY

OF

C.H. JENNER. M.C.

LIEUT COLONEL ~~G.B. EDWARDS. D.S.O.~~

OFFICER COMMANDING 72ND FIELD AMBULANCE.

FROM MAY 1ST 1918 TO MAY 31ST 1918

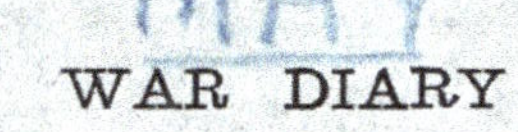

Army Form C. 2118.

Instructions regarding War Diaries and Intelligence Summaries are contained in F. S. Regs., Part II. and the Staff Manual respectively. Title pages will be prepared in manuscript.

WAR DIARY
or
~~INTELLIGENCE SUMMARY.~~

(Erase heading not required.)

Place	Date	Hour	Summary of Events and Information	Remarks and references to Appendices
AIX NOULETTE R22 a.2.6 Sh. 36B	1/5/18	Thurs	Orders received from 72 Inf. Bde that Brigade moves to following areas this day. LES BREBIS SAINS. BULLY GRENAY. Arranged for three Ambulances to follow each battalion viz 1st North Stafford Regt 8 Roy. West Kent. 9th East Surrey Regt as they passed thro' DIVION. Preparatory taking over Ambulance Site from 9th Canadian Field Amblce. Reported ADMS move completed	AD.
"	2/5/18	Wed.	Detailed Maj: W J Webster with 2 NCOs + 36 ORs to report to OC 73rd Fd Amblce. Their duty being to clear sick & wounded of 72nd Infy Bde in the line. ~~[illegible]~~ Visited following posts ADS, Cite St Pierre (M 11.c.8.9) RAP Lens Hosp (N 7.c.1.7) RAP Junction (M.12.a.9.5) Eddie Relay Post. RAP NETLEY (N.1.b.1.7) Netley Relay (N.1.a.4.0) Martyr Relay (M.6.d.3.4) Arranged for clearing Sick of Bde. at SAINS. LES BREBIS & Bully Grenay.	Map Ref 36B France 1-40.000. AD.
"	4/5/18	Satur.	Ambulance inspected by GOC Divn (Maj Genl Daly). Two detailed for duty at ADMS Office SAINS en GOHELLE. Visited 72 Infy Bde HQrs at M 11.a.6.1 Sheet 36B	AD.
"	5/5/18	Sund.	Large Car (Sunbeam) detailed for Temp duty with 73rd FA. Visited personnel ADS St Pierre RAP Junction LENS Hosp. manned by 1 MO Capt WILKINSON + 40 ORs man the posts. Commenced cultivation of ½ acres of land adjacent to Amblce Hdqrs AIX NOULETTE	AD.

T2134. Wt. W708–776. 500000. 4/15. Sir J. C. & S.

Instructions regarding War Diaries and Intelligence Summaries are contained in F. S. Regs., Part II. and the Staff Manual respectively. Title pages will be prepared in manuscript.

WAR DIARY
or
INTELLIGENCE SUMMARY.
(Erase heading not required.)

Army Form C. 2118.

Place	Date	Hour	Summary of Events and Information	Remarks and references to Appendices
ARK NOULETTE R22 a 2 6 Sh 36c	6/5/18	Mon	CAPT S.A. WILKINSON Camc detailed for daily instruction under Maj. W J Webster Rame at ADS Cite St Pierre. The latter relieved this night by CAPT WILKINSON on account of illness (PUO). Lt Col. Cunningham OC 73rd FA notified instruction from ADMS to prepare to receive Scabies	[illegible]
"	7/5/18	Tues	Detailed to Nursing orderlies for duty at 8 CCS WAYRANS (M 26 central) under instructions from ADMS 24 Divn. Applied to 18 Corps Agricultural Officer for Potatoes Seeds etc for cultivation. Applied OC 24 Divn Train for a Farrier [illegible] [illegible] evacuated to CCS. Under ADMS ref. Scabies Officers suffering from Scabies to be sent to 12th Stationary Hospl for treatment. Commenced building Drying ~~Room~~ treatment & Clean Clothing Room & Incinerator	[illegible]
"	9/5/18	Thurs	Conference ADMS (Sains en Gohelle). Took over WWCP (M 8 b 1 2 Sh 36c 1.40,000) at Fosse 11 from 73 FA Personnel Maj Cathcart 2 NCO and 6 ORs. Maj Cathcart relieved Lt Cant [illegible] MORC at Fosse 11. 5 Wheeled Stretcher carriers sent to WWCP Shell dressings & Water. ADS [illegible] of [illegible] Equipment & [illegible] Comforts. Capt Harland [illegible] (T) rejoined Unit from 18 Corps. Detailed 1 Runner to [illegible] to Traffic Control ARK Noulette also 2 orderlies with 1 wheeled Stretcher.	[illegible]

T2134. Wt. W708–776. 500000. 4/15. Sir J. C. & S.

Instructions regarding War Diaries and Intelligence Summaries are contained in F. S. Regs., Part II. and the Staff Manual respectively. Title pages will be prepared in manuscript.

WAR DIARY
or
INTELLIGENCE SUMMARY.
(Erase heading not required.)

Army Form C. 2118.

Place	Date	Hour	Summary of Events and Information	Remarks and references to Appendices
AIX NOULETTE	9/5/18	Thurs	Contd. Medical Arrangements – Evacuation of walking wounded. By Light Railway from Fosse 11 to AIX NOULETTE thence to R.25.d. Sh 36B & from latter to CCS by motor lorry. 1 NCO & 1 OR to be in medical charge of the train. Maj. W J Webber MC RAMC evacuated to No 12 Stationary Hospl. St Pol this day.	AB
"	10/5/18	Frid	ADMS (Col McKenzie) inspected Fosse 11 (WWCP) with CRE 30th Divn. Arranged to take over cellars of YMCA for walking wounded Dressing Station. Lying cases to be dealt with at Dressing Station near Fosse 11 Road. ADMS arranged with RE's for electric lighting & Divisional Gas Officer for protection against Gas.	AB
"	11/5/18	Sat	DDMS XVIII Corps (Col Pryne) inspected WWCP Fosse 11 (Sh 36c SW1 1.10,000) M8.b.12 with ADMS. Capt HARLAND RAMC(T) proceeded to Hospital to DDMS (DIEPPE) under instructions from ADMS. The No. 4. Bearers of B Squad. sent up line for instruction.	AB
"	13/5/18	Mon	Inspected WWCP at Fosse 11 also visited Capt Wilkinson CAMC ADS Cité St Pierre. Capt Walker attd 9 East Surrey Bn established RAP for Bn in support at M11c 8.8.5. Sh 36c S.W.1 LENS. 1.10,000 near Cité St Pierre Church.	

T2134. Wt. W708–776. 500000. 4/15. Sir J. C. & S.

Instructions regarding War Diaries and Intelligence Summaries are contained in F. S. Regs., Part II. and the Staff Manual respectively. Title pages will be prepared in manuscript.

WAR DIARY
or
INTELLIGENCE SUMMARY.
(Erase heading not required.)

Army Form C. 2118.

Place	Date	Hour	Summary of Events and Information	Remarks and references to Appendices
AIX NOULETTE	13/5/18	Mon	Arrangements of 72nd Inf Bde from today 1 Bn in Line RAP Lens Hosp. Bn in Support Cite St Pierre Bn in Reserve BULLY GRENAY.	AD
"	15/5/18	Wed.	C Section bearers relieved B Section at following Posts. RAP Lens Hosp (Line) 4 Bearers; RAP Junction (Line) 12 Bearers 2 Runners 2 NCOs; RAP Cite St Pierre (near Church) 4 Bearers; ADS of 73 FA Cite St Pierre 1 NCO 4 Bearers; 72 Inf Bde HQrs 2 Runners	AD
			Maj. T W Webber reports arrival from No 12 Stationary Hosp.	
"	17/5/18	Fri.	1 NCO & 30 other ranks detailed as a working party to fill in ~~[illegible]~~ ground floor of YMCA Fosse 11 with pit props for protection.	AD
"	18/5/18	Sat.	Capt Grey RAMC(SR) reports arrival for duty this day. W.W.C.P. Fosse 11 recently completed Electric lighting put in by Div. Support Water also laid on which is pumped up from well at R.L. Road. Reserve water supply provided of this fact also [illegible] of electric light fails	AD

T2134. Wt. W708-776. 500000. 4/15. Sir J. C. & S.

Instructions regarding War Diaries and Intelligence Summaries are contained in F. S. Regs., Part II. and the Staff Manual respectively. Title pages will be prepared in manuscript.

WAR DIARY
or
~~INTELLIGENCE SUMMARY.~~

(Erase heading not required.)

Army Form C. 2118.

Place	Date	Hour	Summary of Events and Information	Remarks and references to Appendices
AIX NOULETTE	19/5/18	Sun	CAPT J D Hickley RAMC (T) reported arrival for duty. Rendered report re Bully Switch Line (Reserve) on RAP's German bombed and shelled AIX NOULETTE 1 Casualty slight. Commenced 10 pm & continued till 1.15 am. HWCP at Fosse 11 completed & ready to function.	[illegible]
"	21/5/18	Tues	Pte Muzzell RAMC relieved by Pte Haslem at No 8 CCS. WAVRANS L/Cpl Actg Sgt Graves & Pte Porter noted in DRO as receiving MM.	[illegible]
"	22/5/18	Wed	Bearers at RAP's Lens Road, Junction & Walker Post relieved by 73 FA. Bearers with the exception of Capt Wilkinson Bearer MO, Sgt Queeny & 4 OR at ADS Cite St Pierre. Visited ~~the~~ ADS Cite St Pierre with Capt Grey RAMC. Took ambulance car up to Double Crassier Rd.	[illegible]
"	23/5/18	Thurs	Went up by Light Tramway to Cite St Pierre & visited RAP: Lens Road, Junction & Walker Post with Capt Grey. All bearers from front area relieved by 73 FA. Inspected Transport Lines at Gd Servins where heavy baggage had been transferred.	[illegible]

T2134. Wt. W708—776. 500000. 4/15. Sir J. C. & S.

Instructions regarding War Diaries and Intelligence Summaries are contained in F.S. Regs., Part II. and the Staff Manual respectively. Title pages will be prepared in manuscript.

WAR DIARY
or
INTELLIGENCE SUMMARY.
(Erase heading not required.)

Army Form C. 2118.

Place	Date	Hour	Summary of Events and Information	Remarks and references to Appendices
[illegible]	24/5/18	Fri.	Arranged with OC 74 FA to mobilise personnel of Transport (Horse) with TAB & OC 73 FA to mobilise MT Transport temporarily attached to OC 74 & 73 FA's respectively	[illegible]
"	25/5/18	Sat.	Drew 1 mule from — under arrangements with 74 Infy Bde from Horse [illegible]. Pte Morgan RAMC reported for duty from the Base	
"	26/5/18	Sun.	Maj. Cathcart RAMC & Lt Campbell MORC relieved at [illegible] this day by Maj. Webster MC RAMC & Capt Lockley RAMC (T). Maj. Cathcart rejoined HQrs. Capt Wilkinson relieved by Lt Campbell MORC at Cte St Pierre ADS & rejoined HQrs. Building of a drying Room completed [illegible] supplying heat.	[illegible]
"	27/5/18	Mon.	CAPT GREY detailed for Tempy Duty 18 Corps School under instructions from ADMS 24 Divn.	[illegible]
"	28/5/18	Tue.	CAPT W.R. CATHCART mentioned in despatches "London Gazette" May 25th 1918. [illegible] Horse Lines (Tempy) at [illegible]	
"	30/5/18	Thur.	CAPT WILKINSON CAMC detailed for Tempy Duty with 106 Bde RFA. ADMS [illegible]	
"	31/5/18	Fri.	ADMS inspected HQrs 72 FA. Brick fly proof refuse holder completed, also [illegible]	[illegible]

T2134. Wt. W708-776. 500000. 4/15. Sir J. C. & S.

21

June 1918

MEDICAL

VR 34

140/3076.

CONFIDENTIAL

War Diary

OF

Lieut.-Colonel C.H. DENYER M.C. ~~G.B. EDWARDS. D.S.O.~~

Officer Commanding 72nd. FIELD AMBULANCE

From JUNE 1st. 1918 To JUNE 30th 1918

Instructions regarding War Diaries and Intelligence Summaries are contained in F. S. Regs., Part II. and the Staff Manual respectively. Title pages will be prepared in manuscript.

WAR DIARY
or
~~INTELLIGENCE SUMMARY.~~
(Erase heading not required.)

Army Form C. 2118.

Place	Date	Hour	Summary of Events and Information	Remarks and references to Appendices
			— JUNE —	
Aix Noulette	1/6/18	Sat	89245 Sgt SMILLIE reported arrival from Base. Taken on strength & posted to C Section	
"	2/6/18	Sun	Maj Cathcart relieves Maj Webster MC. at WWCP Fosse 11. Capt Heatley relieves Lt Campbell at ADS Cite St Pierre & returns to Ambulance Hdqrs AIX NOULETTE. Pte Crews detailed for duty with ADMS at Divl Hdqrs SAINS en Gohelle & struck off strength of the unit. Personnel pass out.	[initials]
"	~~4/6/18~~	Mon.	65160 A/Sgt QUERNEY. D. RAMC reported absent from about 11 pm 2/6/18	
"	5/6/18	Wed	No. M2/100900 A/Sgt Summer ASC MT arrived for duty with unit. Dr Parker ASC MT proceeds to 24 Div Cav ASC MT. Received official notification that A/Sgt Querney RAMC was admitted to No 1 CCS (Can) [midnight 2/3 June] suffering from Fractured Skull. Also received statement from Capt Snelling RAMC 3rd FA in reference to Sgt Querney RAMC	[initials]
"	7/6/18	Friday	1st Lt Peck HA. MRC taken on strength & posted to 18 Corps School of Instruction for duty. Capt Grey detailed to report for duty to O.C. 45 CCS. Forwarded A.F. W. 3428	[initials]

Instructions regarding War Diaries and Intelligence Summaries are contained in F. S. Regs., Part II. and the Staff Manual respectively. Title pages will be prepared in manuscript.

WAR DIARY
or
INTELLIGENCE SUMMARY.
(Erase heading not required.)

Army Form C. 2118.

Place	Date	Hour	Summary of Events and Information	Remarks and references to Appendices
Aix Noulette	7/6/18	Frid	(accidental Injury) ref. Sgt. Guerney RAMC to ADMS 24 Division	
"	9/6/18	Sund.	Maj. Webber MC & Lt Campbell relieved Maj. Cathcart & party of B Section. Capt. Leckley rejoined H.Qrs from ADS Cite St Pierre. Visited W.W. Entrainment Siding (in event of Active Operations) at R 25 d. 3.5 Sh. 44B with Sgt Cavanagh RAMC & Corpl Gunton RAMC. Visited Sgt Guerney RAMC at No 1 Can. CCS. He is improving but memory is still defective. Capt. Pullenger MORC was the Surgeon who operated on Sgt Guerney for fractured Skull	[initials]
"	10/6/18	Mon.	Corpl. Harlem & Pte Edwards RAMC transferred to 24 DRS with NYD.P. (Influenzal Type) from Zone 11 WWCP. Dug outs & billets at Ambulance HQrs as well as Zone 11 WWCP sprayed with Cresol & personnel ordered Gargles daily.	[initials]
"	12/6/18	Wed.	An Influenzal Type of Pyrexia appeared in the Division during last few days. Chief Symptoms Severe frontal head ache pain in back & limbs, weakness, high temperature rapid pulse, harsh dry Cough, little expectoration conjunctival injection & occasionally nausea & vomiting. Corpl Harlem & Pte Edwards RAMC have these Symptoms	[initials]
"	13/6/18	Thur.	Maj. Webster MC RAMC - Bar to MC. 24 Div. Orders & 19 Corps No 1R. 144/3470 d/11/6/18. NYDP (Inf) admitted 9	
"	14/6/18	Frid	Lt H.A. Peck MORC reported arrival for duty from 18 Corps School NYD P admitted 6.	[initials]
"	15/6/18	Sat.	Lt & QM. J.T. Cooke Sick with NYD.P. NYD P admitted = 14	

T2134. Wt. W708—776. 500000. 4/15. Sir J. C. & S.

Instructions regarding War Diaries and Intelligence Summaries are contained in F. S. Regs., Part II. and the Staff Manual respectively. Title pages will be prepared in manuscript.

WAR DIARY
or
INTELLIGENCE SUMMARY.
(Erase heading not required.)

Army Form C. 2118.

Place	Date	Hour	Summary of Events and Information	Remarks and references to Appendices
Aix Noulette	16/6/18	Sun	Pyrexias admitted 26	
"	17/6/18	Mon	Lt. Campbell more mild type of pyrexia. NYD. P. admitted = 26	
"	18/6/18	Tues	Lt Peck MORC detailed for Tempy duty with 3rd Inf. Bde. CAPT Wilkinson Carne rejoined unit from Tempy Duty 106 Bde RFA. Sgt Major Coggins RAMC placed on Sick list NYD.P. QMSgt Clarke detailed as a/Sgt Major whilst latter is on Sick list. Adj. Bouzy French Interpreter placed on sick list NYD.P. NYD P Cases admitted = 20	[illegible]
"	19/6/18	Wed	ADMS Mc Dwn visited Aix Noulette & requires accommodation for 150 pyrexias in the 4 Hospital Nissen Huts & 80 in Tents totalling 230. NYD P cases admitted = 22	[illegible]
"	20/6/18	Thur	Maj Webster MC Rame from Zone 4 admitted Hospl with NYD.P. Relieved party at Zone 4 with exception of (lower?) 1 NCO 1 cook 2 nursing Orderlies & 6 Bearers. CAPT Wilkinson Carne detailed for Tempy Duty with 9th East Surreys & Lt Campbell 1st Roy. Irish Fusiliers. 1 marquee & 12 Bell Tents received from Mc Dwn & erected. Received 150 Stretchers 1400 blankets from 18 Corps. Received 175 Cases NYD P. from 73 Field Amb Zone 10. NYD. P cases admitted Hospl = 195	[illegible]

T2134. Wt. W708–776. 500000. 4/15. Sir J. C. & S.

Army Form C. 2118.

Instructions regarding War Diaries and Intelligence Summaries are contained in F. S. Regs., Part II. and the Staff Manual respectively. Title pages will be prepared in manuscript.

WAR DIARY
or
INTELLIGENCE SUMMARY.
(Erase heading not required.)

Place	Date	Hour	Summary of Events and Information	Remarks and references to Appendices
Aix Noulette	21/6/18	Fri	Auxiliary Hospl for NYD P. Cases formed at SAINS en GOHELLE for 100 beds. Personnel – Capt Mortimer (MO i/c 106 Bde RFA) 72 FA. {2 NCOs – 8 Nursing Orderlies 1 QO (Sanitary) 1 Water Cart / 1 Clerk 2 Cooks 1 QO (Supervision of Rations) driver + Orderly. Separate Daily State rendered for above patients but admitted on Books (A&D) of 72 FA. NYD.P admitted Ambulance = 65	[illegible]
"	22/6/18	Sat.	Capt. [illegible] admitted [illegible] CCS NYD P on 14.6.18 discharged 21.6.18. He was during a Course of Instruction at 1st Army School. WAYRANS [illegible] CCS [illegible] MC + Adv. [illegible] discharged Hospl. this day. 11 NYD P convalescent patients transferred to 24 Div. Reception Camp. Marœuil [illegible]. NYD P cases admitted Hospl = 100	[illegible]
"	23/6/18	Sun.	46 NYD P. patients transferred to 24 Div. Reception Camp today. Message from ADMS 24 Div. No further cases of NYD P. to be retained at 72 Fld Ambce but to be evacuated to CCS. Pernes. Arrangements having been made from Base Hospl to take these cases of Pyrexia of Influenzal Type. Convalescent Patients NYD P. transferred to 24 Divl. Reception Camp = 46	[illegible]
"	24/6/18	Mon.	ADMS instructions all PUO cases to be evacuated to CCS. in Pernes + Aubigny Areas with the exception of RE Signals if latter can be possibly retained. Convalescent NYD P. cases to 24 D.R Camp = 26.	

T2134. Wt. W703–776. 500000. 4/15. Sir J. C. & S.

Instructions regarding War Diaries and Intelligence Summaries are contained in F. S. Regs., Part II. and the Staff Manual respectively. Title pages will be prepared in manuscript.

WAR DIARY
or
INTELLIGENCE SUMMARY.
(Erase heading not required.)

Army Form C. 2118.

Place	Date	Hour	Summary of Events and Information	Remarks and references to Appendices
Aix Noulette	25/6/18	Tues	DDMS. (18 Corps). Col. Pepme inspects the Unit.	
"	26/6/18	Wed.	Lt Campbell MORC rejoins from temporary duty with 1st Roy. Inniskillin. Capt McConkey reports arrival from No 4 CCS Cau. Pernes as a convalescent after NYDP. (Influenzal) Type	A.D.
"	27.6.18	Thur	Capt Lickley posted to W.W.C.P. Fosse 11. for duty.	
"	29/6/18	Sat.	Work in progress, improving bomb screen round horse lines & Hospl. & men huts. Hay sifter made for stables. Roofs of two billets rendered rain proof. Roof being built for Incinerator & Disinfector	A.D.
"	30	Sun.	Routine duties. Visited W.W. C.P. Fosse 11. Capt McConkey rejoins 3rd Rifle Bde.	

A. D. [illegible] Lt Col. R.A.M.C.
O.C. 72 F.A.

T2134. Wt. W708–776. 500000. 4/15. Sir J. C. & S.

24

July 1918.

MEDICAL.

Vol 35

140/3131.

CONFIDENTIAL

War Diary

Of

C. H. DENYER. M.C.

~~Lieut.-Colonel G. B. EDWARDS D.S.O.~~

Officer Commanding 72nd. FIELD AMBULANCE

From JULY 1st 1918

To JULY 31st 1918

JULY

WAR DIARY
or
~~INTELLIGENCE SUMMARY.~~
(Erase heading not required.)

Army Form C. 2118.

Instructions regarding War Diaries and Intelligence Summaries are contained in F. S. Regs., Part II. and the Staff Manual respectively. Title pages will be prepared in manuscript.

Place	Date	Hour	Summary of Events and Information	Remarks and references to Appendices
Aix Noulette	1/7/18	Mon.	Routine Duties.	
R22.a.2.6 Sheet 44B France 1.40,000	2/7/18	Tues	CAPT. LICKLEY RAMC (TF) placed on Sick list. CAPT WILKINSON CAMC. detailed for duty at Fosse 11. W.W.C.P. Lt CAMPBELL MORC. detailed for Temporary Duty with Royal Engineers 24 Div. Instructions from ADMS (Col McKenzie) to prepare to receive 10 Contacts Cerebro Spinal meningitis. Marquee erected & Contacts (9th Roy Sussex R) isolated. ~~Sains~~ Auxiliary Hospl. at SAINS-en-GOHELLE which was opened for Pyrexia of Influenzal Type & worked by 72nd Fd Ambce Closed this day. Personnel at W.W.C.P. Fosse 11 relieved this day.	AD.
"	3/7/18	Wed.	The C.S.M. Contacts Cases Sent to No 2 Mob. Lab. AUBIGNY for Examination. Verbal message from ADMS to arrange to keep 100 Cases in Field Ambulance.	AD.
"	4/7/18	Thur	CAPT LICKLEY evac'd to No 1 CCS Cav. Pyrexia with N.Y.D.P. (Influenzal Type)	
"	6/7/18	Sat.	1st Lt HA. PECK MORC Struck off the Strength of the unit to Lyons Office 1st ARMY DMS office Struck off Strength. CAPT WILKINSON detailed for Temp'y Duty 12 Sherwoods - MAROC.	AD.

T2134. Wt. W708-776. 500000. 4/15. Sir J. C. & S.

Instructions regarding War Diaries and Intelligence Summaries are contained in F. S. Regs., Part II. and the Staff Manual respectively. Title pages will be prepared in manuscript.

WAR DIARY
or
~~INTELLIGENCE SUMMARY.~~
(Erase heading not required.)

Army Form C. 2118.

Place	Date	Hour	Summary of Events and Information	Remarks and references to Appendices
AIX NOULETTE	7/7/18	Sun.	1 NCO + 24 ORs detailed to proceed to Fosse 11. Walking Wounded Collecting Post for the purpose of making a road to Collecting Post, under Supervision of an Engineer Officer. German plane brought down at CARENCY the fight ~~between~~ with one of our planes occurred over AIX NOULETTE.	[initials]
"	8/7/18	Mon	4811 Cpl. Franklin RAMC proceeded to 1st Army Rest Camp for 14 days. Lt H. RUBIN MORC attached to the unit this day. At present Sick in at 73 Field Ambulance PETIT SAINS. CAPT J.D. LICKLEY struck off strength. evacuated to the Base this day.	[initials]
"	11/7/18	Thurs	No 12081 CPL GUNTON H. RAMC transferred to 30 CCS. for duty 10/7/18. No 58096 CPL TURBAYNE J. joins for duty vice CPL Gunton.	[initials]
"	13/7/18	Sat	Received orders from ADMS. In the event of active Operations the Advanced Dressing Stations at Fort Glatz (Loos) & Cite St Pierre with Ammun + form an ADS at the Walking Wounded Collecting Post Fosse 11.	[initials]

T2134. Wt. W708–776. 500000. 4/15. Sir J. C. & S.

Instructions regarding War Diaries and Intelligence Summaries are contained in F. S. Regs., Part II. and the Staff Manual respectively. Title pages will be prepared in manuscript.

WAR DIARY
or
INTELLIGENCE SUMMARY.
(Erase heading not required.)

Army Form C. 2118.

Place	Date	Hour	Summary of Events and Information	Remarks and references to Appendices
Aux Roulette	13/7/18	Sat	The 72 Fld Ambce will be in Reserve with Exception of detached 1 Bearer Officer & 36 O.Rs for clearing the sick & wounded of the affiliated Brigade	
"	14/7/18	Sun	Lt H.A. Peck MORC USA rejoined the unit this day from the Base.	[illegible]
"	16/7/18	Tues	Visited 1st Army School of Instruction WAYRANS. also personnel of this unit doing duty there being 2 NCOs & 12 O.Rs. Maj. Cathcart W.R. Rame proceeded on 14 days leave. The w/m have been evacuated wounded from W.W.C.P. Zone 11 (MAROC) No 53486 Pte PARTIS Jn. Rame 65187 " Titimus H. J. " & the w/m admitted Hospital wounded & discharged to duty on same day 15.7.18 No 364170 Pte Williams AC Rame " 38401 " Galloway (H) HLI att.	[illegible] [illegible]

T2134. Wt. W708—776. 500000. 4/15. Sir J. C. & S.

Instructions regarding War Diaries and Intelligence Summaries are contained in F. S. Regs., Part II. and the Staff Manual respectively. Title pages will be prepared in manuscript.

WAR DIARY
or
INTELLIGENCE SUMMARY.
(Erase heading not required.)

Army Form C. 2118.

Place	Date	Hour	Summary of Events and Information	Remarks and references to Appendices
Aix Noulette	18/7/18	Thu.	Reconnoitred road from ADS Fosse Glatz passed the Double Crassier K.S. east corner of Maroc. (Loos) wounded would have to go down by trolley on Light Tramway Lines. Lt H.A. Peak accompanied	A.R.
"	19/7/18	Wed.	The u/m ASC M.T. joined for duty on 18/7/18 & taken on strength M/2 099375 Pte McIlveen J. M/2 100767 " Orr M/2 019531 " Thompson	A.R.
"	20/7/18		Took Capt Rubin MORC & Sgt Hunt to reconnoitre ADS Fosse Glatz Loos & RAPs Tosh Keep, Martyr, & Junction (two medical officers at latter post.) also ADS Cite ST Pierre (Lens). ADMS with CRE visited the Head Quarters of the Unit with a view to removing the Lt Hosp'l Nissen Bow Huts. Visited 73 F.A. with Lt & Quarter Cooke Sgt-Major Cargues ~~with a~~ in event (state of camp) of taking over from 73 Fd Amb	A.R.

T2134. Wt. W708—776. 500000. 4/15. Sir J. C. & S.

Instructions regarding War Diaries and Intelligence Summaries are contained in F. S. Regs., Part II. and the Staff Manual respectively. Title pages will be prepared in manuscript.

WAR DIARY
or
INTELLIGENCE SUMMARY.
(Erase heading not required.)

Army Form C. 2118.

Place	Date	Hour	Summary of Events and Information	Remarks and references to Appendices
Aix Noulette	23/7/18	Tues	Inspection Sanitary of 10 Group 1st Army Field Survey Coy. Sanitation of cook houses & latrines requires improvement. Proceeded with Maj Webster MC & Lt Peck MORC to lecture on Wound Shock by Capt Parker. Called at MDS 73 Field Ambulance Pte Sains. Visited WW CP Fosse 11 & arranged for medical equipment for ADS Pannier to be completed as far as possible & held in Reserve. Also Reserve Dressings for 500 wounded to be kept with Reserve Ration for the same number consisting of Oxo Cafe au lait etc.	AB
"	25/7/18	Thurs	Following officers report for duty. Capt A G Hopper Rame (TF) Capt A.J. Ireland (T.C) & Lt F.S. Mansfield (T.C). Detailed Lt H.A. Peck to proceed to 1st Army School of Instruction for the day for lectures.	AB
"	27/7/18	Sat	The u/m (is promoted) Warrant Officer Class II from 15-1-16 inclusive in accordance with Army Order No 194 d/22/6/18 No 49426 QMS Clark T.W. Lt Mansfield proceeded to 74 Field Ambulance for duty this day. 1918	AB
"	28/7/18	Sun	1st Lt H.A. Peck detailed for Tempy Duty with 29th Forward Depot RE SAVY.	AB

T2134. Wt. W708—776. 500000. 4/15. Sir J. C. & S.

Instructions regarding War Diaries and Intelligence Summaries are contained in F. S. Regs., Part II. and the Staff Manual respectively. Title pages will be prepared in manuscript.

WAR DIARY
or
INTELLIGENCE SUMMARY.
(Erase heading not required.)

Army Form C. 2118.

Place	Date	Hour	Summary of Events and Information	Remarks and references to Appendices
AUX NOULETTE	29/7/18	[illegible]	[illegible] DENVER MC proceeds on 10 days leave to PARIS 30/7/18 to 8/8/18. The [illegible] returns from leave to United Kingdom on 28th inst. 508068 Pte GANDY E.E. [illegible]	[initials]
"	30/7/18	[illegible]	The [illegible] NCO is appointed "Acting Sgt" with pay from 6.6.18 [illegible] 900 Cpl Summers A.W. (ASC MT) Auth. 19/13706/ASC/OB2 d/30/7/18 A.G.'s Office Base.	[initials]
"	31/7/18	[illegible]	The [illegible] detailed to attend at 1st Army School of Instruction to-day for lectures CAPT A.T. IRELAND. Sgt [illegible] Coggins A.F. 50237 Pte Johnson F 79874 Sgt Hunt A.F. 49895 " Lagu[illegible]. 100649 Pte Gilchrist	[initials]

[signature] Lt. Col. R.A.M.C.
O.C. 72 [illegible]

D. D. & L., London, E.C.
(A7883) Wt. W809/M1672 350,000 4/17 Sch. 52a Forms C/2118/14

19

MEDICAL.

Aug. 1918.

WR 36

140/3 200

CONFIDENTIAL

War Diary

of

Lieut.-Colonel ~~C. B. EDWARDS. D.S.O.~~ C.H. DENYER M.C.

Officer Commanding 72nd. FIELD AMBULANCE

From AUGUST 1918 To AUGUST 31ST 1918

Army Form C. 2118.

AUGUST

WAR DIARY
or
INTELLIGENCE SUMMARY.
(Erase heading not required.)

Instructions regarding War Diaries and Intelligence Summaries are contained in F. S. Regs., Part II. and the Staff Manual respectively. Title pages will be prepared in manuscript.

Place	Date	Hour	Summary of Events and Information	Remarks and references to Appendices
AIX NOULETTE	1/8/18	Thurs	Detailed for duty at No 1 CCS 508188 Pte Gorschalk R.J. Capt Hopper AC & Cpl Franklin detailed to	
R22.a.2.6			attend lectures 1st Army School of Instruction. 508068 Pte Gandy G.G. Returned from leave to U.K. 89245 Sgt Smallies T	
Sh 44B France 1:40,000			Maj. W. B. Cultcart Kane returned from 14 days leave to Ireland this day.	AD
"	3/8/18	Sat.	Maj. W. J. Webster MC proceeded on leave to Scotland from 3.8.18 to 17/8/18. Capt H. Rubin	
			MORC USA returned from 1st Army School of Instruction this day. Test in regard to manning	
			Battle Stations carried out. - Satisfactory. Staff Sgt Thomas & Sgt Hedley returned from Paris leave (10 days)	AD
"	4/8/18	Sun	ADMS inspected Hdqrs of Ambulance & considered Sanitation very Satisfactory.	
"	5/8/18	Mon.	Personnel at Fosse 11 W.W.C.P. & Sick Collecting Post Bully Grenay relieved this day.	
"	7/8/18	Wed.	The f/m proceeded to First Army Rest Camp Ambleteuse this day for 14 days	AD
			53466 Cpl. March E.J. Capt A.J. Ireland relieved Capt Wilkinson S.A.	
			73017 Pte Jones R at Fosse 11 W.W.C.P. this day.	
"	8/8/18	Thurs	The f/m O.Rs having been evacuated to Base from No 1 CCS on 4/8/18 are struck off the strength of	AD
			the unit 508135 Pte Harrison L.P. & 74086 Pte Price W.	

D. D. & L., London, E.C. (A7883) Wt. W803/M1672 350,000 4/17 Sch. 52a Forms/C/2118/14

Instructions regarding War Diaries and Intelligence Summaries are contained in F. S. Regs., Part II. and the Staff Manual respectively. Title pages will be prepared in manuscript.

WAR DIARY
or
INTELLIGENCE SUMMARY.
(Erase heading not required.)

Army Form C. 2118.

Place	Date	Hour	Summary of Events and Information	Remarks and references to Appendices
Aix Noulette	10/8/18	Sat	Returned from leave to Paris three days. Capt Wilkinson C.A.M.C. relieved Lt H.A. Peck MORC USA at No 29 Forward Depot RE. until return of MO (14/8/18).	AO
"	11/8/18	Sun.	Capt Hopper detailed for course at 1st Army School of Instruction Pernes Course 10 days. Capt Rubin detailed for duty with 3rd Rif. Bde vice Capt McConkey proceeding on leave. 1 NCO & 6 ORs detailed as picket as requested by Town Major Aix Noulette for guarding crops.	AO
"	12/8/18	Mon.	Capt A.J. Ireland rejoins H.Q.rs. from W.W.C.P. Zone 11.	
"	13/8/18	Tues	W.W.C.P. & A.D.S. Zone 11 handed over to 73 Field Amblce with reserve Rations & dressings for 500, surplus splints etc. Personnel at the Car Relay Post reduced by 5 ORs. Capt IRELAND proceeded to 1st Army School of Instruction No 1 C.C.S. Pernes. Lieut Peck. MA. proceeds on 14 days leave to UK. Period 13.8.18 to 27.8.18.	AO
"	15/8/18	Thurs	German plane bombed AIX NOULETTE between 10 & 10.30 pm 5 Casualties from 110 Bty RGA. visited Car Relay Post Zone 11.	AO

D. D. & L., London, E.C. (A7883) Wt. W809/M1672 350,000 4/17 Sch. 52a Forms/C/2118/14

Army Form C. 2118.

WAR DIARY
or
INTELLIGENCE SUMMARY.
(Erase heading not required.)

Instructions regarding War Diaries and Intelligence Summaries are contained in F. S. Regs., Part II. and the Staff Manual respectively. Title pages will be prepared in manuscript.

Place	Date	Hour	Summary of Events and Information	Remarks and references to Appendices
AIX NOULETTE	16/8/18	Fri	Inspection of the Ambulance by DMS 1st Army Maj-Genl Thompson who expressed great satisfaction with the work & improvement carried out by the unit.	[initials]
"	17/8/18	Sat	German plane bombed the Ambulance, blew roof off the baths - no casualties. Inspected Sanitation of 34 Balloon Coy, No 4 Special Coy RE, Section 84 DAC.	[initials]
"	18/8/18	Sun.	Maj. J.W. Webster returned from leave to the United Kingdom. Personnel relieved at Cen Relay Post Zone 11.	[initials]
"	20/8/18	Tues	The [illegible] NCO & men are detailed to proceed to the 1st Army Rest Camp Ambleteuse tomorrow for 14 days. Cpl Horsley J.H. Pte Foster J. Pte Oldham J. Pte Wood W. " Cutting C. " Hawkes J.	[initials]
"	23/8/18		Visited new RAP VALLEY M17.c.6.4 St Nazaire Rivers Sh. 1.20,000. Reconnoitred route for walking wounded from RAP VALLEY M17.c.6.4 to M17c.1.3. to M.16 d 8.6, M.16, b.10.2 along track to M16 c 6 9 to RAILWAY POST M.15.b.10.3 & thence by Railway Track to Zone 11.	

D. D. & L., London, E.C. (A7883) Wt. W809/M1672 350,000 4/17 Sch. 52a Forms/C/2118/14

Instructions regarding War Diaries and Intelligence Summaries are contained in F. S. Regs., Part II. and the Staff Manual respectively. Title pages will be prepared in manuscript.

WAR DIARY
or
~~INTELLIGENCE~~ SUMMARY.
(Erase heading not required.)

Army Form C. 2118.

Place	Date	Hour	Summary of Events and Information	Remarks and references to Appendices
AIX NOULETTE				
"	24/8/18	Sat.	CAPT IRELAND & HOPPER RAMC returned from 1st Army School of Instruction.	
"	25/8/18	Sun.	CAPT HOPPER detailed for duty with 9 R. Sussex Regt. Capt WILKINSON RAMC detailed for Tempy duty with 12th Sherwoods	[illegible]
"	27/8/18	Tues	Following were taken over from 62nd F.A. 20th Divn night 27/28.	
			ADS Colonial Post M33.a.2.8 (ANGRES)	
			Car Post White Chatn - M28.b.7.1 (LIEVIN)	[illegible]
			(Lt) RAP (CROCUS HOUSE) M23.d.3.7. (LIEVIN)	
			(Rt) RAP (QUARRY) M29.c.6.5 (Bois de RAIUMONT)	
			MAP Ref. 44A 1.40,000	
			CAPT. LAWLOR RAMC reported for duty with the Ambulance	
"	29/8/18	Thurs	Lt H.A. Peck MORC detailed for duty at ADS. Colonial Post ANGRES.	[illegible]
			Visited ADS Colonial Post & Car Post White Chatn	
			" Car Relay Post Nine 11.	

D. D. & L., London, E.C.
(A7883) Wt. W809/M1672 350,000 4/17 Sch. 52a Forms/C/2118/14

Instructions regarding War Diaries and Intelligence Summaries are contained in F. S. Regs., Part II. and the Staff Manual respectively. Title pages will be prepared in manuscript.

WAR DIARY
or
~~INTELLIGENCE~~ SUMMARY.
(Erase heading not required.)

Army Form C. 2118.

Place	Date	Hour	Summary of Events and Information	Remarks and references to Appendices
Aix Noulette	31/8/18	Sat^d	The Germans put about 80, 5.9 shells high velocity into Aix Noulette last evening. Casualties Pte 73017 Jones RAMC Killed.	
			(4811) Cpl. Franklin RAMC wounded Hd & Rt. Shoulder.	
			Pte 47076 Jones Slight wound head.	
			Cpl 44474 LAMB RAMC Slight wound Rt Foot.	[initials]
			One shell went through dugout containing Maj. W. T. Webster Lt. J. T. Cooke & Lt Col. Dwyer RAMC – No casualties. The shell burst between two layers of elephant iron in which was earth & then passed through floor of dugout breaking Lt Cooke's wooden bed.	
			Pte Jones RAMC was buried this day in Aix Noulette Cemetery.	
			MAP Ref. R.16.d.5.7. St NAZAIRE RIVER 1.20.000.	

A. H. Dwyer Lt Col. RAMC
O.C. 72 Field Amblce

D. D. & L., London, E.C. (A7883) Wt. W809/M1672 350,000 4/17 Sch. 52a Forms/C/2118/14

MEDICAL

Sept 1918 9

VIII 37

140/3259

CONFIDENTIAL

War Diary

Of

Lieut.-Colonel ~~G.B. EDWARDS. D.S.O.~~ G.H. Denyer M.C

Officer Commanding 72nd. FIELD AMBULANCE

From Sept 1st 1918 — To Sept 1st 1918

Army Form C. 2118.

Instructions regarding War Diaries and Intelligence Summaries are contained in F. S. Regs., Part II. and the Staff Manual respectively. Title pages will be prepared in manuscript.

SEPTEMBER

WAR DIARY
or
INTELLIGENCE SUMMARY.
(Erase heading not required.)

Place	Date	Hour	Summary of Events and Information	Remarks and references to Appendices
AIX NOULETTE MAP. REF R.22.a.2.b.	1.9.18	Sund.	Attended ADMS (Col. C.T. Mackenzie) Conference Divisional Hdqrs. SAINS-EN-GOHELLE. Detailed extra stretcher squads for work between ADS & RAP. in event of an advance.	
			Visited Relay Post & Car Stand Fosse 11 de BETHUNE & ADS. (Colonels Post) ANGRES (near VIMY RIDGE)	A.D.
"	2.9.18	Tues	Lt T.T. COOKE proceeded on 1 mths leave to United Kingdom.	
			Visited RAP. CROCUS HOUSE. (M23.d.4.8. Sh. 44ª 1.40,000 France) M.O. Capt Hopper 9th Sussex.	
			" " QUARRY. (M29.c.6.5 " " " ") M.O. Capt Kennedy Northampton Regt.	A.D.
			Collecting Post & Car Stand - (M28.b.7.1 " " " ")	
			ADS Colonels Post. (M26.d.9.1 " " " ")	
"	3.9.18	Wed.	Received instructions to post 2 Runners with 72nd Bde HQrs. at Fosse 11. also to get into touch with Regimental MO's in regard to Relay Posts & Testing of water in event of withdrawal of the enemy.	A.D.
"	4.9.18	Thurs	Lt T.T. COOKE Rank promoted CAPTAIN Aug. 28th 1918 Auth: London Gazette August 31st 1918	A.D.

D. D. & L., London, E.C.
(A7883) Wt. W809/M1672 350,000 4/17 Sch. 52a Forms/C/2118/14

Army Form C. 2118.

Instructions regarding War Diaries and Intelligence Summaries are contained in F. S. Regs., Part II. and the Staff Manual respectively. Title pages will be prepared in manuscript.

WAR DIARY
or
INTELLIGENCE SUMMARY.
(Erase heading not required.)

Place	Date	Hour	Summary of Events and Information	Remarks and references to Appendices
Aix Noulette	4.9.18	Wed	Contd. Visited 72 Bde HQrs, OC 8 East Surreys 9 R.W. Kents with Maj. Webster MC with a view to making provisional forward Regimental Aid Posts.	AD
"	6.9.18	Fri	Visited ADS Colonels Post. Considerable number of Mustard Gas Cases coming down from Northamptonshire Regt. The enemy shelled round Collecting Post White House (M28.b.1.7 Sh. 44A) for several hours between 12 am & 2 am. No casualties in RAMC personnel.	AD
"	8.9.18	Sun	Major Webster & Capt Lawlor with "B" Section relieved Maj. Cathcart & Lt Peck with "C" Section at RAP's Crocus & Quarry & Collecting Post White House (HEVIN) & ADS Colonels Post. ANGRES.	AD
			Commenced reconstruction of Stables. Maj. W.B. Cathcart detailed as a Judge for Water Carts etc of 24th Division for Corps Commanders Cup.	AD
"	11.9.18	Wed.	CAPT. IRELAND RAMC returned from Temporary Duty with 67 Bde RGA. 24 Pioneers (Sherwood Foresters) Constructing De-Gassing Chamber at ADS. ANGRES. Enemy put a few Shell into Aix Noulette this morning.	

D. D. & L., London, E.C. (A7883) Wt. W809/M1672 350,000 4/17 Sch. 52a Forms/C/2118/14

Instructions regarding War Diaries and Intelligence Summaries are contained in F. S. Regs., Part II. and the Staff Manual respectively. Title pages will be prepared in manuscript.

WAR DIARY
or
~~INTELLIGENCE SUMMARY.~~
(Erase heading not required.)

Army Form C. 2118.

Place	Date	Hour	Summary of Events and Information	Remarks and references to Appendices
Aix Noulette	11.9.18		RAP Quarry. Bois du Raimmont moved from M29c.6.5 to M23.b.6.7 at ROLLECOURT.	[illegible]
"	13.9.18		Lt Col. Hammond Searle 60th F.A. 20 Divn visited the ambulance this day	[illegible]
"	16.9.18		RAP CROCUS moved to RAP VALLEY by CAPT KENNEDY MO. i/c 13 Middlesx. Reconnoitred provisional RAP in 72 Infy Bde Area at N.8.a.10.4 N.1.a.9.1 St Nazaire River 1.10.000. With Major W. J. Webster MC & Capt Lawlor. RAMC.	[illegible]
"	18.9.18		Capt Lawlor posted for duty to 1st North Staffords. Capt Rubin moved to 12 Sherwood Foresters. Capt Wilkinson proceeded to 7 Canadian Genl. Hospl. under instructions from DGMS. Detailed 1 NCO & 4 ORs to proceed to Adv. RAP N.1.d.9.1 (SCROUNGERS REST) & N.8.c.0.9 (ANGELS REST) for purpose of cleaning & holding.	[illegible]

D. D. & L., London, E.C. (A7883) Wt. W809/M1672 350,000 4/17 Sch. 52a Forms/C/2118/14

Instructions regarding War Diaries and Intelligence Summaries are contained in F. S. Regs., Part II. and the Staff Manual respectively. Title pages will be prepared in manuscript.

WAR DIARY
or
INTELLIGENCE SUMMARY.
(Erase heading not required.)

Army Form C. 2118.

Place	Date	Hour	Summary of Events and Information	Remarks and references to Appendices
Aix Noulette	20.9.18	Friday	Two men detailed to work on new RAP N.8.c.0.9 (ANGES REST) for cleaning & holding & helping Sappers to put up stretcher racks.	AD
Aix Noulette	21.9.18	Saturday	Reconnoitred the trolley lines to Provisional RAP, SCROUNGERS REST & ANGELS Post with Major Cathcart. Arranged with Col. Davidson OC 74th Field Amblce for 6 trolleys to clear from SCROUNGERS REST & ANGELS Post which will be handed over to O/c Bearers (Major W. J. Webster) in event of Active Operations.	AD
"	22.9.18	Sun.	Major Webster MC. i/c B Section relieved Major Cathcart O/c C Section at ADS ANGRES Collecting Post White Chat[eau] & RAP: this Amb.	
"	23.9.18	Mon	Handed over Temporary Command of the Ambulance to Major W. B. Cathcart this day with Imprest Account 367 frs. 25 cent.	[signature] OC [illegible]
"	24.9.18	Tues	Attended conference of OC's Fld Ambs at ADMS' Office 12 noon. Visited ADS.	
	25.9.18	Wed	Programme of 7 days training sent to ADMS. Sgt Cavanagh attended ADS for instruction in de-gassing patients clothing.	WBC
	26.9.18	Thurs	DADMS visited HQ Fld Amb., Visited ADS. Lieut F. G. Riley USA MORC joined Unit for duty	WBC

D. D. & L., London, E.C.
(A7883) Wt. W809/M1672 350,000 4/17 Sch. 52a Forms/C/2118/14

Instructions regarding War Diaries and Intelligence Summaries are contained in F. S. Regs., Part II. and the Staff Manual respectively. Title pages will be prepared in manuscript.

Army Form C. 2118.

WAR DIARY
or
INTELLIGENCE SUMMARY.
(Erase heading not required.)

Place	Date	Hour	Summary of Events and Information	Remarks and references to Appendices
Aisc NOULETTE	27	Frid	1st Lieut PECK USA MRC detailed for temp. duty with 24th M.G. Btn by ADMS whilst MO on leave. Visited ADS. Sgt Cavanagh proceeded to ADS as gas NCO for duty at Chlorinating Chamber. Under instructions from ADMS 472 Blankets sent to VIII Corps Skin Centre. OC of 2/1 Home Counties Fld Amb with other Officers visited & were shown round.	WBC
"	28 10/18	Sat	Visited ADS & 72nd Brigade. Major WARD 2/1 Home Counties Fld Amb arrived with 1 Sgt & 1 OR & proceeded to ADS as advance party.	WBC
"	29 10/18	Sund	Relieved in the line by 2/1 Home Counties Fld Amb (Lt Col FALWASSER) relief completed by 4 pm. after which Unit marched to Billets in HERSIN & stayed one night.	WBC
HERSIN	30 10/18	Mond	Transport left HERSIN at 8 am under Capt IRELAND (TO) marching under Brigade orders. Dismounted party marched to HERSIN Station & entrained at 12 noon & detrained at BOUQUEMAISON 5.15 pm & marched to billets at WARLUZEL arriving 8 pm. MAJOR W.J. WEBSTER having come in advance as billeting Officer with M.T. section & had billets ready. Billets were an old C.R.S	WBC

W B Cathcart
Major RAMC
o/c 72 F.Amb.

D. D. & L., London, E.C.
(A7883) Wt. W809/M1672 350,000 4/17 Sch. 52a Forms/C/2118/14

16 MEDICAL

Oct 1918 CONFIDENTIAL Vol 38

140/3327

War Diary

Of

C.H. DENYER M.C.

Lieut-Colonel ~~C.B. EDWARDS.~~ D.S.O.

Officer Commanding 72nd FIELD AMBULANCE

From Oct 1st 1918 To Oct 31st 1918

Instructions regarding War Diaries and Intelligence Summaries are contained in F. S. Regs., Part II. and the Staff Manual respectively. Title pages will be prepared in manuscript.

WAR DIARY
or
~~INTELLIGENCE~~ SUMMARY.
(*Erase heading not required.*)

Army Form C. 2118.

Place	Date	Hour	Summary of Events and Information	Remarks and references to Appendices
WARLUZEL	1/10/18		Transport arrived from HERSIN at 10 am. ADMS (Col. Mackenzie) inspected Ambulance	
			Sgt Ackerman [illegible] & party returned 7 CCS.	
"	2/10/18		Commenced training of RAMC personnel	[initials]
"	3/10/18		ADMS visited Ambulance. Capt J.T. Cooke returned from leave to United Kingdom	
"	4/10/18		Sgt Ackerman & 3 O.R. detailed as Advanced Party to LOUVERAL Area.	
"	5/10/18		Proceeded with Major Webber & Capt Cooke to Louveral to arrange to	
			take over CMDS from an Ambulance 63 RN Divn. Left Corpl Hammond	[initials]
			& Sgt. Dawson. Capt Ireland proceeded with Transport under Brigade	
			Orders to BOISLEUX AU MONT. Transport to entrain tomorrow under Maj.	
			W.J. Webber	
LOUVERAL	6/10/18		Entrained at MONDICOURT at 12 noon - detrained at RUBECOURT.	
			Capt Cooke & Cars proceeded at 10 am arrived at CMDS (17th) at 12.30	
			& was informed that the unit would not relieve 63rd Div. Amblce	[initials]
			Proceeded with ADMS to DDMS 17th Corps (Col [illegible]) & was ordered to detail	
			1 Tent Sub Division for CMDS in morning. Orders from ADMS to send two	
			runners to 72 Infy Bde.	

D. D. & L., London, E.C.
(A7883) Wt. W803/M1672 350,000 4/17 Sch. 52a Forms/C/2118/14

Instructions regarding War Diaries and Intelligence Summaries are contained in F. S. Regs., Part II. and the Staff Manual respectively. Title pages will be prepared in manuscript.

WAR DIARY
or
INTELLIGENCE SUMMARY.
(*Erase heading not required.*)

Army Form C. 2118.

Place	Date	Hour	Summary of Events and Information	Remarks and references to Appendices
BOULON WOOD	7.10.18		'C' Section Tent Sub Divn. detailed under Capt. Riley to report to 17th Corps Main Dressing Station, for temporary duty. Orders from DDMS 17th Corps to proceed to F.19.d Sh. 57c & erect during dusk & twilight an Advanced Corps MDS 'B' Section Bearers sent up to 72 Infy Bde.	[initials]
"	10.10.18		Returned from 14 days leave to U.K. Rejoined Unit which was running CMDS opposite BOULON Wood. F.19.d. Sh. 57c.	
"	11.10.18		CMDS was closed this day & an Advanced CMDS was opened by 59 FA 19th Divn at B.7.a Sh. 57b NE. of Cambrai 1 Tent Sub. Divn with Capt. REILLY MORE 72 FA. & Capt BARWICK 74 FA detailed Cpl. Pont Rame & 20 ORs for duty at Stone Dump near Sucherie between Fontaine Notre Dame & BOURSES on Cambrai Bapaume Rd. Received instructions from DDMS 17th Corps to remain at F.19.d & be prepared to move at short notice	[initials]
"	14.10.18		Under instructions from DDMS 17th Corps reconnoitred AVESNES les AUBERT Area for an Adv. Corps Main Dressing Station. Found a suitable building which had been a German CCS. Map ref V28 a. 0.8	[initials]

D. D. & L., London, E.C. (A7883) Wt. W809/M1672 350,000 4/17 Sch. 52a Forms/C/2118/14

Instructions regarding War Diaries and Intelligence Summaries are contained in F. S. Regs., Part II, and the Staff Manual respectively. Title pages will be prepared in manuscript.

WAR DIARY
or
INTELLIGENCE SUMMARY.
(Erase heading not required.)

Army Form C. 2118.

Place	Date	Hour	Summary of Events and Information	Remarks and references to Appendices
BOULON WOOD	15/10/18		Detailed Advance Party consisting of Sgt ACKERMAN + 60 OR's to proceed to AVESNES les AUBERT to take over new 17 C.M.D.S.	
"	16/10/18		Visited Avesnes les Aubert Schools. This is being cleared up of the filth left by the GERMANS. Visited Col Bray DDMS 17 Corps at the SUCRERIE B.8.b.8.8 Sh. 57B	
"	17/10/18		Instructions from DDMS 17 Corps to move when ready to the COLLEGE CAMBRAI.	
"	18/10/18		Unit was billeted at Notre Dame de GRACE [illegible] Motor Ambulance Cooks by lorry in advance to prepare food for unit on arrival. Sent remainder of 17 Corps material of a Main Dressing Station on to Avesnes les Aubert.	
"	19/10/18		The unit vacated the site opposite Boulon Wood this day & marched to AVESNES les Aubert via CAMBRAI. The Main [illegible] under Major W. T. Wickham MC [illegible] at Notre Dame de Grace Cambrai (17 Corps Rest Station) & also the Motor Ambulance [illegible]. CAPT COOKE instructed the Road [illegible] for walking wounded at E.22.b. Sh. 57c	

D. D. & L., London, E.C.
(A7883) Wt. W809/M1672 350,000 4/17 Sch. 52a Forms/C/2118/14

Instructions regarding War Diaries and Intelligence Summaries are contained in F. S. Regs., Part II. and the Staff Manual respectively. Title pages will be prepared in manuscript.

WAR DIARY

or

INTELLIGENCE SUMMARY.

(Erase heading not required.)

Army Form C. 2118.

Place	Date	Hour	Summary of Events and Information	Remarks and references to Appendices
[illegible]	[illegible]		[illegible]	[illegible]
"	[illegible]		[illegible]	[illegible]
"	[illegible]		[illegible]	[illegible]

(A7092). Wt. W12839/M1293. 750,000. 1/17. D. D. & L., Ltd. Forms/C.2118/14.

Instructions regarding War Diaries and Intelligence Summaries are contained in F. S. Regs., Part II. and the Staff Manual respectively. Title pages will be prepared in manuscript.

WAR DIARY
or
INTELLIGENCE SUMMARY.
(Erase heading not required.)

Army Form C. 2118.

Place	Date	Hour	Summary of Events and Information	Remarks and references to Appendices
AVESNES le SEC [illegible]	23/10/18		Total Casualties from 6 pm 22.10.18 to [illegible] 23.10.18 Wounded 142 Sick = 130 Instruction from DDMS [illegible] Corps to send [illegible] (on being wounded) to AVESNES GROOP CCS	
"	24/10/18		Casualties from 6 am to 6 pm Wounded 533 of which 48 [illegible] Sick 215 Total 748 CAPT. TAYLOR RAMC reported for duty from [illegible] Field Amb[illegible]	
"	25/10/18		Casualties from [illegible] to 6 pm Wounded 63 of which [illegible] Sick 62 Adv. Dressing Station of [illegible] moved from HAUSSY to Q20.a.1.4. The 51st [illegible] [illegible] [illegible] Horse Ambulance Wagons for [illegible] duty [illegible] CCS under instructions from DDMS. Visited ADS of [illegible] at HAUSSY. Received instructions from ADMS [illegible] Div. for [illegible] Officer (Maj. W.R. Cathcart) to get into touch with [illegible] Inf. Bde. Casualties from 6 pm to 6 am 26/10/18 from 6 am to 6 pm 26.10.18 Wounded 50 Wounded 31 Sick 78 Sick 44 [illegible] 75	

(A7092). Wt. W12339/M1293. 750,000. 1/17. D. D. & L., Ltd. Forms/C.2118/14.

Army Form C. 2118.

Instructions regarding War Diaries and Intelligence Summaries are contained in F. S. Regs., Part II. and the Staff Manual respectively. Title pages will be prepared in manuscript.

WAR DIARY
or
INTELLIGENCE SUMMARY.

(Erase heading not required.)

Place	Date	Hour	Summary of Events and Information	Remarks and references to Appendices
Avesnes [illegible]	27/10/18		Casualties 6 p.m. to 6 a.m. 26/27.10.18 [illegible] Wounded [illegible] Sick [illegible] 173 — 6 a.m. to 6 p.m. Wounded 29 Sick 96 125. [illegible]	[initials]
"	28/10/18		[illegible]	[initials]
"	29/10/18		[illegible] 6 p.m. to 6 a.m. 28/29/10/18 Wounded 12 Sick 99 111 — 6 a.m. to 6 p.m. 29/10/18 Wounded 65 [illegible] Sick 91	[initials]
"	30/10/18		Casualties 6 p.m. to 6 a.m. 29/30/10/18 Wounded – 100 [illegible] 52 Sick 69 169 — 6 a.m. to 6 p.m. 30/10/18 Wounded – [illegible] Sick – 72 [illegible]	[initials]

(A7092). Wt. W12839/M1293. 750,000. 1/17. D. D. & L., Ltd. Forms/C.2118/14.

Instructions regarding War Diaries and Intelligence Summaries are contained in F. S. Regs., Part II. and the Staff Manual respectively. Title pages will be prepared in manuscript.

~~WAR DIARY~~

or

INTELLIGENCE SUMMARY.

(Erase heading not required.)

Army Form C. 2118.

Place	Date	Hour	Summary of Events and Information	Remarks and references to Appendices
Avesnes les Aubert	31/10/18		Casualties [illegible] 30th/31/10/18 [illegible]	
			Reported officially that [illegible] Vendegies [illegible] CMDS at [illegible] ADS at VENDIGIES + POMMEREUIL [illegible]	[illegible]

[illegible signature]

[illegible]

(A7092). Wt. W12839/M1293. 750,000. 1/17. D. D. & L., Ltd. Forms/C.2118/14.

19

ORIGINAL

VR 39

140/3401

Nov. 1918

CONFIDENTIAL

War Diary

Of

C.H. DENNER M.C.

Lieut.-Colonel ~~G.B. EDWARDS. D.S.O.~~

Officer Commanding 72nd. FIELD AMBULANCE

From 1st Nov 1918 NOVEMBER To 30th Nov 1918

WAR DIARY
or
INTELLIGENCE SUMMARY.
(Erase heading not required.)

Army Form C. 2118.

Instructions regarding War Diaries and Intelligence Summaries are contained in F. S. Regs., Part II. and the Staff Manual respectively. Title pages will be prepared in manuscript.

Place	Date	Hour	Summary of Events and Information	Remarks and references to Appendices
Avesnes les Aubert	1/11/18		61st Division attacked this morning & captured MARESCHES many prisoners & Boche wounded brought in. DDMS 3rd ARMY Genl. MURRAY IRVINE visited 17 CMDS & expressed satisfaction	
	2/11/18		Ambulance Car detailed to report to OC 73 FA for duty under instructions from ADMS XVII Corps [?]	[illegible]
			36 Bearers detailed for duty with the Battns of 72 Infy Bde viz	
			1st North Staffords 12 Bearers	
			8 [illegible]	
			9 R.W. Kent	
			Col. Wingate ADMS 24 Div & Major Chubb DADMS visited the Divisional Station	
"	3/11/18		Major B. Cathcart with Bearers proceeded to join the 72 Inf Bde this afternoon. 17 CMDS at Avesnes les Aubert closed at 6 pm & Adv CMDS with OC 59 Field Ambce Lt Col. Mackenzie opened at Ferme Ormonne [?] P.4.b.8.6 Sh 51A	[illegible]
			Tent Sub Divns 19 & 61 Divns [illegible] with their Officers proceeded to Ferme Ormonne [?]	

(A7092). Wt. W12839/M1293. 750,000. 1/17. D. D. & L., Ltd. Forms/C.2118 14.

Instructions regarding War Diaries and Intelligence Summaries are contained in F. S. Regs., Part II. and the Staff Manual respectively. Title pages will be prepared in manuscript.

WAR DIARY
or
INTELLIGENCE SUMMARY.
(Erase heading not required.)

Army Form C. 2118.

Place	Date	Hour	Summary of Events and Information	Remarks and references to Appendices
[illegible]	2/11/18		The Unit vacated the billets at LA MARLE AVESNES les Aubert and [illegible] marched to [illegible] Camp & pitched [illegible] next to the [illegible] Dressing Station. [illegible] WARE [illegible] Col Bray for [illegible] C.M.S. [illegible] Capt Taylor [illegible] detailed for [illegible] duty with 74 Field Ambulance	[illegible]
"	5/11/18		[illegible] WARGNIES le PETIT with Capt [illegible] MAC. Reported to Col Bray DDMS 17 Corps [illegible] to move [illegible] to the [illegible] at WARGNIES [illegible] to [illegible] Corps [illegible] to report tomorrow at 6 a.m. MAC Car to report [illegible] to take [illegible] Comfort to WARGNIES to [illegible] a Soup Kitchen for the French Civilians [illegible]	[illegible]
WARGNIES le PETIT The Chateau	6/11/18		[illegible] at 8 a.m. for Wargnies le Petit [illegible] a [illegible] shell in the roof of the Ch[illegible] killing 5 civilians [illegible] wounding 13	[illegible]
"	8/11/18		Opened Corps MAC [illegible] officially at 12 noon. Casualties [illegible] Sick [illegible] Wounded	
"	9/11/18		Casualties [illegible] 8/9/11/18 [illegible] Sick – 57 Wounded – 77 134 [illegible] Sick – 168 Wounded – 30 198	[illegible]

(A7092). Wt. W12839/M1293. 750,000. 1/17. D. D. & L., Ltd. Forms/C.2118/14.

Army Form C. 2118.

Instructions regarding War Diaries and Intelligence Summaries are contained in F. S. Regs., Part II. and the Staff Manual respectively. Title pages will be prepared in manuscript.

WAR DIARY
or
~~INTELLIGENCE SUMMARY.~~
(Erase heading not required.)

Place	Date	Hour	Summary of Events and Information	Remarks and references to Appendices
WARGNIES les PETIT The Chateau	10/11/18		Casualties 9/10/11/18 6 pm to 6 am Sick - 31 Wounded 18 = 49. 10.11.18 6 am to 6 pm Sick - 107 Wounded - 15 = 122	
			Maj. Scott-Williamson 2/1 Fld Amble rejoined his unit this day & was relieved by Capt. O'Connor	AB.
"	11/11/18		Casualties 10/11/11/18 6 pm to 6 am Sick 34 Wounded 4 = 38. 11/11/18 6 am to 6 pm Sick 112 Wounded 1 = 113	
			Official word received of ARMISTACE. - Hostilities will cease with Germany at 11 am today 11.11.1918 Troops will assume the defensive on the line reached at that time & there will be no fraternisation with the enemy	AB
			The Band of the 61st Division played in the courtyard of the (17 Corps Main Dressing Chateau). All civilians were invited & tea given them afterwards. The Band Programme finished with the Marseillaise & God Save the King. which was sung by all civilians & soldiers present. to commemorate the Armistice.	
"	12/11/18		Casualties 6 pm to 6 am 11/12/11/18 Sick 42 Wounded ~~2~~ = 44. 6 am to 6 pm 12/11/18 Sick ~~103~~ 103* Wounded - 3 = 106 ~~All these were cases that were passed previously.~~	AB.
"	13/11/18		Casualties 6 pm to 6 am 12/13/11/18 Sick - 40 Wounded - 0 = 40. 6 am to 6 pm 13/11/18. Sick - 99 Wounded - 6* all previously passed = 105	AB

(A7092). Wt. W12839/M1293. 750,000. 1/17. D. D. & L., Ltd. Forms/C.2118/14.

Army Form C. 2118.

Instructions regarding War Diaries and Intelligence Summaries are contained in F. S. Regs., Part II. and the Staff Manual respectively. Title pages will be prepared in manuscript.

WAR DIARY
or
~~INTELLIGENCE SUMMARY.~~
(Erase heading not required.)

Place	Date	Hour	Summary of Events and Information	Remarks and references to Appendices
WARGNIES les PETIT The Chateau	14/11/18		Casualties 6pm to 6am 13/11/18 Sick – 54, Wounded – 0, [total] 54. The 17th Corps Main Dressing Station in the Chateau at WARGNIES les PETIT closed down at 6 am this morning.	
			Received instructions from DDMS 17th Corps to return Corps material to Ordnance. Received instructions from ADMS 24th Divn. to see Town Major of ST WAAST re billets. No accomodation. Arranged with 72 Inf Bde to stay at WARGNIES les PETIT until the Brigade moves.	CAD
"	15/11/18		Surplus medical Stores returned to No 16 ADM Stores. Capt Taylor H.L. rejoined unit from temporary duty with 74 Field Ambulance.	CAD
"	16/11/18		Warning order from ADMS to join 72 Bde Group tomorrow. Bde moves to SEPMARIES & MARASCHES	
WARGNIES to MARESCHES	17/11/18	Sunday	The unit moved off at 10am for MARESCHES & arrived at 1 pm. Billets for men & beasts good on the whole though the village is very considerably damaged by shell fire. Received movement order from 72 Inf Bde to ROEULX AREA.	CAD
MARESCHES to ROEULX	18/11/18		The unit moved off with 72 Inf Bde. at 7.45 am & arrived at ROEULX at 2.15 pm. Very good billets. Received orders from 72 Inf Bde re moving to ECAILLON - BRUILLE AREA tomorrow	CAD

(A7092). Wt. W12839/M1293. 750,000. 1/17. D. D. & L., Ltd. Forms/C.2118/14.

Army Form C. 2118.

Instructions regarding War Diaries and Intelligence Summaries are contained in F. S. Regs., Part II. and the Staff Manual respectively. Title pages will be prepared in manuscript.

WAR DIARY
or
INTELLIGENCE SUMMARY.
(Erase heading not required.)

Place	Date	Hour	Summary of Events and Information	Remarks and references to Appendices
RAULX to BRUILLE	19/11/18		Unit marches off at 11.5 am & arrives at BRUILLE at 3 pm Billets fair	
BRUILLE to MASNY	21/11/18		The unit followed the 8th Roy West Kents to MASNY this day. The unit marched off at 10.15 & arrived at 11.15 am.	[initials]
MASNY	23/11/18		Received warning order from Bde ref moving to LANDAS on 25/11/18	[initials]
"	24/11/18		Sgt Ackerman & Pte Woodhouse detailed as Advance Party to LANDAS at 9am on 25/11/18.	
MASNY to LANDAS	25/11/18		Unit marches off with 72 Infy Bde at 6.45 am & arrives LANDAS at 1pm. Billets good.	[initials]
LANDAS to OUVIGNIES	26/11/18		Unit marches off from LANDAS at 10 am & arrives at OUVIGNIES at 1.30 am. Billets good on the whole.	[initials]
OUVIGNIES	26/11/18		Went to TOURNAI with Lt HARVEY 72 Inf Bde Billeting Officer. Arranged to take over Convent School in the FAUBERG de LILLE from 22.9 Field Ambulce	[initials]
"	30/11/18		Had a meeting of the Field Ambulance Canteen Committee in reference to arranging to buy material for (recd) men XMAS Dinner. Extra Vegetables are now been bought out of Canteen Funds.	[initials]

(A7092). Wt. W12839/M1293. 750,000. 1/17. D. D. & L., Ltd. Forms/C.2118/14.

Dec 1918 4

MEDICAL

CONFIDENTIAL

M 40

146/3181

War Diary

of

C. H. DENYER. M.C.

Lieut-Colonel ~~C. B. EDWARDS. D.S.O.~~

Officer Commanding 72nd FIELD AMBULANCE

From 1st Dec 1918 DECEMBER To 31 Dec 18

DECEMBER

Army Form C. 2118.

WAR DIARY
or
~~INTELLIGENCE~~ SUMMARY.
(*Erase heading not required.*)

Instructions regarding War Diaries and Intelligence Summaries are contained in F. S. Regs., Part II. and the Staff Manual respectively. Title pages will be prepared in manuscript.

Place	Date	Hour	Summary of Events and Information	Remarks and references to Appendices
OUNIGNIES	1/12/18	Sun.	No 20748 Pte Elliot A evacuated CCS with Influenza.	RD
G4 a 2.8	2/12/18	Mon	Routine Duties	
Sh. 44.	3/12/18	Tues	Route march for NCOs & men. Unit inspected for Scabies – Report Nil	
Belgium & Part of France 1.40,000	4/12/18	Wed.	Baths instituted & clothes disinfected for men of Unit	RD
			M2 101217 Pte Rummer W. ASC MT. with Ambulance reported for duty from 24 Divl MT Coy. Maj. Webster MC & Lt Peck MORC reported from 10 days Paris leave	
	5/12/18	Thur	Placed house adjacent to QM Stores civilian child sick ? Diphtheria out of bounds	RD
	6/12/18	Fri.	115504 Dr. SIDDONS B. ASC MT. evacuated to 39 Stationary Hospl LILLE ? Diphtheria. Contacts segregated. billets disinfected. ~~threads~~ clothes disinfected. OC. No 2 Mobile Laboratory asked to arrange examination of Contacts. Lt HA. Peck MORC detailed for Temporary duty with 9 East Surrey Regt. in relief of Capt Wallace proceeding on leave.	RD
	8/12/18		Routine duties.	
	9/12/18		The following NCO & men with a Talbot Ambulance were detailed for temporary duty with the Divisional Post Office. ADMS instructions. Red Cross was painted out for time being Sgt Heal HP Rame Pte Douglas D ASC. MT. Pte Scotcher G	RD

(A7092). Wt. W12839/M1293. 750,000. 1/17. D. D. & L., Ltd. Forms/C.2118/14.

Instructions regarding War Diaries and Intelligence Summaries are contained in F. S. Regs., Part II. and the Staff Manual respectively. Title pages will be prepared in manuscript.

WAR DIARY
or
INTELLIGENCE SUMMARY.
(Erase heading not required.)

Army Form C. 2118.

Place	Date	Hour	Summary of Events and Information	Remarks and references to Appendices
OUVIGNIES	12/12/18		Routine duties. The Unit proceeded from OUVIGNIES to TOURNAI by motor lorries to the DAMES REPARATRICE F. de LILLE TOURNAI	
TOURNAI	14/12/18		The undermentioned men proceeded to CHISLEDON (via Corps Concentration Camp Tournai) on the 13th inst for the purpose of demobilization as miners and are accordingly struck off the strength of this unit on 13th inst 20872 Pte PITTS B RAMC 364096 " CLARK A " "	[initials]
	15/12/18		The u/m proceeded to DUDDINGSTON (via 1st C. Conc Camp Tournai) on 14th inst. for the purpose of demobilization as miners & has been struck off the strength of the unit 318505 Pte McDONALD R.J.	[initials]
	16/12/18		The u/m proceeded to SHORNECLIFFE (via 1st Corps Concentratn Camp TOURNAI) on 15th inst for purpose of demobilization as miners & have been struck off the strength of this unit. 490916 Pte JONES E. RAMC 040841 Dr HUNT E (ASC. H.T). The u/m proceeded on Special leave to England on 15th inst 53465 Pte HASSALL W. The u/m proceeded on leave to England on 16th inst 49459 Cpl. HORSLEN J.H. RAMC 319984 Pte SANDILANDS J. (HLI att) T4/040618 Dr. WILKIE D (ASC att)	[initials]
	18/12/18 19/12/18		Routine duties The u/m NCO & man proceeded to RIPON (via 1st C.C. Camp Tournai) for demobilization as miners & struck off the strength of this unit. T4/040960 Sgt. EARLE F ASC. HT 3/10413 Pte HALLIWELL D. (Q.R. Surrey)	[initials]

(A7092). Wt. W12839/M1293. 750,000. 1/17. D. D. & L., Ltd. Forms/C.2118/14.

Army Form C. 2118.

WAR DIARY
or
INTELLIGENCE SUMMARY.
(Erase heading not required.)

Instructions regarding War Diaries and Intelligence Summaries are contained in F. S. Regs., Part II. and the Staff Manual respectively. Title pages will be prepared in manuscript.

Place	Date	Hour	Summary of Events and Information	Remarks and references to Appendices
TOURNAI	22/12/18		Routine duties. The w/m proceeded on Special leave to England today 13.31.90 Pte RENNIE R.M. RAMC The w/m proceeded to Base this day to report to O.C. Reinforcements ETAPLES for transfer to England for duty, & is struck off the Strength accordingly.	A.D.
"	23/12/18		Routine duties	A.D.
"	24/12/18		Routine duties continued.	A.D.

A.L. Dunga... Lt. Col. RAMC
O.C. 72 Fd Amb lce

(A7092). Wt. W12839/M1293. 750,000. 1/17. D. D. & L., Ltd. Forms/C.2118/14.

Instructions regarding War Diaries and Intelligence Summaries are contained in F. S. Regs., Part II. and the Staff Manual respectively. Title pages will be prepared in manuscript.

Army Form C. 2118.

WAR DIARY
or
INTELLIGENCE SUMMARY.
(Erase heading not required.)

Place	Date	Hour	Summary of Events and Information	Remarks and references to Appendices
TOURNAI	24/12/18		The o/m returned from leave to UK. 23rd inst. Cpl. Pont. H.W. RAMC, Pte Pevrons H. RAMC. The following proceeding on leave to England L/Cpl. Grimes S.H. RAMC, Dr. Wilford C (ASC. H.T.), Dr. Gibson W (ASC. H.T.)	
			The o/m NCO proceeded to 1st Corps Concentration Camp TOURNAI for duty on 23 inst. Sgt. T. Smillie RAMC.	A.D.
	25/12/18		XMAS. Day – the personnel had an excellent Xmas Dinner. Turkeys provided out of Cant. fund.	A.D.
	27/12/18		Routine Duties.	A.D.
	29/12/18		The o/m returned from leave to U.K. this day. Dr Woodward W. ASC H.T.	A.D.
	30/12/18		The o/m proceeded to RIPON (via Corps Concentration Camp TOURNAI) today for the purpose of demobilization as MINERS & have been struck off the strength of this unit accordingly. Pte PITT. W.E. RAMC, " LAVERICK J.M. ", " BLANEY J ", " Long R. ", " GIBSON "; Dr THEW P ASC HT, " SIDDONS " , Pte HODGENT. RAMC, Pte JONES J.O "	A.D.
	31/12/18		Educational Training – a History Demonstration was given today.	A.D.

A.H. [illegible] Lt.Col. RAMC.
O.C. 72 Fld Amb[ulan]ce

(A7092). Wt. W12839/M1293. 750,000. 1/17. D. D. & L., Ltd. Forms/C.2118/14

16/3

January

JANUARY

MEDICAL.

CONFIDENTIAL

WO 95/1 [illegible] 41

War Diary

140/5524

24th DIV

Box 1952

Of

C. H. DENYER M.C.

Lieut.-Colonel ~~C. B. EDWARD. D.S.O.~~

Officer Commanding 72nd. FIELD AMBULANCE.

From Jan. 1st. 1919 To Jan. 31st 1919

Army Form C. 2118.

Instructions regarding War Diaries and Intelligence Summaries are contained in F. S. Regs., Part II. and the Staff Manual respectively. Title pages will be prepared in manuscript.

JANUARY 1919

WAR DIARY
or
~~INTELLIGENCE SUMMARY.~~
(Erase heading not required.)

Place	Date	Hour	Summary of Events and Information	Remarks and references to Appendices
TOURNAI	1/1/1919	Wed.	The u/m proceeded on leave to England on 31/12/18 Pte JOHNSON W. RAMC Pte MACDONALD D. " Pte PETTIT T.R. " The u/m returned from leave on the 31 inst Pte BAYFIELD. E. RAMC.	[initials]
"	3/1/19	Fri	Routine duties. Took over duties of A/ADMS 24 DIV. whilst [illegible] Cunningham proceeded on leave	[initials]
"	4/1/19	Sat.	The u/m proceeded on leave to England this day. Pte Gower A. RAMC " Pike J.E. " " McDOUGALL D. "	[initials]
"	6/1/19	Mond.	The u/m Officer returned from Temporary Duty with 1st N. Stafford Regt on 4.1.19. CAPT G.L. LAWLOR RAMC French Class held today - by Sgt. H.D. AKERMAN RAMC.	[initials]
"	8.1.19	Wes.	Under authority from H.M. The King the u/m Officer has been awarded the Military Cross Major W.B. Cathcart M.C. RAMC Spec. Res. Auth Supplement London Gazette d/1/1/19.	[initials]
"	10.1.19	Frid	Routine duties.	[initials]
"	12.1.19	Sun.	The u/m proceeded on leave to England on 11th inst period 11/1/19 to 25/1/19 508185 Pte Apps 65165 " Cutting 368077 " Kent The u/m Officer returned from leave today Period 27.12.18 to 9.1.18 MAJ. W.J. WEBSTER, M.C	[initials]

(A7092). Wt. W12839/M1293. 750,000. 1/17. D. D. & L., Ltd. Forms/C.2118/14.

Instructions regarding War Diaries and Intelligence Summaries are contained in F. S. Regs., Part II. and the Staff Manual respectively. Title pages will be prepared in manuscript.

Army Form C. 2

WAR DIARY
or
INTELLIGENCE SUMMARY.
(Erase heading not required.)

JANUARY.

Place	Date	Hour	Summary of Events and Information	Remarks and references to Appendices
TOURNAI	13.1.19	Mon.	The ufw proceeded to Clipstone via Concentration Camp Tournai for Demobilisation and were Struck off Strength accordingly. 78517 Pte Emery C. 49022 L/C Woodhead C.W. 70126 Pte Sudgen J.B.	[initials]
"	15.1.19	Wed.	A dance was given for the Warrant Officers NCO & men in the Concert Room men invited their Belgian friends. It was a Successful event.	[initials]
"	17.1.19	Fri.	Routine Duties. A whist drive was got up for the men.	
"	18.1.19	Sat.	Routine Duties	
"	19.1.19	Sun.	Horses to proceed to Div. HQrs (24) for inspection by the Veterinary Authorities in respect to Demobilisation.	[initials]
"	20.1.19	Mon.	Col. Mackenzie returned to duty from 39 Stationary Hospl. Lille & took over the duties of A.D.M.S. T/19972. S/S/M. Gathery R.S. RASC joined this unit for duty 20.1.19.	
"	21.1.19	Tues.	Proceeding on leave to U.K. Period 22/1/19 to 21/2/19 Special Leave. Handed over Imprest Account to Major Webster (W.J.) M.C. RAMC Amount handed over 2008 fr 25 Major W. B. Cathcart proceeded on leave to U.K. Capt. Lubin M.O.R.C., U.S. reported for duty from 12th Batt. Sherwood Foresters.	[initials] Major LB Rowe

(A7092). Wt. W12839/M1293. 750,000. 1/17. D. D. & L., Ltd. Forms/C.2118/14.

Instructions regarding War Diaries and Intelligence Summaries are contained in F. S. Regs., Part II. and the Staff Manual respectively. Title pages will be prepared in manuscript.

WAR DIARY
or
INTELLIGENCE SUMMARY.
(Erase heading not required.)

Army Form C. 2118.

Place	Date	Hour	Summary of Events and Information	Remarks and references to Appendices
Tournai	22/1/19	Wed	Capt Lubin, M.O.R.C detailed for temporary duty at 1st Corps Officers' Rest Station Tournai, in relief of Capt Twist RAMC on leave to U.K. The personnel held another successful dance.	
"	23/1/19	Thurs	The undermentioned proceeded on leave to U.K. (period 22/1/19 to 6/2/19) No 111071 Pte Booker. J.H., No T4 040597 Driver Vines. A (ASC. H.T.) No 58096 Sgt. Tarbayne J. was detailed to work with the Divisional Foden Disinfector and make necessary arrangements with each unit to which it is attached	
"	26/1/19	Sun	The undermentioned proceeded on leave to U.K. (period 26/1/19 to 9/2/19) M/38574 Pte Poulton RASC (M.T.) and 66841 Pte Goss. W. H.	
"	27/1/19	Mon.	A party of 1 N.C.O and 24 O.R was detailed to load Ambulance Train at Tournai Station	
"	28/1/19	Tues	A.D.M.S, 24th Division visited and inspected the unit.	
"	29/1/19	Wed	Surgeon-General Thompson, D.M.S. First Army accompanied by D.D.M.S and ADMS visited the unit. Sergeant Goddard, RASC (H.T.) proceeded to 24th Div. Train for duty on becoming surplus to establishment	
"	30/1/19	Thurs	The undermentioned proceeded on leave to U.K (period 29/1/19 to 12/2/19) 53931 Pte Shone. G.H. and 47964 Pte Hadfield. J.	
"	31/1/19	Frid		

1/2/19

W. J. Webster [signature]
Major RAMC
O/C 72 Fd A.

(A7092). Wt. W12839/M1293. 750,000. 1/17. D. D. & L., Ltd. Forms/C.2118/14.

Feb 1919

144 9/3524

No 72 Field Ambulance

FEBRUARY 1919. **WAR DIARY**

~~or~~

~~INTELLIGENCE SUMMARY.~~

(Erase heading not required.)

Army Form C. 2118.

Instructions regarding War Diaries and Intelligence Summaries are contained in F. S. Regs., Part II. and the Staff Manual respectively. Title pages will be prepared in manuscript.

42

Place	Date	Hour	Summary of Events and Information	Remarks and references to Appendices
TOURNAI, BELGIUM.	2/2/19		A loading party of 1 N.C.O. and 24 men was detailed to load Ambulance Train at Tournai Station. Cpl Huckle. E.E. discharged to duty from 51 C.C.S. & rejoined unit.	W.J.W.
	3/2/19.		The undermentioned proceeded to dispersal centres for demobilization this day and are struck off the strength accordingly — S/Sergt. Newham. E.C., Cpl Elliot. J., Pte Derrick.	W.J.W.
	5/2/19.		The w/m proceeded on leave to U.K. period 5/2/19 to 19/2/19:— 61173 Pte Beet. Y.G. 65181 Pte Phillips. R., 69053 Pte Taylor R.H., 65188 Pte Smith. F.J.	W.J.W.
			The personnel held a successful dance in the evening.	
	8/2/19.		The undermentioned proceeded to England via 10th Corps Concentration Camp, Tournai for demobilization:- S-Major Coggins. A.J., Sergt Hedley. W., Pte Henderson. R., Pte Keedy. F.	W.J.W.
			Pte Aussee. F. returned from leave to England today.	
	9/2/19.		Pte Booker returned from leave to England today.	W.J.W.
	11/2/19.		The following men proceeded on leave to U.K. today:— Pte Rowe N.B. (period 12/2/19 to 14/3/19), Pte Towner. A.E. (period 12/2/19 to 14/3/19), Pte Longthorne. A. (period 12/2/19 to 26/2/19).	W.J.W.
	12/2/19		Pte Ingham returned from leave to U.K. today. A loading party of 1 N.C.O. and 24 men was detailed to load ambulance train at Tournai station.	W.J.W.
	13/2/19.		The following returned from leave today:- Pte Kemb. Driver Vines R.A.S.C. H.T. Pte Goss. M.H. The following proceeded to England for demobilization via Corps Concentration Camp Tournai - 19109 Cpl Pont. H.W., 11817 Pte Brewer. J., 92362 PTE Green. E.	W.J.W.

(A7092). Wt. W12839/M1293. 750,000. 1/17. D. D. & L., Ltd. Forms/C.2118/14.

FEBRUARY 1919. (2).

Army Form C. 2[illegible]

Instructions regarding War Diaries and Intelligence Summaries are contained in F. S. Regs., Part II. and the Staff Manual respectively. Title pages will be prepared in manuscript.

WAR DIARY
or
~~INTELLIGENCE~~ SUMMARY.

(Erase heading not required.)

Place	Date	Hour	Summary of Events and Information	Remarks and references to Appendices
Tournai, Belgium	14/II/19.		The following returned from leave to U.K this day. Pte Cutting. C. H., Pte Storey. J.	W.J.W.
			The following proceeded on leave to U.K. period 15/2/19 to 1/3/19. Pte Warburton. A., Pte Stanworth. T., Driver Barlow. (RASC H.T.).	
	15/II/19		A Court of Inquiry was held at 24th Div. M.T. Coy this day to investigate the loss of a Talbot ambulance car from 72nd Field Ambulance on 8/II/19.	W.J.W.
			The following men reported back from leave to U.K.:– Pte Poulton RASC M.T. and Pte Hatfield. J.	
	16/II/19.		The undermentioned returned from leave to U.K. this day:– Major W. B. Cathcart, M.C.; Pte Cocker. R. W., Pte Shone G. H.	
	17/II/19.		The following N.C.O. proceeded on 14 days leave to U.K:– Sergt. Cavanagh. C.	W.J.W.
			A loading party of 1 N.C.O. and 24 men was on duty with an Ambulance Train at Tournai Station today.	
	19/II/19.		Capt & Q.M. J.T. Cooke proceeded on leave to U.K (period 20/II/19 to 6/III/19.)	W.J.W.
			The personnel held a dance in the evening.	
	21/2/19		The u/m Officer proceeded on leave to U.K. Capt. H.L. Taylor Period – 21/2/19 to 7/3/19.	
			The u/m proceeded to 1st Corps Concentration Camp for duty vice Sgt Smillie – Cpl. Balen[illegible]	
			" " " " 57 CCS for duty 20/2/19 Pte Jackson, " Grant, " McDowall	[initials]

(A7092). Wt. W12839/M1293. 750,000. 1/17. D. D. & L., Ltd. Forms/C.2118/14.

FEBRUARY (3)
1919

Instructions regarding War Diaries and Intelligence Summaries are contained in F. S. Regs., Part II. and the Staff Manual respectively. Title pages will be prepared in manuscript.

WAR DIARY
or
~~INTELLIGENCE SUMMARY.~~
(Erase heading not required.)

Army Form C. 2118.

Place	Date	Hour	Summary of Events and Information	Remarks and references to Appendices
Tournai Belgium		23/2/19	The u/m proceed on leave today to U.K. period 23/2/19 to 9.3.19 49477 Pte McNaughton J M2/134014 " Donaldson D.	AB
			The u/m returned from leave on 22/2/19 Lt Col. C.H. Dwyer MC. 22/1/19 to 21/2/19 49053 Pte R.H. Taylor 5/2/19 to 19/2/19	
"		24/2/19	The u/m proceeded on leave to U.K. 23.2.19 47947 Pte Gore. Period 24/2/19 to 10/3/19	AB
"		25/2/19	The u/m proceeded to 30 CCS 24/2/19 for duty & struck off strength accordingly 508188 Pte Gosschalk R.J. 508107 " Bartlett H.J 64887 " Forbes A The u/m proceeded on leave to UK on 24.2.19 Pte Punchard E. Period 25/2/19 to 11/3/19	AB
"		26/2/19	The u/m proceeded on leave to U.K. Period 26/2/19 to 12/3/19 Pte Ross C.J. " " " to 24th Divn. HQrs "G" for duty 25/2/19. " Armitage. 65195 Pte Cocker W.K The Personnel of Unit had a successful Dance – Belgian Civilians invited This unit won the Inter-Ambulance Associatn. Football match of the 24th Division (72, 73, 74 F.A.'s).	AB
"		28/2/19	The u/m Officer rejoined this unit from 1st Corps Officers Rest Station Tournai this day Capt. H. Rubin, MORC.	AB

C.H. Dwyer Lt Col. Comdg
O.C. 72 Field Ambulance

(A7092). Wt. W12839/M1293. 750,000. 1/17. D. D. & L., Ltd. Forms/C.2118/14.

140/3557.

Mar. 1919

72nd 7. a

26

MEDICAL
~~DUPLICATE~~
ORIGINAL

CONFIDENTIAL

WAR DIARY

OF

LIEUT COLONEL C. H DENYER MC

OFFICER COMMDING 72ND FIELD AMBULANCE

FROM ~~NOVBR 1ST 18~~ MARCH 1st 1919 TO ~~NOVBR 30TH 18~~ MARCH 31st 1919

MARCH.

Instructions regarding War Diaries and Intelligence Summaries are contained in F. S. Regs., Part II. and the Staff Manual respectively. Title pages will be prepared in manuscript.

WAR DIARY
or
~~INTELLIGENCE~~ SUMMARY.

(Erase heading not required.)

Army Form C. 2118.

Vol 43

Place	Date	Hour	Summary of Events and Information	Remarks and references to Appendices
TOURNAI Belgium O27.a.9.8 Sheet 37 1/40,000		1/3/19	The u/m proceeded to England for re engagements for three years for Post Bellum Army 52008 A/Cpl/Sgt Grimes RAMC 73324 Pte Devine "	[initials]
			The undermentioned returned from leave 26/2/19 from UK 61173 Pte Best V.G. RAMC.	
"		3/3/19	The u/m proceeded to England 1/3/19 for demobilisation Pte Clear RAMC Pte Payne RAMC " Fox " Eardley	[initials]
"			28 Animals (horses & mules) were demobilised 2/3/19 proceeding to a Camp near Abbeville by train from Tournai.	
"		4/3/19	The u/m Officer proceeded to 9 Bn East Surrey Regt for duty this day & is accordingly struck off the strength of this unit. Capt. C. L. Lawlor RAMC	
			1 NCO & 15 men proceeded to Station Tournai for purpose of loading patients from 51 CCS (Highland).	[initials]
"		5/3/19	The u/m returned from leave Period 15.2.19 to 2.3.19 49514 Pte Stanworthy	
			The u/m Officer joined this unit for duty on 4/3/19 from 9 East Surrey Regt Capt. R. D. L. WALLACE MC RAMC	

(A7092). Wt. W12839/M1293. 750,000. 1/17. D. D. & L., Ltd. Forms/C.2118/14.

Instructions regarding War Diaries and Intelligence Summaries are contained in F. S. Regs., Part II. and the Staff Manual respectively. Title pages will be prepared in manuscript.

WAR DIARY
or
~~INTELLIGENCE~~ SUMMARY.
(Erase heading not required.)

Army Form C. 2118.

Place	Date	Hour	Summary of Events and Information	Remarks and references to Appendices
Tournai Belgium		7 3/19	The u/m returned from leave in France 6 3/19 Period 3 3/19 to 6 3/19 81513 Pte MUIR. A RAMC The u/m returned from leave to U.K. T4/040730 Dr. BARLOW H. RASC. H.T. The u/m N.C.O. is struck off this unit from 6 3/19 and taken on the strength of 51 CCS from the same date 9217 Sgt STIRZAKER. T.G. RAMC.	AD
"		8 3/19	The u/m returned from leave to U.K. 6 3/19 Period 18 2/19 to 4 3/19 52023 Sgt CAVANAGH. C.	
"		9 3/19	The u/m returned from leave CAPT J.T. COOKE on 8 3/19 Period 20.2.19 to 6.3.19. 47836 Pte LONGTHORNE on 7/3/19 Period 12.2.19 to 6.3.19 The u/m proceeded to 1st Corps Concentration Camp on 8 3/19 for demobilization CAPT R.W.L. WALLACE RAMC. 65323 Sgt Davidson A.T. RAMC 65212 Pte Holyman E. " 49099 " Ingham J. " 49147 " Shuttleworth J. "	AD

(A7092). Wt. W12839/M1293. 750,000. 1/17. D. D. & L., Ltd. Forms/C.2118 14.

Army Form C. 2118.

Instructions regarding War Diaries and Intelligence Summaries are contained in F. S. Regs., Part II. and the Staff Manual respectively. Title pages will be prepared in manuscript.

WAR DIARY
or
INTELLIGENCE SUMMARY.
(Erase heading not required.)

Place	Date	Hour	Summary of Events and Information	Remarks and references to Appendices
Tournai Belgium	11/3/19		Routine duties.	
"	12/3/19		1. NCO + 14 O.R. proceeded to Station Tournai for purpose of loading Ambulance Train with sick for Base from 51 CCS.	[initials]
"	13/3/19		The u/m proceeded on leave from Tournai to U.K. 12/3/19 Period 13/3/19 to 27/3/19. 52013 Sgt. Catlow J. A. RAMC 53470 a/C. Tanner E.C. " 49216 Pte Foster J " 93278 " Pilcher L " The u/m returned from leave to UK 11/3/19 Period 24/2/19 to 10/3/19 47947 Pte Gore J. RAMC	[initials]
"	14/3/19		The u/m proceeded to 1st Corps Concentration Camp 13.3.19 for Demobilization RASC: 94974 L/C Gamb W.B.; 104330 Pte Wrightson H.J.; 368077 " Kent J.W.; 5874 " Cripps RAMC: 69133 Pte Richards; 44907 " Crossland; 364170 " Williams; 65195 " Cocker T4/040898 Dr Exalby RASC The u/m for temporary duty under ADMS 24th Divn: 63265 Pte Woodhouse RAMC	[initials]
"	15/3/19		No 61173 Pte Best V.G. evacuated sick to 51 CCS. Tournai 14.3.19 and struck off strength accordingly. The u/m NCO & men proceeded to ADMS 20th Divn 52023 Sgt Cavanagh; 111071 Pte Booker; 130969 " Herbert } RAMC	
"	16/3/19		The u/m returned from leave to U.K 14/3/19 Period 27.2.19 – 13.3.19 130920 Pte Armitage E. Under instructions from Division as much transport as possible to be despatched to Vehicle Park Basieux Station. M.18.a.7.2 Sh. 37. Following were sent: Horse Ambulances 2, G.S. Wagons 4, Water Carts	[initials]

A5834 Wt. W4973/M687 750,000 8/16 D. D. & L. Ltd. Forms/C.2118/13.

Instructions regarding War Diaries and Intelligence Summaries are contained in F. S. Regs., Part II. and the Staff Manual respectively. Title pages will be prepared in manuscript.

WAR DIARY
or
INTELLIGENCE SUMMARY.
(*Erase heading not required.*)

Army Form C. 2118.

Place	Date	Hour	Summary of Events and Information	Remarks and references to Appendices
Tournai Belgium	17/3/19		The o/r returned from leave to UK 16/3/19 Period 12.2.19 to 14.3.19	
			77 Pte Towner RAMC	
			The o/r proceeded on leave to UK Period 17.3.19 to 31.3.19	[illegible]
			25832 Cpl Rice RAMC	
			49196 Pte Bartram RAMC	
"	20/3/19		The Unit paraded for inspection this day in full marching order.	[illegible]
"	22/3/19		Routine Duties	
"	23/3/19		Routine Duties The o/r proceeded to 1st Corps Concentration Camp Tournai this day	
	24/3/19		for Demobilization. 70492 L/Cpl. Lawrence A.J. RAMC 69384 Pte Parsons H. RAMC	
			73301 Pte Marsden L.W. " 103074 " Rothwell S. "	
			53431 " Shore G.H " 26834 " Jones S.G. "	
			219841 " Hitchen J " 457106 " Crews J "	
"	25/3/19		The o/r proceeded to 1st Corps Concentration Camp this day for Demobilization	[illegible]
			T4/036596 Dr Flanagan H.J. RASC HT. Maj. W.J. Cathcart proceeded for duty as MO i/c of 24 DAC & 107 Bde & 48 Bde RFA. billeting with DAC.	
			T4/040796 " Daft E.G. — " —	
TOURNAI to GRUSON FRANCE M.33.a. Sh 37 1.40,000 Belgium pt of France	26/3/19		The unit vacated its billets in LES DAMES REPATATRICES (Convent) Chassée de Lille Tournai & marched to GRUSON taking over billets vacated by 74th Field Ambulance.	[illegible]
			Ordnance Stores & Horse Transport of C Section viz: 1 Horse Ambulance, 1 G.S. Wagon, 1 Water Cart [illegible], 1 Limber Cart — handed into Ordnance in accordance with New Mobilization Table d	

D. D. & L., London, E.C.
(A7883) Wt. W809/M1672 350,000 4/17 Sch. 52a Forms/C/2118/14

Instructions regarding War Diaries and Intelligence Summaries are contained in F. S. Regs., Part II. and the Staff Manual respectively. Title pages will be prepared in manuscript.

WAR DIARY
or
INTELLIGENCE SUMMARY.
(Erase heading not required.)

Army Form C. 2118.

Place	Date	Hour	Summary of Events and Information	Remarks and references to Appendices
GROSON FRANCE	27/3/19		Maj. W. J. Webster MC. detailed to inspect Staff drill of following units	
M.33.a.5l.37			1st N. Staffs Regt. CAMPLIN 2nd M.G. Corps MARQUAIN	
Belgium Ypl. & France			5 R.W. Kents LAMAIN 12 Sherwood Frstrs ORCQ.	A.B.
"	28.3.19		Nil report.	
"	29.3.19		The u/m proceeded to No 51 CCS for temporary duty this day at Tournai: No. 27589 Cpl. Huckle GE. RAMC; " 66841 Pte Gow W.A. "; " 46519 " Jago L.G. "; " 75864 " Ram W.H. ". The u/m returned from 14 days leave U.K. 52013 Sgt Catton, 49206 Pte Foster, 53470 L/Cpl Tanner, 93278 Pte Fletcher } RAMC	A.B.
"	30.3.19		The u/m proceeded to 1st Corps Concentration Camp Tournai for Demobilization: 58096 Sgt Turbayne J RAMC; 104544 Pte Rowe "; 14422 " Preston "; 81613 " Muir "; 47586 " Longthorne "; 50892 " Hunt "; 122089 " Gledden "; 66884 " Dudgeon "; 47943 " Holden "; 53968 Pte Warburton; 478817 " Stretcher; 65787 " Phillips; 49134 " Freestone; 49477 " McNaughton; 77983 " Jones; 47964 " Hadfield; 32857 " Farrington; 61173 " Best. The u/m proceeded to 1st Corps Conc. Camp for transfer to England on 3 mths leave having re-engaged to serve. 418581 Dr. Brunson A. (RASC. H.T.) The u/m proceeded to No 2 CCS Valenciennes for duty 130920 Pte Armitage E (RAMC) The u/m Officers are struck off the Unit from 29.3.19 & shown on strength of No 1 Area Maj. W. J. Webster MC. " W. B. Cathcart MC.	A.B.
"	31.3.19		Nil report	

[signature]

O.C. 72 [illegible] Field Ambulance

D. D. & L., London, E.C. (A7883) Wt. W809/M1672 350,000 4/17 Sch. 52a Forms/C/2118/14

Medical
Duplicate

Original Copy

Confidential

War Diary

Of

Lieut Colonel C. H. Denyer M.C.

Officer Commd^ing^ 72nd Field Ambulance

April 1st. 19 — April 30th 19.

From ~~Nov^br.^~~ 1st ~~18~~ To ~~Nov^br^~~ 30th 18

Apr 1919

Army Form C. 2118.

APRIL

WAR DIARY
or
~~INTELLIGENCE~~ SUMMARY.
(Erase heading not required.)

Instructions regarding War Diaries and Intelligence Summaries are contained in F. S. Regs., Part II. and the Staff Manual respectively. Title pages will be prepared in manuscript.

Place	Date	Hour	Summary of Events and Information	Remarks and references to Appendices
GRUSON M 33 a 36.37 Belgium pt. of France	1.4.1919		Routine duties	A.D.
"	2.4.19		Nil report.	A.D.
"	3.4.19		Nil report	A.D.
"	4.4.19		~~Nil report~~. The after returned from leave today 25832 Cpl Rice RAMC; 49196 Pte Bertram "	A.D.
"	5.4.19		Nil report.	
"	6.4.19		Nil report	
"	7.4.19		Arranged to take over duties of ADMS Dvl. Bde Groups temporarily. Took over	
"	"		74 Field Ambulance as a temporary measure from Lt Col. Davidson.	A.D.
"			Pte Smith S.J. relieves Pte Culling C.A. at Vehicle Pk. Basieux.	
			Pte Lumsden G " Oldham J	
"	8.4.19		~~[illegible] at 74th Dvl. Vehicle Park Basieux [illegible]~~ Nil report	A.D.
"	9.4.19		No 70197 Pte Oldham J. proceeded to No 51 CCS today for temporary duty in relief of 66841 Pte W.H. Cross to rejoin this unit. For temporary duty to ADMS Douai Central Office 65191 Pte Hardiman H. No 88102 Pte Lumsden rejoined unit from 74th Dvl. Veh. Park Basieux this day.	A.D.
"	10.4.19		The after proceeded on 14 days leave to UK on 9.4.19 Period 10.4.19 to 24.4.19 21959 Pte King RAMC 101794 " Leach " 467043 " Londer " M2/131326 L/c Brown DC RASC MT.	A.D.

D. D. & L., London, E.C. (A7883) Wt. W809/M1672 350,000 4/17 Sch. 52a Forms/C/2118/14

Army Form C. 2118.

Instructions regarding War Diaries and Intelligence Summaries are contained in F. S. Regs., Part II. and the Staff Manual respectively. Title pages will be prepared in manuscript.

April.

WAR DIARY
~~or~~
~~INTELLIGENCE SUMMARY.~~
(Erase heading not required.)

Place	Date	Hour	Summary of Events and Information	Remarks and references to Appendices
Gruson M33a Sh.37 Belgium part of France	11.4.19		League match 72nd FA & 9 R. Sussex in favour of 72 FA by 1 goal to nil.	AD
	12.4.19		Nil report.	AD
	13.4.19		Nil report	AD
"	14.4.19		The u/m rejoined this unit from ADMS DOUAI Cadre 'A' on 13.4.19 65191 Pte Hardiman. H.	AD
"	15.4.19		The 34 Divl. Bde Group H.Q. have arranged trips for NCOs & men to Brussels, Waterloo, Louvain, Antwerp & Zeebrugge.	AD
"	16.4.19		The u/m are detailed for temporary duty at 34th Divisional Reception Camp Tournai No T4/040987 Dr Brown RASC att 72 FA. No T2/14480 " Holt RASC " " 14 days leave to UK. Period 16.4.19 to 30.4.19 65191 Pte Hardiman H RAMC T4/040753 Dr Hughes A RASC.	AD AD
"	17.4.19		Nil report	AD
"	18.4.19		Nil report, with exception of football match played between 72 FA & 3rd Bn Rifle Bgde in 34 Divisional Group. The ambulance lost 4 to nil.	AD
"	19.4.19		Nil report	AD
"	20.4.19		Nil report.	AD
"	21.4.19		The u/m NCO for temporary duty 24th Divl. Reception Camp Rue Royale Tournai on 20.4.19 25832 Cpl. Rice RAMC also " " in relief 27589 Cpl. Huckle proceeding on leave to U.K. Period 21.4.19 to 5.5.19.	AD
"	22.4.19		The u/m proceeded on 14 days leave to UK Period 22.4.19 to 6.5.19 52013 S/Sgt Catton RAMC RAMC {26690 Cpl. Cooper, 49157 Pte Smith} 93498 Pte Allen RAMC M2/131233 Dr Cleary MT	AD

D. D. & L., London, E.C.
(A7883) Wt. W803/M1672 350,000 4/17 Sch. 52a Forms/C/2118/14

Army Form C. 2118.

Instructions regarding War Diaries and Intelligence Summaries are contained in F. S. Regs., Part II, and the Staff Manual respectively. Title pages will be prepared in manuscript.

WAR DIARY
or
INTELLIGENCE SUMMARY.
(Erase heading not required.)

Place	Date	Hour	Summary of Events and Information	Remarks and references to Appendices
Gruson M33a Sh. 37 Bel. & part of France	23.4.19		The u/m officer proceeded on leave (14 days) to UK. Period 23.4.19 to 7.5.19	
			Maj. W. J. Webster MC. RAMC.	AD
	24.4.19		106434 Pte Coupland to 57 CCS for temporary duty in relief of 465729 Pte Jago	
			proceeding on leave.	AD
	25.4.19		The u/m proceeded on 14 days leave to UK on 24th Period 25.4.19 to 9.5.19	
			73281 Pte McKie	
			The u/m on 72 hours leave to Brussels on 24th:	
			T4/040790 Dr Barlow RASC MT	
			T4/036872 " Wands " "	
			T4/040671 " Woodward " "	
			The u/m officer rejoined the unit from "sec" Divl. Duty on 23.4.19	
			Capt. W.B. Cathcart.	
			No M2/136014 Pte Douglas D. RASC MT reported to OC 24 Divl MT with Sunbeam Car	
			No 15122 on 23.4.19 & is struck off the strength	AD
	26.4.19		The u/m proceeded on 72 hours leave to Brussels to day	
			78495 Pte Howell RAMC	
			65190 " Hawkes "	AD
			53467 " Storey "	
	27.4.19		Nil report.	AD
	28.4.19		3 ORs returned from 3 days leave to Brussels.	AD
	29.4.19		The u/m returned from leave to UK 28.4.19. Pte Louder, Leach & King RAMC Period 10.4.19 to 24.4.19	AD
	30.4.19		The u/m returned from leave to Brussels.	AD
			Pte Hawkes Howell & Storey RAMC.	

D. D. & L., London, E.C.
(A7883) Wt. W809/M1672 350,000 4/17 Sch. 52a Forms/C/2118/14